GW01471635

1991 Census

County report

Laid before Parliament pursuant to Section 4(1)
Census Act 1920

Hampshire
part 2

London: HMSO

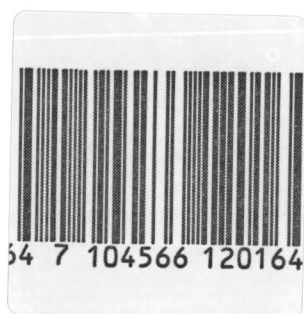

HMSO
Standing order service

Placing a standing order with HMSO BOOKS enables a
customer to receive future titles in this series automatically
as published. This saves the time, trouble and expense of
placing individual orders and avoids the problem of
knowing when to do so. For details please write to HMSO
BOOKS (PC 13A/1), Publications Centre, PO Box 276,
London SW8 5DT quoting reference 02 02 009. The
standing order service also enables customers to receive
automatically as published all material of their choice
which additionally saves extensive catalogue research. The
scope and selectivity of the service has been extended by
new techniques, and there are more than 3,500
classifications to choose from. A special leaflet describing
the service in detail may be obtained on request.

Cover illustration by Guy Eves

Contents

1 Introduction

1.1 This volume is the second part of the Report for Hampshire from the Census of Great Britain which took place on 21 April 1991. It is published and laid before Parliament under the authority of, and to meet the requirements of, section 4(1) of the Census Act 1920.

1.2 The 1991 Census was the nineteenth in a series begun in 1801, and carried out every tenth year except 1941, and the ninth in which there have been reports for each county.

1.3 The Report contains statistical tables on all topics covered by the 1991 Census. Part 1 includes the results based on processing all Census returns, prefaced by a summary of the main results. This second part includes results based on the subsequent processing of a one in ten sample of the returns. Each of the main tables is presented for the county as a whole and for each local authority district within the county.

1.4 A similar two-part Report is being made for each county in England and Wales, and for each Region and Islands Area in Scotland, published in a series during 1992 and 1993. To complete the series, there is a Report for Great Britain as a whole, including figures for Scotland as a whole, Wales as a whole, and for each of the standard statistical regions in England.

1.5 The contents of the Reports were designed, after extensive consultations, to meet needs for statistical facts in consistent form over the whole country on population, housing, employment, health, education, and transport. The series of Reports will serve: local and health authorities; the elected representatives of the community; business and commerce; academic research; education and teaching; local community groups; and, taking the series of Reports as a whole, central government and other national organisations.

1.6 In addition, the forms of table included in this Report were designed to be the basis of standard sets of *statistical abstracts* available, under the terms of section 4(2) of the Census Act 1920, for areas such as wards which are smaller than a local authority. Thus the results of the Census can be analysed for counties, for local authority areas, and for still smaller local areas with comparability throughout Great Britain.

1.7 The text of this second part of the Report is similar to that in the first part and gives brief background information on the 1991 Census, an introduction to the detailed content of the report, and guidance to assist the user. It also includes a summary of the complete programme of reports and other results from the Census. There is guidance on how to obtain further information.

1.8 This Report was made possible by the co-operation of the households and other members of the public in Hampshire in responding to the Census, by the hard work of the many members of the temporary Census field staff who delivered and collected the Census forms, and by other help given locally. The Registrar General is most grateful for all these contributions. They will be repaid by the value of the results of the Census both to people and organisations in Hampshire and more widely.

2 The 1991 Census

2.1 The Census was held on Sunday 21 April 1991, when every household in Great Britain was required by law to complete a census form. In England there were five questions on housing and 19 questions on each person, while in Wales there was one additional question, and in Scotland two further questions. People in communal establishments such as hospitals, hotels, and prisons were also included. The forms were delivered shortly before Census day by some 118,000 'enumerators', each responsible for a precisely defined area, and then collected in the following days. Enumeration went well over Great Britain as a whole, although some households, mainly in inner city areas, proved difficult to contact.

2.2 The first results of the Census were published in July 1991 in *Preliminary Reports* for England and Wales and for Scotland. These results were derived from summary records made by the field staff. The main processing of the Census began in June 1991. The publication of County and Region Reports is scheduled to be completed during 1993.

2.3 Preparations for the Census began well in advance, and included trials in the field. Consultation on the topics to be included took place in 1987/8 and the Government issued its plans in a Parliamentary White Paper in July 1988[1]. Parliament debated and approved plans for the Census at the end of 1989 and they became law shortly afterwards. Consultation on the form of statistical output began in August 1988, and, for the County Reports, was completed by mid 1990.

*The 1991 Census Reports to Parliament will be concluded by a **General Report** covering all aspects of the conduct of the Census; in the meantime more information may be obtained from the addresses given in section 13.*

3 Local results from the Census

3.1 Results have been published for local areas of Great Britain from every census since the first in 1801. Reports for each county have been published from censuses in this century. These reports have covered most of the questions asked in each successive census, but there were innovations in the way the 1991 Census County Reports were prepared.

3.2 The Census Offices planned from the outset that the 1991 County Reports should provide results from *all* the topics covered by the Census, and that there should be a single base of standard statistical tables for the Reports and for the associated statistical abstracts which would be made available for smaller areas. It was therefore possible, for the

first time, to consult with users of local statistics with a focus on one main objective.

3.3 The Census Offices prepared initial proposals for the local statistics based on those produced from the 1981 Census, and invited comment from advisory groups representing government departments and local and health authorities. Meetings, which were open to all those with an interest, were also held in various parts of the country to discuss the proposals, and written comments were invited. The form of the local statistics was then developed and refined through two further rounds of consultations.

3.4 It was decided to produce two tiers of local statistics. The upper tier is the set of main tables appearing in this Report - they are also known as the 'Local Base Statistics'. This upper tier is also available as statistical abstracts for wards in England and Wales and for postcode sectors in Scotland, provided that the wards or sectors are above a minimum population size. The lower tier - known as the 'Small Area Statistics' (SAS) - is a set of some 80 tables which, for comparability, are either whole or abbreviated versions of the upper tier tables. The SAS are available as statistical abstracts for smaller areas. More information is given in Annex B.

4 The range of information in the Report

4.1 This Report gives Census results for Hampshire, and for the local authority districts within it, *as constituted on 21 April 1991*. The county and district boundaries are shown on the map which forms section 14. There have been changes in the boundaries of Basingstoke and Dean, East Hampshire, Eastleigh, Hart, Havant, Rushmoor, Test Valley, and Winchester districts since the Census on 5 April 1981, and these are summarised in Annex A which follows the main tables.

4.2 The starting point of the topics covered in this Report is the Census form itself. There are facsimiles of the forms used in the Census in the volume of *1991 Census Definitions* - see section 7. All the topics in the 1981 Census were included in the 1991 Census, with the exception of a separate question on outside WCs. However, the answer categories in questions like tenure and economic position (whether in work, etc) were updated. There were also new questions on ethnic group, limiting long-term illness, term-time address of students and schoolchildren, and central heating; a question on weekly hours worked was reintroduced; and information was collected to give a count of dwellings and building types. As in the 1981 and previous censuses, a number of 'hard to code' questions, such as occupation, name and business of employer, and workplace, have been processed only for a 10 per cent sample of households or a 10 per cent sample of people in communal establishments - see section 8.2.

---

[1]*1991 Census of Population* (Cm 430). HMSO, 1988 ISBN 010 104302 3

4.3 The Census questions for all people, whether they were in households or in communal establishments like hospitals and hotels, were:

> age (date of birth)
> sex
> marital status
> relationship to head of household*/position in
> establishment
> whereabouts on Census night - asked in households only
> usual address
> term-time address of students and schoolchildren
> usual address one year ago (migration)
> country of birth
> ethnic group
> long-term illness;

and for all those aged 16 or over:

> economic activity in preceding week and employment
> status (self-employed, employee, etc)
> hours worked weekly*
> occupation*
> industry of employment (name and business of
> employer)*
> address of work-place*
> means of daily journey to work*
> higher qualifications*.

* Analysed for a 10 per cent sample of the population - see section 8.

In Wales there was a question on the Welsh language and in Scotland a question on Gaelic.

4.4 In addition, the person filling in the form in each household was asked about:

> number of rooms
> 'shared' accommodation
> tenure
> amenities (WC, bath, central heating)
> number of cars and vans available
> lowest floor of accommodation - Scotland only.

The name and address of the household was recorded on the form, but, apart from the postcode of the address, this information was not included in the processing operation.

4.5 If a household was absent, or no contact was made with a household which appeared to be present on Census day, the census enumerators recorded the type of accommodation and an estimate of the number of rooms and the number of residents. Absent households were asked to complete a census form voluntarily on return. Where they did so, the data from the forms have been included in the results; where they did not, data about such households have been imputed with the exception of those data processed only for the 10 per cent sample of the population. The effect of this exception is discussed in section 8.

4.6 Each topic on the Census form is covered by tables in this Report. But one of the strengths of the Census is the facility to derive additional variables from a number of questions asked at one time. Examples of derived variables for individuals are 'socio-economic group' and 'social class' (based on occupation) and, for households, an example is the type of household by composition.

5 Finding information in the Report

The tables

5.1 Each Report contains the following tables:

Summary tables in (Part 1)

A to L	All parts of Great Britain
M	Areas in Wales or Scotland only (Welsh or Gaelic language)

Main tables in (Part 1)

1 to 66	All parts of Great Britain
67	Areas in Wales or Scotland only (Welsh or Gaelic language)
68-70	Areas in Scotland only (special housing tables)

Main tables in (Part 2)

71-99	All parts of Great Britain

The *main tables* are either *cross-tabulations*, that is where each element in the population is counted only once in the matrix of table *cells*, or groupings of two or more cross-tabulations of related statistics. Some additional counts are given in *single cells* which do not form part of the matrix of a cross-tabulation.

5.2 Each of the main tables has a short *key word title* which appears at the head of each page and indicates the main feature of the table, but not necessarily every aspect included. These key word titles are listed in table number order in section 15. The tables are grouped into six main subject areas:

in part 1 of the Report:

1-18	Demographic and economic characteristics
19-27	Housing
28-53	Households and household composition
54-66	Household spaces and dwellings
67-70	Scotland and Wales only tables;

and, in part 2 of the Report:

71-99   Socio-economic characteristics (tables based on the
        10 per cent sample)

The *Topic and key word index* in section 15 shows where
topics and cross-tabulations of topics are found.

Table conventions

5.3   In each table, the figures for the county as a whole are
given first, with the local authority areas following in
alphabetical order. In the larger tables, the margins are
repeated for each area. To make the table content clear, the
wording in the table margins is as comprehensive as possible,
and abbreviations have been kept to a minimum. There are
also a number of standard conventions used in the tables.

Margins (row and column headings)

> The *population base* or *bases* for each table - see
> section 6, are shown in the banner heading over the
> column headings; when the table contains two or more
> bases, these are separated by semi-colons.

> Indentation in row headings indicates that counts in that
> row are *sub-totals* of counts in the previous non-
> indented rows (equivalent to the sub-divisions of
> column headings).

> Text set in italics signifies either that no counts will
> appear for that row/column, or that counts in that
> row/column are a *sub-set* of a previous row/column and
> should not be added to other rows/columns when
> totalling.

> *Total rows/columns* are indicated by text in capital
> letters.

Counts

> Counts based on full processing (Tables 1 to 70) are
> given without modification; a cell where the count is
> zero, but where a non-zero count was possible, is
> shown with a dash, whereas a cell for which a non-zero
> count is impossible is left blank. Some cells obviously
> duplicating others are also left blank.

> Counts based on the one in ten sample of returns (Tables
> 71 to 99) are given as the count obtained in the sample
> without modification; the count must be multiplied by
> an appropriate factor of around ten to provide an
> estimated figure for the enumerated population as a
> whole; a cell with no member of the sample population
> is shown with a dash, but this is not necessarily an
> estimate of a nil value in the population as a whole.
> Section 8 gives fuller guidance.

> Cross-tabulations, that is where an element of the
> population is counted only once, are separated by *ruled
> lines* within tables, as are single cell counts; where a
> table has a total row or column common to a number of
> cross-tabulations, it is usually shown only for the first
> cross-tabulation.

6   The populations covered in the Report

6.1   Each cross-tabulation in this Report has a *population
base*, that is the total population distributed among the
tabulation cells - using the term 'population' in the wider
statistical sense of the items being counted. Most of the bases
count people or households, but some count other items, and
many tabulations have bases which are sub-sets of populations as a whole.

6.2   The tabulations count people in an area in one of two
basic ways - those who were *present* on Census night, and
those who were *resident* whether or not they were present.
The method of counting people present is unchanged from
previous censuses; the method of enumerating people resident
was revised for the 1991 Census to provide a more complete
count.

6.3   The Census placed a legal obligation on every
household in which someone was present on Census night,
and on every person present in a communal establishment, to
complete a census form whether they were resident there or
a visitor resident elsewhere in Great Britain or outside
Britain. Additionally in 1991, for the first time in a British
census, there was an arrangement to enumerate, on a
voluntary basis, households where nobody was present on
Census night - 'wholly absent households'. Census forms
and reply paid envelopes were left for completion on the
return of such households. (This part of the enumeration was
on a voluntary basis because members of the absent
households either would have fulfilled their legal obligation
by filling in forms if they were elsewhere in Britain, or, if
they were outside Britain, had no such obligation.)

6.4   In all cases of wholly absent households, or where no
contact was made with a household which appeared to have
been present on Census day, the census enumerator recorded
the type of accommodation and an estimate of the number of
rooms and residents. Where a wholly absent household did
not subsequently return a form or where no contact was
made with a household, values for the fully processed parts
of the Census form were imputed during computer processing
using the basic information returned and data on households
nearby. The number of people in an area, included either on
the basis of voluntary returns or by imputation, is shown in
Table 1 in part 1 of the Report, with more detail in Table 18;
the number of households included by imputation is shown
in Table 19 in part 1 of the Report. Table 71 in this part of
the Report also shows the number of residents and
households imputed.

6.5   The addition of data from wholly absent households
and non-contacted households is an improvement compared
with the 1981 Census, when people from absent households
were only enumerated where they were present on Census
night (if in Britain). In 1981, people in wholly absent
households, although included in the counts of people
present, were excluded from the tables with a base of

residents in the 1981 County Reports. The change to the base does, however, slightly affect comparisons between 1981 and 1991 - see section 10.

Population bases

6.6   The main population bases used in cross-tabulations in this Report are defined in full in the volume *1991 Census Definitions* - see section 7. In summary they are as follows:

Persons present in the area on the night of 21 April 1991.

Residents of the area, who are:

- people both present and resident in a household or communal establishment;

- people resident in, but absent on the night of 21 April 1991, from a household in which one or more other people were present (people resident in communal establishments but absent on Census night are *not* included since the Census forms for communal establishments covered only those people present on Census night);

- people resident in wholly absent households who returned a census form; and

- people imputed as resident in wholly absent households and in households where no contact was made (Tables A to M and 1 to 70 only, and excluded from Tables 72 to 99).

Households with residents.

Households with people present but no residents.

Household spaces occupied by a household, or unoccupied.

Dwellings - structurally separate premises (a building or part of one) designed for occupation by a single household.

Figure 1 below shows the relationship between the elements in the population bases of *persons present* and *residents*.

6.7   In addition, there are bases of: *families* of resident persons; units of *non-permanent accommodation*; units of *converted or shared accommodation*; *rooms*; *cars in* (available to) *households*; and *communal establishments*.

6.8   Many tabulations count sub-sets of the main bases, for example, residents in households (that is, excluding those in communal establishments). Two tabulations - Tables 10 and 26 - combine more than one sub-set by including both students who were residents and those whose usual addresses were elsewhere. *Bases should therefore be checked before making comparisons between tabulations.*

Fig 1   Inter-relationship of population bases

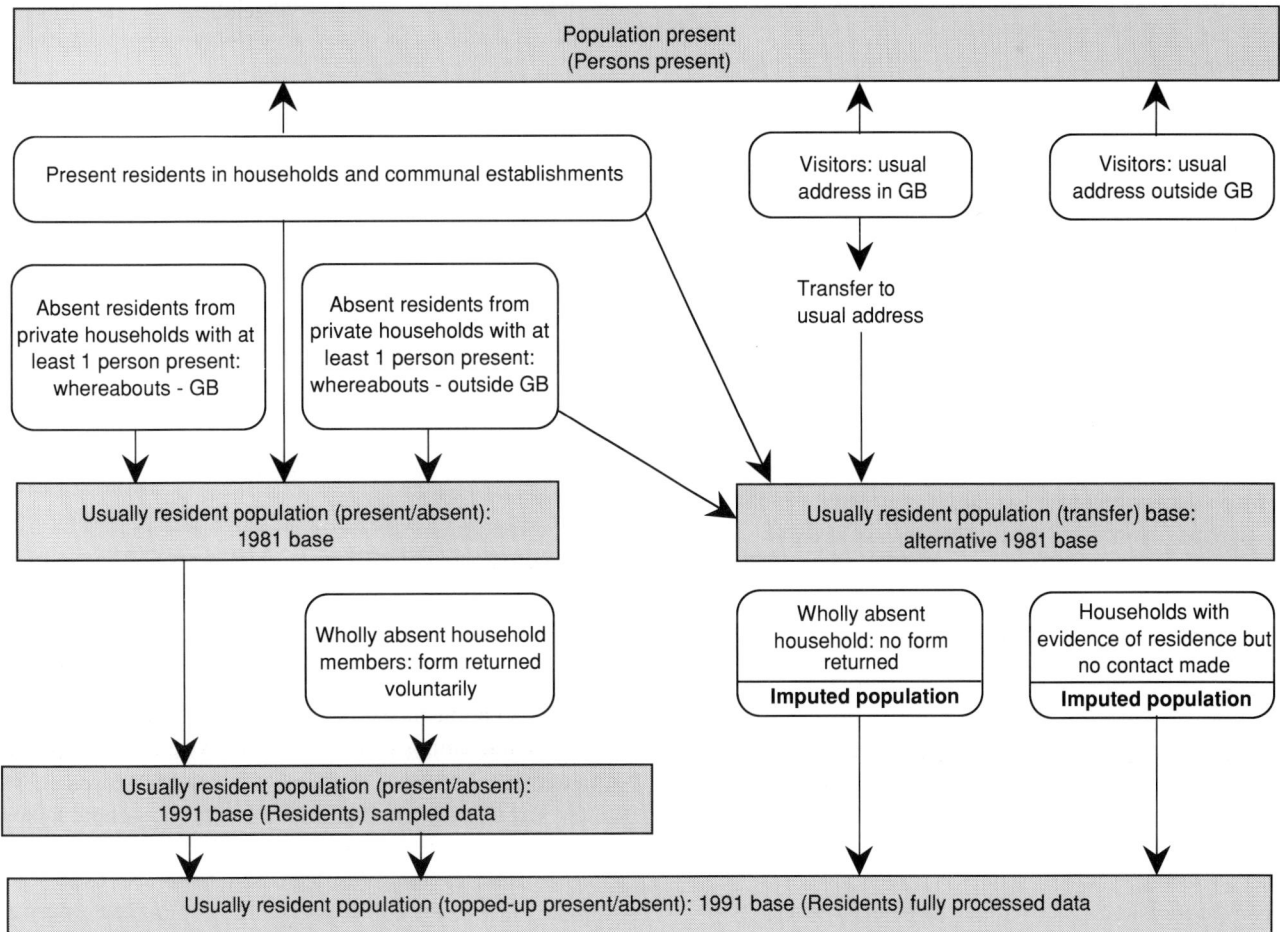

7 Definitions and explanatory notes

7.1 Definitions of all the terms used in the tables in this Report are given in *1991 Census Definitions* published by HMSO[2]. There are too many such definitions for them to be included in the text of this Report.

7.2 The margins of tables in this Report have been made as self-explanatory as possible, with as few abbreviations as possible. But they do not provide a complete definition of the statistics tabulated, and reference should also be made to the *1991 Census Definitions*. Reference may also need to be made to the volumes of *Definitions* for previous censuses if comparisons are being made, or to the appropriate definitions of terms in non-census sources.

7.3 Explanatory notes for the main tables in this part of the Report, including a general note on overstatement of the numbers of people on a government employment or training scheme, are given in Annex C after the main tables. Explanatory notes for tables 1 to 70 are in part 1 of the Report.

8 The '10 per cent' sample
(Tables 71-99)

8.1 The answers to certain census questions, mainly those which are difficult to code because of a wide range of written responses, have been processed for a sample of a nominal one in ten returns. The questions are identified in the list in section 4. The sample is drawn from the edited records prepared during the processing of all the returns. Thus the processing of the sample follows after the full processing, and the results are published somewhat later.

8.2 The sample is drawn by randomly selecting one complete enumerated (but not imputed) household from each 'stratum' of ten sequentially numbered forms, together with one person randomly selected from each stratum of ten sequentially numbered individual forms in communal establishments. This method of sampling avoids the types of bias that can occur in field sampling, and the stratification improves the geographical spread of households included in the sample. However, the clustering of people within households tends to reduce the precision of estimates for variables such as migration or mode of travel to work where the characteristics of individuals within the same household tend to be inter-dependent. Data are not imputed for the sampled topics. *Imputed wholly absent households - see section 6 - are therefore not included in the '10 per cent' tables and the sample is therefore slightly fewer than 10 per cent of the households included in the '100 per cent' tables.*

Estimating '100 per cent' figures

8.3 The conversion of a sample count, as given in tables 71 to 99 in this part of the Report, to an estimate of the figure for the population as a whole (100 per cent) can be obtained by multiplying the sample count by a sampling factor. The factors, both for residents and for households will be slightly over 10 in most cases, for the reasons given in paragraph 8.2, and will vary slightly from area to area. In addition, the factor for residents may be somewhat affected for small populations by the clustering of individuals within sampled households; this may also affect estimates of characteristics within households (see paragraphs 8.2 and 8.5).

8.4 The sampling factor is essentially the ratio of the 100 per cent count to the sample count. This allows for the omission of imputed households and residents in the 10 per cent sample (see paragraph 8.2). For the total population for an area, the sampling factor can be determined from Table 71:

$$\text{for residents} = \frac{\text{row 1, column b}}{\text{row 2, column b}}$$

and,

$$\text{for households} = \frac{\text{row 1, columns f and g}}{\text{row 2, column f}}$$

8.5 In most cases the method in paragraph 8.4 will give sufficiently accurate results. However, the factors given there do no take into account any variation in sampling factors specific to the variable being analysed, for example, by the clustering effect (see paragraphs 8.2 and 8.3). To take this additional variation into account, it is often possible to calculate a sampling factor for a sub-population. Many of the tables in this part of the Report contain statistics for a sub-population for which a 100 per cent count is given in tables 1 to 70 in part 1 of the Report. In these cases, the sampling factor can be more accurately determined as the ratio of the relevant 100 per cent count to the sample count. As an example, suppose an estimate of the 100 per cent count of all male corporate managers and administrators aged 30-44 (from Table 74), which is a group within the sub-population of male employees and self-employed, is required for a particular area. The most accurate sampling factor would be given by:

$$\frac{\begin{array}{c}\text{100\% count of all male employees}\\\text{and self-employed aged 30-44}\end{array}}{\begin{array}{c}\text{Sample count of all male employees}\\\text{and self-employed aged 30-44}\end{array}}$$

$$= \frac{\text{Table 8 (males) rows 2 to 5, columns j to l}}{\text{Table 74 row 1, column f}}$$

8.6 In those tables in which no comparable 100 per cent sub-population count is available (Tables 80, 86 (part), 88, 89, 96, and 97), the total resident and total household factors (see paragraph 8.4) should be used. Alternatively, a close approximation to the sub-population could be used - for example, the factor for residents in employment (derived

---

[2]OPCS/GRO(S). *1991 Census Definitions, Great Britain.* HMSO, 1992

from Tables 8 and 72) could be used for Table 96. For counts of families in tables 80, 86 (part), 88, and 89, household factors should be used.

8.7 Further information and guidance on the use of 10 per cent statistics, will be given in 1991 Census User Guides to be published later in 1993.

9   Evaluation of the results

9.1 The results presented in this Report will inevitably contain some inaccuracies arising from deficiencies and errors in coverage or response. The main causes are:

(a) failure to identify all residential accommodation;

(b) failure to identify all households and household spaces within accommodation;

(c) failure to enumerate all persons present or resident within households or communal establishments;

(d) errors in the estimates of numbers of persons in wholly absent households or where no contact was made;

(e) mis-classification of accommodation, for example, classifying wholly absent households as vacant, or vice versa;

(f) errors of double counting persons recorded as resident at more than one address;

(g) incorrect information supplied by filling in the forms, including missing responses; and

(h) errors introduced when processing the forms, including the imputation of data.

Steps are taken to assess the prevalence of these inaccuracies; but, because of the impracticability of conducting a very large number of one-to-one checks, the results are fairly broad estimates. These provide the basis of allowances for inaccuracies in the Census when the Registrar General's mid-year population estimates are made, and provide users of the Census with indications of the degree of confidence that may be placed in the Census results. The figures in Census Reports themselves are *not* adjusted.

9.2 The main check on the completeness and quality of response to the 1991 Census is provided by a Census Validation Survey (CVS). This was a voluntary sample survey conducted soon after the Census in 1,200 Census Enumeration Districts by interviewers employed in the Social Survey by the Office of Population Censuses and Surveys (OPCS). The sampling fraction for the CVS was higher in Inner and Outer London, and in the Metropolitan Counties and Glasgow.

9.3 The checks on *coverage* assessed whether:

(a) any household spaces in accommodation in the sampled areas had been missed;

(b) any of a sample of unoccupied household spaces had been mis-classified;

(c) any household in a sample of multi-occupied buildings had been missed; and whether

(d) anyone was present on Census night in a sample of households reported to have been wholly absent.

A sample of households where no contact had been made was also checked. On the basis of the coverage checks, estimates of under- or over-enumeration have been made for Inner London, Outer London, Glasgow, other Metropolitan Counties as a whole, the remaining parts of England and Wales as a whole, and the remaining parts of Scotland as a whole.

9.4 The check on the *quality* of response is provided by a further sample of households taken in the sampled Enumeration Districts. As well as checking whether everybody in the household had been included on the Census form (as part of the coverage check), the interviewer checked the accuracy of responses on the form by asking further questions, noting any explanations for differences. Analyses of gross and net differences will be prepared.

9.5 All estimates from the CVS will, of course, be subject to sampling error. Also, the CVS cannot provide a complete check on coverage and quality, even for the households included in the sample, because of changes in the circumstances of respondents between the Census and the CVS and because of incomplete response to the CVS. Despite these inherent limitations, the CVS provides valuable information about the coverage and quality of the Census.

9.6 Results of the CVS are published as they become available. The *Census Newsletter* - see section 13 - includes summaries of the main findings, and initial results of the coverage check for Great Britain were published in October 1992 in *Census Newsletter* 24. The full report on the CVS is scheduled to be published early in 1994.

9.7 The Registrar General's mid-year estimates for local authorities in 1991 (and subsequent years) take the Census counts of usual residents given in the County Reports as the starting point. The Census counts are adjusted as necessary in the calculation of the estimates, the main adjustments being as follows:

(a) allowances for any estimated under- (or over-) enumeration indicated by the CVS and any other appropriate evidence, including estimates 'rolled forward' from the 1981 Census;

(b) allowances for differences in the definition of 'residents' between the Census and the estimates; in particular, students are included in the estimates at term-time addresses (an extra question was included in the 1991 Census to provide a better basis for this adjustment);

(c) allowances in respect of armed forces personnel and their dependants; and

(d) the lapse of time between the Census and mid-year 1991.

The counts of residents in this Report and the 1991 mid-year population estimates will therefore not be identical. Differences should be interpreted in the light of the adjustments described above.

9.8   A comparison between the results of the 1991 Census for Great Britain, England and Wales, and Scotland and the provisional mid-1991 population estimates was published in December 1992 as Annex A in the *1991 Census National Monitor: Great Britain*[3]. This showed some 1,166 thousand fewer residents counted in the Census than in the estimate of 50,055 thousand residents in Great Britain, and, after allowances for the different basis of the estimate, this suggested an under-coverage in the Census of some 1,053 thousand residents (a level of 1.9 per cent). The comparison, together with brief guidance on taking account of under-coverage when using 1991 Census figures, is also published in section 7 of the 1991 Census Report *Sex, Age and Marital Status*[4] and will be repeated in other topic reports - see Annex B. The *General Report* on the 1991 Census - see section 2 - will contain an overview of the evaluation of the Census.

10 Comparisons of results with those of earlier censuses

10.1   The population of Hampshire at successive censuses from 1891 to 1991 is given in summary Table A in section 15 of part 1 of the Report. Comparisons between 1981 and 1991 are also given for selected variables in other tables in section 15 of part 1.

10.2   Further comparisons between censuses are affected by changes in: the geographic base; the topics included in the censuses; and the definition of counts presented in the tables. The detail of changes over the long series of censuses is complex, and there is no single guide for users. Reports since the 1901 Census have listed intercensal boundary changes - on the lines of Annex A in this Report, and the *Guide to Census Reports*[5] describes the general changes in censuses up to 1966.

10.3   A guide to the detailed comparability of the 1971 and 1981 Census Small Area Statistics was issued after the 1981 Census (OPCS *1981 User Guide 84*[6]), but it does not cover

comparison between 1971 and 1981 County Reports where they differ from the Small Area Statistics for those years. There is a similar guide on the detailed comparability of 1981 Small Area Statistics and 1991 Local and Small Area Statistics (OPCS/GRO(S) *1991 User Guide 28*[7]), and, although the Guide is not specific to the 1981 County Reports - the content of which differed somewhat from the Small Area Statistics, OPCS *1981 User Guide 86*[8] gives the link between 1981 SAS and 1981 County Report tables. It is therefore possible to determine where comparisons can be made between figures in the 1981 and 1991 County Report tables, and where comparisons must be qualified.

11 Further results from the 1991 Census

11.1   The results of the Census are made available in two ways:

(a) in printed reports made to Parliament and sold by HMSO bookshops (or, in a few cases, directly from the Census Offices); or

(b) in statistical abstracts available, on request and for a charge, from the Census Offices.

11.2   The results also tend to fall into two broad types: local statistics which cover the full range of census topics - such as this Report - or a summary selection of all topics; and topic statistics which focus on a particular census topic in more detail, mainly at national and regional level. There are also other products which provide further information from the Census. All the main results and products are described in *Prospectuses* in the OPCS/GRO(S) 1991 *User Guide* series, available from the addresses given in section 13. A brief guide to sources of comparable local statistics for other areas, and to sources of more detailed results on particular census topics, together with relevant *Prospectuses,* is included at Annex B.

[3]OPCS/GRO(S). *1991 Census National Monitor: Great Britain.* OPCS Monitor Cen 91, CM 56. OPCS, 1992. ISBN 1 85774 056 4

[4]OPCS/GRO(S). *1991 Census Sex, Age and Marital Status: Great Britain.* HMSO, 1993.

[5]OPCS/GRO(S). *Guide to Census reports, Great Britain 1801-1966.* HMSO, 1977. ISBN 0 11 690638 3

[6]OPCS. *Guide to Statistical Comparability 1971-81: England and Wales.* User Guide 84, OPCS Census Customer Services, 1984

[7]OPCS. *Guide to Statistical Comparability of 1981 Small Area Statistics and 1991 Local Base and Small Area Statistics - Prospectus.* User Guide 28, OPCS Census Customer Services, 1992

[8]OPCS. *1981 Small Area Statistics/County Reports. A guide to comparison.* User Guide 86, OPCS Census Customer Services, 1982

12 Copyright and reproduction of material from this Report

12.1 All text, statistical and other material in this Report and information of any kind derived from the statistics or other material in the Report is CROWN COPYRIGHT and may be reproduced only with the permission of the Office of Population Censuses and Surveys (OPCS).

12.2 OPCS is prepared to allow extracts of statistics or other material from this Report to be reproduced without a licence provided that these form part of a larger work not primarily designed to reproduce the extracts *and* provided that any extract of statistics represents only a limited part of a table or tables *and* provided that Crown Copyright and the source are prominently acknowledged. OPCS reserves its rights in all circumstances and should be consulted in any case of uncertainty. Enquiries about the reproduction of material should be directed to OPCS at the address given in section 13, and reproduction may require a licence and payment of fees.

13 Further information

13.1 Any *queries* about the content of this Report or on the interpretation of the results in the Report should be made to:

Census Division
OPCS
St Catherine's House
10 Kingsway
London WC2B 6JP

telephone 071 396 2008

Please quote the topic(s) and/or table(s) which are the subject of the enquiry and ask, if necessary, to be put in touch with the member of staff with responsibility for the topic(s) or the subject of the table(s) concerned.

13.2 All *Prospectuses/User Guides* mentioned in this Report may be obtained (by those in England and Wales, or outside Great Britain) from:

Census Customer Services
OPCS
Segensworth Road
Titchfield
Fareham
Hants PO15 5RR

telephone 0329 813800

or (by those in Scotland) from:

Census Customer Services
General Register Office for Scotland
Ladywell House
Ladywell Road
Edinburgh EH12 7TF

telephone 031 314 4254

Census Customer Services will also arrange the supply of any statistical abstracts required.

Request to reproduce material from this Report - see section 12, should be made to Census Customer Services at OPCS.

Reports published by HMSO may be purchased from the addresses shown on the back cover of this Report.

Census Newsletter

*News on all aspects of the Census, including the availability of results, is provided by the **Census Newsletter** issued several times a year by the Census Offices and distributed without charge. Names may be added to the mailing list by contacting Census Customer Services. It is also possible to register with Census Customer Services as a user of the Census to obtain details of relevant products automatically and to ensure inclusion in consultation over future developments.*

14 Reference map

14.1 The map on the following page shows the boundaries of districts covered by this Report, and the boundaries of neighbouring counties. The map is reproduced from the Ordnance Survey 1:250,000 map with the permission of the Controller of Her Majesty's Stationery Office, Crown Copyright reserved.

14.2 The highlighted county/county district boundary lines were drawn by OPCS and reflect, as accurately as possible, the boundaries as constituted at 21 April 1991. As the base maps supplied by Ordnance Survey may not always reflect the latest boundary changes, the county boundary lines on the base map and the highlighted boundaries will not always correspond exactly.

9

© Crown copyright

15 Indexes and main tables

Tables by key word title

Summary tables (Section 15, Part 1)

Main tables (Part 1)

Main tables (Part 2)

Topic and key word index (Part 2)

Full table titles

The following notes describe how to interpret the titles, which are constructed in standard forms. Titles of simple tables which are generally a *cross-tabulation* with a single variable in the rows, but possibly have more than one variable in the columns, follow the form:

(row variable) "by" (column variable(s))

Table 7 is an example.

Titles of tables with more than one variable in the rows have the general form:

(row variables) "all by" (column variable(s))

Where cross-tabulations share a common set of total counts, this 'concatenation' is separated by a comma. Different tabulations *within* a table are separated by a semi-colon (for example, where a set of counts shares only the same population base but no common variables). Table 47 illustrates these features:

An example of a complex table illustrates these features.

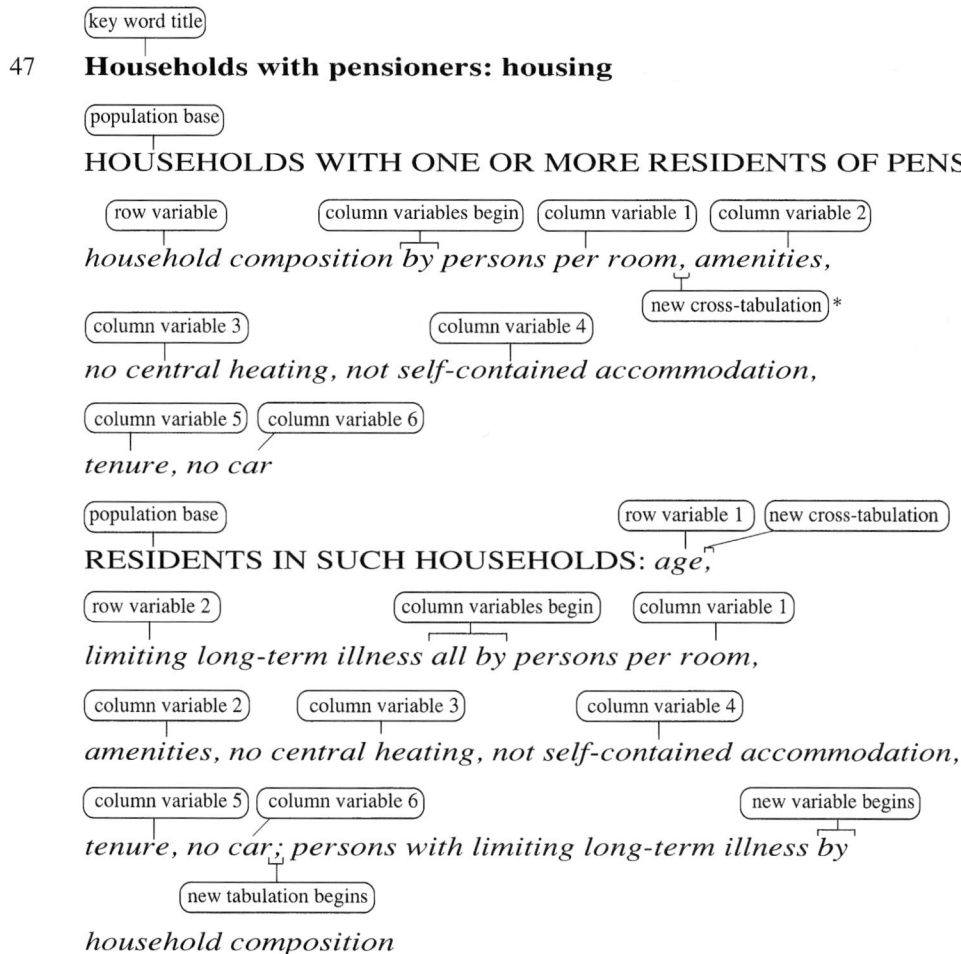

[key word title]

47 **Households with pensioners: housing**

[population base]

HOUSEHOLDS WITH ONE OR MORE RESIDENTS OF PENSIONABLE AGE:

[row variable] [column variables begin] [column variable 1] [column variable 2]

household composition by persons per room, amenities,

[new cross-tabulation] *

[column variable 3] [column variable 4]

no central heating, not self-contained accommodation,

[column variable 5] [column variable 6]

tenure, no car

[population base] [row variable 1] [new cross-tabulation]

RESIDENTS IN SUCH HOUSEHOLDS: *age,*

[row variable 2] [column variables begin] [column variable 1]

limiting long-term illness all by persons per room,

[column variable 2] [column variable 3] [column variable 4]

amenities, no central heating, not self-contained accommodation,

[column variable 5] [column variable 6] [new variable begins]

tenure, no car; persons with limiting long-term illness by

[new tabulation begins]

household composition

* refers to all commas

Where row or column variables are 'nested', that is where one variable is broken down by another along one axis of a table, they are separated by the word "by". Where this 'nesting' occurs in the rows axis, the 'nested' variables will be followed by "all by". Table 73 illustrates these features:

[key word title]

73 **Industry (10% sample)**

[population base]

RESIDENTS AGED 16 AND OVER, EMPLOYEES AND SELF-EMPLOYED:

[nested variables] [column variables begin]

sex by age all by industry divisions

Main tables (Part 1)

Page numbers for tables are given in Part 1 of the report published separately.

I *Demographic and Economic characteristics*

1 **Population bases**

PERSONS PRESENT PLUS ABSENT RESIDENTS IN HOUSEHOLDS: *whether present or absent residents or visitors, 1971, 1981 and 1991 population base counts by whether in a household by sex*

2 **Age and marital status**

RESIDENTS: *age by sex by marital status*

3 **Communal establishments**

ESTABLISHMENTS: *number of establishments by type*
PERSONS PRESENT NOT IN HOUSEHOLDS: *type of establishment by status in establishment by sex*

4 **Medical and care establishments**

RESIDENTS (NON-STAFF) PRESENT NOT IN HOUSEHOLDS: *type of establishment by age by sex, migrants, limiting long-term illness, ethnic group*

5 **Hotels and other establishments**

RESIDENTS (NON-STAFF) PRESENT NOT IN HOUSEHOLDS: *type of establishment by age by sex, economic position, migrants, ethnic group*

6 **Ethnic group**

RESIDENTS: *age by sex, born in UK, limiting long-term illness by sex all by ethnic group, born in Ireland*

7 **Country of birth**

RESIDENTS: *country of birth by sex*

8 **Economic position**

RESIDENTS AGED 16 AND OVER: *sex by marital status for females by economic position all by age*

9 **Economic position and ethnic group**

RESIDENTS AGED 16 AND OVER: *sex by economic position all by ethnic group, born in Ireland*

10 **Term-time address**

STUDENTS (16 AND OVER) PRESENT PLUS ABSENT RESIDENT STUDENTS (16 AND OVER): *residence status by term-time address all by age, born outside UK*

11 **Persons present**

PERSONS PRESENT: *age by whether enumerated in a household or not by sex, status if not in a household by sex*

Main tables (Part 1) - *continued*

12 **Long-term illness in households**

RESIDENTS IN HOUSEHOLDS WITH LIMITING LONG-TERM ILLNESS: *age by sex*

13 **Long-term illness in communal establishments**

PERSONS PRESENT NOT IN HOUSEHOLDS WITH LIMITING LONG-TERM ILLNESS: *age by type of establishment by sex, status in establishment by sex for residents*

14 **Long-term illness and economic position**

RESIDENTS AGED 16 AND OVER WITH LIMITING LONG-TERM ILLNESS: *economic position by age*

15 **Migrants**

RESIDENTS WITH DIFFERENT ADDRESS ONE YEAR BEFORE CENSUS: *all migrants by age, migrants in households by age, all by type of move by sex*

16 **Wholly moving households**

WHOLLY MOVING HOUSEHOLDS: *type of household by type of move*
RESIDENTS IN SUCH HOUSEHOLDS: *type of household by type of move*

17 **Ethnic group of migrants**

RESIDENTS AGED 1 AND OVER: *total persons, migrants all by ethnic group, born in Ireland*

18 **Imputed residents**

IMPUTED RESIDENTS OF WHOLLY ABSENT HOUSEHOLDS: *age, marital status, limiting long-term illness, economic position, ethnic group all by sex*

II *Housing*

19 **Imputed households**

WHOLLY ABSENT HOUSEHOLDS WITH IMPUTED RESIDENTS: *tenure, amenities, no central heating, no car, lone 'parent' households all by number of persons in household*
IMPUTED RESIDENTS IN SUCH HOUSEHOLDS: *tenure, amenities, central heating, no car, lone 'parent' households*

20 **Tenure and amenities**

HOUSEHOLDS WITH RESIDENTS: *amenities, no car all by tenure of households in permanent accommodation, non-permanent accommodation, no car*
RESIDENTS IN HOUSEHOLDS: *amenities, no car all by tenure of households in permanent accommodation, non-permanent accommodation, no car*

Main tables (Part 1) - *continued*

21 **Car availability**

HOUSEHOLDS WITH RESIDENTS: *household composition, by number of cars available*
RESIDENTS IN HOUSEHOLDS: *household composition; all persons and persons aged 17 and over all by number of cars available*
CARS IN HOUSEHOLDS: *household composition*

22 **Rooms and household size**

HOUSEHOLDS WITH RESIDENTS: *tenure by number of persons all by number of rooms*
RESIDENTS IN HOUSEHOLDS: *tenure by number of rooms*
ROOMS IN HOUSEHOLD SPACES: *tenure by number of persons*

23 **Persons per room**

HOUSEHOLDS WITH RESIDENTS: *tenure of households in permanent buildings, non-permanent accommodation all by number of persons per room*
RESIDENTS IN HOUSEHOLDS: *tenure of households in permanent buildings, non-permanent accommodation all by number of persons per room*

24 **Residents 18 and over**

HOUSEHOLDS WITH RESIDENTS: *number of persons by number of persons aged 18 and over*
RESIDENTS IN HOUSEHOLDS: *total persons by number of persons aged 18 and over; total persons aged 18 and over by number of persons*

25 **Visitor households**

HOUSEHOLDS WITH PERSONS PRESENT BUT NO RESIDENTS: *household composition by amenities, no central heating, not self-contained accommodation, tenure*
PERSONS PRESENT IN SUCH HOUSEHOLDS: *total persons, total students all by amenities, no central heating, not self-contained accommodation, tenure; total students by household composition*
CARS IN SUCH HOUSEHOLDS: *household composition*
ROOMS IN SUCH HOUSEHOLDS: *household composition*

26 **Students in households**

HOUSEHOLDS WITH RESIDENTS: *household composition, number of students in household all by amenities, no central heating, not self-contained accommodation, tenure, number of persons present or resident*
RESIDENTS IN HOUSEHOLDS, PERSONS PRESENT IN HOUSEHOLDS: *total persons present or resident, total students present or resident all by amenities, no central heating, not self-contained accommodation, tenure, number of persons present or resident, household composition, number of students in household all by total student visitors, total student residents*
ROOMS IN HOUSEHOLD SPACES: *household composition, number of students in household*
CARS IN HOUSEHOLDS: *household composition, number of students in household*

Main tables (Part 1) - *continued*

27 **Households: 1971/81/91 bases**

HOUSEHOLDS WITH PERSONS PRESENT (1971 POPULATION BASE): *number of persons*
HOUSEHOLDS (1981 POPULATION BASE): *number of persons*
HOUSEHOLDS ENUMERATED OR ABSENT (1991 POPULATION BASE): *number of persons*
PRESENT RESIDENTS AND VISITORS (1971 POPULATION BASE): *total*
PRESENT AND ABSENT RESIDENTS (1981 POPULATION BASE): *total*
PRESENT AND ABSENT RESIDENTS AND IMPUTED MEMBERS OF WHOLLY ABSENT HOUSEHOLDS (1991 POPULATION BASE): *total*
ROOMS: *in 1971, 1981, and 1991 population base households*

III *Households and household composition*

28 **Dependants in households**

HOUSEHOLDS WITH RESIDENTS: *household composition by economic position of non-dependants*
RESIDENTS IN HOUSEHOLDS: *non-dependants, dependants all by economic position of non-dependants*

29 **Dependants and long-term illness**

HOUSEHOLDS WITH RESIDENTS: *household composition*
DEPENDANTS IN HOUSEHOLDS: *household composition by dependency type*

30 **'Carers'**

HOUSEHOLDS WITH RESIDENTS: *number of non-dependants by sex by age all by ages in combination of dependants*
RESIDENTS IN HOUSEHOLDS WITH DEPENDANTS: non-dependants, dependants all by number, age and sex of non-dependants

31 **Dependent children in households**

HOUSEHOLDS WITH RESIDENTS: *number of adults by sex all by number of dependent children by age*
RESIDENTS IN HOUSEHOLDS: *number of adults in household by sex all by whether dependent children in household by economic activity*

32 **Children aged 0-15 in households**

HOUSEHOLDS WITH RESIDENTS: *number of persons aged 16 and over by sex all by number of persons aged 0-15 by age*
RESIDENTS IN HOUSEHOLDS: *number of persons aged 16 and over in household by sex all by whether persons aged 0-15 in household by economic activity*

33 **Women in 'couples': economic position**

FEMALES RESIDENT IN HOUSEHOLDS OF ONE MALE AGED 16 OR OVER AND ONE FEMALE AGED 16 OR OVER WITH OR WITHOUT PERSONS AGED 0-15: *ages in combination of persons aged under 16 by economic activity*
PERSONS AGED 0-15 IN SUCH HOUSEHOLDS: *age by economic position of female aged 16 or over*

19

Main tables (Part 1) - *continued*

34 **Economic position of household residents**

RESIDENTS AGED 16 AND OVER IN HOUSEHOLDS: *economic position by sex by marital status*

35 **Age and marital status of household residents**

RESIDENTS IN HOUSEHOLDS: *age by sex by marital status*

36 **'Earners' and dependent children**

HOUSEHOLDS WITH RESIDENTS: *number and economic position of adults all by number of dependent children*
RESIDENT ADULTS: *economic position by number of dependent children in household*
RESIDENT DEPENDENT CHILDREN: *number and economic position of adults in household*

37 **Young adults**

RESIDENTS AGED 16-24 IN HOUSEHOLDS: *age by marital status, lone 'parents' with children aged 0-15, economic position*

38 **Single years of age**

RESIDENTS IN HOUSEHOLDS: *age by sex*

39 **Headship**

RESIDENTS IN HOUSEHOLDS: *age by sex by marital status; persons by household head's age, sex and marital status*

40 **Lone 'parents'**

LONE 'PARENTS' AGED 16 AND OVER IN HOUSEHOLDS OF ONE PERSON AGED 16 AND OVER WITH PERSON(S) AGED 0-15: *ages of children in combination by sex by economic position*
PERSONS AGED 0-15 IN SUCH HOUSEHOLDS: *age by sex by economic position of lone 'parent'*

41 **Shared accommodation**

HOUSEHOLDS WITH RESIDENTS NOT IN SELF-CONTAINED ACCOMMODATION: *number of persons by persons per room, amenities, central heating, no car*
ROOMS IN SUCH HOUSEHOLDS: *number of persons*

42 **Household composition and housing**

HOUSEHOLDS WITH RESIDENTS: *household composition by persons per room, amenities, no central heating, not self-contained accommodation, tenure, car availability*
DEPENDENT CHILDREN IN HOUSEHOLDS: *age by persons per room, amenities, no central heating, not self-contained accommodation, tenure, car availability*

Main tables (Part 1) - *continued*

43 Household composition and ethnic group

HOUSEHOLDS WITH RESIDENTS: *household composition, pensioner households all by ethnic group of head of household, household head born in Ireland*
RESIDENTS IN HOUSEHOLDS: *age by ethnic group of head of household, household head born in Ireland*

44 Household composition and long-term illness

HOUSEHOLDS CONTAINING PERSONS WITH LIMITING LONG-TERM ILLNESS: *household composition, economic position of household members*
RESIDENTS IN SUCH HOUSEHOLDS: *household composition, economic position of household members, economic position all by limiting long-term illness by age by sex*

45 Migrant household heads

HOUSEHOLDS WITH RESIDENTS: *tenure by household heads, economic activity all by age by sex of migrant heads, age by sex of all household heads*

46 Households with dependent children: housing

HOUSEHOLDS WITH DEPENDENT CHILDREN: *household composition by persons per room, amenities, no central heating, not self-contained accommodation, tenure, no car*
RESIDENTS IN SUCH HOUSEHOLDS: *household composition by age all by persons per room, amenities, no central heating, not self-contained accommodation, tenure, no car; household composition*

47 Households with pensioners: housing

HOUSEHOLDS WITH ONE OR MORE RESIDENTS OF PENSIONABLE AGE: *household composition by persons per room, amenities, no central heating, not self-contained accommodation, tenure, no car*
RESIDENTS IN SUCH HOUSEHOLDS: *age, limiting long-term illness all by persons per room, amenities, no central heating, not self-contained accommodation, tenure, no car; persons with limiting long-term illness by household composition*

48 Households with dependants: housing

HOUSEHOLDS WITH RESIDENTS: *non-dependants and dependants by age of youngest and oldest dependants in combination all by persons per room, amenities, no central heating, not self-contained accommodation, no car*

49 Ethnic group: housing

HOUSEHOLDS WITH RESIDENTS: *persons per room, tenure, amenities, no central heating, not self-contained accommodation, no car, containing person(s) with limiting long-term illness all by ethnic group of household head, country of birth of household head*
RESIDENTS IN HOUSEHOLDS: *persons per room, amenities, no central heating, not self-contained accommodation, no car all by ethnic group of household head, country of birth of household head*

50 Country of birth: household heads and residents

RESIDENTS IN HOUSEHOLDS: *country of birth of household head by age, by country of birth of persons*
HOUSEHOLD HEADS: *country of birth*

Main tables (Part 1) - *continued*

51   **Country of birth and ethnic group**

RESIDENTS IN HOUSEHOLDS: *country of birth by ethnic group; country of birth of household heads by ethnic group of persons*
HOUSEHOLD HEADS: *country of birth by ethnic group*

52   **Language indicators**

RESIDENTS: *whether in a household by age all by country of birth, country of birth of household head*

53   **'Lifestages'**

RESIDENTS AGED 16 AND OVER IN HOUSEHOLDS: *age and household composition (lifestage category) all by whether in a 'couple' household*

IV *Household spaces and dwellings*

54   **Occupancy (occupied, vacant, and other accommodation)**

HOUSEHOLD SPACES: *occupancy type*
ROOMS IN HOUSEHOLD SPACES: *occupancy type*
ROOMS IN HOTELS AND BOARDING HOUSES: *total*

55   **Household spaces and occupancy**

HOUSEHOLD SPACES IN PERMANENT BUILDINGS: *occupancy type by number of household spaces in dwelling, unattached household spaces (not in a dwelling)*
DWELLINGS: *number of household spaces in dwelling*

56   **Household space type and occupancy**

HOUSEHOLD SPACES: *occupancy type by household space type in permanent buildings, non-permanent accommodation*

57   **Household space type: rooms and household size**

HOUSEHOLDS WITH RESIDENTS: *number of rooms, number of persons, persons per room all by household space type in permanent buildings, non-permanent accommodation, with migrant head*
RESIDENTS IN HOUSEHOLDS: *household space type in permanent buildings, non-permanent accommodation, with migrant head*
ROOMS IN HOUSEHOLD SPACES: *household space type in permanent buildings, non-permanent accommodation, with migrant head*

58   **Household space type: tenure and amenities**

HOUSEHOLDS WITH RESIDENTS: *tenure, amenities all by household space type in permanent buildings, non-permanent accommodation*

59   **Household space type: household composition**

HOUSEHOLDS WITH RESIDENTS: *household composition, pensioner households all by household space type in permanent buildings, non-permanent accommodation, with migrant head*
RESIDENTS IN HOUSEHOLDS: *age by household space type in permanent buildings, non-permanent accommodation, with migrant head; persons in households with migrant head by household composition, pensioner households*

Main tables (Part 1) - *continued*

60 **Dwellings and household spaces**

CONVERTED OR SHARED ACCOMMODATION (MULTI-OCCUPIED BUILDINGS): *number and type of dwellings*
DWELLINGS: *number and type in building by number of household spaces*
HOUSEHOLD SPACES: *number and type of dwellings in building by unattached household spaces, household space type*
ROOMS IN SUCH ACCOMMODATION: *number and type of dwellings in building*

61 **Dwelling type and occupancy**

DWELLINGS: *occupancy type by type of dwelling*
NON-PERMANENT ACCOMMODATION: *occupancy type*

62 **Occupancy and tenure of dwellings**

DWELLINGS WITH PERSONS PRESENT OR RESIDENT: *occupancy type by tenure*

63 **Dwelling type and tenure**

DWELLINGS WITH RESIDENTS: *tenure by type of dwelling*
NON-PERMANENT ACCOMMODATION: *tenure*

64 **Tenure of dwellings and household spaces**

DWELLINGS: *tenure or occupancy type by type of dwelling*
HOUSEHOLD SPACES IN DWELLINGS: *tenure or occupancy type of dwelling by tenure or occupancy type of household spaces*

65 **Occupancy of dwellings and household spaces**

DWELLINGS: *occupancy type by type of dwelling*
HOUSEHOLD SPACES IN DWELLINGS: *occupancy type of dwelling by occupancy type of household spaces*

66 **Shared dwellings**

SHARED DWELLINGS: *number of household spaces within dwelling*
HOUSEHOLD SPACES IN SHARED DWELLINGS: *number of household spaces in dwelling by type of household spaces*

V *Wales only tables*

67 **Welsh language**

RESIDENTS: *age, not in households, born in Wales all by speaking, reading, writing Welsh, sex*

Main Tables (Part 2)   Page

VI *10 per cent topics*

RESIDENTS: *100% and 10% sample counts all by whether in households, whether imputed residents in a wholly absent household*
HOUSEHOLDS WITH RESIDENTS: *100% and 10% counts all by whether imputed wholly absent households*

Main tables (Part 2) - *continued*

Page

Main tables (Part 2) - *continued*

Main tables (Part 2) - *continued*

Main Tables

Explanatory notes for tables appear in Annex C, after the tables. Notes are in the numerical order of the tables.

Table 71   Comparison of 100% and 10% counts   **County, districts**

71. Residents; households with residents

	Residents				Households	
	TOTAL	Not in households	In households		Enumerated	Imputed
			Enumerated	Imputed		
a	b	c	d	e	f	g
HAMPSHIRE						
100% counts	1,541,547	29,509	1,495,287	16,751	594,624	8,633
10% sample counts	152,415	2,965	149,450		59,458	
Basingstoke & Deane						
100% counts	144,790	1,512	141,945	1,333	53,678	645
10% sample counts	14,314	147	14,167		5,369	
East Hampshire						
100% counts	103,460	2,125	100,384	951	38,685	473
10% sample counts	10,130	215	9,915		3,873	
Eastleigh						
100% counts	105,999	701	104,226	1,072	40,690	529
10% sample counts	10,507	72	10,435		4,073	
Fareham						
100% counts	99,262	1,655	97,084	523	38,090	279
10% sample counts	9,903	166	9,737		3,810	
Gosport						
100% counts	75,061	1,357	72,984	720	29,005	351
10% sample counts	7,426	138	7,288		2,899	
Hart						
100% counts	80,921	1,907	78,324	690	28,731	342
10% sample counts	8,040	192	7,848		2,875	
Havant						
100% counts	119,697	1,400	117,257	1,040	45,637	514
10% sample counts	11,717	136	11,581		4,562	
New Forest						
100% counts	160,456	2,852	155,775	1,829	64,411	1,000
10% sample counts	15,788	296	15,492		6,429	
Portsmouth						
100% counts	174,697	4,967	166,818	2,912	71,042	1,548
10% sample counts	17,362	494	16,868		7,101	
Rushmoor						
100% counts	82,526	3,405	78,205	916	30,078	445
10% sample counts	8,156	341	7,815		3,008	

71. Residents; households with residents

a	Residents				Households	
	TOTAL	Not in households	In households		Enumerated	Imputed
			Enumerated	Imputed		
a	b	c	d	e	f	g
Southampton						
100% counts	196,864	2,998	190,831	3,035	79,505	1,635
10% sample counts	19,411	303	19,108		7,955	
Test Valley						
100% counts	101,428	1,965	98,459	1,004	37,863	528
10% sample counts	10,118	197	9,921		3,781	
Winchester						
100% counts	96,386	2,665	92,995	726	37,209	344
10% sample counts	9,543	268	9,275		3,723	

Table 72   Economic and employment status (10% sample)   **County, districts**

72. Residents aged 16 and over   (10% sample)

Economic position and employment status	TOTAL PERSONS	Males	Females	Students (economically active or inactive)
a	b	c	d	e

HAMPSHIRE

TOTAL PERSONS	**121,979**	**58,818**	**63,161**	**5,157**
Economically active	**78,033**	**45,053**	**32,980**	**862**
In employment	72,521	41,184	31,337	847
of which - working 31 or more hours per week	*54,601*	*37,343*	*17,258*	*56*
of which - working 30 or fewer hours per week	*14,992*	*1,940*	*13,052*	*766*
Employees	63,216	34,046	29,170	842
of which - working 31 or more hours per week	*47,772*	*31,494*	*16,278*	*55*
of which - working 30 or fewer hours per week	*13,767*	*1,501*	*12,266*	*762*
Managers	12,653	8,667	3,986	54
Large establishments	4,935	3,623	1,312	14
Small establishments	7,718	5,044	2,674	40
Foremen and supervisors	3,773	2,132	1,641	23
Non-manual	1,633	542	1,091	15
Manual	2,140	1,590	550	8
Professional employees	4,072	3,451	621	49
Other employees	62,472	28,705	33,767	1,937
Self-employed	8,657	6,744	1,913	5
of which - working 31 or more hours per week	*6,829*	*5,849*	*980*	*1*
of which - working 30 or fewer hours per week	*1,225*	*439*	*786*	*4*
Without employees	6,128	4,833	1,295	4
With employees	2,529	1,911	618	1
Large establishments	48	39	9	-
Small establishments	2,481	1,872	609	1
On a Government scheme	648	394	254	
Unemployed	5,512	3,869	1,643	15
Seeking work	5,296	3,748	1,548	12
Waiting to start a job	216	121	95	3
Economically active students (included above)	*862*	*380*	*482*	
Economically inactive	**43,946**	**13,765**	**30,181**	**4,295**
Students	4,295	2,144	2,151	4,295
Permanently sick	3,038	1,706	1,332	
Retired	21,506	9,575	11,931	
Other inactive	15,107	340	14,767	

72. Residents aged 16 and over   (10% sample)

Economic position and employment status	TOTAL PERSONS	Males	Females	Students (economically active or inactive)
a	b	c	d	e

Basingstoke & Deane

TOTAL PERSONS	**11,279**	**5,595**	**5,684**	**444**
Economically active	**7,992**	**4,587**	**3,405**	**83**
In employment	7,529	4,268	3,261	80
of which - working 31 or more hours per week	*5,898*	*3,953*	*1,945*	*4*
of which - working 30 or fewer hours per week	*1,404*	*173*	*1,231*	*75*
Employees	6,650	3,586	3,064	79
of which - working 31 or more hours per week	*5,239*	*3,378*	*1,861*	*4*
of which - working 30 or fewer hours per week	*1,293*	*138*	*1,155*	*74*
Managers	1,369	914	455	5
Large establishments	563	378	185	2
Small establishments	806	536	270	3
Foremen and supervisors	389	231	158	3
Non-manual	167	61	106	2
Manual	222	170	52	1
Professional employees	478	394	84	1
Other employees	6,075	2,773	3,302	166
Self-employed	822	651	171	1
of which - working 31 or more hours per week	*659*	*575*	*84*	*-*
of which - working 30 or fewer hours per week	*111*	*35*	*76*	*1*
Without employees	599	472	127	1
With employees	223	179	44	-
Large establishments	6	5	1	-
Small establishments	217	174	43	-
On a Government scheme	57	31	26	
Unemployed	463	319	144	3
Seeking work	451	312	139	2
Waiting to start a job	12	7	5	1
Economically active students (included above)	*83*	*37*	*46*	
Economically inactive	**3,287**	**1,008**	**2,279**	**361**
Students	361	180	181	361
Permanently sick	207	107	100	
Retired	1,536	695	841	
Other inactive	1,183	26	1,157	

72. Residents aged 16 and over   (10% sample)

Economic position and employment status	TOTAL PERSONS	Males	Females	Students (economically active or inactive)
a	b	c	d	e
East Hampshire				
TOTAL PERSONS	8,047	3,858	4,189	347
Economically active	5,238	3,010	2,228	51
In employment	4,995	2,845	2,150	49
of which - working 31 or more hours per week	*3,753*	*2,585*	*1,168*	*7*
of which - working 30 or fewer hours per week	*1,030*	*132*	*898*	*40*
Employees	4,155	2,215	1,940	49
of which - working 31 or more hours per week	*3,126*	*2,058*	*1,068*	*7*
of which - working 30 or fewer hours per week	*925*	*99*	*826*	*40*
Managers	1,039	768	271	1
Large establishments	356	292	64	-
Small establishments	683	476	207	1
Foremen and supervisors	222	120	102	-
Non-manual	84	26	58	-
Manual	138	94	44	-
Professional employees	285	244	41	2
Other employees	3,686	1,532	2,154	110
Self-employed	801	606	195	-
of which - working 31 or more hours per week	*627*	*527*	*100*	*-*
of which - working 30 or fewer hours per week	*105*	*33*	*72*	*-*
Without employees	568	430	138	-
With employees	233	176	57	-
Large establishments	2	2	-	-
Small establishments	231	174	57	-
On a Government scheme	39	24	15	
Unemployed	243	165	78	2
Seeking work	230	155	75	-
Waiting to start a job	13	10	3	2
Economically active students (included above)	*51*	*28*	*23*	
Economically inactive	2,809	848	1,961	296
Students	296	134	162	296
Permanently sick	134	73	61	
Retired	1,289	614	675	
Other inactive	1,090	27	1,063	

72. Residents aged 16 and over   (10% sample)

Economic position and employment status	TOTAL PERSONS	Males	Females	Students (economically active or inactive)
a	b	c	d	e
Eastleigh				
TOTAL PERSONS	8,326	4,046	4,280	344
Economically active	5,521	3,165	2,356	63
In employment	5,239	2,964	2,275	63
of which - working 31 or more hours per week	*3,948*	*2,723*	*1,225*	*6*
of which - working 30 or fewer hours per week	*1,129*	*144*	*985*	*57*
Employees	4,642	2,496	2,146	63
of which - working 31 or more hours per week	*3,493*	*2,324*	*1,169*	*6*
of which - working 30 or fewer hours per week	*1,059*	*122*	*937*	*57*
Managers	933	622	311	3
Large establishments	334	242	92	-
Small establishments	599	380	219	3
Foremen and supervisors	283	154	129	1
Non-manual	148	47	101	1
Manual	135	107	28	-
Professional employees	268	234	34	3
Other employees	4,450	2,053	2,397	134
Self-employed	563	449	114	-
of which - working 31 or more hours per week	*455*	*399*	*56*	*-*
of which - working 30 or fewer hours per week	*70*	*22*	*48*	*-*
Without employees	405	323	82	-
With employees	158	126	32	-
Large establishments	4	3	1	-
Small establishments	154	123	31	-
On a Government scheme	34	19	15	
Unemployed	282	201	81	-
Seeking work	270	195	75	-
Waiting to start a job	12	6	6	-
Economically active students (included above)	*63*	*31*	*32*	
Economically inactive	2,805	881	1,924	281
Students	281	146	135	281
Permanently sick	192	108	84	
Retired	1,354	614	740	
Other inactive	978	13	965	

72. Residents aged 16 and over   (10% sample)

Economic position and employment status	TOTAL PERSONS	Males	Females	Students (economically active or inactive)
a	b	c	d	e

Fareham

TOTAL PERSONS	7,924	3,770	4,154	329
Economically active	5,087	2,906	2,181	60
In employment	4,837	2,732	2,105	59
of which - working 31 or more hours per week	3,656	2,497	1,159	2
of which - working 30 or fewer hours per week	1,005	118	887	54
Employees	4,242	2,282	1,960	59
of which - working 31 or more hours per week	3,226	2,129	1,097	2
of which - working 30 or fewer hours per week	919	94	825	54
Managers	963	695	268	6
Large establishments	426	337	89	1
Small establishments	537	358	179	5
Foremen and supervisors	257	147	110	-
Non-manual	125	49	76	-
Manual	132	98	34	-
Professional employees	296	249	47	-
Other employees	4,020	1,738	2,282	137
Self-employed	548	416	132	-
of which - working 31 or more hours per week	430	368	62	-
of which - working 30 or fewer hours per week	86	24	62	-
Without employees	384	297	87	-
With employees	164	119	45	-
Large establishments	3	2	1	-
Small establishments	161	117	44	-
On a Government scheme	47	34	13	
Unemployed	250	174	76	1
Seeking work	239	168	71	1
Waiting to start a job	11	6	5	-
Economically active students (included above)	60	25	35	
Economically inactive	2,837	864	1,973	269
Students	269	126	143	269
Permanently sick	192	102	90	
Retired	1,394	620	774	
Other inactive	982	16	966	

72. Residents aged 16 and over   (10% sample)

Economic position and employment status	TOTAL PERSONS	Males	Females	Students (economically active or inactive)
a	b	c	d	e
Gosport				
TOTAL PERSONS	5,773	2,719	3,054	217
Economically active	3,711	2,130	1,581	36
In employment	3,434	1,954	1,480	36
of which - working 31 or more hours per week	*2,533*	*1,758*	*775*	*3*
of which - working 30 or fewer hours per week	*722*	*72*	*650*	*30*
Employees	3,130	1,727	1,403	36
of which - working 31 or more hours per week	*2,323*	*1,577*	*746*	*3*
of which - working 30 or fewer hours per week	*686*	*61*	*625*	*30*
Managers	442	289	153	2
Large establishments	199	142	57	1
Small establishments	243	147	96	1
Foremen and supervisors	178	99	79	1
Non-manual	74	20	54	1
Manual	104	79	25	-
Professional employees	108	94	14	1
Other employees	3,385	1,634	1,751	74
Self-employed	260	204	56	-
of which - working 31 or more hours per week	*210*	*181*	*29*	*-*
of which - working 30 or fewer hours per week	*36*	*11*	*25*	*-*
Without employees	190	149	41	-
With employees	70	55	15	-
Large establishments	1	-	1	-
Small establishments	69	55	14	-
On a Government scheme	44	23	21	
Unemployed	277	176	101	-
Seeking work	266	172	94	-
Waiting to start a job	11	4	7	-
Economically active students (included above)	*36*	*11*	*25*	
Economically inactive	2,062	589	1,473	181
Students	181	83	98	181
Permanently sick	143	81	62	
Retired	990	414	576	
Other inactive	748	11	737	

72. Residents aged 16 and over   (10% sample)

Economic position and employment status	TOTAL PERSONS	Males	Females	Students (economically active or inactive)
a	b	c	d	e
Hart				
TOTAL PERSONS	6,327	3,171	3,156	363
Economically active	4,442	2,630	1,812	68
In employment	4,242	2,499	1,743	67
of which - working 31 or more hours per week	*3,263*	*2,309*	*954*	*7*
of which - working 30 or fewer hours per week	*863*	*118*	*745*	*60*
Employees	3,692	2,085	1,607	67
of which - working 31 or more hours per week	*2,858*	*1,959*	*899*	*7*
of which - working 30 or fewer hours per week	*765*	*90*	*675*	*60*
Managers	1,043	736	307	5
Large establishments	422	319	103	2
Small establishments	621	417	204	3
Foremen and supervisors	150	85	65	3
Non-manual	67	24	43	2
Manual	83	61	22	1
Professional employees	354	297	57	4
Other employees	3,007	1,302	1,705	145
Self-employed	530	400	130	-
of which - working 31 or more hours per week	*405*	*350*	*55*	-
of which - working 30 or fewer hours per week	*98*	*28*	*70*	-
Without employees	378	278	100	-
With employees	152	122	30	-
Large establishments	1	1	-	-
Small establishments	151	121	30	-
On a Government scheme	20	14	6	
Unemployed	200	131	69	1
Seeking work	188	124	64	1
Waiting to start a job	12	7	5	-
Economically active students (included above)	*68*	*36*	*32*	
Economically inactive	1,885	541	1,344	295
Students	295	149	146	295
Permanently sick	84	45	39	
Retired	751	340	411	
Other inactive	755	7	748	

72. Residents aged 16 and over   (10% sample)

Economic position and employment status	TOTAL PERSONS	Males	Females	Students (economically active or inactive)
a	b	c	d	e

Havant

TOTAL PERSONS	**9,363**	**4,447**	**4,916**	**359**
Economically active	**5,742**	**3,325**	**2,417**	**60**
In employment	5,237	2,957	2,280	60
of which - working 31 or more hours per week	*3,885*	*2,685*	*1,200*	*3*
of which - working 30 or fewer hours per week	*1,130*	*129*	*1,001*	*56*
Employees	4,545	2,405	2,140	59
of which - working 31 or more hours per week	*3,384*	*2,241*	*1,143*	*3*
of which - working 30 or fewer hours per week	*1,045*	*96*	*949*	*55*
Managers	835	573	262	-
Large establishments	362	280	82	-
Small establishments	473	293	180	-
Foremen and supervisors	286	155	131	-
Non-manual	126	44	82	-
Manual	160	111	49	-
Professional employees	313	279	34	1
Other employees	4,815	2,213	2,602	129
Self-employed	632	513	119	1
of which - working 31 or more hours per week	*501*	*444*	*57*	*-*
of which - working 30 or fewer hours per week	*85*	*33*	*52*	*1*
Without employees	450	375	75	1
With employees	182	138	44	-
Large establishments	5	4	1	-
Small establishments	177	134	43	-
On a Government scheme	60	39	21	
Unemployed	505	368	137	-
Seeking work	484	355	129	-
Waiting to start a job	21	13	8	-
Economically active students (included above)	*60*	*22*	*38*	
Economically inactive	**3,621**	**1,122**	**2,499**	**299**
Students	299	157	142	299
Permanently sick	302	167	135	
Retired	1,707	768	939	
Other inactive	1,313	30	1,283	

72. Residents aged 16 and over

(10% sample)

Economic position and employment status	TOTAL PERSONS	Males	Females	Students (economically active or inactive)
a	b	c	d	e

New Forest

TOTAL PERSONS	**12,979**	**6,074**	**6,905**	**511**
Economically active	**7,421**	**4,218**	**3,203**	**92**
In employment	6,932	3,864	3,068	90
of which - working 31 or more hours per week	*5,067*	*3,486*	*1,581*	*4*
of which - working 30 or fewer hours per week	*1,611*	*229*	*1,382*	*81*
Employees	5,859	3,060	2,799	90
of which - working 31 or more hours per week	*4,254*	*2,806*	*1,448*	*4*
of which - working 30 or fewer hours per week	*1,449*	*161*	*1,288*	*81*
Managers	1,353	953	400	3
Large establishments	433	334	99	2
Small establishments	920	619	301	1
Foremen and supervisors	361	221	140	-
Non-manual	133	38	95	-
Manual	228	183	45	-
Professional employees	332	290	42	-
Other employees	5,889	2,606	3,283	179
Self-employed	1,035	787	248	-
of which - working 31 or more hours per week	*813*	*680*	*133*	-
of which - working 30 or fewer hours per week	*162*	*68*	*94*	-
Without employees	696	542	154	-
With employees	339	245	94	-
Large establishments	7	6	1	-
Small establishments	332	239	93	-
On a Government scheme	38	17	21	
Unemployed	489	354	135	2
Seeking work	473	344	129	2
Waiting to start a job	16	10	6	-
Economically active students (included above)	*92*	*46*	*46*	
Economically inactive	**5,558**	**1,856**	**3,702**	**419**
Students	419	179	240	419
Permanently sick	264	164	100	
Retired	3,094	1,471	1,623	
Other inactive	1,781	42	1,739	

72. Residents aged 16 and over (10% sample)

Economic position and employment status	TOTAL PERSONS	Males	Females	Students (economically active or inactive)
a	b	c	d	e

Portsmouth

Economic position and employment status	TOTAL PERSONS	Males	Females	Students
TOTAL PERSONS	14,097	6,795	7,302	526
Economically active	8,599	4,993	3,606	87
In employment	7,677	4,361	3,316	85
of which - working 31 or more hours per week	*5,718*	*3,857*	*1,861*	*6*
of which - working 30 or fewer hours per week	*1,530*	*203*	*1,327*	*77*
Employees	6,735	3,639	3,096	84
of which - working 31 or more hours per week	*5,073*	*3,311*	*1,762*	*6*
of which - working 30 or fewer hours per week	*1,422*	*156*	*1,266*	*76*
Managers	982	629	353	12
Large establishments	372	239	133	1
Small establishments	610	390	220	11
Foremen and supervisors	448	250	198	3
Non-manual	197	77	120	2
Manual	251	173	78	1
Professional employees	352	304	48	9
Other employees	7,454	3,650	3,804	214
Self-employed	828	649	179	1
of which - working 31 or more hours per week	*645*	*546*	*99*	*-*
of which - working 30 or fewer hours per week	*108*	*47*	*61*	*1*
Without employees	602	489	113	1
With employees	226	160	66	-
Large establishments	6	5	1	-
Small establishments	220	155	65	-
On a Government scheme	114	73	41	
Unemployed	922	632	290	2
Seeking work	889	619	270	2
Waiting to start a job	33	13	20	-
Economically active students (included above)	*87*	*33*	*54*	
Economically inactive	5,498	1,802	3,696	439
Students	439	235	204	439
Permanently sick	516	279	237	
Retired	2,923	1,242	1,681	
Other inactive	1,620	46	1,574	

72. Residents aged 16 and over　　　　　　　　　　　　　　　　　　　　　　　　　　　　　　　　(10% sample)

Economic position and employment status	TOTAL PERSONS	Males	Females	Students (economically active or inactive)
a	b	c	d	e

Rushmoor

TOTAL PERSONS	**6,454**	**3,170**	**3,284**	**228**
Economically active	**4,622**	**2,650**	**1,972**	**39**
In employment	4,368	2,483	1,885	38
of which - working 31 or more hours per week	*3,363*	*2,221*	*1,142*	*1*
of which - working 30 or fewer hours per week	*776*	*93*	*683*	*37*
Employees	3,966	2,165	1,801	38
of which - working 31 or more hours per week	*3,068*	*1,959*	*1,109*	*1*
of which - working 30 or fewer hours per week	*732*	*79*	*653*	*37*
Managers	705	463	242	3
Large establishments	321	220	101	2
Small establishments	384	243	141	1
Foremen and supervisors	232	124	108	-
Non-manual	101	33	68	-
Manual	131	91	40	-
Professional employees	253	218	35	2
Other employees	3,738	1,747	1,991	94
Self-employed	367	299	68	-
of which - working 31 or more hours per week	*295*	*262*	*33*	*-*
of which - working 30 or fewer hours per week	*44*	*14*	*30*	*-*
Without employees	287	240	47	-
With employees	80	59	21	-
Large establishments	-	-	-	-
Small establishments	80	59	21	-
On a Government scheme	35	19	16	
Unemployed	254	167	87	1
Seeking work	243	162	81	1
Waiting to start a job	11	5	6	-
Economically active students (included above)	*39*	*13*	*26*	
Economically inactive	**1,832**	**520**	**1,312**	**189**
Students	189	86	103	189
Permanently sick	136	64	72	
Retired	857	357	500	
Other inactive	650	13	637	

72. Residents aged 16 and over   (10% sample)

Economic position and employment status	TOTAL PERSONS	Males	Females	Students (economically active or inactive)
a	b	c	d	e

Southampton

TOTAL PERSONS	**15,585**	**7,521**	**8,064**	**689**
Economically active	**9,506**	**5,523**	**3,983**	**91**
In employment	8,404	4,692	3,712	91
of which - working 31 or more hours per week	*6,267*	*4,234*	*2,033*	*6*
of which - working 30 or fewer hours per week	*1,782*	*236*	*1,546*	*84*
Employees	7,420	3,923	3,497	89
of which - working 31 or more hours per week	*5,558*	*3,624*	*1,934*	*5*
of which - working 30 or fewer hours per week	*1,657*	*182*	*1,475*	*83*
Managers	1,079	666	413	5
Large establishments	356	224	132	-
Small establishments	723	442	281	5
Foremen and supervisors	526	304	222	5
Non-manual	215	64	151	2
Manual	311	240	71	3
Professional employees	471	384	87	22
Other employees	8,278	4,028	4,250	253
Self-employed	900	720	180	2
of which - working 31 or more hours per week	*709*	*610*	*99*	*1*
of which - working 30 or fewer hours per week	*125*	*54*	*71*	*1*
Without employees	699	569	130	1
With employees	201	151	50	1
Large establishments	-	-	-	-
Small establishments	201	151	50	1
On a Government scheme	84	49	35	
Unemployed	1,102	831	271	-
Seeking work	1,072	811	261	-
Waiting to start a job	30	20	10	-
Economically active students (included above)	*91*	*45*	*46*	
Economically inactive	**6,079**	**1,998**	**4,081**	**598**
Students	598	333	265	598
Permanently sick	564	353	211	
Retired	2,951	1,250	1,701	
Other inactive	1,966	62	1,904	

72. Residents aged 16 and over   (10% sample)

Economic position and employment status	TOTAL PERSONS	Males	Females	Students (economically active or inactive)
a	b	c	d	e

Test Valley

TOTAL PERSONS	**8,019**	**3,935**	**4,084**	**354**
Economically active	**5,343**	**3,124**	**2,219**	**71**
In employment	5,069	2,940	2,129	70
of which - working 31 or more hours per week	*3,856*	*2,697*	*1,159*	*2*
of which - working 30 or fewer hours per week	*1,024*	*132*	*892*	*65*
Employees	4,362	2,384	1,978	70
of which - working 31 or more hours per week	*3,316*	*2,225*	*1,091*	*2*
of which - working 30 or fewer hours per week	*939*	*104*	*835*	*65*
Managers	954	684	270	1
Large establishments	393	310	83	-
Small establishments	561	374	187	1
Foremen and supervisors	256	139	117	4
Non-manual	105	26	79	3
Manual	151	113	38	1
Professional employees	231	187	44	2
Other employees	4,103	1,882	2,221	143
Self-employed	668	531	137	-
of which - working 31 or more hours per week	*540*	*472*	*68*	-
of which - working 30 or fewer hours per week	*85*	*28*	*57*	-
Without employees	434	349	85	-
With employees	234	182	52	-
Large establishments	5	5	-	-
Small establishments	229	177	52	-
On a Government scheme	39	25	14	
Unemployed	274	184	90	1
Seeking work	261	177	84	1
Waiting to start a job	13	7	6	-
Economically active students (included above)	*71*	*28*	*43*	
Economically inactive	**2,676**	**811**	**1,865**	**283**
Students	283	161	122	283
Permanently sick	138	72	66	
Retired	1,241	562	679	
Other inactive	1,014	16	998	

72. Residents aged 16 and over   (10% sample)

Economic position and employment status	TOTAL PERSONS	Males	Females	Students (economically active or inactive)
a	b	c	d	e
Winchester				
TOTAL PERSONS	**7,806**	**3,717**	**4,089**	**446**
Economically active	**4,809**	**2,792**	**2,017**	**61**
In employment	4,558	2,625	1,933	59
of which - working 31 or more hours per week	*3,394*	*2,338*	*1,056*	*5*
of which - working 30 or fewer hours per week	*986*	*161*	*825*	*50*
Employees	3,818	2,079	1,739	59
of which - working 31 or more hours per week	*2,854*	*1,903*	*951*	*5*
of which - working 30 or fewer hours per week	*876*	*119*	*757*	*50*
Managers	956	675	281	8
Large establishments	398	306	92	3
Small establishments	558	369	189	5
Foremen and supervisors	185	103	82	3
Non-manual	91	33	58	2
Manual	94	70	24	1
Professional employees	331	277	54	2
Other employees	3,572	1,547	2,025	159
Self-employed	703	519	184	-
of which - working 31 or more hours per week	*540*	*435*	*105*	-
of which - working 30 or fewer hours per week	*110*	*42*	*68*	-
Without employees	436	320	116	-
With employees	267	199	68	-
Large establishments	8	6	2	-
Small establishments	259	193	66	-
On a Government scheme	37	27	10	
Unemployed	251	167	84	2
Seeking work	230	154	76	2
Waiting to start a job	21	13	8	-
Economically active students (included above)	*61*	*25*	*36*	
Economically inactive	**2,997**	**925**	**2,072**	**385**
Students	385	175	210	385
Permanently sick	166	91	75	
Retired	1,419	628	791	
Other inactive	1,027	31	996	

Table 73 Industry (10% sample)　　County, districts

73. Residents aged 16 and over, employees and self-employed　　(10% sample)

Sex and age	TOTAL PERSONS	Agriculture, forestry and fishing	Energy and water	Mining	Manufacturing metal etc	Other manufacturing	Construction	Distribution and catering	Transport	Banking and finance etc	Other services	Not stated, inadequately described or workplace outside UK
a	b	c	d	e	f	g	h	i	j	k	l	m
HAMPSHIRE												
TOTAL PERSONS	71,873	1,122	988	1,281	8,405	3,649	5,687	14,461	4,128	9,092	22,548	512
Males aged 16 and over	40,790	869	781	808	6,376	2,303	5,146	6,741	3,127	4,572	9,737	330
16 - 19	2,086	40	29	20	201	107	255	733	58	143	483	17
20 - 29	9,904	195	155	181	1,469	536	1,423	1,821	642	1,140	2,276	66
30 - 44	15,090	225	308	346	2,350	860	1,876	2,242	1,264	1,791	3,716	112
45 - 64	12,932	336	288	258	2,299	764	1,530	1,755	1,128	1,395	3,064	115
65 and over	778	73	1	3	57	36	62	190	35	103	198	20
Females aged 16 and over	31,083	253	207	473	2,029	1,346	541	7,720	1,001	4,520	12,811	182
16 - 19	1,857	5	12	20	110	75	24	715	52	339	490	15
20 - 29	7,944	55	77	160	616	340	127	1,884	347	1,616	2,685	37
30 - 44	11,443	75	66	186	684	481	217	2,702	354	1,619	4,999	60
45 - 59	8,436	81	45	100	570	407	141	2,032	212	835	3,957	56
60 and over	1,403	37	7	7	49	43	32	387	36	111	680	14
Basingstoke & Deane												
TOTAL PERSONS	7,472	132	68	183	836	417	577	1,584	348	1,189	2,094	44
Males aged 16 and over	4,237	112	40	106	617	273	519	801	277	629	838	25
16 - 19	222	3	1	1	23	17	29	81	7	23	34	3
20 - 29	1,058	20	9	30	143	49	158	236	74	154	178	7
30 - 44	1,577	33	15	47	232	106	181	276	115	255	313	4
45 - 64	1,303	42	15	28	212	99	145	195	78	186	293	10
65 and over	77	14	-	-	7	2	6	13	3	11	20	1
Females aged 16 and over	3,235	20	28	77	219	144	58	783	71	560	1,256	19
16 - 19	179	-	2	1	11	10	2	61	3	39	49	1
20 - 29	864	3	7	26	75	41	13	214	27	210	242	6
30 - 44	1,208	7	10	26	84	47	23	257	25	198	527	4
45 - 59	841	6	9	23	44	40	17	205	13	98	380	6
60 and over	143	4	-	1	5	6	3	46	3	15	58	2

Table 73 Industry (10% sample) – **continued**

73. Residents aged 16 and over, employees and self-employed

(10% sample)

Sex and age	TOTAL PERSONS	Agriculture, forestry and fishing	Energy and water	Mining	Manufacturing metal etc	Other manufacturing	Construction	Distribution and catering	Transport	Banking and finance etc	Other services	Not stated, inadequately described or workplace outside UK
a	b	c	d	e	f	g	h	i	j	k	l	m
East Hampshire												
TOTAL PERSONS	4,956	176	58	87	460	287	405	949	237	718	1,549	30
Males aged 16 and over	2,821	136	49	53	341	191	365	479	160	395	635	17
16 - 19	138	5	1	1	14	7	7	42	3	9	47	2
20 - 29	609	34	6	11	71	36	106	112	30	77	121	5
30 - 44	1,069	39	23	26	122	83	133	165	68	170	232	8
45 - 64	939	50	19	15	127	63	117	143	56	128	219	2
65 and over	66	8	-	-	7	2	2	17	3	11	16	-
Females aged 16 and over	2,135	40	9	34	119	96	40	470	77	323	914	13
16 - 19	115	2	1	3	4	7	1	46	3	15	31	2
20 - 29	487	6	3	11	37	23	7	108	30	99	162	1
30 - 44	829	17	3	17	39	33	20	164	26	131	375	4
45 - 59	593	13	2	3	37	30	7	124	15	71	288	3
60 and over	111	2	-	-	2	3	5	28	3	7	58	3
Eastleigh												
TOTAL PERSONS	5,205	55	86	66	740	259	458	1,095	363	692	1,362	29
Males aged 16 and over	2,945	41	59	46	610	172	397	502	271	335	492	20
16 - 19	147	4	4	1	13	10	20	60	7	10	18	-
20 - 29	692	12	15	18	116	38	105	135	65	86	98	4
30 - 44	1,162	8	22	17	246	61	159	183	106	134	218	8
45 - 64	900	15	18	9	232	59	110	112	91	98	148	8
65 and over	44	2	-	1	3	4	3	12	2	7	10	-
Females aged 16 and over	2,260	14	27	20	130	87	61	593	92	357	870	9
16 - 19	113	-	3	-	5	3	1	48	1	28	24	-
20 - 29	580	5	9	10	29	24	16	160	28	128	169	2
30 - 44	868	4	6	5	50	27	24	211	40	129	367	5
45 - 59	629	4	7	5	40	31	18	157	20	68	277	2
60 and over	70	1	2	-	6	2	2	17	3	4	33	-

Industry

Table 73 Industry (10% sample) – continued

County, districts

(10% sample)

73. Residents aged 16 and over, employees and self-employed

Fareham

Sex and age	TOTAL PERSONS	Industry										Not stated, inadequately described or workplace outside UK
		Agriculture, forestry and fishing	Energy and water	Mining	Manufacturing metal etc	Other manufacturing	Construction	Distribution and catering	Transport	Banking and finance etc	Other services	
a	b	c	d	e	f	g	h	i	j	k	l	m
TOTAL PERSONS	4,790	45	51	92	674	209	365	808	231	562	1,717	36
Males aged 16 and over	2,698	33	41	55	523	130	320	357	165	263	783	28
16 - 19	116	5	2	2	16	2	10	40	3	2	34	-
20 - 29	528	6	5	2	94	21	77	85	40	54	139	5
30 - 44	1,054	6	20	28	187	44	128	123	71	113	323	11
45 - 64	961	14	14	22	224	59	100	100	48	87	282	11
65 and over	39	2	-	1	2	4	5	9	3	7	5	1
Females aged 16 and over	2,092	12	10	37	151	79	45	451	66	299	934	8
16 - 19	132	-	-	-	9	5	-	43	6	26	42	1
20 - 29	470	5	3	10	37	15	13	100	15	101	169	2
30 - 44	766	4	4	14	53	31	14	150	21	108	365	2
45 - 59	642	2	3	13	50	26	15	136	22	59	313	3
60 and over	82	1	-	-	2	2	3	22	2	5	45	-

Gosport

Sex and age	TOTAL PERSONS	c	d	e	f	g	h	i	j	k	l	m
TOTAL PERSONS	3,390	20	21	126	418	136	201	606	117	260	1,461	24
Males aged 16 and over	1,931	18	17	49	318	87	186	240	90	110	801	15
16 - 19	98	3	1	1	8	3	13	31	-	3	34	1
20 - 29	536	3	6	11	81	26	57	64	21	36	229	2
30 - 44	744	6	5	23	115	37	65	82	35	41	328	7
45 - 64	532	6	5	14	112	20	50	60	34	30	197	4
65 and over	21	-	-	-	2	1	1	3	-	-	13	1
Females aged 16 and over	1,459	2	4	77	100	49	15	366	27	150	660	9
16 - 19	89	-	-	2	6	5	2	33	1	14	25	1
20 - 29	428	-	3	27	37	12	5	80	11	63	186	4
30 - 44	543	1	1	35	27	17	3	144	10	54	249	2
45 - 59	356	1	-	13	28	14	5	95	4	17	177	2
60 and over	43	-	-	-	2	1	-	14	1	2	23	-

Table 73 Industry (10% sample) – continued

County, districts

73. Residents aged 16 and over, employees and self-employed

(10% sample)

Sex and age	TOTAL PERSONS	Agriculture, forestry and fishing	Energy and water	Mining	Manufacturing metal etc	Other manufacturing	Construction	Distribution and catering	Transport	Banking and finance etc	Other services	Not stated, inadequately described or workplace outside UK
a	b	c	d	e	f	g	h	i	j	k	l	m
Hart												
TOTAL PERSONS	4,222	68	46	76	398	181	264	826	276	797	1,260	30
Males aged 16 and over	2,485	52	37	50	294	133	232	389	216	438	627	17
16 - 19	142	3	1	4	5	7	11	52	2	20	36	1
20 - 29	583	12	7	7	70	33	68	88	36	93	166	3
30 - 44	920	11	19	23	109	43	80	142	87	177	224	5
45 - 64	790	22	10	16	106	48	70	102	86	136	188	6
65 and over	50	4	-	-	4	2	3	5	5	12	13	2
Females aged 16 and over	1,737	16	9	26	104	48	32	437	60	359	633	13
16 - 19	92	-	-	4	7	1	2	39	1	15	21	2
20 - 29	403	6	3	6	31	16	3	97	23	108	108	2
30 - 44	676	3	3	6	37	19	16	152	25	151	259	5
45 - 59	502	2	3	9	27	11	8	134	10	77	217	4
60 and over	64	5	-	1	2	1	3	15	1	8	28	-
Havant												
TOTAL PERSONS	5,177	37	71	107	994	314	479	992	238	486	1,425	34
Males aged 16 and over	2,918	28	48	55	677	184	439	442	179	240	609	17
16 - 19	131	2	3	2	24	9	21	36	6	6	22	-
20 - 29	646	8	9	13	143	44	108	122	42	64	92	1
30 - 44	1,036	5	17	19	227	67	167	138	68	80	240	8
45 - 64	1,061	11	19	21	277	64	140	131	63	83	246	6
65 and over	44	2	-	-	6	-	3	15	-	7	9	2
Females aged 16 and over	2,259	9	23	52	317	130	40	550	59	246	816	17
16 - 19	149	1	2	4	29	4	1	54	3	19	32	-
20 - 29	482	2	9	16	77	28	7	120	17	64	138	4
30 - 44	811	4	6	21	100	42	19	204	22	91	299	3
45 - 59	707	2	5	10	103	53	11	142	13	63	298	7
60 and over	110	-	1	1	8	3	2	30	4	9	49	3

Table 73 Industry (10% sample) – **continued**

County, districts

73. Residents aged 16 and over, employees and self-employed

(10% sample)

Sex and age	TOTAL PERSONS	Agriculture, forestry and fishing	Energy and water	Mining	Manufacturing metal etc	Other manufacturing	Construction	Distribution and catering	Transport	Banking and finance etc	Other services	Not stated, inadequately described or workplace outside UK
a	b	c	d	e	f	g	h	i	j	k	l	m
New Forest												
TOTAL PERSONS	6,894	174	223	180	671	345	572	1,550	446	919	1,744	70
Males aged 16 and over	3,847	134	199	161	515	225	506	694	323	456	586	48
16 - 19	173	6	7	1	15	12	18	85	3	12	13	1
20 - 29	830	27	40	29	110	59	123	171	47	99	119	6
30 - 44	1,438	38	78	68	199	83	196	220	137	169	228	22
45 - 64	1,316	51	74	63	183	64	158	204	136	162	203	18
65 and over	90	12	-	-	8	7	11	14	-	14	23	1
Females aged 16 and over	3,047	40	24	19	156	120	66	856	123	463	1,158	22
16 - 19	198	-	-	-	3	15	3	80	5	37	52	3
20 - 29	682	6	11	5	44	26	19	178	41	149	197	6
30 - 44	1,150	12	8	13	57	37	26	312	42	164	472	7
45 - 59	847	15	5	1	46	37	12	230	30	97	370	4
60 and over	170	7	-	-	6	5	6	56	5	16	67	2
Portsmouth												
TOTAL PERSONS	7,563	18	95	77	865	428	594	1,554	492	676	2,699	65
Males aged 16 and over	4,288	16	70	45	638	228	556	702	377	306	1,305	45
16 - 19	209	-	2	2	15	12	27	75	3	12	61	-
20 - 29	1,271	5	12	17	215	61	181	219	76	105	370	10
30 - 44	1,509	7	30	15	227	86	198	207	156	90	481	12
45 - 64	1,221	4	26	10	177	66	144	178	135	91	369	21
65 and over	78	-	-	1	4	3	6	23	7	8	24	2
Females aged 16 and over	3,275	2	25	32	227	200	38	852	115	370	1,394	20
16 - 19	172	-	2	4	8	7	-	84	5	23	37	2
20 - 29	1,021	1	11	12	101	49	12	219	41	155	418	2
30 - 44	1,150	1	9	13	66	85	17	306	39	121	486	7
45 - 59	790	-	2	2	50	53	8	202	24	62	380	7
60 and over	142	-	1	1	2	6	1	41	6	9	73	2

Table 73 Industry (10% sample) – continued

73. Residents aged 16 and over, employees and self-employed

(10% sample)

Sex and age	TOTAL PERSONS	Agriculture, forestry and fishing	Energy and water	Mining	Manufacturing metal etc	Other manufacturing	Construction	Distribution and catering	Transport	Banking and finance etc	Other services	Not stated, inadequately described or workplace outside UK
a	b	c	d	e	f	g	h	i	j	k	l	m

Rushmoor

Sex and age	b	c	d	e	f	g	h	i	j	k	l	m
TOTAL PERSONS	4,333	11	47	67	428	144	300	820	293	596	1,599	28
Males aged 16 and over	2,464	7	41	29	287	82	283	381	207	273	856	18
16 - 19	176	-	1	-	11	1	17	45	5	11	83	2
20 - 29	800	6	10	10	78	18	94	122	45	96	317	4
30 - 44	834	1	16	12	119	26	98	118	75	107	258	4
45 - 64	624	-	14	7	78	35	71	87	82	56	188	6
65 and over	30	-	-	-	1	2	3	9	-	3	10	2
Females aged 16 and over	1,869	4	6	38	141	62	17	439	86	323	743	10
16 - 19	144	-	1	1	8	2	2	55	7	25	43	-
20 - 29	556	1	2	14	38	13	3	128	35	149	172	1
30 - 44	658	2	2	14	55	21	8	136	30	95	288	7
45 - 59	427	-	1	7	35	22	3	100	12	51	194	2
60 and over	84	1	-	2	5	4	1	20	2	3	46	-

Southampton

Sex and age	b	c	d	e	f	g	h	i	j	k	l	m
TOTAL PERSONS	8,320	23	130	97	956	417	721	1,893	699	889	2,439	56
Males aged 16 and over	4,643	18	101	68	780	273	670	878	556	408	856	35
16 - 19	221	-	3	2	28	13	44	81	12	16	20	2
20 - 29	1,227	7	26	19	167	75	184	269	122	153	191	14
30 - 44	1,719	6	35	30	294	111	231	293	222	138	351	8
45 - 64	1,397	5	37	17	285	70	204	205	193	95	277	9
65 and over	79	-	-	-	6	4	7	30	7	6	17	2
Females aged 16 and over	3,677	5	29	29	176	144	51	1,015	143	481	1,583	21
16 - 19	224	-	1	1	10	5	6	78	7	51	64	1
20 - 29	1,063	2	13	12	47	41	15	281	61	204	384	3
30 - 44	1,287	2	8	10	54	63	13	351	38	150	592	6
45 - 59	938	1	6	5	59	33	15	254	34	63	458	10
60 and over	165	-	1	1	6	2	2	51	3	13	85	1

Table 73 Industry (10% sample) – continued

73. Residents aged 16 and over, employees and self-employed

(10% sample)

Sex and age	TOTAL PERSONS	Industry										Not stated, inadequately described or workplace outside UK
		Agriculture, forestry and fishing	Energy and water	Mining	Manufacturing metal etc	Other manufacturing	Construction	Distribution and catering	Transport	Banking and finance etc	Other services	
a	b	c	d	e	f	g	h	i	j	k	l	m
Test Valley												
TOTAL PERSONS	5,030	168	50	76	549	338	385	987	219	679	1,541	38
Males aged 16 and over	2,915	126	41	59	437	220	350	484	179	343	651	25
16 - 19	169	9	2	1	19	10	16	57	5	13	34	3
20 - 29	663	28	5	9	121	57	91	112	25	65	146	4
30 - 44	1,062	24	11	30	138	72	120	169	75	157	257	9
45 - 64	957	55	22	19	156	80	117	126	71	104	199	8
65 and over	64	10	1	-	3	1	6	20	3	4	15	1
Females aged 16 and over	2,115	42	9	17	112	118	35	503	40	336	890	13
16 - 19	141	1	-	-	6	9	-	59	5	29	30	2
20 - 29	509	7	3	8	41	30	5	111	8	119	175	2
30 - 44	789	5	2	8	35	34	19	182	17	124	360	3
45 - 59	587	25	2	1	29	42	10	134	8	56	275	5
60 and over	89	4	2	-	1	3	1	17	2	8	50	1
Winchester												
TOTAL PERSONS	4,521	195	42	47	416	174	366	797	169	629	1,658	28
Males aged 16 and over	2,598	148	38	32	339	105	323	392	127	376	698	20
16 - 19	144	-	1	2	10	4	22	48	2	6	47	2
20 - 29	461	27	5	5	60	19	71	86	19	58	110	1
30 - 44	966	41	17	8	135	41	120	126	49	160	263	6
45 - 64	931	61	15	17	130	37	104	112	55	139	255	6
65 and over	96	19	-	-	4	4	6	20	2	13	23	5
Females aged 16 and over	1,923	47	4	15	77	69	43	405	42	253	960	8
16 - 19	109	1	-	-	4	2	4	35	5	18	40	-
20 - 29	399	11	-	3	22	22	9	88	10	67	165	2
30 - 44	708	13	4	4	27	25	15	133	19	103	360	5
45 - 59	577	10	-	8	22	15	12	119	7	53	330	1
60 and over	130	12	-	-	2	5	3	30	1	12	65	-

Table 74 Occupation (10% sample)

74. Residents aged 16 and over, employees and self-employed

(10% sample)

HAMPSHIRE

Standard Occupational Classification Sub-major Groups	TOTAL PERSONS	Males aged 16 and over						Females aged 16 and over					
		Total	16 - 19	20 - 29	30 - 44	45 - 64	65 and over	Total	16 - 19	20 - 29	30 - 44	45 - 59	60 and over
a	b	c	d	e	f	g	h	i	j	k	l	m	n
ALL OCCUPATIONS	71,873	40,790	2,086	9,904	15,090	12,932	778	31,083	1,857	7,944	11,443	8,436	1,403
1a Corporate managers and administrators	8,237	5,872	27	763	2,759	2,240	83	2,365	24	704	1,029	546	62
1b Managers/proprietors in agriculture and services	3,933	2,387	27	455	938	862	105	1,546	30	417	583	426	90
2a Science and engineering professionals	2,462	2,251	-	572	947	715	17	211	-	96	92	21	2
2b Health professionals	389	243	-	18	117	95	13	146	-	40	80	20	6
2c Teaching professionals	2,237	784	2	62	356	354	10	1,453	-	186	708	500	59
2d Other professional occupations	1,401	955	1	173	411	344	26	446	-	131	186	110	19
3a Science and engineering associate professionals	2,504	1,973	76	636	780	474	7	531	11	201	218	98	3
3b Health associate professionals	1,566	141	2	30	67	38	4	1,425	21	398	567	382	57
3c Other associate professional occupations	2,737	1,670	41	310	671	616	32	1,067	22	319	435	258	33
4a Clerical occupations	8,079	2,428	207	774	684	718	45	5,651	469	1,732	1,887	1,378	185
4b Secretarial occupations	3,496	105	6	17	33	46	3	3,391	169	886	1,197	1,006	133
5a Skilled construction trades	1,888	1,860	78	492	649	621	20	28	-	5	16	6	1
5b Skilled engineering trades	3,135	3,040	177	810	1,066	961	26	95	7	31	33	22	2
5c Other skilled trades	4,466	3,891	309	1,083	1,330	1,104	65	575	32	141	211	170	21
6a Protective service occupations	3,035	2,752	240	1,068	1,046	370	28	283	44	124	75	34	6
6b Personal service occupations	4,924	1,014	114	332	231	291	46	3,910	329	883	1,491	1,014	193
7a Buyers, brokers and sales representatives	1,362	1,015	20	249	394	329	23	347	12	132	127	66	10
7b Other sales occupations	3,935	832	286	241	147	132	26	3,103	423	686	986	861	147
8a Industrial plant and machine operators, assemblers	3,671	2,409	131	616	827	808	27	1,262	98	343	408	375	38
8b Drivers and mobile machinery operators	2,321	2,159	20	392	812	898	37	162	4	42	75	38	3
9a Other occupations in agriculture, forestry and fishing	433	326	22	78	93	119	14	107	20	33	25	22	7
9b Other elementary occupations	5,166	2,371	282	671	634	681	103	2,795	134	374	949	1,026	312
Occupation not stated or inadequately described	496	312	18	62	98	116	18	184	8	40	65	57	14

Table 74　Occupation (10% sample) – continued

74. Residents aged 16 and over, employees and self-employed

(10% sample)

Basingstoke & Deane

Standard Occupational Classification Sub-major Groups	TOTAL PERSONS	Males aged 16 and over						Females aged 16 and over					
		Total	16 - 19	20 - 29	30 - 44	45 - 64	65 and over	Total	16 - 19	20 - 29	30 - 44	45 - 59	60 and over
a	b	c	d	e	f	g	h	i	j	k	l	m	n
ALL OCCUPATIONS	7,472	4,237	222	1,058	1,577	1,303	77	3,235	179	864	1,208	841	143
1a Corporate managers and administrators	1,028	703	3	105	338	249	8	325	4	118	137	61	5
1b Managers/proprietors in agriculture and services	313	198	4	44	83	58	9	115	2	36	43	32	2
2a Science and engineering professionals	337	296	-	81	142	72	1	41	-	24	10	6	1
2b Health professionals	30	17	-	1	8	7	1	13	-	7	5	1	-
2c Teaching professionals	164	48	-	6	18	24	-	116	-	12	60	41	3
2d Other professional occupations	146	100	1	19	43	35	2	46	-	13	26	7	-
3a Science and engineering associate professionals	303	237	11	81	96	48	1	66	1	30	24	11	-
3b Health associate professionals	146	19	-	1	10	8	-	127	1	32	48	39	7
3c Other associate professional occupations	278	165	4	42	73	44	2	113	2	43	45	20	3
4a Clerical occupations	1,011	323	35	101	84	99	4	688	52	202	234	174	26
4b Secretarial occupations	458	12	-	1	8	3	-	446	19	118	167	125	17
5a Skilled construction trades	187	185	10	53	60	62	-	2	-	1	1	-	-
5b Skilled engineering trades	307	302	15	89	100	95	3	5	1	1	3	-	-
5c Other skilled trades	425	387	31	113	131	102	10	38	-	9	15	11	3
6a Protective service occupations	126	114	2	23	43	41	5	12	-	4	3	2	3
6b Personal service occupations	429	118	16	41	22	33	6	311	23	47	145	78	18
7a Buyers, brokers and sales representatives	135	101	2	25	43	29	2	34	1	11	15	6	1
7b Other sales occupations	357	86	29	28	16	10	3	271	43	71	72	72	13
8a Industrial plant and machine operators, assemblers	403	269	20	65	86	93	5	134	12	39	46	32	5
8b Drivers and mobile machinery operators	264	249	2	56	90	96	5	15	1	3	6	4	1
9a Other occupations in agriculture, forestry and fishing	64	55	1	14	17	20	3	9	1	2	5	1	-
9b Other elementary occupations	512	220	34	62	53	65	6	292	15	36	93	115	33
Occupation not stated or inadequately described	49	33	2	7	13	10	1	16	1	5	5	3	2

Table 74 Occupation (10% sample) – continued

74. Residents aged 16 and over, employees and self-employed (10% sample)

East Hampshire

Standard Occupational Classification Sub-major Groups	TOTAL PERSONS	Males aged 16 and over						Females aged 16 and over					
		Total	16 - 19	20 - 29	30 - 44	45 - 64	65 and over	Total	16 - 19	20 - 29	30 - 44	45 - 59	60 and over
a	b	c	d	e	f	g	h	i	j	k	l	m	n
ALL OCCUPATIONS	4,956	2,821	138	609	1,069	939	66	2,135	115	487	829	593	111
1a Corporate managers and administrators	673	511	1	46	247	206	11	162	1	53	64	36	8
1b Managers/proprietors in agriculture and services	357	233	1	41	90	89	12	124	3	23	61	24	13
2a Science and engineering professionals	167	156	-	35	63	57	1	11	-	1	9	1	-
2b Health professionals	35	21	-	2	9	9	1	14	-	1	9	3	1
2c Teaching professionals	230	67	1	5	29	32	-	163	-	22	77	60	4
2d Other professional occupations	116	85	-	14	34	32	5	31	-	7	16	7	1
3a Science and engineering associate professionals	129	97	4	28	45	19	1	32	2	9	13	8	-
3b Health associate professionals	98	6	-	-	2	3	1	92	1	15	37	32	7
3c Other associate professional occupations	230	141	4	19	55	61	2	89	3	28	34	21	3
4a Clerical occupations	441	122	15	35	30	39	3	319	24	87	116	83	9
4b Secretarial occupations	280	5	-	1	-	4	-	275	11	67	104	79	14
5a Skilled construction trades	153	151	3	50	48	47	3	2	-	-	1	1	-
5b Skilled engineering trades	167	156	9	39	61	44	3	11	-	3	7	1	-
5c Other skilled trades	310	265	17	66	77	100	5	45	2	7	18	17	1
6a Protective service occupations	200	183	30	71	70	11	1	17	5	5	5	2	-
6b Personal service occupations	339	52	4	17	12	18	1	287	20	69	111	68	19
7a Buyers, brokers and sales representatives	102	77	1	15	33	27	1	25	1	7	11	5	1
7b Other sales occupations	208	49	15	11	14	5	4	159	27	31	50	40	11
8a Industrial plant and machine operators, assemblers	202	131	10	35	50	35	1	71	2	21	28	20	-
8b Drivers and mobile machinery operators	125	113	1	17	44	50	1	12	-	4	2	6	-
9a Other occupations in agriculture, forestry and fishing	69	51	4	15	15	14	3	18	4	8	2	4	-
9b Other elementary occupations	298	135	17	44	35	34	5	163	8	18	47	71	19
Occupation not stated or inadequately described	27	14	1	3	6	3	1	13	1	1	7	4	-

Table 74 Occupation (10% sample) – continued

(10% sample)

74. Residents aged 16 and over, employees and self-employed

Eastleigh

Standard Occupational Classification Sub-major Groups	TOTAL PERSONS	Males aged 16 and over						Females aged 16 and over					
		Total	16 - 19	20 - 29	30 - 44	45 - 64	65 and over	Total	16 - 19	20 - 29	30 - 44	45 - 59	60 and over
a	b	c	d	e	f	g	h	i	j	k	l	m	n
ALL OCCUPATIONS	5,205	2,945	147	692	1,162	900	44	2,260	113	580	868	629	70
1a Corporate managers and administrators	619	436	2	65	210	156	3	183	2	47	79	51	4
1b Managers/proprietors in agriculture and services	254	146	1	28	68	46	3	108	2	35	43	26	2
2a Science and engineering professionals	164	158	-	38	71	48	1	6	-	2	4	-	-
2b Health professionals	18	9	-	-	9	-	-	9	-	2	6	1	-
2c Teaching professionals	179	77	-	4	40	32	1	102	-	7	57	35	3
2d Other professional occupations	106	70	-	17	30	22	1	36	-	15	11	8	2
3a Science and engineering associate professionals	222	176	7	56	72	40	1	46	1	16	20	9	-
3b Health associate professionals	112	11	-	3	5	3	-	101	2	30	46	20	3
3c Other associate professional occupations	194	119	1	33	50	32	3	75	-	29	28	18	-
4a Clerical occupations	641	179	22	44	59	52	2	462	30	131	167	118	16
4b Secretarial occupations	300	9	-	3	2	4	-	291	17	74	100	96	4
5a Skilled construction trades	108	105	1	20	51	32	1	3	-	1	1	1	-
5b Skilled engineering trades	257	255	13	77	95	68	2	2	-	1	1	-	-
5c Other skilled trades	364	335	32	84	123	94	2	29	1	10	8	10	-
6a Protective service occupations	96	88	2	23	39	23	1	8	1	2	5	5	-
6b Personal service occupations	312	53	6	16	13	17	1	259	18	56	104	71	10
7a Buyers, brokers and sales representatives	137	103	2	30	42	28	1	34	1	23	7	2	1
7b Other sales occupations	324	69	24	16	16	11	2	255	28	58	82	80	7
8a Industrial plant and machine operators, assemblers	259	183	10	35	70	63	5	76	5	17	31	21	2
8b Drivers and mobile machinery operators	191	181	3	42	48	84	4	10	-	2	5	3	-
9a Other occupations in agriculture, forestry and fishing	12	10	1	5	1	2	1	2	-	2	-	-	-
9b Other elementary occupations	313	160	20	51	43	38	8	153	5	18	57	58	15
Occupation not stated or inadequately described	23	13	-	2	5	5	1	10	-	2	6	1	1

Table 74 Occupation (10% sample) – continued

(10% sample)

74. Residents aged 16 and over, employees and self-employed

Fareham

Standard Occupational Classification Sub-major Groups	TOTAL PERSONS	Males aged 16 and over						Females aged 16 and over					
		Total	16 - 19	20 - 29	30 - 44	45 - 64	65 and over	Total	16 - 19	20 - 29	30 - 44	45 - 59	60 and over
a	b	c	d	e	f	g	h	i	j	k	l	m	n
ALL OCCUPATIONS	4,790	2,698	116	528	1,054	961	39	2,092	132	470	766	642	82
1a Corporate managers and administrators	659	497	-	58	232	204	3	162	1	36	75	45	5
1b Managers/proprietors in agriculture and services	229	131	2	22	53	51	3	98	1	27	40	25	5
2a Science and engineering professionals	199	177	-	27	75	73	2	22	-	9	11	2	-
2b Health professionals	25	18	-	2	10	4	2	7	-	3	2	1	1
2c Teaching professionals	181	61	-	2	26	33	-	120	-	9	59	47	5
2d Other professional occupations	88	54	-	10	24	17	3	34	-	7	14	13	-
3a Science and engineering associate professionals	176	136	5	29	57	45	-	40	2	19	17	2	-
3b Health associate professionals	138	14	-	5	6	3	-	124	2	33	50	32	7
3c Other associate professional occupations	213	143	6	17	52	64	4	70	5	14	27	24	-
4a Clerical occupations	524	129	6	48	39	34	2	395	36	98	128	122	11
4b Secretarial occupations	239	2	-	-	-	2	-	237	13	52	88	79	5
5a Skilled construction trades	93	93	3	23	32	33	2	-	-	-	-	-	-
5b Skilled engineering trades	222	218	11	40	76	90	1	4	-	2	-	2	-
5c Other skilled trades	285	249	24	62	78	80	5	36	4	9	12	11	-
6a Protective service occupations	279	251	16	61	133	38	3	28	2	10	13	2	1
6b Personal service occupations	270	38	7	10	10	11	-	232	23	55	75	65	14
7a Buyers, brokers and sales representatives	90	58	-	15	21	21	1	32	2	10	11	8	1
7b Other sales occupations	239	46	15	16	3	11	1	193	26	31	60	65	11
8a Industrial plant and machine operators, assemblers	187	121	4	27	38	52	-	66	4	15	21	25	1
8b Drivers and mobile machinery operators	116	109	-	22	42	42	3	7	-	3	-	4	-
9a Other occupations in agriculture, forestry and fishing	9	5	1	-	2	2	-	4	1	2	1	-	-
9b Other elementary occupations	300	129	15	31	40	40	3	171	10	23	58	65	15
Occupation not stated or inadequately described	29	19	1	1	5	11	1	10	-	3	4	3	-

Table 74 Occupation (10% sample) – **continued**

74. Residents aged 16 and over, employees and self-employed

(10% sample)

Gosport

Standard Occupational Classification Sub-major Groups	TOTAL PERSONS	Males aged 16 and over						Females aged 16 and over					
		Total	16 - 19	20 - 29	30 - 44	45 - 64	65 and over	Total	16 - 19	20 - 29	30 - 44	45 - 59	60 and over
a	b	c	d	e	f	g	h	i	j	k	l	m	n
ALL OCCUPATIONS	3,390	1,931	98	536	744	532	21	1,459	89	428	543	356	43
1a Corporate managers and administrators	273	187	2	20	99	65	1	86	2	27	36	21	1
1b Managers/proprietors in agriculture and services	138	73	-	16	27	30	-	65	2	18	18	25	2
2a Science and engineering professionals	65	60	-	26	14	20	-	5	-	5	-	-	-
2b Health professionals	11	9	-	1	4	3	1	2	-	-	1	1	-
2c Teaching professionals	59	22	-	3	9	9	1	37	-	7	19	10	1
2d Other professional occupations	28	20	-	1	7	12	-	8	-	2	5	-	1
3a Science and engineering associate professionals	89	70	4	17	27	22	-	19	-	8	6	5	-
3b Health associate professionals	74	5	-	2	2	1	-	69	2	26	27	12	2
3c Other associate professional occupations	101	68	1	10	29	27	1	33	-	8	17	6	2
4a Clerical occupations	370	94	3	31	28	32	-	276	27	93	93	59	4
4b Secretarial occupations	115	6	-	2	3	1	-	109	4	37	40	26	2
5a Skilled construction trades	69	68	3	20	23	22	-	1	-	-	1	-	-
5b Skilled engineering trades	216	212	14	53	72	70	3	4	2	-	2	-	-
5c Other skilled trades	206	180	18	46	65	50	1	26	2	3	13	7	1
6a Protective service occupations	455	409	17	165	185	41	1	46	5	24	12	4	1
6b Personal service occupations	260	44	6	13	11	9	5	216	14	59	83	52	8
7a Buyers, brokers and sales representatives	36	27	1	8	12	6	-	9	-	4	3	2	-
7b Other sales occupations	214	37	11	10	8	8	-	177	16	40	72	46	3
8a Industrial plant and machine operators, assemblers	228	135	4	44	57	30	-	93	8	33	31	21	-
8b Drivers and mobile machinery operators	92	82	-	21	27	34	-	10	-	4	5	1	-
9a Other occupations in agriculture, forestry and fishing	7	4	-	2	-	2	-	3	-	1	2	-	-
9b Other elementary occupations	257	103	12	22	31	31	7	154	3	24	56	55	16
Occupation not stated or inadequately described	27	16	2	3	4	7	-	11	2	5	1	3	-

57

Table 74 Occupation (10% sample) – continued

(10% sample)

74. Residents aged 16 and over, employees and self-employed

Hart

Standard Occupational Classification Sub-major Groups	TOTAL PERSONS	Males aged 16 and over						Females aged 16 and over					
		Total	16 - 19	20 - 29	30 - 44	45 - 64	65 and over	Total	16 - 19	20 - 29	30 - 44	45 - 59	60 and over
a	b	c	d	e	f	g	h	i	j	k	l	m	n
ALL OCCUPATIONS	4,222	2,485	142	583	920	790	50	1,737	92	403	676	502	64
1a Corporate managers and administrators	733	548	5	65	243	225	10	185	2	59	87	35	2
1b Managers/proprietors in agriculture and services	234	149	6	23	62	52	6	85	2	31	23	24	5
2a Science and engineering professionals	233	211	-	40	87	81	3	22	-	10	9	2	1
2b Health professionals	30	18	-	-	9	9	-	12	-	2	9	1	-
2c Teaching professionals	139	35	-	3	18	13	1	104	-	11	53	37	3
2d Other professional occupations	120	79	-	13	30	36	-	41	-	15	18	7	1
3a Science and engineering associate professionals	150	111	6	43	43	19	-	39	-	9	19	11	-
3b Health associate professionals	81	3	-	-	-	3	-	78	1	13	31	27	6
3c Other associate professional occupations	192	117	3	20	46	43	5	75	1	22	31	18	3
4a Clerical occupations	402	100	14	25	23	35	3	302	21	78	118	77	8
4b Secretarial occupations	238	6	-	-	1	4	1	232	6	51	80	90	5
5a Skilled construction trades	79	77	4	26	22	24	1	2	-	-	2	-	-
5b Skilled engineering trades	156	152	7	34	55	55	1	4	-	-	2	2	-
5c Other skilled trades	205	184	15	51	64	50	4	21	3	6	4	6	2
6a Protective service occupations	224	212	16	110	72	12	2	12	2	3	5	1	1
6b Personal service occupations	229	55	8	24	10	10	3	174	16	31	64	51	12
7a Buyers, brokers and sales representatives	109	85	2	16	42	24	1	24	3	7	11	3	-
7b Other sales occupations	204	43	23	11	6	2	1	161	27	30	46	53	5
8a Industrial plant and machine operators, assemblers	115	84	6	26	21	29	2	31	5	6	8	11	1
8b Drivers and mobile machinery operators	102	95	1	22	33	37	2	7	-	1	4	2	-
9a Other occupations in agriculture, forestry and fishing	23	16	2	3	6	5	-	7	-	2	1	3	1
9b Other elementary occupations	201	90	23	24	21	18	4	111	2	14	49	39	7
Occupation not stated or inadequately described	23	15	1	4	6	4	-	8	1	2	2	2	1

Table 74 Occupation (10% sample) – continued

74. Residents aged 16 and over, employees and self-employed

(10% sample)

Havant

Standard Occupational Classification Sub-major Groups	TOTAL PERSONS	Males aged 16 and over						Females aged 16 and over					
		Total	16 - 19	20 - 29	30 - 44	45 - 64	65 and over	Total	16 - 19	20 - 29	30 - 44	45 - 59	60 and over
a	b	c	d	e	f	g	h	i	j	k	l	m	n
ALL OCCUPATIONS	5,177	2,918	131	646	1,036	1,061	44	2,259	149	482	811	707	110
1a Corporate managers and administrators	541	374	4	34	164	166	6	167	1	38	65	53	10
1b Managers/proprietors in agriculture and services	235	146	3	31	53	55	4	89	2	20	36	28	3
2a Science and engineering professionals	190	182	-	43	70	68	1	8	-	4	3	1	-
2b Health professionals	24	14	-	1	5	7	1	10	-	3	6	1	-
2c Teaching professionals	150	53	-	1	21	31	-	97	-	5	42	43	7
2d Other professional occupations	78	55	-	4	22	28	1	23	-	4	10	8	1
3a Science and engineering associate professionals	210	168	9	45	62	51	1	42	2	13	16	11	-
3b Health associate professionals	93	8	-	-	6	2	-	85	1	24	30	26	4
3c Other associate professional occupations	168	108	5	15	40	47	1	60	1	15	22	21	1
4a Clerical occupations	532	177	8	53	49	66	1	355	33	97	110	107	8
4b Secretarial occupations	199	8	-	-	1	7	-	191	11	32	75	64	9
5a Skilled construction trades	165	159	7	33	61	57	1	6	-	1	2	3	-
5b Skilled engineering trades	278	262	12	73	91	85	1	16	1	6	3	6	-
5c Other skilled trades	374	309	21	81	104	100	3	65	4	14	26	21	-
6a Protective service occupations	117	109	2	24	48	35	-	8	-	3	2	3	-
6b Personal service occupations	360	71	10	20	18	18	5	289	30	58	106	78	17
7a Buyers, brokers and sales representatives	101	69	1	13	28	23	4	32	2	10	11	6	3
7b Other sales occupations	327	52	15	14	7	14	2	275	32	53	105	71	14
8a Industrial plant and machine operators, assemblers	448	234	14	65	69	82	4	214	19	51	73	65	6
8b Drivers and mobile machinery operators	159	146	1	29	57	59	-	13	1	2	6	3	1
9a Other occupations in agriculture, forestry and fishing	12	8	1	2	1	4	-	4	1	1	1	1	-
9b Other elementary occupations	371	179	17	60	53	43	6	192	7	25	57	80	23
Occupation not stated or inadequately described	45	27	1	5	6	13	2	18	1	3	4	7	3

Table 74 Occupation (10% sample) – continued

County, districts

(10% sample)

74. Residents aged 16 and over, employees and self-employed

New Forest

Standard Occupational Classification Sub-major Groups	TOTAL PERSONS	Males aged 16 and over						Females aged 16 and over					
		Total	16 - 19	20 - 29	30 - 44	45 - 64	65 and over	Total	16 - 19	20 - 29	30 - 44	45 - 59	60 and over
a	b	c	d	e	f	g	h	i	j	k	l	m	n
ALL OCCUPATIONS	**6,894**	**3,847**	**173**	**830**	**1,438**	**1,316**	**90**	**3,047**	**198**	**682**	**1,150**	**847**	**170**
1a Corporate managers and administrators	735	538	2	54	258	213	11	197	1	49	89	52	6
1b Managers/proprietors in agriculture and services	502	289	2	50	107	116	14	213	6	46	81	70	10
2a Science and engineering professionals	192	178	-	45	73	57	3	14	-	5	8	1	-
2b Health professionals	53	37	-	3	15	16	3	16	-	3	12	1	1
2c Teaching professionals	199	67	-	2	30	34	1	132	-	14	60	52	6
2d Other professional occupations	121	90	-	14	40	33	3	31	-	8	11	11	1
3a Science and engineering associate professionals	222	193	6	49	78	60	-	29	-	11	10	8	-
3b Health associate professionals	152	12	-	2	5	5	-	140	1	24	62	46	7
3c Other associate professional occupations	292	186	3	32	71	74	6	106	-	26	46	30	4
4a Clerical occupations	715	199	21	55	56	60	7	516	45	156	176	118	21
4b Secretarial occupations	382	12	2	-	4	5	1	370	20	94	129	104	23
5a Skilled construction trades	199	196	7	57	61	68	3	3	-	-	3	-	-
5b Skilled engineering trades	282	274	11	68	95	96	4	8	1	3	2	1	1
5c Other skilled trades	452	387	32	111	152	87	5	65	5	19	22	16	3
6a Protective service occupations	124	109	2	45	43	19	-	15	1	7	4	3	-
6b Personal service occupations	556	98	17	36	18	22	5	458	46	84	187	114	27
7a Buyers, brokers and sales representatives	139	110	-	28	43	36	3	29	1	9	10	7	2
7b Other sales occupations	415	81	30	17	16	16	2	334	41	64	103	100	26
8a Industrial plant and machine operators, assemblers	361	282	9	63	108	99	3	79	9	20	22	26	2
8b Drivers and mobile machinery operators	219	207	-	31	76	95	5	12	1	3	6	1	1
9a Other occupations in agriculture, forestry and fishing	73	54	4	10	15	22	3	19	5	3	5	4	2
9b Other elementary occupations	457	214	24	53	60	70	7	243	15	31	96	75	26
Occupation not stated or inadequately described	52	34	1	5	14	13	1	18	-	3	6	7	2

Table 74 Occupation (10% sample) – continued

74. Residents aged 16 and over, employees and self-employed

(10% sample)

Portsmouth

Standard Occupational Classification Sub-major Groups	TOTAL PERSONS	Males aged 16 and over						Females aged 16 and over					
		Total	16 - 19	20 - 29	30 - 44	45 - 64	65 and over	Total	16 - 19	20 - 29	30 - 44	45 - 59	60 and over
a	b	c	d	e	f	g	h	i	j	k	l	m	n
ALL OCCUPATIONS	7,563	4,288	209	1,271	1,509	1,221	78	3,275	172	1,021	1,150	790	142
1a Corporate managers and administrators	603	388	3	77	172	129	7	215	-	79	84	50	2
1b Managers/proprietors in agriculture and services	398	239	3	52	89	83	12	159	2	53	55	37	12
2a Science and engineering professionals	228	209	-	69	87	52	1	19	-	13	6	-	-
2b Health professionals	27	16	-	1	5	9	1	11	-	7	1	2	1
2c Teaching professionals	192	80	-	8	44	28	-	112	-	26	51	25	10
2d Other professional occupations	99	60	-	16	20	22	2	39	-	11	16	12	-
3a Science and engineering associate professionals	240	198	2	84	75	37	-	42	-	21	16	5	-
3b Health associate professionals	191	19	-	5	8	5	1	172	3	70	57	38	4
3c Other associate professional occupations	258	157	1	37	54	63	2	101	1	30	46	17	7
4a Clerical occupations	858	272	16	96	84	69	7	586	36	219	198	115	18
4b Secretarial occupations	276	9	1	2	1	5	-	267	11	98	86	58	14
5a Skilled construction trades	228	227	15	68	74	69	1	1	-	-	1	-	-
5b Skilled engineering trades	362	352	15	106	130	99	2	10	-	5	4	1	-
5c Other skilled trades	495	397	28	111	141	111	6	98	5	25	41	23	4
6a Protective service occupations	450	418	38	179	134	60	7	32	5	20	5	2	-
6b Personal service occupations	608	156	16	59	41	36	4	452	31	135	159	116	11
7a Buyers, brokers and sales representatives	109	86	1	32	29	22	2	23	-	10	9	4	-
7b Other sales occupations	490	108	26	34	26	18	4	382	55	82	139	92	14
8a Industrial plant and machine operators, assemblers	413	261	9	85	79	86	2	152	8	53	41	44	6
8b Drivers and mobile machinery operators	279	256	2	42	105	107	-	23	-	8	10	5	-
9a Other occupations in agriculture, forestry and fishing	9	8	-	2	2	3	1	1	-	-	1	-	-
9b Other elementary occupations	689	331	31	98	97	90	15	358	14	55	116	136	37
Occupation not stated or inadequately described	61	41	2	8	12	18	1	20	1	1	8	8	2

Table 74 Occupation (10% sample) – continued

County, districts

(10% sample)

74. Residents aged 16 and over, employees and self-employed

Rushmoor

Standard Occupational Classification Sub-major Groups	TOTAL PERSONS	Males aged 16 and over						Females aged 16 and over					
		Total	16 - 19	20 - 29	30 - 44	45 - 64	65 and over	Total	16 - 19	20 - 29	30 - 44	45 - 59	60 and over
a	b	c	d	e	f	g	h	i	j	k	l	m	n
ALL OCCUPATIONS	4,333	2,464	176	800	834	624	30	1,869	144	556	658	427	84
1a Corporate managers and administrators	494	336	-	59	171	103	3	158	4	53	70	25	6
1b Managers/proprietors in agriculture and services	165	100	1	31	37	29	2	65	-	22	25	14	4
2a Science and engineering professionals	180	164	-	40	74	50	-	16	-	6	8	2	-
2b Health professionals	9	4	-	1	3	-	-	5	-	1	4	-	-
2c Teaching professionals	80	20	1	1	10	6	2	60	-	7	39	12	2
2d Other professional occupations	51	31	-	8	14	9	-	20	-	9	6	5	-
3a Science and engineering associate professionals	149	113	5	44	42	22	-	36	-	14	11	10	1
3b Health associate professionals	74	12	1	4	5	1	1	62	1	18	26	14	3
3c Other associate professional occupations	163	92	6	21	34	30	1	71	3	27	23	18	-
4a Clerical occupations	549	152	15	57	31	45	4	397	36	146	123	86	6
4b Secretarial occupations	205	6	-	2	2	2	-	199	12	49	72	58	8
5a Skilled construction trades	105	104	7	33	36	27	1	1	-	1	-	-	-
5b Skilled engineering trades	197	190	12	59	61	58	-	7	1	2	2	2	2
5c Other skilled trades	219	190	14	63	59	53	1	29	-	8	11	8	2
6a Protective service occupations	468	412	57	220	115	17	3	56	15	30	9	2	-
6b Personal service occupations	282	59	4	17	12	25	1	223	23	69	73	48	10
7a Buyers, brokers and sales representatives	87	58	4	17	18	19	-	29	1	7	13	7	1
7b Other sales occupations	195	47	22	18	2	5	-	148	29	33	36	40	10
8a Industrial plant and machine operators, assemblers	191	107	13	31	35	28	-	84	4	18	28	29	5
8b Drivers and mobile machinery operators	117	107	1	20	34	49	3	10	1	2	4	3	-
9a Other occupations in agriculture, forestry and fishing	4	2	-	-	2	-	-	2	1	-	1	-	-
9b Other elementary occupations	326	142	11	48	32	44	7	184	13	33	69	43	26
Occupation not stated or inadequately described	23	16	2	6	5	2	1	7	-	1	5	1	-

Table 74 Occupation (10% sample) – continued

74. Residents aged 16 and over, employees and self-employed

(10% sample)

Southampton

Standard Occupational Classification Sub-major Groups	TOTAL PERSONS	Males aged 16 and over						Females aged 16 and over					
		Total	16 - 19	20 - 29	30 - 44	45 - 64	65 and over	Total	16 - 19	20 - 29	30 - 44	45 - 59	60 and over
a	b	c	d	e	f	g	h	i	j	k	l	m	n
ALL OCCUPATIONS	8,320	4,643	221	1,227	1,719	1,397	79	3,677	224	1,063	1,287	938	165
1a Corporate managers and administrators	611	400	-	87	189	119	5	211	3	76	80	44	8
1b Managers/proprietors in agriculture and services	413	233	3	57	94	74	5	180	2	48	67	50	13
2a Science and engineering professionals	196	178	-	75	74	29	-	18	-	7	9	2	-
2b Health professionals	49	32	-	4	20	8	-	17	-	7	8	1	1
2c Teaching professionals	269	133	-	20	58	55	-	136	-	35	64	32	5
2d Other professional occupations	161	104	-	32	45	25	2	57	-	16	27	10	4
3a Science and engineering associate professionals	301	230	11	84	88	45	2	71	3	29	29	8	2
3b Health associate professionals	220	19	-	5	12	1	1	201	5	71	77	43	5
3c Other associate professional occupations	283	154	4	29	69	52	-	129	4	42	56	25	2
4a Clerical occupations	1,001	362	24	129	113	88	8	639	62	217	201	129	30
4b Secretarial occupations	374	27	3	5	10	9	-	347	22	117	100	92	16
5a Skilled construction trades	271	268	12	58	98	98	2	3	-	1	2	-	-
5b Skilled engineering trades	402	387	31	96	138	120	2	15	-	3	4	7	1
5c Other skilled trades	571	518	34	168	173	133	10	53	3	12	21	15	2
6a Protective service occupations	126	100	5	19	37	36	3	26	1	9	8	8	-
6b Personal service occupations	645	153	10	45	38	52	8	492	46	116	180	131	19
7a Buyers, brokers and sales representatives	149	113	2	29	43	34	5	36	-	21	9	6	-
7b Other sales occupations	563	113	33	35	22	21	2	450	47	133	134	120	16
8a Industrial plant and machine operators, assemblers	447	324	12	74	120	117	1	123	5	33	43	38	4
8b Drivers and mobile machinery operators	385	353	4	55	151	136	7	32	-	7	20	5	-
9a Other occupations in agriculture, forestry and fishing	10	6	-	2	3	1	-	4	1	2	1	-	-
9b Other elementary occupations	807	395	32	106	111	133	13	412	20	52	142	162	36
Occupation not stated or inadequately described	66	41	1	13	13	11	3	25	-	9	5	10	1

Table 74 Occupation (10% sample) – continued

(10% sample)

74. Residents aged 16 and over, employees and self-employed

Test Valley

Standard Occupational Classification Sub-major Groups	TOTAL PERSONS	Males aged 16 and over						Females aged 16 and over					
		Total	16 - 19	20 - 29	30 - 44	45 - 64	65 and over	Total	16 - 19	20 - 29	30 - 44	45 - 59	60 and over
a	b	c	d	e	f	g	h	i	j	k	l	m	n
ALL OCCUPATIONS	5,030	2,915	169	663	1,062	957	64	2,115	141	509	789	587	89
1a Corporate managers and administrators	631	482	3	48	223	199	9	149	3	39	74	32	1
1b Managers/proprietors in agriculture and services	337	222	-	34	87	91	10	115	4	29	41	37	4
2a Science and engineering professionals	128	115	-	24	47	43	1	13	-	4	8	1	-
2b Health professionals	38	25	-	-	14	10	1	13	-	2	9	1	1
2c Teaching professionals	171	54	-	3	25	23	3	117	-	13	58	42	4
2d Other professional occupations	119	85	-	12	46	24	3	34	-	12	10	9	3
3a Science and engineering associate professionals	171	136	3	42	55	36	-	35	-	12	19	4	-
3b Health associate professionals	88	1	-	-	1	-	-	87	-	22	36	27	2
3c Other associate professional occupations	170	97	1	13	47	35	1	73	2	20	32	17	2
4a Clerical occupations	594	176	14	60	44	55	3	418	40	123	137	101	17
4b Secretarial occupations	227	1	-	-	1	-	-	226	13	59	86	64	4
5a Skilled construction trades	122	120	2	26	44	45	3	2	-	-	1	1	-
5b Skilled engineering trades	192	186	20	57	56	52	1	6	-	4	2	-	-
5c Other skilled trades	314	277	24	79	87	84	3	37	2	8	11	15	1
6a Protective service occupations	206	198	25	88	68	16	1	8	-	2	4	2	-
6b Personal service occupations	309	50	5	12	17	15	1	259	21	52	111	64	11
7a Buyers, brokers and sales representatives	108	80	3	16	27	33	1	28	-	10	9	9	-
7b Other sales occupations	205	49	23	12	7	5	2	156	27	28	45	51	5
8a Industrial plant and machine operators, assemblers	296	190	12	50	60	66	2	106	14	30	27	34	1
8b Drivers and mobile machinery operators	156	150	2	25	64	55	4	6	-	3	3	-	-
9a Other occupations in agriculture, forestry and fishing	65	51	7	11	11	20	2	14	3	3	1	5	2
9b Other elementary occupations	344	149	23	47	28	40	11	195	11	31	58	66	29
Occupation not stated or inadequately described	39	21	2	4	3	10	2	18	1	3	7	5	2

Table 74 Occupation (10% sample) – continued

County, districts

(10% sample)

74. Residents aged 16 and over, employees and self-employed

Winchester

Standard Occupational Classification Sub-major Groups	TOTAL PERSONS	Males aged 16 and over						Females aged 16 and over					
		Total	16 - 19	20 - 29	30 - 44	45 - 64	65 and over	Total	16 - 19	20 - 29	30 - 44	45 - 59	60 and over
a	b	c	d	e	f	g	h	i	j	k	l	m	n
ALL OCCUPATIONS	4,521	2,598	144	461	966	931	96	1,923	109	399	708	577	130
1a Corporate managers and administrators	637	472	2	45	213	206	6	165	-	30	89	41	5
1b Managers/proprietors in agriculture and services	358	228	1	26	88	88	25	130	2	29	50	34	15
2a Science and engineering professionals	183	167	-	29	70	65	3	16	-	6	7	3	-
2b Health professionals	40	23	-	2	6	13	2	17	-	2	8	6	1
2c Teaching professionals	224	67	-	4	28	34	1	157	-	18	69	64	6
2d Other professional occupations	168	122	-	13	56	49	4	46	-	12	16	13	5
3a Science and engineering associate professionals	142	108	3	34	40	30	1	34	-	10	18	6	-
3b Health associate professionals	99	12	1	3	5	3	-	87	1	20	40	26	-
3c Other associate professional occupations	195	123	2	22	51	44	4	72	-	15	28	23	6
4a Clerical occupations	441	143	14	40	44	44	1	298	27	85	86	89	11
4b Secretarial occupations	203	2	-	1	-	-	1	201	10	38	70	71	12
5a Skilled construction trades	109	107	4	25	39	37	2	2	-	-	1	-	1
5b Skilled engineering trades	97	94	7	19	36	29	3	3	1	1	1	-	-
5c Other skilled trades	246	213	19	48	76	60	10	33	1	11	9	10	2
6a Protective service occupations	164	149	28	40	59	21	1	15	7	5	-	3	-
6b Personal service occupations	325	67	5	22	9	25	6	258	18	52	93	78	17
7a Buyers, brokers and sales representatives	60	48	1	5	13	27	2	12	-	3	8	1	2
7b Other sales occupations	194	52	20	19	4	6	3	142	25	32	42	31	12
8a Industrial plant and machine operators, assemblers	121	88	8	16	34	28	2	33	3	7	9	9	5
8b Drivers and mobile machinery operators	116	111	3	10	41	54	3	5	-	-	4	1	-
9a Other occupations in agriculture, forestry and fishing	76	56	1	12	18	24	1	20	3	7	4	4	2
9b Other elementary occupations	291	124	23	25	30	35	11	167	11	14	51	61	30
Occupation not stated or inadequately described	32	22	2	1	6	9	4	10	-	2	5	3	-

Table 75 Hours worked (10% sample)

75. Residents aged 16 and over, employees and self-employed

(10% sample)

HAMPSHIRE

Sex, age, marital status and long-term illness	TOTAL PERSONS	Hours worked weekly											Not stated
		3 and under	4 - 7	8 - 15	16 - 21	22 - 23	24 - 30	31 - 35	36 - 40	41 - 50	51 - 60	61 and over	
a	b	c	d	e	f	g	h	i	j	k	l	m	n
TOTAL PERSONS	**71,873**	**231**	**1,304**	**4,555**	**4,390**	**696**	**3,816**	**5,300**	**35,924**	**8,995**	**2,773**	**1,609**	**2,280**
Males													
16 - 19	2,086	17	67	240	54	3	36	112	1,129	216	45	39	128
20 - 24	4,527	1	7	35	33	1	51	289	2,845	747	195	101	222
25 - 29	5,377	1	3	25	20	2	45	299	3,342	959	307	165	209
30 - 34	5,116	-	5	13	17	2	40	280	3,065	958	341	213	182
35 - 39	4,673	-	5	14	14	3	54	241	2,690	964	351	185	152
40 - 44	5,301	1	2	15	15	3	58	254	3,054	1,142	388	188	181
45 - 49	4,293	1	2	20	16	2	67	202	2,497	861	330	149	146
50 - 54	3,596	2	1	14	24	5	63	157	2,202	720	203	106	99
55 - 59	3,033	1	9	28	47	9	75	165	1,881	501	148	97	72
60 - 64	2,010	2	14	54	72	15	74	89	1,230	283	71	41	65
65 and over	778	5	30	144	119	22	101	39	175	51	27	14	51
Females													
16 - 19	1,857	11	136	279	54	13	60	206	926	104	14	2	52
20 - 24	3,990	4	43	153	128	20	144	622	2,394	285	61	26	110
25 - 29	3,954	16	96	383	312	53	233	519	1,926	263	48	31	74
30 - 34	3,441	32	176	591	464	72	321	296	1,160	172	38	33	86
35 - 39	3,618	33	161	570	572	80	476	308	1,063	178	52	35	90
40 - 44	4,384	28	163	547	696	101	616	416	1,374	228	61	57	97
45 - 49	3,640	16	81	409	579	115	490	356	1,254	162	34	55	89
50 - 54	2,757	13	102	370	492	75	377	221	862	113	28	36	68
55 - 59	2,039	15	76	292	372	63	276	160	635	61	18	18	53
60 - 64	946	13	62	220	204	29	120	52	183	21	8	12	22
65 and over	457	19	63	139	86	8	39	17	37	6	5	6	32
Total males	**40,790**	**31**	**145**	**602**	**431**	**67**	**664**	**2,127**	**24,110**	**7,402**	**2,406**	**1,298**	**1,507**
Single, widowed or divorced	13,985	19	86	353	175	20	225	775	8,554	2,125	657	386	610
Married	26,805	12	59	249	256	47	439	1,352	15,556	5,277	1,749	912	897
Total females	**31,083**	**200**	**1,159**	**3,953**	**3,959**	**629**	**3,152**	**3,173**	**11,814**	**1,593**	**367**	**311**	**773**
Single, widowed or divorced	11,175	37	330	747	545	105	692	1,460	5,888	785	173	97	316
Married	19,908	163	829	3,206	3,414	524	2,460	1,713	5,926	808	194	214	457
Persons with limiting long-term illness													
Total	**2,459**	**12**	**74**	**204**	**200**	**28**	**158**	**138**	**1,161**	**252**	**108**	**43**	**81**
Males	1,512	3	14	63	55	7	59	65	857	208	91	36	54
Females	947	9	60	141	145	21	99	73	304	44	17	7	27

Table 75 Hours worked (10% sample) – continued

75. Residents aged 16 and over, employees and self-employed   (10% sample)

Basingstoke & Deane

Sex, age, marital status and long-term illness	TOTAL PERSONS	3 and under	4 - 7	8 - 15	16 - 21	22 - 23	24 - 30	31 - 35	36 - 40	41 - 50	51 - 60	61 and over	Not stated
a	b	c	d	e	f	g	h	i	j	k	l	m	n
TOTAL PERSONS	**7,472**	**17**	**112**	**433**	**405**	**63**	**374**	**582**	**3,989**	**919**	**290**	**118**	**170**
Males													
16 - 19	222	1	7	27	5	-	4	15	127	24	2	2	8
20 - 24	508	-	-	2	1	-	4	36	336	92	19	6	12
25 - 29	550	-	-	3	-	-	3	29	352	91	44	5	23
30 - 34	517	-	-	1	1	1	6	38	327	77	34	21	11
35 - 39	509	-	-	-	-	-	5	26	308	101	40	22	7
40 - 44	551	-	-	2	1	-	4	37	328	112	39	18	10
45 - 49	435	-	-	1	4	-	4	23	253	92	34	13	11
50 - 54	365	-	-	4	2	2	2	13	224	75	25	6	12
55 - 59	309	-	1	2	4	2	4	18	204	49	10	6	9
60 - 64	194	-	-	7	5	-	5	6	127	31	6	3	4
65 and over	77	-	3	16	9	1	17	2	18	4	3	-	4
Females													
16 - 19	179	1	15	26	5	-	3	21	92	10	2	-	4
20 - 24	429	1	1	15	8	-	5	68	274	35	3	2	17
25 - 29	435	1	6	42	28	8	19	55	231	30	5	3	7
30 - 34	361	2	13	54	62	8	36	25	128	22	3	2	6
35 - 39	388	4	20	63	48	7	47	35	134	18	6	3	3
40 - 44	459	4	12	44	63	9	70	46	175	22	6	1	7
45 - 49	370	-	3	35	56	11	54	50	138	15	3	1	4
50 - 54	276	1	10	27	45	5	38	19	106	13	3	3	6
55 - 59	195	-	10	25	30	4	28	15	77	3	1	1	1
60 - 64	96	1	5	21	18	5	12	4	24	3	1	-	2
65 and over	47	1	6	16	10	-	4	1	6	-	1	-	2
Total males	**4,237**	**1**	**11**	**65**	**32**	**6**	**58**	**243**	**2,604**	**748**	**256**	**102**	**111**
Single, widowed or divorced	1,482	1	8	38	12	1	24	98	947	216	66	27	44
Married	2,755	-	3	27	20	5	34	145	1,657	532	190	75	67
Total females	**3,235**	**16**	**101**	**368**	**373**	**57**	**316**	**339**	**1,385**	**171**	**34**	**16**	**59**
Single, widowed or divorced	1,128	5	30	64	41	12	55	145	633	86	18	8	31
Married	2,107	11	71	304	332	45	261	194	752	85	16	8	28
Persons with limiting long-term illness													
Total	**211**	**2**	**5**	**14**	**14**	**2**	**15**	**10**	**104**	**27**	**9**	**3**	**6**
Males	142	-	-	6	5	1	4	4	79	26	9	3	5
Females	69	2	5	8	9	1	11	6	25	1	-	-	1

Table 75 Hours worked (10% sample) – continued

75. Residents aged 16 and over, employees and self-employed

(10% sample)

East Hampshire

Sex, age, marital status and long-term illness	TOTAL PERSONS	Hours worked weekly											
		3 and under	4 - 7	8 - 15	16 - 21	22 - 23	24 - 30	31 - 35	36 - 40	41 - 50	51 - 60	61 and over	Not stated
a	b	c	d	e	f	g	h	i	j	k	l	m	n
TOTAL PERSONS	4,956	20	124	304	260	49	273	374	2,236	775	238	130	173
Males													
16 - 19	138	-	3	18	2	-	2	6	70	25	1	1	10
20 - 24	274	-	1	1	1	-	8	15	161	48	14	10	15
25 - 29	335	-	1	1	-	1	1	19	197	78	22	7	8
30 - 34	337	-	1	-	-	-	1	13	183	87	25	17	10
35 - 39	328	-	-	1	-	-	2	14	170	90	27	15	9
40 - 44	404	-	-	-	2	-	1	24	219	97	29	16	16
45 - 49	331	-	-	1	-	-	8	19	168	70	39	13	13
50 - 54	237	-	-	1	3	-	3	8	139	56	12	8	7
55 - 59	206	-	1	3	3	1	6	10	117	37	15	9	4
60 - 64	165	-	1	6	6	1	4	10	96	27	5	4	5
65 and over	66	-	6	9	10	1	10	1	14	4	2	2	7
Females													
16 - 19	115	-	9	19	3	1	6	17	48	5	4	-	3
20 - 24	234	-	2	7	10	1	3	39	133	27	5	1	6
25 - 29	253	2	7	16	15	6	18	35	118	27	5	4	-
30 - 34	250	3	15	39	28	4	26	21	79	19	3	2	11
35 - 39	271	6	11	43	32	6	36	21	77	16	10	4	9
40 - 44	308	2	19	35	38	9	47	35	73	27	6	9	8
45 - 49	257	-	6	30	34	8	31	35	75	13	7	7	16
50 - 54	200	4	11	26	35	2	35	14	49	11	3	2	8
55 - 59	136	-	13	23	22	5	15	12	33	6	2	1	4
60 - 64	69	1	10	18	10	1	6	4	11	3	2	1	2
65 and over	42	2	7	7	6	2	4	2	6	2	-	2	2
Total males	**2,821**	**-**	**14**	**41**	**27**	**4**	**46**	**139**	**1,534**	**619**	**191**	**102**	**104**
Single, widowed or divorced	908	-	8	22	9	1	16	41	497	190	47	34	43
Married	1,913	-	6	19	18	3	30	98	1,037	429	144	68	61
Total females	**2,135**	**20**	**110**	**263**	**233**	**45**	**227**	**235**	**702**	**156**	**47**	**28**	**69**
Single, widowed or divorced	741	4	31	52	39	6	45	103	338	70	20	9	24
Married	1,394	16	79	211	194	39	182	132	364	86	27	19	45
Persons with limiting long-term illness													
Total	**152**	**-**	**12**	**15**	**12**	**-**	**9**	**9**	**63**	**16**	**9**	**3**	**4**
Males	85	-	1	7	4	-	3	5	41	11	6	3	4
Females	67	-	11	8	8	-	6	4	22	5	3	-	-

Table 75 Hours worked (10% sample) – continued

75. Residents aged 16 and over, employees and self-employed (10% sample)

Eastleigh

Sex, age, marital status and long-term illness	TOTAL PERSONS	Hours worked weekly											
		3 and under	4 - 7	8 - 15	16 - 21	22 - 23	24 - 30	31 - 35	36 - 40	41 - 50	51 - 60	61 and over	Not stated
a	b	c	d	e	f	g	h	i	j	k	l	m	n
TOTAL PERSONS	5,205	13	104	354	303	61	294	446	2,609	607	189	97	128
Males													
16 - 19	147	-	7	21	4	1	2	9	85	11	-	-	7
20 - 24	316	-	1	-	5	-	2	24	216	39	13	5	11
25 - 29	376	-	-	1	1	-	5	22	231	74	22	13	7
30 - 34	378	-	1	1	1	-	4	22	236	68	28	10	7
35 - 39	382	-	-	1	1	1	6	23	229	69	20	20	12
40 - 44	402	-	-	1	1	-	11	22	240	78	30	8	11
45 - 49	296	-	-	-	1	-	9	14	171	66	17	11	7
50 - 54	270	-	-	-	3	1	5	17	167	48	14	8	8
55 - 59	197	-	-	2	4	-	3	11	124	38	8	3	3
60 - 64	137	-	2	3	2	-	4	7	87	18	7	3	4
65 and over	44	1	1	9	3	1	11	4	11	1	1	-	1
Females													
16 - 19	113	1	9	19	2	-	5	11	56	8	-	-	2
20 - 24	276	-	6	14	4	1	6	47	172	14	6	1	5
25 - 29	304	-	9	31	15	6	18	49	145	21	4	1	5
30 - 34	257	1	19	47	32	8	17	32	81	11	2	2	5
35 - 39	291	1	19	59	48	10	34	28	64	9	7	2	10
40 - 44	320	3	9	34	53	8	49	30	101	13	7	4	9
45 - 49	284	1	9	35	53	10	42	34	83	10	1	2	4
50 - 54	203	2	4	31	34	7	32	19	59	7	1	2	5
55 - 59	142	1	4	24	20	4	24	16	40	4	1	1	3
60 - 64	49	1	1	13	10	3	4	4	11	-	-	1	1
65 and over	21	1	3	8	6	-	1	1	-	-	-	-	1
Total males	**2,945**	**1**	**12**	**39**	**26**	**4**	**62**	**175**	**1,797**	**510**	**160**	**81**	**78**
Single, widowed or divorced	948	-	8	26	13	3	21	60	603	129	35	19	31
Married	1,997	1	4	13	13	1	41	115	1,194	381	125	62	47
Total females	**2,260**	**12**	**92**	**315**	**277**	**57**	**232**	**271**	**812**	**97**	**29**	**16**	**50**
Single, widowed or divorced	745	2	24	53	30	4	41	115	398	44	14	5	15
Married	1,515	10	68	262	247	53	191	156	414	53	15	11	35
Persons with limiting long-term illness													
Total	**164**	**-**	**3**	**16**	**9**	**2**	**10**	**13**	**83**	**18**	**5**	**4**	**1**
Males	95	-	1	3	1	-	6	3	59	16	2	4	-
Females	69	-	2	13	8	2	4	10	24	2	3	-	1

Table 75 Hours worked (10% sample) – continued

(10% sample)

75. Residents aged 16 and over, employees and self-employed

Fareham

Sex, age, marital status and long-term illness	TOTAL PERSONS	Hours worked weekly											
		3 and under	4 - 7	8 - 15	16 - 21	22 - 23	24 - 30	31 - 35	36 - 40	41 - 50	51 - 60	61 and over	Not stated
a	b	c	d	e	f	g	h	i	j	k	l	m	n
TOTAL PERSONS	**4,790**	21	92	283	318	48	243	344	2,469	565	171	107	129
Males													
16 - 19	116	3	7	11	5	-	2	9	58	9	4	3	5
20 - 24	241	-	-	1	2	-	3	12	171	31	10	5	6
25 - 29	287	-	-	2	-	-	3	17	177	51	19	11	7
30 - 34	361	-	1	-	2	-	1	18	233	52	23	20	11
35 - 39	322	-	-	1	-	-	2	23	183	66	24	13	10
40 - 44	371	-	1	-	-	-	6	11	210	92	23	13	15
45 - 49	319	-	-	1	2	-	5	16	191	63	19	9	13
50 - 54	260	-	2	-	-	1	5	13	177	46	11	3	4
55 - 59	245	-	-	2	5	1	7	14	155	35	10	9	5
60 - 64	137	-	-	5	6	2	3	5	91	16	3	3	3
65 and over	39	-	3	6	8	1	-	2	13	-	2	-	4
Females													
16 - 19	132	3	7	22	3	2	6	15	60	7	1	-	6
20 - 24	211	-	1	6	8	2	7	32	127	18	4	1	5
25 - 29	259	1	5	28	23	3	18	33	121	12	5	3	7
30 - 34	228	1	15	38	29	5	21	19	89	7	2	1	1
35 - 39	218	4	5	32	38	5	23	19	71	12	3	2	4
40 - 44	320	2	17	39	62	5	40	28	102	15	3	2	5
45 - 49	278	3	7	24	34	8	35	29	101	19	2	8	8
50 - 54	220	-	7	27	41	5	26	18	74	12	3	-	7
55 - 59	144	4	7	13	34	7	19	9	46	2	-	1	2
60 - 64	61	-	5	16	12	1	9	-	17	-	-	-	1
65 and over	21	-	2	9	4	-	2	2	2	-	-	-	-
Total males	**2,698**	**3**	**14**	**29**	**30**	**5**	**37**	**140**	**1,659**	**461**	**148**	**89**	**83**
Single, widowed or divorced	754	3	9	15	9	2	11	43	472	105	37	28	20
Married	1,944	-	5	14	21	3	26	97	1,187	356	111	61	63
Total females	**2,092**	**18**	**78**	**254**	**288**	**43**	**206**	**204**	**810**	**104**	**23**	**18**	**46**
Single, widowed or divorced	675	3	18	42	36	9	40	82	368	45	8	5	19
Married	1,417	15	60	212	252	34	166	122	442	59	15	13	27
Persons with limiting long-term illness													
Total	**138**	**-**	**4**	**6**	**14**	**3**	**10**	**8**	**70**	**13**	**6**	**1**	**3**
Males	87	-	1	2	3	2	2	4	53	12	5	1	2
Females	51	-	3	4	11	1	8	4	17	1	1	-	1

Table 75 Hours worked (10% sample) – **continued**

75. Residents aged 16 and over, employees and self-employed

(10% sample)

Gosport

Sex, age, marital status and long-term illness	TOTAL PERSONS	Hours worked weekly											
		3 and under	4 - 7	8 - 15	16 - 21	22 - 23	24 - 30	31 - 35	36 - 40	41 - 50	51 - 60	61 and over	Not stated
a	b	c	d	e	f	g	h	i	j	k	l	m	n
TOTAL PERSONS	**3,390**	**8**	**65**	**221**	**237**	**26**	**165**	**235**	**1,700**	**404**	**114**	**80**	**135**
Males													
16 - 19	98	-	3	8	-	-	2	6	52	10	1	5	11
20 - 24	243	-	-	2	1	-	-	16	157	38	11	10	8
25 - 29	293	-	-	-	-	-	1	22	176	47	16	11	20
30 - 34	298	-	-	1	-	-	2	17	159	57	19	13	30
35 - 39	229	-	-	1	2	1	1	11	134	45	15	7	12
40 - 44	217	1	-	1	-	-	1	4	134	50	12	6	8
45 - 49	185	-	-	-	1	-	6	3	124	32	9	5	5
50 - 54	137	-	-	-	-	-	4	3	79	29	12	6	4
55 - 59	127	-	-	1	3	-	3	8	83	17	9	2	1
60 - 64	83	-	-	2	2	2	5	1	58	8	2	1	2
65 and over	21	1	1	4	6	-	3	1	3	1	-	1	-
Females													
16 - 19	89	-	13	7	5	-	3	8	48	1	1	1	3
20 - 24	225	-	1	13	9	2	15	41	113	18	4	4	5
25 - 29	203	-	5	20	30	3	13	26	91	7	1	1	7
30 - 34	171	1	8	41	24	5	20	12	43	11	1	2	3
35 - 39	166	2	9	26	31	2	14	14	58	4	-	1	5
40 - 44	206	1	5	27	40	4	26	19	63	13	1	3	4
45 - 49	175	-	5	21	35	2	23	7	70	8	1	2	1
50 - 54	105	-	2	19	19	4	12	7	33	6	-	-	3
55 - 59	76	1	6	14	18	1	10	4	18	2	-	-	2
60 - 64	34	1	6	9	9	-	-	4	4	-	-	-	1
65 and over	9	-	1	4	2	-	1	1	-	-	-	-	-
Total males	**1,931**	**2**	**4**	**20**	**15**	**3**	**28**	**92**	**1,159**	**334**	**106**	**67**	**101**
Single, widowed or divorced	607	-	3	12	5	1	5	31	384	92	20	21	33
Married	1,324	2	1	8	10	2	23	61	775	242	86	46	68
Total females	**1,459**	**6**	**61**	**201**	**222**	**23**	**137**	**143**	**541**	**70**	**8**	**13**	**34**
Single, widowed or divorced	507	-	24	33	34	2	40	59	254	36	5	5	15
Married	952	6	37	168	188	21	97	84	287	34	3	8	19
Persons with limiting long-term illness													
Total	**130**	**1**	**2**	**9**	**18**	**1**	**11**	**5**	**64**	**12**	**4**	**1**	**2**
Males	79	-	1	1	6	1	3	3	47	10	4	1	2
Females	51	1	1	8	12	-	8	2	17	2	-	-	-

Table 75 Hours worked (10% sample) – **continued**

County, districts

75. Residents aged 16 and over, employees and self-employed

(10% sample)

Hart

Sex, age, marital status and long-term illness	TOTAL PERSONS	Hours worked weekly											
		3 and under	4 - 7	8 - 15	16 - 21	22 - 23	24 - 30	31 - 35	36 - 40	41 - 50	51 - 60	61 and over	Not stated
a	b	c	d	e	f	g	h	i	j	k	l	m	n
TOTAL PERSONS	**4,222**	**19**	**74**	**272**	**250**	**48**	**200**	**346**	**1,948**	**659**	**212**	**98**	**96**
Males													
16 - 19	142	1	9	19	7	-	1	16	62	17	3	3	4
20 - 24	275	-	-	3	1	-	3	24	145	63	19	8	9
25 - 29	308	-	-	-	-	-	3	16	170	81	18	12	8
30 - 34	288	-	-	1	2	-	1	19	151	76	26	10	2
35 - 39	298	-	-	1	-	-	2	18	167	70	24	11	5
40 - 44	334	-	-	1	1	-	5	14	173	81	43	8	8
45 - 49	281	-	-	1	1	-	1	21	153	63	23	11	7
50 - 54	227	-	-	1	2	-	2	9	131	52	12	11	7
55 - 59	184	-	-	-	4	-	4	17	105	34	10	6	4
60 - 64	98	-	-	3	7	-	6	6	55	13	3	1	4
65 and over	50	-	1	12	9	1	2	4	14	3	1	3	-
Females													
16 - 19	92	2	12	13	2	1	1	7	45	6	1	-	2
20 - 24	211	-	1	3	5	1	8	28	125	21	10	2	7
25 - 29	192	1	7	13	10	1	8	36	93	17	5	-	1
30 - 34	181	6	7	35	28	5	13	13	56	9	3	1	5
35 - 39	221	2	13	36	39	6	31	20	52	13	4	-	5
40 - 44	274	-	12	33	49	8	36	27	82	16	4	1	6
45 - 49	230	1	3	41	28	8	30	20	79	9	1	3	7
50 - 54	156	3	4	26	28	7	16	11	49	6	1	2	3
55 - 59	116	-	1	19	17	5	15	15	35	7	-	1	1
60 - 64	42	1	2	7	7	4	8	4	6	1	-	2	-
65 and over	22	2	2	4	3	1	4	1	-	1	1	2	1
Total males	**2,485**	**1**	**10**	**42**	**34**	**1**	**30**	**164**	**1,326**	**553**	**182**	**84**	**58**
Single, widowed or divorced	794	1	9	25	11	-	8	65	445	129	51	28	22
Married	1,691	-	1	17	23	1	22	99	881	424	131	56	36
Total females	**1,737**	**18**	**64**	**230**	**216**	**47**	**170**	**182**	**622**	**106**	**30**	**14**	**38**
Single, widowed or divorced	565	5	16	30	19	9	27	76	291	52	18	6	16
Married	1,172	13	48	200	197	38	143	106	331	54	12	8	22
Persons with limiting long-term illness													
Total	**121**	**-**	**3**	**8**	**13**	**2**	**4**	**6**	**55**	**11**	**10**	**4**	**5**
Males	75	-	1	3	3	-	-	3	41	9	9	3	3
Females	46	-	2	5	10	2	4	3	14	2	1	1	2

Table 75 Hours worked (10% sample) – continued

75. Residents aged 16 and over, employees and self-employed (10% sample)

Havant

Sex, age, marital status and long-term illness	TOTAL PERSONS	3 and under	4 - 7	8 - 15	16 - 21	22 - 23	24 - 30	31 - 35	36 - 40	41 - 50	51 - 60	61 and over	Not stated
	b	c	d	e	f	g	h	i	j	k	l	m	n
TOTAL PERSONS	**5,177**	**14**	**88**	**338**	**351**	**55**	**284**	**271**	**2,789**	**543**	**180**	**102**	**162**
Males													
16 - 19	131	1	2	14	1	-	3	5	83	6	6	1	9
20 - 24	296	-	-	7	1	-	4	14	207	33	12	3	15
25 - 29	350	-	-	3	2	-	5	17	235	49	18	15	6
30 - 34	342	-	-	1	-	-	1	10	242	53	14	10	11
35 - 39	329	-	-	2	1	-	4	8	201	64	28	13	8
40 - 44	365	-	-	2	-	-	5	16	226	65	27	10	14
45 - 49	308	1	-	2	-	-	3	10	191	51	24	8	18
50 - 54	310	1	-	1	-	-	7	13	211	53	13	4	6
55 - 59	253	-	1	1	1	-	12	9	167	32	10	12	4
60 - 64	190	1	2	3	5	1	3	9	110	37	6	4	8
65 and over	44	-	1	8	4	1	5	3	13	2	-	2	5
Females													
16 - 19	149	1	9	28	2	-	5	13	77	7	-	-	7
20 - 24	255	-	1	8	12	3	4	32	170	14	4	2	5
25 - 29	227	-	7	21	26	2	19	23	113	8	2	3	3
30 - 34	239	1	13	38	41	7	16	13	89	11	2	3	5
35 - 39	257	-	12	38	49	7	30	15	81	14	2	2	7
40 - 44	315	3	7	47	53	5	50	18	97	19	4	4	8
45 - 49	266	2	3	29	43	12	37	14	111	8	2	1	4
50 - 54	236	-	7	28	44	7	30	15	87	8	2	3	5
55 - 59	205	2	12	28	39	8	24	11	62	8	3	2	6
60 - 64	79	1	5	21	13	2	14	3	14	1	1	-	4
65 and over	31	-	6	8	8	-	3	-	2	-	-	-	4
Total males	**2,918**	**4**	**6**	**44**	**21**	**2**	**52**	**114**	**1,886**	**445**	**158**	**82**	**104**
Single, widowed or divorced	944	1	2	29	6	-	20	48	632	104	44	20	38
Married	1,974	3	4	15	15	2	32	66	1,254	341	114	62	66
Total females	**2,259**	**10**	**82**	**294**	**330**	**53**	**232**	**157**	**903**	**98**	**22**	**20**	**58**
Single, widowed or divorced	786	1	23	72	46	6	42	74	445	42	7	6	22
Married	1,473	9	59	222	284	47	190	83	458	56	15	14	36
Persons with limiting long-term illness													
Total	**205**	**4**	**6**	**16**	**28**	**4**	**12**	**11**	**91**	**16**	**10**	**2**	**5**
Males	112	2	-	5	6	-	3	7	64	11	9	2	3
Females	93	2	6	11	22	4	9	4	27	5	1	-	2

Table 75 Hours worked (10% sample) – continued

County, districts

75. Residents aged 16 and over, employees and self-employed   (10% sample)

New Forest

Sex, age, marital status and long-term illness	TOTAL PERSONS	3 and under	4 - 7	8 - 15	16 - 21	22 - 23	24 - 30	31 - 35	36 - 40	41 - 50	51 - 60	61 and over	Not stated
	b	c	d	e	f	g	h	i	j	k	l	m	n
TOTAL PERSONS	**6,894**	**26**	**147**	**530**	**469**	**58**	**381**	**537**	**3,167**	**901**	**290**	**172**	**216**
Males													
16 - 19	173	-	8	31	8	-	7	8	89	10	4	2	6
20 - 24	373	-	-	2	3	-	6	28	232	57	17	6	22
25 - 29	457	-	-	3	4	-	2	30	272	91	28	16	11
30 - 34	456	-	-	-	2	-	5	22	276	94	26	18	13
35 - 39	443	-	-	1	-	-	9	36	230	96	37	19	15
40 - 44	539	-	1	-	-	1	7	32	289	127	40	25	17
45 - 49	440	-	1	4	2	-	8	27	235	97	33	17	16
50 - 54	361	1	1	3	4	-	7	18	218	64	25	8	13
55 - 59	312	-	-	6	6	1	9	18	166	60	24	15	6
60 - 64	203	-	2	9	13	3	5	15	113	26	7	4	6
65 and over	90	-	4	15	15	2	8	7	17	7	5	3	7
Females													
16 - 19	198	1	14	31	6	-	8	19	102	12	1	-	4
20 - 24	358	1	2	9	6	1	21	59	214	30	3	1	11
25 - 29	324	2	9	37	27	3	17	35	157	24	4	2	7
30 - 34	332	4	17	69	50	8	27	32	91	20	3	5	6
35 - 39	365	3	18	61	68	6	49	27	87	22	9	5	10
40 - 44	453	2	23	65	77	14	58	42	121	22	7	11	11
45 - 49	368	1	10	49	60	5	57	36	106	20	4	8	12
50 - 54	274	-	15	54	50	6	31	19	69	13	6	7	4
55 - 59	205	3	6	30	31	5	21	21	66	7	4	-	11
60 - 64	114	3	10	32	25	3	16	6	15	1	2	-	1
65 and over	56	5	6	19	12	-	3	-	2	1	1	-	7
Total males	**3,847**	**1**	**17**	**74**	**57**	**7**	**73**	**241**	**2,137**	**729**	**246**	**133**	**132**
Single, widowed or divorced	1,198	-	8	38	25	-	27	77	679	187	67	38	52
Married	2,649	1	9	36	32	7	46	164	1,458	542	179	95	80
Total females	**3,047**	**25**	**130**	**456**	**412**	**51**	**308**	**296**	**1,030**	**172**	**44**	**39**	**84**
Single, widowed or divorced	1,032	5	32	76	58	11	74	126	516	81	12	11	30
Married	2,015	20	98	380	354	40	234	170	514	91	32	28	54
Persons with limiting long-term illness													
Total	**244**	**1**	**9**	**24**	**20**	**2**	**19**	**22**	**85**	**30**	**12**	**6**	**14**
Males	157	-	4	8	9	-	9	13	67	24	11	4	8
Females	87	1	5	16	11	2	10	9	18	6	1	2	6

Table 75 Hours worked (10% sample) – continued

75. Residents aged 16 and over, employees and self-employed   (10% sample)

Portsmouth

Sex, age, marital status and long-term illness	TOTAL PERSONS	Hours worked weekly											
		3 and under	4 - 7	8 - 15	16 - 21	22 - 23	24 - 30	31 - 35	36 - 40	41 - 50	51 - 60	61 and over	Not stated
a	b	c	d	e	f	g	h	i	j	k	l	m	n
TOTAL PERSONS	7,563	18	116	447	477	90	382	449	4,030	785	267	187	315
Males													
16 - 19	209	2	6	17	8	1	5	9	113	25	9	7	7
20 - 24	573	-	-	6	4	1	10	29	330	95	33	21	44
25 - 29	698	-	1	2	4	-	5	28	463	102	29	22	42
30 - 34	560	-	1	1	2	-	4	22	350	83	38	25	34
35 - 39	465	-	-	2	2	-	5	17	291	71	30	21	26
40 - 44	484	-	-	2	5	1	6	10	301	82	33	17	27
45 - 49	426	-	-	1	2	1	6	11	271	76	31	16	11
50 - 54	320	-	-	1	3	-	8	15	207	48	11	14	13
55 - 59	286	-	-	5	5	-	5	12	192	39	9	5	14
60 - 64	189	-	-	6	8	2	5	5	125	23	8	2	5
65 and over	78	-	1	13	13	6	9	2	12	13	4	-	5
Females													
16 - 19	172	-	9	24	12	3	7	19	88	6	-	-	4
20 - 24	507	-	13	22	18	4	21	60	329	25	5	3	7
25 - 29	514	3	5	49	46	5	27	53	273	32	3	5	13
30 - 34	379	6	18	57	58	6	43	27	138	13	3	2	8
35 - 39	355	2	13	56	53	6	49	23	121	17	5	1	9
40 - 44	416	2	15	69	61	13	41	40	136	13	5	5	16
45 - 49	327	2	6	31	57	18	38	28	122	9	4	7	5
50 - 54	257	-	12	26	38	14	43	20	81	8	3	7	5
55 - 59	206	-	4	25	42	6	30	13	67	4	2	4	9
60 - 64	92	-	3	21	25	3	11	4	15	1	1	3	5
65 and over	50	1	9	11	11	-	4	2	5	-	1	-	6
Total males	**4,288**	2	9	56	56	12	68	160	2,655	657	235	150	228
Single, widowed or divorced	1,809	2	7	31	26	4	34	73	1,117	259	97	55	104
Married	2,479	-	2	25	30	8	34	87	1,538	398	138	95	124
Total females	**3,275**	16	107	391	421	78	314	289	1,375	128	32	37	87
Single, widowed or divorced	1,383	4	35	94	82	17	104	146	772	60	16	14	39
Married	1,892	12	72	297	339	61	210	143	603	68	16	23	48
Persons with limiting long-term illness													
Total	**290**	-	8	23	22	2	15	8	158	26	9	6	13
Males	188	-	1	4	5	-	7	5	118	24	9	6	9
Females	102	-	7	19	17	2	8	3	40	2	-	-	4

Table 75 Hours worked (10% sample) – **continued**

County, districts

(10% sample)

75. Residents aged 16 and over, employees and self-employed

Rushmoor

Sex, age, marital status and long-term illness	TOTAL PERSONS	Hours worked weekly											
		3 and under	4 - 7	8 - 15	16 - 21	22 - 23	24 - 30	31 - 35	36 - 40	41 - 50	51 - 60	61 and over	Not stated
a	b	c	d	e	f	g	h	i	j	k	l	m	n
TOTAL PERSONS	**4,333**	**15**	**53**	**231**	**230**	**45**	**202**	**320**	**2,195**	**614**	**141**	**93**	**194**
Males													
16 - 19	176	4	8	8	3	-	2	4	90	23	2	9	23
20 - 24	384	1	1	2	2	-	2	19	205	81	13	15	43
25 - 29	416	1	-	3	2	-	4	20	225	87	32	15	27
30 - 34	310	-	-	1	1	-	3	16	184	59	18	15	13
35 - 39	248	-	1	-	1	-	-	11	139	58	14	7	17
40 - 44	276	-	-	-	-	-	3	9	168	63	16	6	11
45 - 49	219	-	-	2	-	-	2	9	139	47	11	4	5
50 - 54	174	-	-	1	1	-	3	7	101	36	10	7	8
55 - 59	139	-	-	-	2	-	4	6	90	28	8	1	-
60 - 64	92	-	-	3	4	1	1	4	58	17	-	2	2
65 and over	30	-	1	9	3	-	3	1	8	3	-	1	1
Females													
16 - 19	144	-	6	23	4	1	5	15	73	12	2	-	3
20 - 24	275	-	1	13	7	-	12	47	158	21	4	1	11
25 - 29	281	3	9	31	18	5	13	43	125	27	2	1	4
30 - 34	236	3	6	31	26	3	22	21	94	15	5	2	8
35 - 39	194	-	4	22	29	3	26	24	64	12	-	2	8
40 - 44	228	-	4	24	38	6	41	18	82	6	3	2	4
45 - 49	189	2	4	16	30	11	17	19	76	9	1	2	3
50 - 54	142	-	3	16	24	4	20	20	50	3	-	-	1
55 - 59	96	-	1	9	17	5	8	5	44	5	-	1	1
60 - 64	55	-	2	9	14	3	7	2	16	2	-	-	-
65 and over	29	1	2	8	4	3	4	-	6	-	-	-	1
Total males	**2,464**	**6**	**11**	**29**	**19**	**1**	**27**	**106**	**1,407**	**502**	**124**	**82**	**150**
Single, widowed or divorced	991	5	10	16	9	-	12	40	573	175	39	32	80
Married	1,473	1	1	13	10	1	15	66	834	327	85	50	70
Total females	**1,869**	**9**	**42**	**202**	**211**	**44**	**175**	**214**	**788**	**112**	**17**	**11**	**44**
Single, widowed or divorced	747	-	15	50	23	5	36	117	408	61	12	1	19
Married	1,122	9	27	152	188	39	139	97	380	51	5	10	25
Persons with limiting long-term illness													
Total	**149**	-	**3**	**17**	**9**	**5**	**5**	**12**	**80**	**14**	**5**	**1**	**3**
Males	90	-	2	6	1	1	1	6	56	10	5	1	2
Females	59	-	1	11	8	4	4	6	24	4	-	-	1

Table 75 Hours worked (10% sample) – continued

75. Residents aged 16 and over, employees and self-employed

(10% sample)

Southampton

Sex, age, marital status and long-term illness	TOTAL PERSONS	Hours worked weekly												
		3 and under	4 - 7	8 - 15	16 - 21	22 - 23	24 - 30	31 - 35	36 - 40	41 - 50	51 - 60	61 and over	Not stated
a	b	c	d	e	f	g	h	i	j	k	l	m	n
TOTAL PERSONS	8,320	19	125	555	559	66	458	657	4,299	864	273	174	271
Males													
16 - 19	221	1	2	29	3	-	2	12	134	20	2	2	14
20 - 24	523	-	4	5	7	-	6	44	345	71	17	3	21
25 - 29	704	-	1	3	2	-	10	43	474	98	29	21	23
30 - 34	639	-	1	3	4	-	10	44	376	118	40	21	22
35 - 39	517	-	3	3	4	-	9	19	310	100	41	14	14
40 - 44	563	-	-	3	4	1	6	28	348	88	36	25	24
45 - 49	442	-	-	6	1	-	7	22	269	76	30	12	19
50 - 54	390	-	-	1	-	-	10	13	260	65	22	11	8
55 - 59	339	-	1	2	4	1	7	18	217	49	10	16	14
60 - 64	226	1	2	4	4	1	10	10	148	27	5	3	11
65 and over	79	1	2	16	15	2	12	4	20	2	2	-	3
Females													
16 - 19	224	-	12	30	5	1	5	32	115	15	2	-	7
20 - 24	532	1	7	26	25	4	23	87	308	28	5	4	14
25 - 29	531	2	16	49	47	7	34	64	257	30	6	7	12
30 - 34	401	2	17	81	54	7	33	43	132	10	3	5	14
35 - 39	423	2	12	67	75	10	65	38	126	11	3	4	10
40 - 44	463	4	14	56	75	8	61	48	155	21	6	8	7
45 - 49	389	-	7	42	75	8	57	35	119	17	7	10	12
50 - 54	304	-	11	37	64	4	40	25	95	11	4	4	9
55 - 59	245	3	3	50	49	8	36	16	64	3	3	4	6
60 - 64	114	2	5	18	32	2	12	10	25	4	-	-	4
65 and over	51	-	5	24	10	2	3	2	2	-	-	-	3
Total males	**4,643**	**3**	**16**	**75**	**48**	**5**	**89**	**257**	**2,901**	**714**	**234**	**128**	**173**
Single, widowed or divorced	1,792	1	8	49	23	2	25	109	1,155	234	72	35	79
Married	2,851	2	8	26	25	3	64	148	1,746	480	162	93	94
Total females	**3,677**	**16**	**109**	**480**	**511**	**61**	**369**	**400**	**1,398**	**150**	**39**	**46**	**98**
Single, widowed or divorced	1,529	3	41	91	86	16	104	217	797	93	20	15	46
Married	2,148	13	68	389	425	45	265	183	601	57	19	31	52
Persons with limiting long-term illness													
Total	**317**	**1**	**9**	**30**	**20**	**5**	**26**	**17**	**152**	**26**	**12**	**4**	**15**
Males	189	1	1	9	6	-	10	7	112	23	7	3	10
Females	128	-	8	21	14	5	16	10	40	3	5	1	5

Table 75 Hours worked (10% sample) – continued

75. Residents aged 16 and over, employees and self-employed

County, districts

(10% sample)

Test Valley

Sex, age, marital status and long-term illness	TOTAL PERSONS	Hours worked weekly											Not stated
		3 and under	4 - 7	8 - 15	16 - 21	22 - 23	24 - 30	31 - 35	36 - 40	41 - 50	51 - 60	61 and over	
a	b	c	d	e	f	g	h	i	j	k	l	m	n
TOTAL PERSONS	**5,030**	**15**	**107**	**310**	**260**	**51**	**281**	**457**	**2,389**	**673**	**214**	**123**	**150**
Males													
16 - 19	169	3	2	20	4	1	2	7	99	14	5	1	11
20 - 24	300	-	-	2	1	-	-	18	203	57	8	5	6
25 - 29	363	-	-	2	4	-	1	25	230	62	16	7	16
30 - 34	340	-	-	2	1	1	1	26	174	74	31	19	12
35 - 39	319	-	1	-	-	1	2	16	181	70	31	12	5
40 - 44	403	-	-	2	1	-	3	26	220	100	27	14	10
45 - 49	319	-	-	-	-	1	4	17	184	65	28	11	9
50 - 54	276	1	-	-	3	1	4	19	148	63	22	11	4
55 - 59	230	-	2	3	1	1	5	11	140	42	13	8	4
60 - 64	132	-	1	-	2	1	10	5	74	18	11	6	4
65 and over	64	1	2	13	9	2	9	4	13	3	2	1	5
Females													
16 - 19	141	1	12	23	2	2	4	22	61	8	1	-	5
20 - 24	265	1	4	7	8	1	9	58	143	15	4	3	12
25 - 29	244	-	8	30	14	2	16	43	102	18	2	2	7
30 - 34	218	2	21	33	21	4	31	22	62	8	3	4	7
35 - 39	247	1	12	46	31	7	44	26	56	15	1	4	4
40 - 44	324	2	9	34	44	6	54	43	104	16	5	2	5
45 - 49	259	2	11	24	34	10	37	27	89	12	-	6	7
50 - 54	198	-	9	26	41	8	17	21	53	8	1	4	10
55 - 59	130	-	4	14	27	2	18	14	41	5	1	-	4
60 - 64	53	-	4	16	8	1	8	4	9	-	1	1	1
65 and over	36	1	5	13	4	-	2	3	3	-	1	2	2
Total males	**2,915**	**5**	**8**	**44**	**26**	**8**	**41**	**174**	**1,666**	**568**	**194**	**95**	**86**
Single, widowed or divorced	946	4	3	26	13	3	5	55	597	147	42	22	29
Married	1,969	1	5	18	13	5	36	119	1,069	421	152	73	57
Total females	**2,115**	**10**	**99**	**266**	**234**	**43**	**240**	**283**	**723**	**105**	**20**	**28**	**64**
Single, widowed or divorced	690	1	20	48	21	5	41	134	326	52	12	5	25
Married	1,425	9	79	218	213	38	199	149	397	53	8	23	39
Persons with limiting long-term illness													
Total	**182**	**-**	**2**	**10**	**11**	**3**	**11**	**9**	**95**	**23**	**6**	**7**	**5**
Males	122	-	-	5	4	2	5	3	72	19	6	4	2
Females	60	-	2	5	7	1	6	6	23	4	-	3	3

Table 75 Hours worked (10% sample) – continued

75. Residents aged 16 and over, employees and self-employed

(10% sample)

Winchester

Sex, age, marital status and long-term illness	TOTAL PERSONS	Hours worked weekly											
		3 and under	4 - 7	8 - 15	16 - 21	22 - 23	24 - 30	31 - 35	36 - 40	41 - 50	51 - 60	61 and over	Not stated
a	b	c	d	e	f	g	h	i	j	k	l	m	n
TOTAL PERSONS	4,521	26	97	277	271	36	279	282	2,104	686	194	128	141
Males													
16 - 19	144	1	3	17	4	-	2	6	67	22	6	3	13
20 - 24	221	-	-	2	4	-	3	10	137	42	9	4	10
25 - 29	240	-	-	2	1	1	2	11	140	48	14	10	11
30 - 34	290	-	-	2	1	-	1	13	174	60	19	14	6
35 - 39	284	-	-	1	3	-	7	19	147	64	20	11	12
40 - 44	392	-	-	1	-	-	-	21	198	107	33	22	10
45 - 49	292	-	1	-	2	1	4	10	148	63	32	19	12
50 - 54	269	-	-	1	2	1	3	9	140	85	14	9	5
55 - 59	206	-	1	1	1	1	6	13	121	41	12	5	4
60 - 64	164	-	4	3	7	1	13	6	88	22	8	5	7
65 and over	96	1	4	14	15	4	12	4	19	8	5	1	9
Females													
16 - 19	109	1	9	14	3	2	2	7	61	7	-	1	2
20 - 24	212	-	3	10	8	-	10	24	128	19	4	1	5
25 - 29	187	1	3	16	13	2	13	24	100	10	4	-	1
30 - 34	188	-	7	28	11	2	16	16	78	16	5	2	7
35 - 39	222	6	13	21	31	5	28	18	72	15	2	5	6
40 - 44	298	3	17	40	43	6	43	22	83	25	4	5	7
45 - 49	248	2	7	32	40	4	32	22	85	13	2	3	6
50 - 54	186	3	7	27	29	2	37	13	57	7	-	2	2
55 - 59	143	1	5	18	26	3	28	9	42	5	1	2	3
60 - 64	88	2	4	19	21	1	13	3	16	5	-	4	-
65 and over	42	5	9	8	6	-	4	2	3	2	-	-	3
Total males	**2,598**	**2**	**13**	**44**	**40**	**9**	**53**	**122**	**1,379**	**562**	**172**	**103**	**99**
Single, widowed or divorced	812	1	3	26	14	3	17	35	453	158	40	27	35
Married	1,786	1	10	18	26	6	36	87	926	404	132	76	64
Total females	**1,923**	**24**	**84**	**233**	**231**	**27**	**226**	**160**	**725**	**124**	**22**	**25**	**42**
Single, widowed or divorced	647	4	21	42	30	3	43	66	342	63	11	7	15
Married	1,276	20	63	191	201	24	183	94	383	61	11	18	27
Persons with limiting long-term illness													
Total	**156**	**3**	**8**	**16**	**10**	**2**	**11**	**8**	**61**	**20**	**11**	**1**	**5**
Males	91	-	1	4	2	1	6	2	48	13	9	1	4
Females	65	3	7	12	8	1	5	6	13	7	2	-	1

Table 76 Occupation and industry (10% sample)

76. Residents aged 16 and over, employees and self-employed

(10% sample)

HAMPSHIRE

Standard Occupational Classification Sub-major Groups	TOTAL PERSONS	Industry										Not stated, inadequately described or workplace outside UK	Working outside district of usual residence
		Agriculture, forestry and fishing	Energy and water	Mining	Manufacturing metal etc	Other manufacturing	Construction	Distribution and catering	Transport	Banking and finance etc	Other services		
a	b	c	d	e	f	g	h	i	j	k	l	m	n
ALL OCCUPATIONS	71,873	1,122	988	1,281	8,405	3,649	5,687	14,461	4,128	9,092	22,548	512	26,966
1a Corporate managers and administrators	8,237	18	109	238	1,353	527	677	1,039	531	1,726	1,979	40	4,692
1b Managers/proprietors in agriculture and services	3,933	349	7	7	14	34	1	2,768	74	250	424	5	1,299
2a Science and engineering professionals	2,462	6	74	73	781	47	146	89	67	504	663	12	1,529
2b Health professionals	389	-	-	2	-	-	-	58	-	3	324	2	166
2c Teaching professionals	2,237	-	-	-	-	-	1	1	-	3	2,223	9	988
2d Other professional occupations	1,401	2	15	11	61	19	47	26	17	690	510	3	717
3a Science and engineering associate professionals	2,504	4	95	100	737	73	133	138	82	519	613	10	1,392
3b Health associate professionals	1,566	-	-	5	7	-	-	52	-	7	1,489	6	668
3c Other associate professional occupations	2,737	1	43	25	147	151	64	104	159	823	1,203	17	1,276
4a Clerical occupations	8,079	16	174	137	689	350	206	1,186	610	2,179	2,517	15	3,152
4b Secretarial occupations	3,496	31	26	52	323	118	181	425	175	1,126	1,026	13	1,288
5a Skilled construction trades	1,888	4	7	10	42	42	1,621	74	10	10	65	3	273
5b Skilled engineering trades	3,135	8	171	70	1,265	121	511	259	336	97	288	9	1,463
5c Other skilled trades	4,466	289	56	70	768	911	946	869	99	64	376	18	1,429
6a Protective service occupations	3,035	1	5	1	18	19	2	23	21	166	2,775	4	494
6b Personal service occupations	4,924	11	2	9	12	22	9	1,264	141	64	3,367	23	1,091
7a Buyers, brokers and sales representatives	1,362	2	19	43	223	114	53	462	29	355	52	10	664
7b Other sales occupations	3,935	9	17	3	19	70	15	3,645	25	79	49	4	893
8a Industrial plant and machine operators, assemblers	3,671	19	105	341	1,536	754	313	234	88	94	175	12	1,349
8b Drivers and mobile machinery operators	2,321	16	27	45	129	143	205	412	1,038	102	192	12	881
9a Other occupations in agriculture, forestry and fishing	433	318	2	-	1	3	-	13	-	14	79	3	58
9b Other elementary occupations	5,166	15	33	32	257	120	529	1,277	611	181	2,084	27	1,105
Occupation not stated or inadequately described	496	3	1	7	23	11	27	43	15	36	75	255	99
Working outside district of usual residence	26,966	164	524	519	4,201	1,432	1,681	4,631	1,841	4,376	7,415	182	

Table 76 Occupation and industry (10% sample) – **continued**

County, districts

76. Residents aged 16 and over, employees and self-employed

(10% sample)

Basingstoke & Deane

| Standard Occupational Classification Sub-major Groups | TOTAL PERSONS | Industry | | | | | | | | | | Not stated, inadequately described or workplace outside UK | Working outside district of usual residence |
| | | Agriculture, forestry and fishing | Energy and water | Mining | Manufacturing metal etc | Other manufacturing | Construction | Distribution and catering | Transport | Banking and finance etc | Other services | | |
a	b	c	d	e	f	g	h	i	j	k	l	m	n
ALL OCCUPATIONS	7,472	132	68	183	836	417	577	1,584	348	1,189	2,094	44	2,237
1a Corporate managers and administrators	1,028	4	7	38	160	70	74	178	41	257	198	1	501
1b Managers/proprietors in agriculture and services	313	34	1	1	1	3	-	204	6	25	38	-	96
2a Science and engineering professionals	337	-	4	13	80	5	12	20	5	79	118	1	204
2b Health professionals	30	-	-	-	-	-	-	3	-	-	27	-	6
2c Teaching professionals	164	-	-	-	-	-	-	1	-	-	163	-	45
2d Other professional occupations	146	-	-	2	6	4	2	5	-	83	43	1	66
3a Science and engineering associate professionals	303	-	3	12	59	5	12	39	11	80	82	-	133
3b Health associate professionals	146	-	-	6	-	-	-	2	-	-	142	2	30
3c Other associate professional occupations	278	1	4	6	12	14	8	14	10	100	108	1	101
4a Clerical occupations	1,011	-	19	16	103	49	23	171	39	276	312	3	272
4b Secretarial occupations	458	6	4	11	45	28	21	66	15	137	125	-	108
5a Skilled construction trades	187	1	-	-	1	5	166	6	1	2	5	-	18
5b Skilled engineering trades	307	-	6	8	117	12	49	34	37	7	36	1	115
5c Other skilled trades	425	35	4	8	47	69	104	97	6	15	39	1	100
6a Protective service occupations	126	-	-	-	1	8	-	3	1	26	87	-	54
6b Personal service occupations	429	1	1	-	2	4	-	117	17	8	276	3	69
7a Buyers, brokers and sales representatives	135	-	1	8	25	11	6	43	-	34	7	-	52
7b Other sales occupations	357	1	-	-	3	3	2	337	-	8	3	-	35
8a Industrial plant and machine operators, assemblers	403	-	7	44	140	98	29	44	9	7	22	3	69
8b Drivers and mobile machinery operators	264	-	1	9	12	18	22	58	99	20	25	-	71
9a Other occupations in agriculture, forestry and fishing	64	48	-	-	1	1	1	1	-	3	9	1	5
9b Other elementary occupations	512	1	6	6	19	9	44	135	50	16	223	3	79
Occupation not stated or inadequately described	49	-	-	1	2	1	3	6	1	6	6	23	8
Working outside district of usual residence	2,237	20	30	28	255	102	127	368	138	471	687	11	

Table 76 Occupation and industry (10% sample) – continued

County, districts

76. Residents aged 16 and over, employees and self-employed

(10% sample)

East Hampshire

Standard Occupational Classification Sub-major Groups	TOTAL PERSONS	Industry										Not stated, inadequately described or workplace outside UK	Working outside district of usual residence
		Agriculture, forestry and fishing	Energy and water	Mining	Manufacturing metal etc	Other manufacturing	Construction	Distribution and catering	Transport	Banking and finance etc	Other services		
a	b	c	d	e	f	g	h	i	j	k	l	m	n
ALL OCCUPATIONS	4,956	176	58	87	460	287	405	949	237	718	1,549	30	2,043
1a Corporate managers and administrators	673	3	5	18	116	48	58	79	48	156	139	3	469
1b Managers/proprietors in agriculture and services	357	57	1	1	-	5	-	236	10	17	28	2	131
2a Science and engineering professionals	167	2	6	6	46	6	9	5	3	53	31	-	107
2b Health professionals	35	-	-	-	-	-	-	5	-	-	30	-	15
2c Teaching professionals	230	-	-	-	-	-	-	1	-	1	227	2	116
2d Other professional occupations	116	1	1	1	4	2	3	1	1	68	34	-	66
3a Science and engineering associate professionals	129	1	5	2	34	1	6	7	4	41	27	1	82
3b Health associate professionals	98	-	-	1	-	-	-	2	-	3	90	2	54
3c Other associate professional occupations	230	-	4	1	8	16	4	12	7	79	97	2	101
4a Clerical occupations	441	1	11	15	32	20	14	71	36	130	111	-	195
4b Secretarial occupations	280	3	1	8	25	8	9	38	6	93	89	-	109
5a Skilled construction trades	153	1	-	-	-	1	142	5	-	-	4	-	13
5b Skilled engineering trades	167	1	10	-	63	11	30	18	18	6	10	-	79
5c Other skilled trades	310	44	3	7	31	67	48	77	1	3	28	1	68
6a Protective service occupations	200	-	-	-	-	1	-	1	-	5	192	1	31
6b Personal service occupations	339	3	-	-	2	2	-	73	15	7	236	1	83
7a Buyers, brokers and sales representatives	102	-	-	6	20	8	4	29	3	29	3	-	49
7b Other sales occupations	208	-	1	-	1	6	-	192	-	4	4	-	77
8a Industrial plant and machine operators, assemblers	202	2	8	15	64	62	23	8	8	4	8	-	64
8b Drivers and mobile machinery operators	125	-	1	2	2	16	18	24	50	2	10	-	47
9a Other occupations in agriculture, forestry and fishing	69	55	-	-	-	-	-	1	-	1	11	1	12
9b Other elementary occupations	298	1	1	4	10	5	35	61	27	14	136	4	67
Occupation not stated or inadequately described	27	1	-	-	2	2	2	4	-	2	4	10	8
Working outside district of usual residence	2,043	18	42	43	267	93	102	377	127	395	568	11	

Table 76 Occupation and industry (10% sample) – continued

County, districts

76. Residents aged 16 and over, employees and self-employed

(10% sample)

Eastleigh

Standard Occupational Classification Sub-major Groups	TOTAL PERSONS	Agriculture, forestry and fishing	Energy and water	Mining	Manufacturing metal etc	Other manufacturing	Construction	Distribution and catering	Transport	Banking and finance etc	Other services	Not stated, inadequately described or workplace outside UK	Working outside district of usual residence
a	b	c	d	e	f	g	h	i	j	k	l	m	n
ALL OCCUPATIONS	5,205	55	86	66	740	259	458	1,095	363	692	1,362	29	2,760
1a Corporate managers and administrators	619	-	6	16	101	44	79	88	41	119	124	1	420
1b Managers/proprietors in agriculture and services	254	10	-	1	3	3	1	180	8	19	29	-	121
2a Science and engineering professionals	164	1	2	3	68	5	10	10	6	36	22	1	122
2b Health professionals	18	-	-	-	-	-	-	3	-	-	15	-	12
2c Teaching professionals	179	-	-	-	-	-	-	1	2	-	179	-	111
2d Other professional occupations	106	-	4	-	5	-	9	1	2	48	37	-	75
3a Science and engineering associate professionals	222	-	8	6	73	8	19	8	8	41	49	2	159
3b Health associate professionals	112	-	-	-	-	-	-	4	-	1	107	-	85
3c Other associate professional occupations	194	-	5	-	9	10	8	7	15	69	71	-	123
4a Clerical occupations	641	2	24	4	71	22	27	102	50	172	167	-	367
4b Secretarial occupations	300	4	2	4	20	4	14	39	17	101	95	-	177
5a Skilled construction trades	108	-	-	1	1	2	93	3	3	-	5	-	19
5b Skilled engineering trades	257	2	14	4	118	5	50	18	27	10	7	2	121
5c Other skilled trades	364	23	5	5	84	63	79	65	17	1	20	2	150
6a Protective service occupations	96	1	-	-	4	-	-	1	-	7	82	1	61
6b Personal service occupations	312	-	-	-	1	3	1	85	12	3	206	1	122
7a Buyers, brokers and sales representatives	137	1	4	7	22	12	8	44	3	29	7	-	70
7b Other sales occupations	324	1	2	-	2	6	1	296	3	9	3	1	130
8a Industrial plant and machine operators, assemblers	259	1	7	9	116	55	21	18	10	12	9	1	104
8b Drivers and mobile machinery operators	191	-	1	3	23	7	6	40	92	3	13	3	99
9a Other occupations in agriculture, forestry and fishing	12	9	-	-	-	-	-	-	-	-	3	-	5
9b Other elementary occupations	313	-	2	3	17	9	30	82	47	12	110	1	97
Occupation not stated or inadequately described	23	-	-	-	2	1	2	1	2	-	2	13	10
Working outside district of usual residence	2,760	22	63	35	389	110	181	491	177	451	827	14	

Table 76 Occupation and industry (10% sample) – **continued**

County, districts

76. Residents aged 16 and over, employees and self-employed

(10% sample)

Fareham

Standard Occupational Classification Sub-major Groups	TOTAL PERSONS	Industry										Not stated, inadequately described or workplace outside UK	Working outside district of usual residence
		Agriculture, forestry and fishing	Energy and water	Mining	Manufacturing metal etc	Other manufacturing	Construction	Distribution and catering	Transport	Banking and finance etc	Other services		
a	b	c	d	e	f	g	h	i	j	k	l	m	n
ALL OCCUPATIONS	**4,790**	**45**	**51**	**92**	**674**	**209**	**365**	**808**	**231**	**562**	**1,717**	**36**	**2,392**
1a Corporate managers and administrators	659	-	4	25	128	39	54	59	36	116	191	7	421
1b Managers/proprietors in agriculture and services	229	12	-	-	1	7	-	165	2	6	36	-	107
2a Science and engineering professionals	199	1	2	10	73	-	19	4	4	37	49	-	150
2b Health professionals	25	-	-	-	-	-	-	6	-	-	19	-	14
2c Teaching professionals	181	-	-	-	-	-	-	-	-	-	181	-	104
2d Other professional occupations	88	-	1	-	9	-	5	1	1	41	30	-	54
3a Science and engineering associate professionals	176	-	9	5	86	2	9	5	6	18	35	1	143
3b Health associate professionals	138	-	-	-	2	-	-	5	-	-	130	1	91
3c Other associate professional occupations	213	-	3	2	18	9	6	3	13	61	93	5	134
4a Clerical occupations	524	-	6	7	46	18	10	60	46	132	198	1	276
4b Secretarial occupations	239	2	2	5	25	5	17	27	9	76	71	-	118
5a Skilled construction trades	93	-	-	-	4	4	75	4	1	-	4	1	18
5b Skilled engineering trades	222	-	9	6	102	5	36	13	9	8	32	2	139
5c Other skilled trades	285	22	3	2	64	65	63	37	8	1	17	3	125
6a Protective service occupations	279	-	-	-	-	1	-	3	2	9	264	-	65
6b Personal service occupations	270	-	-	-	-	1	-	65	4	2	197	1	77
7a Buyers, brokers and sales representatives	90	-	-	6	17	3	3	26	2	28	4	1	47
7b Other sales occupations	239	-	1	-	-	8	1	219	1	4	5	-	46
8a Industrial plant and machine operators, assemblers	187	1	9	22	74	26	22	12	5	5	10	1	110
8b Drivers and mobile machinery operators	116	-	2	2	6	8	9	21	53	3	12	-	60
9a Other occupations in agriculture, forestry and fishing	9	5	-	-	-	-	-	-	-	-	3	-	-
9b Other elementary occupations	300	2	-	-	18	8	36	68	27	10	130	1	81
Occupation not stated or inadequately described	29	-	-	-	1	-	-	5	2	4	6	11	12
Working outside district of usual residence	2,392	2	44	77	461	120	127	296	141	300	802	22	

Table 76 Occupation and industry (10% sample) – continued

76. Residents aged 16 and over, employees and self-employed

(10% sample)

Gosport

Standard Occupational Classification Sub-major Groups	TOTAL PERSONS	Industry											Working outside district of usual residence
		Agriculture, forestry and fishing	Energy and water	Mining	Manufacturing metal etc	Other manufacturing	Construction	Distribution and catering	Transport	Banking and finance etc	Other services	Not stated, inadequately described or workplace outside UK	
a	b	c	d	e	f	g	h	i	j	k	l	m	n
ALL OCCUPATIONS	3,390	20	21	126	418	136	201	606	117	260	1,461	24	1,290
1a Corporate managers and administrators	273	-	-	13	50	14	13	16	5	43	119	-	142
1b Managers/proprietors in agriculture and services	138	3	-	1	3	1	-	96	2	7	25	-	51
2a Science and engineering professionals	65	-	2	5	23	-	1	3	4	5	21	1	37
2b Health professionals	11	-	-	-	-	-	-	1	-	-	10	-	3
2c Teaching professionals	59	-	-	-	-	-	-	-	-	-	58	1	29
2d Other professional occupations	28	-	-	-	2	-	-	-	-	9	16	1	14
3a Science and engineering associate professionals	89	-	3	7	27	2	3	6	1	8	31	1	48
3b Health associate professionals	74	-	-	1	1	-	-	2	-	-	70	-	33
3c Other associate professional occupations	101	-	1	2	9	7	2	2	7	22	48	1	58
4a Clerical occupations	370	-	4	19	27	14	5	44	19	72	166	-	176
4b Secretarial occupations	115	1	1	7	10	2	6	7	6	34	40	1	48
5a Skilled construction trades	69	-	-	-	3	-	54	4	-	1	7	-	12
5b Skilled engineering trades	216	1	7	7	98	10	25	16	10	5	37	-	117
5c Other skilled trades	206	9	-	2	39	29	49	39	1	2	35	1	98
6a Protective service occupations	455	-	-	-	3	-	-	-	1	21	430	-	33
6b Personal service occupations	260	1	1	-	1	-	-	52	2	2	200	1	72
7a Buyers, brokers and sales representatives	36	-	-	1	6	2	3	18	-	4	2	-	28
7b Other sales occupations	214	-	-	-	-	3	2	200	1	4	4	-	83
8a Industrial plant and machine operators, assemblers	228	-	-	56	91	40	17	8	-	6	10	-	69
8b Drivers and mobile machinery operators	92	1	-	2	9	6	7	12	41	2	12	-	46
9a Other occupations in agriculture, forestry and fishing	7	4	-	-	-	-	-	-	-	-	3	-	4
9b Other elementary occupations	257	-	2	3	15	6	13	78	17	12	110	1	85
Occupation not stated or inadequately described	27	-	-	-	1	-	1	2	-	1	7	15	4
Working outside district of usual residence	1,290	12	20	16	232	64	75	259	77	148	382	5	

Table 76 Occupation and industry (10% sample) – continued

76. Residents aged 16 and over, employees and self-employed

(10% sample)

Hart

Standard Occupational Classification Sub-major Groups	TOTAL PERSONS	Industry										Not stated, inadequately described or workplace outside UK	Working outside district of usual residence
		Agriculture, forestry and fishing	Energy and water	Mining	Manufacturing metal etc	Other manufacturing	Construction	Distribution and catering	Transport	Banking and finance etc	Other services		
a	b	c	d	e	f	g	h	i	j	k	l	m	n
ALL OCCUPATIONS	4,222	68	46	76	398	181	264	826	276	797	1,260	30	2,484
1a Corporate managers and administrators	733	1	9	22	123	45	45	87	51	198	148	4	547
1b Managers/proprietors in agriculture and services	234	16	-	-	1	-	-	167	4	25	21	-	119
2a Science and engineering professionals	233	-	8	5	49	4	8	11	7	68	72	1	190
2b Health professionals	30	-	-	1	-	-	-	4	-	1	24	1	19
2c Teaching professionals	139	-	-	1	-	-	-	-	-	-	138	1	75
2d Other professional occupations	120	1	1	1	4	4	3	3	3	72	28	-	81
3a Science and engineering associate professionals	150	-	4	7	24	4	9	16	4	49	32	1	109
3b Health associate professionals	81	-	-	-	-	-	-	1	-	-	80	-	56
3c Other associate professional occupations	192	-	1	1	2	11	2	7	22	79	67	-	129
4a Clerical occupations	402	1	6	7	24	18	13	54	37	139	102	1	278
4b Secretarial occupations	238	2	2	2	24	5	7	30	9	91	63	3	147
5a Skilled construction trades	79	-	-	-	-	3	64	6	-	-	6	-	16
5b Skilled engineering trades	156	-	6	3	48	5	16	20	39	7	12	-	120
5c Other skilled trades	205	21	1	4	20	45	45	42	3	3	18	3	85
6a Protective service occupations	224	-	-	-	-	2	1	-	3	7	212	-	28
6b Personal service occupations	229	1	-	3	-	1	1	62	16	6	138	1	72
7a Buyers, brokers and sales representatives	109	-	1	2	22	11	3	34	5	25	2	4	82
7b Other sales occupations	204	1	1	-	1	1	2	191	1	5	1	-	96
8a Industrial plant and machine operators, assemblers	115	-	5	14	51	15	15	6	2	1	6	-	90
8b Drivers and mobile machinery operators	102	3	1	2	1	5	9	19	43	9	10	-	59
9a Other occupations in agriculture, forestry and fishing	23	18	-	-	-	-	-	1	-	-	3	1	4
9b Other elementary occupations	201	3	-	2	4	2	19	62	27	9	73	-	75
Occupation not stated or inadequately described	23	-	-	-	-	-	3	3	-	3	4	10	7
Working outside district of usual residence	2,484	16	42	64	334	128	97	445	225	506	611	16	

Table 76 Occupation and industry (10% sample) – continued

76. Residents aged 16 and over, employees and self-employed (10% sample)

Havant

Standard Occupational Classification Sub-major Groups	TOTAL PERSONS	Industry										Not stated, inadequately described or workplace outside UK	Working outside district of usual residence
		Agriculture, forestry and fishing	Energy and water	Mining	Manufacturing metal etc	Other manufacturing	Construction	Distribution and catering	Transport	Banking and finance etc	Other services		
a	b	c	d	e	f	g	h	i	j	k	l	m	n
ALL OCCUPATIONS	**5,177**	**37**	**71**	**107**	**994**	**314**	**479**	**992**	**238**	**486**	**1,425**	**34**	**2,360**
1a Corporate managers and administrators	541	1	7	13	137	40	49	62	22	86	121	3	311
1b Managers/proprietors in agriculture and services	235	10	1	-	-	1	-	179	3	12	29	-	97
2a Science and engineering professionals	190	-	1	1	95	5	8	1	3	23	53	-	116
2b Health professionals	24	-	-	-	-	-	-	6	-	1	16	1	10
2c Teaching professionals	150	-	-	-	-	-	-	-	-	-	150	-	73
2d Other professional occupations	78	-	-	-	16	2	4	2	-	24	30	-	51
3a Science and engineering associate professionals	210	-	3	6	104	8	9	8	2	31	39	-	146
3b Health associate professionals	93	-	-	-	1	-	-	3	-	1	88	-	64
3c Other associate professional occupations	168	-	2	1	23	12	4	5	11	26	83	1	91
4a Clerical occupations	532	1	23	8	73	31	15	76	30	125	150	-	264
4b Secretarial occupations	199	-	2	4	20	3	11	20	10	62	65	2	88
5a Skilled construction trades	165	-	1	1	4	4	143	6	1	1	4	-	37
5b Skilled engineering trades	278	-	11	7	132	13	44	15	23	6	25	2	171
5c Other skilled trades	374	12	6	4	75	95	79	63	6	6	28	-	153
6a Protective service occupations	117	-	-	1	1	-	-	2	-	14	98	1	40
6b Personal service occupations	360	-	-	-	-	2	-	90	6	4	257	1	122
7a Buyers, brokers and sales representatives	101	-	-	-	28	4	2	37	-	25	5	-	44
7b Other sales occupations	327	1	5	-	2	9	-	300	3	6	1	-	76
8a Industrial plant and machine operators, assemblers	448	1	3	50	239	63	42	13	6	11	18	2	196
8b Drivers and mobile machinery operators	159	2	2	4	9	14	16	22	66	10	13	1	84
9a Other occupations in agriculture, forestry and fishing	12	8	1	-	-	-	-	-	-	1	2	-	6
9b Other elementary occupations	371	-	3	6	29	8	50	77	43	9	145	1	109
Occupation not stated or inadequately described	45	1	-	1	6	-	3	5	3	2	5	19	11
Working outside district of usual residence	2,360	14	32	48	494	177	158	355	130	250	692	10	

Table 76 Occupation and industry (10% sample) – continued

76. Residents aged 16 and over, employees and self-employed — (10% sample)

New Forest

Standard Occupational Classification Sub-major Groups	TOTAL PERSONS	Industry										Not stated, inadequately described or workplace outside UK	Working outside district of usual residence
		Agriculture, forestry and fishing	Energy and water	Mining	Manufacturing metal etc	Other manufacturing	Construction	Distribution and catering	Transport	Banking and finance etc	Other services		
a	b	c	d	e	f	g	h	i	j	k	l	m	n
ALL OCCUPATIONS	6,894	174	223	180	671	345	572	1,550	446	919	1,744	70	2,495
1a Corporate managers and administrators	735	3	24	39	104	48	75	95	67	162	110	8	431
1b Managers/proprietors in agriculture and services	502	57	-	-	1	3	-	340	11	44	46	-	126
2a Science and engineering professionals	192	1	25	13	63	6	14	7	10	36	16	1	105
2b Health professionals	53	-	-	-	-	-	-	6	-	-	47	-	27
2c Teaching professionals	199	-	-	-	-	-	-	-	-	-	199	-	83
2d Other professional occupations	121	-	3	1	-	2	5	3	1	64	41	1	55
3a Science and engineering associate professionals	222	2	34	32	33	3	8	11	19	42	38	-	99
3b Health associate professionals	152	-	-	-	-	-	-	11	-	1	140	-	69
3c Other associate professional occupations	292	-	9	4	11	17	9	12	24	89	114	3	142
4a Clerical occupations	715	5	22	6	57	24	21	87	69	250	171	3	346
4b Secretarial occupations	382	5	6	-	34	15	32	63	23	109	92	3	154
5a Skilled construction trades	199	-	3	1	4	4	171	9	2	1	4	-	20
5b Skilled engineering trades	282	1	33	15	119	12	35	23	24	13	6	1	111
5c Other skilled trades	452	43	9	13	67	93	79	101	12	6	27	2	113
6a Protective service occupations	124	-	3	-	3	-	-	3	-	9	106	-	41
6b Personal service occupations	556	2	-	2	1	-	-	158	7	6	374	6	99
7a Buyers, brokers and sales representatives	139	-	3	4	17	16	1	49	4	38	4	3	79
7b Other sales occupations	415	3	4	1	1	9	1	384	2	3	7	-	97
8a Industrial plant and machine operators, assemblers	361	-	32	45	122	71	27	20	20	9	13	2	111
8b Drivers and mobile machinery operators	219	-	7	4	4	8	26	36	104	11	17	2	87
9a Other occupations in agriculture, forestry and fishing	73	52	-	-	-	1	-	2	-	4	14	-	3
9b Other elementary occupations	457	-	6	-	27	11	66	129	45	16	154	3	86
Occupation not stated or inadequately described	52	-	-	-	3	2	2	1	2	6	4	32	11
Working outside district of usual residence	2,495	9	70	30	322	135	138	469	218	505	570	29	

Table 76 Occupation and industry (10% sample) – continued

County, districts

76. Residents aged 16 and over, employees and self-employed

(10% sample)

Portsmouth

Standard Occupational Classification Sub-major Groups	TOTAL PERSONS	Industry										Not stated, inadequately described or workplace outside UK	Working outside district of usual residence
		Agriculture, forestry and fishing	Energy and water	Mining	Manufacturing metal etc	Other manufacturing	Construction	Distribution and catering	Transport	Banking and finance etc	Other services		
a	b	c	d	e	f	g	h	i	j	k	l	m	n
ALL OCCUPATIONS	7,563	18	95	77	865	428	594	1,554	492	676	2,699	65	1,591
1a Corporate managers and administrators	603	-	8	7	73	34	42	75	55	107	200	2	215
1b Managers/proprietors in agriculture and services	398	1	1	1	2	7	-	307	6	19	52	2	73
2a Science and engineering professionals	228	-	6	-	88	3	17	4	6	22	78	4	93
2b Health professionals	27	-	-	1	-	-	-	5	-	-	20	1	3
2c Teaching professionals	192	-	-	-	-	-	-	5	-	2	188	2	47
2d Other professional occupations	99	-	-	-	4	1	4	5	1	34	50	-	40
3a Science and engineering associate professionals	240	-	8	6	111	9	10	6	8	29	53	-	89
3b Health associate professionals	191	-	-	-	3	-	-	6	-	-	182	-	22
3c Other associate professional occupations	258	-	5	1	20	17	7	14	11	56	126	1	76
4a Clerical occupations	858	-	21	7	76	36	15	126	77	183	316	1	152
4b Secretarial occupations	276	1	1	2	33	12	13	23	20	90	81	-	46
5a Skilled construction trades	228	-	-	4	6	5	183	14	-	-	15	1	33
5b Skilled engineering trades	362	-	23	6	110	25	49	31	40	11	66	1	111
5c Other skilled trades	495	9	8	7	77	124	116	79	11	6	58	-	124
6a Protective service occupations	450	-	-	-	-	1	-	1	4	21	423	-	24
6b Personal service occupations	608	-	-	1	1	2	-	160	23	11	407	3	69
7a Buyers, brokers and sales representatives	109	-	1	3	21	8	7	34	3	26	5	1	40
7b Other sales occupations	490	-	2	-	3	7	-	459	2	11	5	1	40
8a Industrial plant and machine operators, assemblers	413	-	6	26	185	96	38	16	3	11	30	2	156
8b Drivers and mobile machinery operators	279	1	1	3	13	20	20	27	155	8	28	3	54
9a Other occupations in agriculture, forestry and fishing	9	6	-	-	-	-	-	-	-	1	2	-	1
9b Other elementary occupations	689	-	4	2	37	20	67	160	66	25	303	5	81
Occupation not stated or inadequately described	61	-	-	-	2	1	6	2	1	3	11	35	2
Working outside district of usual residence	1,591	5	34	44	313	113	156	254	87	196	376	13	

89

Table 76 Occupation and industry (10% sample) – **continued**

76. Residents aged 16 and over, employees and self-employed

(10% sample)

Rushmoor

Standard Occupational Classification Sub-major Groups	TOTAL PERSONS	Industry										Not stated, inadequately described or workplace outside UK	Working outside district of usual residence
		Agriculture, forestry and fishing	Energy and water	Mining	Manufacturing metal etc	Other manufacturing	Construction	Distribution and catering	Transport	Banking and finance etc	Other services		
a	b	c	d	e	f	g	h	i	j	k	l	m	n
ALL OCCUPATIONS	4,333	11	47	67	428	144	300	820	293	596	1,599	28	1,744
1a Corporate managers and administrators	494	-	7	9	74	26	36	66	38	104	132	2	300
1b Managers/proprietors in agriculture and services	165	1	-	1	-	-	-	131	4	12	16	-	78
2a Science and engineering professionals	180	1	5	2	36	2	7	6	6	37	78	-	110
2b Health professionals	9	-	-	-	-	-	-	3	-	-	6	-	4
2c Teaching professionals	80	-	-	-	-	-	-	-	-	-	80	-	41
2d Other professional occupations	51	-	1	1	2	-	-	1	1	26	19	-	26
3a Science and engineering associate professionals	149	-	2	1	36	1	6	5	7	49	40	2	81
3b Health associate professionals	74	-	-	1	-	-	-	3	-	-	69	1	44
3c Other associate professional occupations	163	-	3	1	9	4	3	9	12	51	70	1	90
4a Clerical occupations	549	1	1	21	39	16	8	78	48	165	171	1	233
4b Secretarial occupations	205	-	1	2	23	8	5	29	18	66	51	2	96
5a Skilled construction trades	105	1	1	-	1	-	99	4	-	-	-	-	9
5b Skilled engineering trades	197	-	7	7	58	3	31	17	39	7	28	-	89
5c Other skilled trades	219	6	4	2	35	39	42	52	5	6	26	2	92
6a Protective service occupations	468	-	-	-	-	1	1	2	6	14	443	1	37
6b Personal service occupations	282	-	-	-	-	1	2	73	10	8	188	-	91
7a Buyers, brokers and sales representatives	87	-	4	1	12	9	1	29	4	26	1	1	38
7b Other sales occupations	195	-	-	-	-	2	-	184	2	4	1	2	51
8a Industrial plant and machine operators, assemblers	191	-	6	13	91	23	17	14	3	5	19	-	79
8b Drivers and mobile machinery operators	117	2	2	4	5	3	12	30	41	3	15	-	54
9a Other occupations in agriculture, forestry and fishing	4	-	-	-	-	-	-	1	-	-	3	-	2
9b Other elementary occupations	326	-	3	1	6	5	30	82	49	11	139	-	94
Occupation not stated or inadequately described	23	-	-	-	1	1	-	1	-	2	4	14	5
Working outside district of usual residence	1,744	9	30	33	251	64	88	320	154	323	461	11	

Table 76 Occupation and industry (10% sample) – continued

76. Residents aged 16 and over, employees and self-employed

(10% sample)

Southampton

Standard Occupational Classification Sub-major Groups	TOTAL PERSONS	Industry											Working outside district of usual residence
		Agriculture, forestry and fishing	Energy and water	Mining	Manufacturing metal etc	Other manufacturing	Construction	Distribution and catering	Transport	Banking and finance etc	Other services	Not stated, inadequately described or workplace outside UK	
a	b	c	d	e	f	g	h	i	j	k	l	m	n
ALL OCCUPATIONS	8,320	23	130	97	956	417	721	1,893	699	889	2,439	56	2,303
1a Corporate managers and administrators	611	-	13	10	75	38	51	106	58	113	145	2	250
1b Managers/proprietors in agriculture and services	413	2	2	-	2	-	-	326	7	20	53	1	101
2a Science and engineering professionals	196	-	5	8	72	2	18	5	9	25	50	2	110
2b Health professionals	49	-	-	-	-	-	-	5	-	1	43	-	15
2c Teaching professionals	269	-	-	-	-	-	-	2	-	-	267	2	67
2d Other professional occupations	161	-	-	3	-	-	4	2	3	67	82	-	45
3a Science and engineering associate professionals	301	1	11	11	64	14	20	17	7	50	105	1	134
3b Health associate professionals	220	-	-	2	-	-	-	7	-	-	211	-	40
3c Other associate professional occupations	283	-	3	-	12	19	4	10	13	69	152	1	63
4a Clerical occupations	1,001	1	26	8	71	41	25	162	111	270	283	3	250
4b Secretarial occupations	374	-	4	4	21	13	16	45	35	113	122	1	70
5a Skilled construction trades	271	-	2	2	15	8	224	9	2	2	6	1	55
5b Skilled engineering trades	402	-	30	5	181	10	85	27	47	3	14	-	165
5c Other skilled trades	571	12	9	5	135	114	118	115	18	6	36	3	197
6a Protective service occupations	126	-	2	-	4	3	1	4	4	20	88	-	26
6b Personal service occupations	645	-	-	3	4	2	5	164	19	2	442	4	104
7a Buyers, brokers and sales representatives	149	-	2	2	8	14	5	61	4	51	2	-	56
7b Other sales occupations	563	-	-	1	1	9	4	520	8	14	6	-	96
8a Industrial plant and machine operators, assemblers	447	1	9	20	214	92	33	38	15	13	11	1	168
8b Drivers and mobile machinery operators	385	-	9	6	28	19	29	75	186	16	16	1	121
9a Other occupations in agriculture, forestry and fishing	10	5	-	-	-	-	-	-	-	-	5	-	5
9b Other elementary occupations	807	1	3	3	47	18	75	185	150	29	292	4	157
Occupation not stated or inadequately described	66	-	-	4	2	1	4	10	3	5	8	29	8
Working outside district of usual residence	2,303	9	53	52	436	163	233	483	192	226	435	21	

Table 76 Occupation and industry (10% sample) – **continued**

County, districts

76. Residents aged 16 and over, employees and self-employed

(10% sample)

Test Valley

Standard Occupational Classification Sub-major Groups	TOTAL PERSONS	Industry										Not stated, inadequately described or workplace outside UK	Working outside district of usual residence
		Agriculture, forestry and fishing	Energy and water	Mining	Manufac- turing metal etc	Other manufac- turing	Construction	Distribution and catering	Transport	Banking and finance etc	Other services		
a	b	c	d	e	f	g	h	i	j	k	l	m	n
ALL OCCUPATIONS	**5,030**	**168**	**50**	**76**	**549**	**338**	**385**	**987**	**219**	**679**	**1,541**	**38**	**1,711**
1a Corporate managers and administrators	631	3	12	19	100	46	42	63	43	130	168	5	336
1b Managers/proprietors in agriculture and services	337	60	-	-	-	-	-	220	4	25	28	-	93
2a Science and engineering professionals	128	-	2	1	40	8	8	3	-	30	35	1	72
2b Health professionals	38	-	-	-	-	-	-	5	-	-	33	-	21
2c Teaching professionals	171	-	-	-	-	-	-	-	-	-	170	1	85
2d Other professional occupations	119	-	2	2	1	2	5	-	1	62	44	-	65
3a Science and engineering associate professionals	171	-	2	3	37	14	11	7	2	47	47	1	106
3b Health associate professionals	88	-	-	-	-	-	-	4	-	-	84	-	53
3c Other associate professional occupations	170	-	2	2	4	7	3	2	8	57	84	1	79
4a Clerical occupations	594	3	8	9	45	42	13	100	29	161	183	1	195
4b Secretarial occupations	227	5	-	3	24	9	12	26	5	81	62	-	82
5a Skilled construction trades	122	1	-	1	3	4	108	2	-	-	3	-	12
5b Skilled engineering trades	192	2	10	1	75	5	42	20	17	10	10	-	69
5c Other skilled trades	314	22	2	6	60	63	64	60	10	6	21	-	67
6a Protective service occupations	206	-	-	-	-	1	-	1	-	6	198	-	27
6b Personal service occupations	309	3	-	-	-	4	-	96	2	3	200	1	69
7a Buyers, brokers and sales representatives	108	1	1	3	18	8	7	36	-	30	4	-	49
7b Other sales occupations	205	-	1	1	3	6	1	183	1	3	6	-	34
8a Industrial plant and machine operators, assemblers	296	9	5	22	111	86	17	25	5	4	12	-	81
8b Drivers and mobile machinery operators	156	6	-	1	12	14	17	31	56	8	9	2	48
9a Other occupations in agriculture, forestry and fishing	65	50	-	-	-	1	-	6	-	2	6	-	3
9b Other elementary occupations	344	3	2	1	16	16	34	95	36	12	126	3	58
Occupation not stated or inadequately described	39	-	1	1	-	2	1	2	-	2	8	22	7
Working outside district of usual residence	1,711	16	36	25	208	80	106	260	89	307	571	13	

Table 76 Occupation and industry (10% sample) – continued

County, districts

(10% sample)

76. Residents aged 16 and over, employees and self-employed

Winchester

Standard Occupational Classification Sub-major Groups	TOTAL PERSONS	Industry										Not stated, inadequately described or workplace outside UK	Working outside district of usual residence
		Agriculture, forestry and fishing	Energy and water	Mining	Manufacturing metal etc	Other manufacturing	Construction	Distribution and catering	Transport	Banking and finance etc	Other services		
a	b	c	d	e	f	g	h	i	j	k	l	m	n
ALL OCCUPATIONS	4,521	195	42	47	416	174	366	797	169	629	1,658	28	1,556
1a Corporate managers and administrators	637	3	7	9	112	35	59	65	26	135	184	2	349
1b Managers/proprietors in agriculture and services	358	86	1	1	-	4	-	217	7	19	23	-	106
2a Science and engineering professionals	183	-	6	6	48	1	15	10	4	53	40	-	113
2b Health professionals	40	-	-	-	-	-	1	6	-	-	34	-	17
2c Teaching professionals	224	-	-	-	-	-	1	-	-	-	223	-	112
2d Other professional occupations	168	-	2	-	8	2	3	2	3	92	56	-	79
3a Science and engineering associate professionals	142	-	3	2	49	2	11	3	3	34	35	-	63
3b Health associate professionals	99	-	-	-	-	-	-	2	-	1	96	-	27
3c Other associate professional occupations	195	-	1	4	10	8	4	7	6	65	90	-	89
4a Clerical occupations	441	1	3	10	25	19	17	55	19	104	187	1	148
4b Secretarial occupations	203	2	-	-	19	6	18	12	2	73	70	1	45
5a Skilled construction trades	109	1	1	-	-	2	99	2	-	3	2	-	11
5b Skilled engineering trades	97	1	5	1	44	5	19	7	6	4	5	-	56
5c Other skilled trades	246	31	2	5	34	45	60	42	1	3	23	-	57
6a Protective service occupations	164	-	-	-	2	1	-	2	-	7	152	-	27
6b Personal service occupations	325	-	-	-	-	-	-	69	8	2	246	-	42
7a Buyers, brokers and sales representatives	60	-	2	-	7	8	3	22	1	10	6	1	30
7b Other sales occupations	194	2	-	-	2	1	1	180	1	4	3	-	32
8a Industrial plant and machine operators, assemblers	121	4	8	5	38	27	12	12	2	6	7	-	52
8b Drivers and mobile machinery operators	116	1	-	3	5	5	14	17	52	7	12	-	51
9a Other occupations in agriculture, forestry and fishing	76	58	1	-	-	-	-	1	-	1	15	-	8
9b Other elementary occupations	291	4	1	1	12	3	30	63	27	6	143	1	36
Occupation not stated or inadequately described	32	1	-	-	1	-	-	1	1	-	6	22	6
Working outside district of usual residence	1,556	12	28	24	239	83	93	254	86	298	433	6	

93

Table 77 Industry and hours worked (10% sample)

(10% sample)

77. Residents aged 16 and over, employees and self-employed

Hours worked weekly	TOTAL PERSONS	Agriculture, forestry and fishing	Energy and water	Mining	Manufacturing metal etc	Other manufacturing	Construction	Distribution and catering	Transport	Banking and finance etc	Other services	Not stated, inadequately described or workplace outside UK
a	b	c	d	e	f	g	h	i	j	k	l	m
HAMPSHIRE												
TOTAL PERSONS	**71,873**	**1,122**	**988**	**1,281**	**8,405**	**3,649**	**5,687**	**14,461**	**4,128**	**9,092**	**22,548**	**512**
3 and under	231	4	1	-	3	12	7	41	2	33	127	1
4 - 7	1,304	20	2	-	17	27	21	479	20	126	581	11
8 - 15	4,555	64	10	23	85	106	95	1,788	93	370	1,904	17
16 - 21	4,390	48	17	58	108	132	91	1,405	101	439	1,979	12
22 - 23	696	7	4	9	41	25	11	204	13	54	328	-
24 - 30	3,816	59	6	18	147	180	102	956	104	353	1,869	22
31 - 35	5,300	37	39	112	234	348	158	613	184	2,195	1,363	17
36 - 40	35,924	480	835	817	6,746	2,104	2,971	5,644	2,199	3,822	10,181	125
41 - 50	8,995	187	43	157	664	447	1,489	1,779	865	988	2,325	51
51 - 60	2,773	80	7	48	162	153	391	701	236	379	588	28
61 and over	1,609	87	6	14	61	49	123	499	162	135	442	31
Not stated	2,280	49	18	25	137	66	228	352	149	198	861	197
Basingstoke & Deane												
TOTAL PERSONS	**7,472**	**132**	**68**	**183**	**836**	**417**	**577**	**1,584**	**348**	**1,189**	**2,094**	**44**
3 and under	17	1	-	-	-	1	-	3	-	5	7	-
4 - 7	112	1	-	-	4	3	2	34	3	9	53	3
8 - 15	433	9	1	4	8	10	10	154	6	40	190	1
16 - 21	405	6	-	4	9	11	6	129	11	42	187	-
22 - 23	63	3	-	2	5	4	-	19	-	12	18	-
24 - 30	374	7	1	-	20	11	14	103	5	42	168	3
31 - 35	582	3	8	14	28	56	18	63	7	288	96	1
36 - 40	3,989	65	52	131	662	228	261	778	194	519	1,085	14
41 - 50	919	19	2	19	68	63	184	176	78	127	181	2
51 - 60	290	9	1	4	18	21	48	63	21	61	42	2
61 and over	118	6	-	1	8	7	13	33	9	22	18	1
Not stated	170	3	3	4	6	2	21	29	14	22	49	17

Industry

Table 77 Industry and hours worked (10% sample) – continued

77. Residents aged 16 and over, employees and self-employed

(10% sample)

Hours worked weekly	TOTAL PERSONS	Agriculture, forestry and fishing	Energy and water	Mining	Manufacturing metal etc	Other manufacturing	Construction	Distribution and catering	Transport	Banking and finance etc	Other services	Not stated, inadequately described or workplace outside UK
a	b	c	d	e	f	g	h	i	j	k	l	m
East Hampshire												
TOTAL PERSONS	4,956	176	58	87	460	287	405	949	237	718	1,549	30
3 and under	20	-	-	-	-	-	1	2	-	3	14	-
4 - 7	124	4	-	-	2	3	1	32	1	11	69	1
8 - 15	304	5	-	-	3	10	12	91	2	35	142	4
16 - 21	260	9	1	1	7	10	5	70	9	18	128	2
22 - 23	49	1	-	1	3	2	1	17	1	2	21	-
24 - 30	273	7	1	-	13	14	11	58	12	27	129	1
31 - 35	374	4	6	6	17	16	8	40	13	146	117	1
36 - 40	2,236	79	44	65	357	155	182	329	122	307	590	6
41 - 50	775	23	2	6	36	52	131	170	49	105	198	3
51 - 60	238	16	-	6	6	18	31	59	12	33	56	1
61 and over	130	18	-	-	6	2	8	47	6	12	29	2
Not stated	173	10	4	2	10	5	14	34	10	19	56	9
Eastleigh												
TOTAL PERSONS	5,205	55	86	66	740	259	458	1,095	363	692	1,362	29
3 and under	13	-	-	-	-	-	1	2	-	3	7	-
4 - 7	104	-	-	-	-	3	-	38	3	9	50	1
8 - 15	354	4	-	2	16	8	3	162	10	30	117	2
16 - 21	303	3	4	-	10	9	7	90	8	32	140	-
22 - 23	61	-	-	-	3	2	-	22	2	3	29	-
24 - 30	294	4	2	3	11	12	8	84	12	25	133	-
31 - 35	446	-	3	5	26	23	27	46	23	193	99	1
36 - 40	2,609	26	72	45	583	144	248	425	195	280	583	8
41 - 50	607	11	3	8	66	32	108	122	61	68	125	3
51 - 60	189	3	-	3	10	13	27	54	22	30	26	1
61 and over	97	4	1	-	6	3	11	36	17	4	12	3
Not stated	128	-	1	-	9	10	18	14	10	15	41	10

Table 77 Industry and hours worked (10% sample) – continued

County, districts

77. Residents aged 16 and over, employees and self-employed

(10% sample)

Hours worked weekly	TOTAL PERSONS	Industry										Not stated, inadequately described or workplace outside UK
		Agriculture, forestry and fishing	Energy and water	Mining	Manufacturing metal etc	Other manufacturing	Construction	Distribution and catering	Transport	Banking and finance etc	Other services	
a	b	c	d	e	f	g	h	i	j	k	l	m
Fareham												
TOTAL PERSONS	4,790	45	51	92	674	209	365	808	231	562	1,717	36
3 and under	21	-	-	-	1	2	-	6	1	2	9	1
4 - 7	92	2	-	-	-	3	-	23	1	10	52	1
8 - 15	283	3	-	1	8	7	6	102	6	15	135	-
16 - 21	318	4	1	3	8	11	8	117	3	26	137	-
22 - 23	48	-	-	1	7	1	1	11	2	3	22	-
24 - 30	243	2	-	2	5	11	3	57	5	28	128	2
31 - 35	344	2	-	19	15	18	11	38	5	141	93	2
36 - 40	2,469	17	45	52	546	109	202	298	135	231	824	10
41 - 50	565	8	3	10	55	22	87	86	42	63	186	3
51 - 60	171	3	-	3	12	13	27	36	10	23	42	2
61 and over	107	-	1	-	6	5	11	20	15	7	39	3
Not stated	129	4	1	1	11	7	9	14	6	13	50	13
Gosport												
TOTAL PERSONS	3,390	20	21	126	418	136	201	606	117	260	1,461	24
3 and under	8	-	-	-	1	-	-	1	1	2	3	-
4 - 7	65	-	-	-	-	1	1	35	-	2	25	1
8 - 15	221	2	-	1	2	3	3	88	4	14	103	1
16 - 21	237	-	-	16	3	6	3	84	2	10	112	-
22 - 23	26	-	-	-	-	1	2	4	1	2	16	-
24 - 30	165	2	-	1	4	4	1	44	5	12	91	1
31 - 35	235	1	-	27	12	4	5	29	-	58	97	2
36 - 40	1,700	10	20	64	348	86	117	196	63	107	682	7
41 - 50	404	4	1	11	29	25	44	69	27	23	169	2
51 - 60	114	-	-	1	5	4	13	32	7	20	31	1
61 and over	80	-	-	2	4	-	7	11	5	6	45	-
Not stated	135	1	-	3	10	2	5	13	2	4	87	8

Table 77 Industry and hours worked (10% sample) – continued

County, districts

(10% sample)

77. Residents aged 16 and over, employees and self-employed

Hours worked weekly	TOTAL PERSONS	Industry										Not stated, inadequately described or workplace outside UK
		Agriculture, forestry and fishing	Energy and water	Mining	Manufacturing metal etc	Other manufacturing	Construction	Distribution and catering	Transport	Banking and finance etc	Other services	
a	b	c	d	e	f	g	h	i	j	k	l	m
Hart												
TOTAL PERSONS	**4,222**	68	46	76	398	181	264	826	276	797	1,260	30
3 and under	19	-	1	-	-	-	-	2	-	5	11	-
4 - 7	74	1	-	-	2	2	2	26	1	9	31	-
8 - 15	272	3	-	1	9	6	5	93	4	39	109	3
16 - 21	250	2	1	1	4	5	9	75	11	68	73	1
22 - 23	48	-	-	2	2	1	-	17	-	4	22	-
24 - 30	200	1	-	-	9	6	9	47	7	28	91	2
31 - 35	346	6	3	7	22	18	8	36	20	149	75	2
36 - 40	1,948	33	34	44	291	94	110	309	162	329	535	7
41 - 50	659	10	4	10	43	34	82	117	44	97	214	4
51 - 60	212	2	2	8	10	6	24	60	11	41	44	4
61 and over	98	7	1	2	2	7	4	26	6	15	27	1
Not stated	96	3	-	1	4	2	11	18	10	13	28	6
Havant												
TOTAL PERSONS	**5,177**	37	71	107	994	314	479	992	238	486	1,425	34
3 and under	14	-	-	-	-	4	-	3	-	2	5	-
4 - 7	88	1	-	-	-	-	3	30	2	12	40	-
8 - 15	338	1	3	1	4	7	15	151	9	22	124	1
16 - 21	351	-	2	11	14	12	5	115	7	41	143	-
22 - 23	55	-	-	2	3	3	-	16	-	2	29	-
24 - 30	284	6	-	1	19	22	5	65	3	33	128	2
31 - 35	271	1	1	1	22	14	8	47	11	93	73	-
36 - 40	2,789	19	63	80	832	204	256	352	118	195	661	9
41 - 50	543	3	1	4	64	28	114	106	42	48	130	3
51 - 60	180	1	-	2	19	6	37	45	20	19	29	2
61 and over	102	2	-	2	5	7	11	38	14	5	18	-
Not stated	162	3	1	3	12	7	25	24	12	14	45	16

Table 77 Industry and hours worked (10% sample) – continued

County, districts

(10% sample)

77. Residents aged 16 and over, employees and self-employed

Hours worked weekly	TOTAL PERSONS	Agriculture, forestry and fishing	Energy and water	Mining	Manufacturing metal etc	Other manufacturing	Construction	Distribution and catering	Transport	Banking and finance etc	Other services	Not stated, inadequately described or workplace outside UK
a	b	c	d	e	f	g	h	i	j	k	l	m

New Forest

TOTAL PERSONS	6,894	174	223	180	671	345	572	1,550	446	919	1,744	70
3 and under	26	-	-	-	-	1	1	2	-	4	17	-
4 - 7	147	3	1	-	2	3	4	59	2	16	56	1
8 - 15	530	11	1	1	9	13	5	233	14	40	202	1
16 - 21	469	7	2	3	11	15	21	152	8	47	201	2
22 - 23	58	2	1	-	2	2	2	11	1	5	32	-
24 - 30	381	8	1	4	10	16	10	84	17	31	195	5
31 - 35	537	7	2	9	22	29	16	73	22	250	104	3
36 - 40	3,167	70	196	112	518	202	311	540	235	348	618	17
41 - 50	901	29	13	36	65	40	139	207	92	99	174	7
51 - 60	290	14	2	10	18	13	34	82	32	37	44	4
61 and over	172	17	1	2	6	3	13	62	11	17	37	3
Not stated	216	6	3	3	8	8	15	45	12	25	64	27

Portsmouth

TOTAL PERSONS	7,563	18	95	77	865	428	594	1,554	492	676	2,699	65
3 and under	18	-	-	-	-	1	1	6	-	1	9	-
4 - 7	116	-	-	-	-	2	-	71	2	9	32	-
8 - 15	447	1	3	2	5	12	6	188	7	30	192	1
16 - 21	477	1	1	-	16	20	5	163	11	32	224	4
22 - 23	90	-	-	-	1	2	2	26	3	12	44	-
24 - 30	382	1	-	3	11	26	8	100	14	22	196	1
31 - 35	449	1	2	6	14	30	16	54	10	158	158	-
36 - 40	4,030	9	86	52	732	268	344	593	278	311	1,343	14
41 - 50	785	3	1	10	52	41	129	160	105	55	223	6
51 - 60	267	-	-	1	14	15	44	74	23	24	66	6
61 and over	187	1	-	1	2	2	9	65	24	7	72	4
Not stated	315	1	2	2	18	9	30	54	15	15	140	29

Table 77 Industry and hours worked (10% sample) – continued

(10% sample)

77. Residents aged 16 and over, employees and self-employed

Hours worked weekly	TOTAL PERSONS	Agriculture, forestry and fishing	Energy and water	Mining	Manufacturing metal etc	Other manufacturing	Industry Construction	Distribution and catering	Transport	Banking and finance etc	Other services	Not stated, inadequately described or workplace outside UK
a	b	c	d	e	f	g	h	i	j	k	l	m
Rushmoor												
TOTAL PERSONS	**4,333**	**11**	**47**	**67**	**428**	**144**	**300**	**820**	**293**	**596**	**1,599**	**28**
3 and under	15	-	-	-	-	-	1	1	-	1	11	1
4 - 7	53	-	-	-	-	1	-	22	-	4	26	-
8 - 15	231	1	-	6	3	5	3	88	7	20	98	-
16 - 21	230	1	-	13	5	4	3	73	6	24	100	1
22 - 23	45	-	-	-	6	1	-	23	-	-	15	-
24 - 30	202	-	-	-	11	3	7	58	6	18	99	-
31 - 35	320	-	4	4	13	17	11	34	14	171	52	-
36 - 40	2,195	6	42	36	338	88	141	339	166	265	768	6
41 - 50	614	3	1	5	33	14	100	114	70	48	222	4
51 - 60	141	-	-	3	8	9	22	29	7	15	47	1
61 and over	93	-	-	-	4	-	3	20	3	17	44	2
Not stated	194	-	-	-	7	2	9	19	14	13	117	13
Southampton												
TOTAL PERSONS	**8,320**	**23**	**130**	**97**	**956**	**417**	**721**	**1,893**	**699**	**889**	**2,439**	**56**
3 and under	19	-	-	-	1	1	-	5	-	1	11	-
4 - 7	125	-	-	-	4	3	2	53	1	9	52	1
8 - 15	555	2	1	-	8	14	14	243	12	37	222	2
16 - 21	559	1	4	3	11	15	9	192	19	47	258	-
22 - 23	66	-	1	1	1	2	-	14	1	3	43	-
24 - 30	458	2	1	2	10	23	8	130	9	28	242	3
31 - 35	657	2	5	7	22	72	13	73	39	243	179	2
36 - 40	4,299	11	110	60	806	223	433	798	351	371	1,126	10
41 - 50	864	1	4	16	51	35	147	198	165	90	153	4
51 - 60	273	1	1	1	15	16	42	84	40	27	44	2
61 and over	174	2	-	2	2	6	17	63	31	14	29	8
Not stated	271	1	3	5	25	7	36	40	31	19	80	24

Table 77 Industry and hours worked (10% sample) – continued

77. Residents aged 16 and over, employees and self-employed

Hours worked weekly	TOTAL PERSONS	Industry											Not stated, inadequately described or workplace outside UK
		Agriculture, forestry and fishing	Energy and water	Mining	Manufacturing metal etc	Other manufacturing	Construction	Distribution and catering	Transport	Banking and finance etc	Other services		
a	b	c	d	e	f	g	h	i	j	k	l	m

Test Valley

	b	c	d	e	f	g	h	i	j	k	l	m
TOTAL PERSONS	5,030	168	50	76	549	338	385	987	219	679	1,541	38
3 and under	15	1	-	-	-	2	-	4	-	1	7	-
4 - 7	107	4	1	-	2	2	3	33	3	14	43	2
8 - 15	310	11	1	2	5	7	5	110	5	27	136	1
16 - 21	260	7	1	1	7	5	4	83	4	23	125	-
22 - 23	51	-	2	-	3	3	2	15	2	5	19	-
24 - 30	281	8	-	2	18	24	6	63	3	28	128	1
31 - 35	457	7	2	4	10	31	11	51	16	199	125	1
36 - 40	2,389	69	38	48	435	208	184	379	99	264	655	10
41 - 50	673	33	3	13	51	37	121	129	48	77	156	5
51 - 60	214	11	1	3	9	13	21	52	22	26	55	1
61 and over	123	11	1	2	1	3	11	41	12	5	33	3
Not stated	150	6	-	1	8	3	17	27	5	10	59	14

Winchester

	b	c	d	e	f	g	h	i	j	k	l	m
TOTAL PERSONS	4,521	195	42	47	416	174	366	797	169	629	1,658	28
3 and under	26	2	-	-	-	-	1	4	-	3	16	-
4 - 7	97	4	-	-	1	1	3	23	1	12	52	-
8 - 15	277	11	-	2	5	4	8	85	7	21	134	-
16 - 21	271	7	-	2	3	9	6	62	2	29	151	-
22 - 23	36	1	-	-	5	1	1	9	-	1	18	-
24 - 30	279	11	-	-	6	8	12	63	6	31	141	1
31 - 35	282	3	3	3	11	20	6	29	4	106	95	2
36 - 40	2,104	66	33	28	298	95	182	308	81	295	711	7
41 - 50	686	40	5	9	51	24	103	125	42	88	194	5
51 - 60	194	20	-	3	18	6	21	31	9	23	62	1
61 and over	128	19	1	-	9	4	5	37	9	4	39	1
Not stated	141	11	-	-	9	2	18	21	8	16	45	11

Table 78 Occupation and hours worked (10% sample)

78. Residents aged 16 and over, employees and self-employed (10% sample)

HAMPSHIRE

Standard Occupational Classification Sub-major Groups	TOTAL PERSONS	Hours worked weekly											
		3 and under	4 - 7	8 - 15	16 - 21	22 - 23	24 - 30	31 - 35	36 - 40	41 - 50	51 - 60	61 and over	Not stated
a	b	c	d	e	f	g	h	i	j	k	l	m	n
ALL OCCUPATIONS	71,873	231	1,304	4,555	4,390	696	3,816	5,300	35,924	8,995	2,773	1,609	2,280
1a Corporate managers and administrators	8,237	8	31	91	119	28	182	822	4,469	1,674	483	166	164
1b Managers/proprietors in agriculture and services	3,933	5	21	91	107	14	159	163	1,366	810	498	529	170
2a Science and engineering professionals	2,462	-	2	16	24	8	16	109	1,908	281	49	18	31
2b Health professionals	389	1	7	17	23	3	23	22	104	55	51	73	10
2c Teaching professionals	2,237	45	95	200	124	17	281	319	514	399	128	25	90
2d Other professional occupations	1,401	1	3	22	56	5	38	152	756	216	69	50	33
3a Science and engineering associate professionals	2,504	-	6	20	43	8	48	221	1,905	186	22	6	39
3b Health associate professionals	1,566	6	22	145	212	41	216	99	724	38	12	16	35
3c Other associate professional occupations	2,737	9	37	80	125	12	135	314	1,382	323	130	79	111
4a Clerical occupations	8,079	20	119	419	708	108	465	1,284	4,415	362	39	13	127
4b Secretarial occupations	3,496	18	75	269	467	89	324	516	1,507	159	9	3	60
5a Skilled construction trades	1,888	2	1	12	6	-	24	60	1,090	463	104	35	91
5b Skilled engineering trades	3,135	-	-	10	17	3	20	65	2,471	362	95	27	65
5c Other skilled trades	4,466	3	16	82	98	11	135	108	2,864	739	195	66	149
6a Protective service occupations	3,035	7	6	52	11	7	23	132	1,410	676	188	191	332
6b Personal service occupations	4,924	32	387	732	656	121	687	257	1,375	368	92	61	156
7a Buyers, brokers and sales representatives	1,362	3	9	34	38	6	33	135	680	260	104	26	34
7b Other sales occupations	3,935	12	193	1,045	745	112	340	133	1,049	166	50	22	68
8a Industrial plant and machine operators, assemblers	3,671	4	8	78	117	20	107	130	2,659	356	88	27	77
8b Drivers and mobile machinery operators	2,321	6	6	35	47	6	52	34	1,281	442	204	120	88
9a Other occupations in agriculture, forestry and fishing	433	1	5	17	11	3	23	10	226	77	29	18	13
9b Other elementary occupations	5,166	47	252	1,065	627	73	467	196	1,636	539	112	23	129
Occupation not stated or inadequately described	496	1	3	23	9	1	18	19	133	44	22	15	208
Working outside district of usual residence	26,966	44	229	926	1,018	189	1,028	2,327	15,557	3,643	1,078	414	513

Table 78 Occupation and hours worked (10% sample) – continued

78. Residents aged 16 and over, employees and self-employed (10% sample)

Basingstoke & Deane

Standard Occupational Classification Sub-major Groups	TOTAL PERSONS	Hours worked weekly											
		3 and under	4 - 7	8 - 15	16 - 21	22 - 23	24 - 30	31 - 35	36 - 40	41 - 50	51 - 60	61 and over	Not stated
a	b	c	d	e	f	g	h	i	j	k	l	m	n
ALL OCCUPATIONS	**7,472**	**17**	**112**	**433**	**405**	**63**	**374**	**582**	**3,989**	**919**	**290**	**118**	**170**
1a Corporate managers and administrators	1,028	-	5	12	10	3	19	109	589	179	67	21	14
1b Managers/proprietors in agriculture and services	313	-	2	11	10	3	14	10	131	64	31	26	11
2a Science and engineering professionals	337	-	1	-	4	-	2	16	263	42	3	4	2
2b Health professionals	30	-	-	3	5	-	-	-	7	3	4	6	2
2c Teaching professionals	164	3	7	16	13	2	27	19	33	31	8	3	2
2d Other professional occupations	146	1	-	1	4	2	2	22	82	16	10	3	3
3a Science and engineering associate professionals	303	-	-	2	2	1	1	36	229	22	4	1	5
3b Health associate professionals	146	-	1	12	24	3	19	8	67	4	3	-	5
3c Other associate professional occupations	278	1	2	10	10	-	12	41	137	32	17	5	11
4a Clerical occupations	1,011	3	11	44	71	14	62	149	593	51	3	-	10
4b Secretarial occupations	458	2	12	26	51	8	43	57	231	19	2	-	7
5a Skilled construction trades	187	-	-	1	-	-	1	6	92	62	16	2	7
5b Skilled engineering trades	307	-	-	1	1	-	-	7	255	30	9	1	3
5c Other skilled trades	425	-	-	10	12	1	14	8	254	91	18	6	11
6a Protective service occupations	126	-	-	6	-	-	2	2	65	24	17	5	5
6b Personal service occupations	429	4	30	58	47	6	47	18	150	36	16	6	11
7a Buyers, brokers and sales representatives	135	-	1	2	3	-	2	15	65	30	8	7	2
7b Other sales occupations	357	1	11	81	60	8	37	17	112	15	5	2	8
8a Industrial plant and machine operators, assemblers	403	1	-	9	11	5	12	17	282	43	14	1	8
8b Drivers and mobile machinery operators	264	-	-	2	4	1	4	4	144	63	21	10	11
9a Other occupations in agriculture, forestry and fishing	64	1	1	2	1	1	6	1	34	8	2	5	2
9b Other elementary occupations	512	-	27	120	62	4	46	18	163	49	10	2	11
Occupation not stated or inadequately described	49	-	1	4	-	1	2	2	11	5	2	2	19
Working outside district of usual residence	2,237	4	8	45	67	5	66	176	1,322	344	119	36	45

Table 78 Occupation and hours worked (10% sample) – continued

County, districts

(10% sample)

78. Residents aged 16 and over, employees and self-employed

East Hampshire

Standard Occupational Classification Sub-major Groups	TOTAL PERSONS	Hours worked weekly											
		3 and under	4 - 7	8 - 15	16 - 21	22 - 23	24 - 30	31 - 35	36 - 40	41 - 50	51 - 60	61 and over	Not stated
a	b	c	d	e	f	g	h	i	j	k	l	m	n
ALL OCCUPATIONS	4,956	20	124	304	260	49	273	374	2,236	775	238	130	173
1a Corporate managers and administrators	673	1	1	3	11	2	20	54	336	175	45	11	14
1b Managers/proprietors in agriculture and services	357	-	1	5	11	1	12	15	105	81	46	54	26
2a Science and engineering professionals	167	-	-	2	-	1	-	12	116	27	4	2	3
2b Health professionals	35	-	3	1	2	-	2	3	6	6	4	6	2
2c Teaching professionals	230	4	10	21	10	2	34	34	49	39	13	7	7
2d Other professional occupations	116	-	1	-	4	-	1	12	55	24	6	7	6
3a Science and engineering associate professionals	129	-	-	1	5	-	3	7	98	10	3	1	1
3b Health associate professionals	98	2	3	12	12	2	17	7	33	4	2	1	3
3c Other associate professional occupations	230	1	4	8	11	2	7	22	107	33	16	8	11
4a Clerical occupations	441	1	15	24	24	9	25	85	231	19	2	1	5
4b Secretarial occupations	280	3	10	31	38	6	22	44	105	14	1	-	6
5a Skilled construction trades	153	-	-	1	1	-	3	4	78	45	11	2	8
5b Skilled engineering trades	167	-	-	1	2	1	4	5	122	23	6	-	3
5c Other skilled trades	310	-	-	9	12	2	13	3	169	56	20	5	21
6a Protective service occupations	200	-	1	1	1	-	-	12	104	59	5	4	13
6b Personal service occupations	339	3	35	53	42	6	46	21	79	32	6	2	14
7a Buyers, brokers and sales representatives	102	-	1	2	1	-	2	6	46	24	13	6	1
7b Other sales occupations	208	-	14	53	38	9	14	5	52	17	3	1	2
8a Industrial plant and machine operators, assemblers	202	-	1	4	6	2	14	9	144	17	-	2	3
8b Drivers and mobile machinery operators	125	-	-	2	4	1	3	1	66	25	14	6	3
9a Other occupations in agriculture, forestry and fishing	69	-	1	1	3	1	2	1	38	9	9	2	2
9b Other elementary occupations	298	5	23	65	22	2	29	9	94	33	7	-	9
Occupation not stated or inadequately described	27	-	-	4	-	-	-	3	3	3	2	2	10
Working outside district of usual residence	2,043	4	28	71	70	19	95	191	1,044	354	92	37	38

Table 78 Occupation and hours worked (10% sample) – continued

County, districts

(10% sample)

78. Residents aged 16 and over, employees and self-employed

Eastleigh

Standard Occupational Classification Sub-major Groups	TOTAL PERSONS	Hours worked weekly											Not stated
		3 and under	4 - 7	8 - 15	16 - 21	22 - 23	24 - 30	31 - 35	36 - 40	41 - 50	51 - 60	61 and over	
a	b	c	d	e	f	g	h	i	j	k	l	m	n
ALL OCCUPATIONS	5,205	13	104	354	303	61	294	446	2,609	607	189	97	128
1a Corporate managers and administrators	619	-	1	6	6	3	16	60	332	129	40	11	15
1b Managers/proprietors in agriculture and services	254	1	1	2	2	4	10	13	95	45	37	39	5
2a Science and engineering professionals	164	-	-	-	-	-	1	9	131	15	5	2	1
2b Health professionals	18	-	-	-	2	1	2	1	4	3	3	2	-
2c Teaching professionals	179	4	10	17	13	2	25	22	39	29	11	-	7
2d Other professional occupations	106	-	-	-	4	-	4	11	66	12	4	3	2
3a Science and engineering associate professionals	222	-	-	2	7	1	7	22	164	14	1	-	4
3b Health associate professionals	112	1	2	9	20	4	10	7	52	2	1	1	3
3c Other associate professional occupations	194	-	3	5	5	-	11	32	101	25	3	2	7
4a Clerical occupations	641	1	7	40	64	11	48	123	312	21	3	-	11
4b Secretarial occupations	300	1	6	29	36	6	26	55	123	17	-	-	1
5a Skilled construction trades	108	1	-	-	-	-	1	6	67	20	5	3	5
5b Skilled engineering trades	257	-	-	-	2	-	-	4	200	28	10	4	9
5c Other skilled trades	364	-	5	4	6	-	5	8	246	56	17	5	12
6a Protective service occupations	96	-	1	1	-	-	-	3	60	21	2	2	6
6b Personal service occupations	312	1	33	57	35	12	45	15	73	22	5	3	11
7a Buyers, brokers and sales representatives	137	-	-	1	2	-	4	22	70	23	11	2	2
7b Other sales occupations	324	1	13	98	50	14	32	13	80	19	2	2	-
8a Industrial plant and machine operators, assemblers	259	-	2	10	13	1	11	6	170	35	6	2	3
8b Drivers and mobile machinery operators	191	-	1	3	1	-	2	4	109	40	12	10	9
9a Other occupations in agriculture, forestry and fishing	12	-	-	-	1	-	-	-	9	1	-	1	-
9b Other elementary occupations	313	2	19	67	34	2	34	9	102	28	9	1	6
Occupation not stated or inadequately described	23	-	-	3	-	-	-	1	4	2	2	2	9
Working outside district of usual residence	2,760	5	33	115	124	26	135	287	1,506	351	101	36	41

Table 78 Occupation and hours worked (10% sample) – continued

78. Residents aged 16 and over, employees and self-employed (10% sample)

Fareham

Standard Occupational Classification Sub-major Groups	TOTAL PERSONS	Hours worked weekly											
		3 and under	4 - 7	8 - 15	16 - 21	22 - 23	24 - 30	31 - 35	36 - 40	41 - 50	51 - 60	61 and over	Not stated
a	b	c	d	e	f	g	h	i	j	k	l	m	n
ALL OCCUPATIONS	4,790	21	92	283	318	48	243	344	2,469	565	171	107	129
1a Corporate managers and administrators	659	-	5	1	7	2	10	60	380	134	32	15	13
1b Managers/proprietors in agriculture and services	229	-	-	9	12	-	14	14	83	38	32	18	9
2a Science and engineering professionals	199	-	-	3	4	1	1	9	145	28	3	2	3
2b Health professionals	25	-	-	3	2	-	-	1	9	3	2	5	-
2c Teaching professionals	181	5	11	8	13	1	27	26	37	33	13	1	6
2d Other professional occupations	88	-	-	-	9	-	3	8	50	12	5	1	-
3a Science and engineering associate professionals	176	-	-	-	2	-	1	10	140	18	-	2	3
3b Health associate professionals	138	-	1	13	17	5	29	8	57	4	-	2	2
3c Other associate professional occupations	213	1	2	5	8	2	8	22	105	29	8	14	9
4a Clerical occupations	524	1	8	25	35	9	31	66	305	35	2	1	6
4b Secretarial occupations	239	3	2	16	40	9	23	37	94	10	-	1	4
5a Skilled construction trades	93	-	-	1	-	-	1	2	54	24	6	3	2
5b Skilled engineering trades	222	-	-	-	1	-	2	8	182	18	5	2	4
5c Other skilled trades	285	1	5	5	8	-	9	7	178	41	13	7	11
6a Protective service occupations	279	-	2	4	1	-	1	21	157	46	14	17	16
6b Personal service occupations	270	1	22	51	44	6	36	8	76	14	3	2	7
7a Buyers, brokers and sales representatives	90	1	-	2	4	-	1	7	45	20	6	1	3
7b Other sales occupations	239	2	10	61	64	6	22	7	55	4	3	3	2
8a Industrial plant and machine operators, assemblers	187	-	-	3	7	-	-	9	144	17	-	2	5
8b Drivers and mobile machinery operators	116	1	-	-	2	1	2	2	70	15	12	6	5
9a Other occupations in agriculture, forestry and fishing	9	-	-	2	1	-	-	-	4	-	1	-	1
9b Other elementary occupations	300	5	24	71	35	6	20	11	89	20	11	2	6
Occupation not stated or inadequately described	29	-	-	-	2	-	2	1	10	2	-	-	12
Working outside district of usual residence	2,392	4	23	65	108	17	91	203	1,432	295	78	37	39

Table 78 Occupation and hours worked (10% sample) – **continued**

County, districts

(10% sample)

78. Residents aged 16 and over, employees and self-employed

Gosport

Standard Occupational Classification Sub-major Groups	TOTAL PERSONS	Hours worked weekly											
		3 and under	4 - 7	8 - 15	16 - 21	22 - 23	24 - 30	31 - 35	36 - 40	41 - 50	51 - 60	61 and over	Not stated
a	b	c	d	e	f	g	h	i	j	k	l	m	n
ALL OCCUPATIONS	**3,390**	**8**	**65**	**221**	**237**	**26**	**165**	**235**	**1,700**	**404**	**114**	**80**	**135**
1a Corporate managers and administrators	273	1	-	1	4	3	8	22	163	42	13	6	10
1b Managers/proprietors in agriculture and services	138	-	-	4	4	-	7	7	55	30	16	12	3
2a Science and engineering professionals	65	-	-	-	1	1	1	2	48	9	1	-	2
2b Health professionals	11	1	-	-	-	1	1	1	2	1	1	-	-
2c Teaching professionals	59	1	3	6	1	-	8	11	12	12	2	-	3
2d Other professional occupations	28	-	-	1	-	-	-	2	15	5	2	3	-
3a Science and engineering associate professionals	89	-	-	1	-	-	2	10	68	8	-	-	-
3b Health associate professionals	74	-	4	2	16	-	8	5	37	1	-	-	1
3c Other associate professional occupations	101	-	1	2	5	-	7	6	59	13	2	4	2
4a Clerical occupations	370	-	5	18	37	3	16	48	209	23	2	1	8
4b Secretarial occupations	115	-	1	8	16	6	9	18	46	7	1	-	3
5a Skilled construction trades	69	-	-	-	-	-	1	3	47	13	-	4	1
5b Skilled engineering trades	216	-	-	-	4	1	1	1	168	29	6	4	2
5c Other skilled trades	206	-	-	2	2	1	5	3	141	28	10	3	11
6a Protective service occupations	455	-	1	3	2	-	3	41	212	78	27	32	56
6b Personal service occupations	260	1	22	36	45	4	38	22	60	19	3	2	8
7a Buyers, brokers and sales representatives	36	-	1	-	-	-	2	3	20	4	4	1	1
7b Other sales occupations	214	-	19	62	45	3	17	5	46	11	4	-	2
8a Industrial plant and machine operators, assemblers	228	-	-	3	12	-	1	11	161	35	3	-	2
8b Drivers and mobile machinery operators	92	1	-	1	3	-	4	1	47	18	9	3	5
9a Other occupations in agriculture, forestry and fishing	7	-	-	-	-	-	-	1	4	-	-	-	2
9b Other elementary occupations	257	3	8	70	39	4	24	11	70	16	7	1	4
Occupation not stated or inadequately described	27	-	-	1	1	-	2	1	10	2	1	-	9
Working outside district of usual residence	1,290	-	14	59	59	8	46	76	784	154	47	20	23

Table 78 Occupation and hours worked (10% sample) – **continued**

County, districts

78. Residents aged 16 and over, employees and self-employed

(10% sample)

Hart

Standard Occupational Classification Sub-major Groups (a)	TOTAL PERSONS (b)	Hours worked weekly											Not stated (n)
		3 and under (c)	4 - 7 (d)	8 - 15 (e)	16 - 21 (f)	22 - 23 (g)	24 - 30 (h)	31 - 35 (i)	36 - 40 (j)	41 - 50 (k)	51 - 60 (l)	61 and over (m)	
ALL OCCUPATIONS	4,222	19	74	272	250	48	200	346	1,948	659	212	98	96
1a Corporate managers and administrators	733	2	3	12	17	1	10	84	362	157	53	16	16
1b Managers/proprietors in agriculture and services	234	-	1	4	6	-	9	7	84	54	33	27	9
2a Science and engineering professionals	233	-	-	3	2	-	2	13	189	17	5	2	-
2b Health professionals	30	-	1	2	2	-	1	2	11	4	5	2	-
2c Teaching professionals	139	5	3	15	5	-	22	16	29	29	9	1	5
2d Other professional occupations	120	-	-	3	4	1	3	17	57	21	5	6	3
3a Science and engineering associate professionals	150	-	2	3	6	-	3	12	109	12	-	2	1
3b Health associate professionals	81	-	2	14	7	3	12	7	28	4	1	1	2
3c Other associate professional occupations	192	1	5	5	14	1	8	27	76	31	17	5	2
4a Clerical occupations	402	4	12	34	50	4	24	59	195	14	2	1	3
4b Secretarial occupations	238	1	8	19	31	14	23	33	93	10	1	-	5
5a Skilled construction trades	79	-	-	-	-	-	1	3	39	26	6	2	2
5b Skilled engineering trades	156	-	-	-	1	-	-	5	117	23	4	1	5
5c Other skilled trades	205	-	1	3	4	-	6	12	102	52	13	7	5
6a Protective service occupations	224	1	-	4	1	-	3	5	78	102	11	12	7
6b Personal service occupations	229	2	15	43	24	10	32	12	52	17	11	2	9
7a Buyers, brokers and sales representatives	109	-	-	5	2	1	3	6	63	14	11	1	3
7b Other sales occupations	204	-	11	54	48	5	10	4	54	10	5	1	2
8a Industrial plant and machine operators, assemblers	115	-	-	2	4	-	3	8	81	8	7	1	1
8b Drivers and mobile machinery operators	102	-	-	-	4	1	5	2	54	23	7	4	2
9a Other occupations in agriculture, forestry and fishing	23	-	1	2	-	-	1	1	13	3	1	1	-
9b Other elementary occupations	201	3	9	44	18	7	19	10	56	24	3	2	6
Occupation not stated or inadequately described	23	-	-	1	-	-	-	1	6	4	2	1	8
Working outside district of usual residence	2,484	6	20	105	98	27	87	251	1,390	329	100	33	38

107

Table 78 Occupation and hours worked (10% sample) – continued

County, districts

78. Residents aged 16 and over, employees and self-employed

(10% sample)

Havant

Standard Occupational Classification Sub-major Groups	TOTAL PERSONS	Hours worked weekly											
		3 and under	4 - 7	8 - 15	16 - 21	22 - 23	24 - 30	31 - 35	36 - 40	41 - 50	51 - 60	61 and over	Not stated
a	b	c	d	e	f	g	h	i	j	k	l	m	n
ALL OCCUPATIONS	5,177	14	88	338	351	55	284	271	2,789	543	180	102	162
1a Corporate managers and administrators	541	-	2	7	13	3	18	48	297	95	26	15	17
1b Managers/proprietors in agriculture and services	235	-	3	4	6	2	8	8	88	48	26	39	3
2a Science and engineering professionals	190	-	-	-	-	-	1	1	164	19	3	1	1
2b Health professionals	24	-	1	-	2	1	3	1	8	4	3	-	1
2c Teaching professionals	150	1	12	14	6	-	16	26	38	24	4	1	8
2d Other professional occupations	78	-	-	1	3	-	2	2	54	12	2	-	2
3a Science and engineering associate professionals	210	-	-	1	2	-	1	8	182	16	-	-	-
3b Health associate professionals	93	-	2	7	21	5	13	3	40	2	-	-	-
3c Other associate professional occupations	168	-	1	6	6	2	10	15	95	11	11	3	8
4a Clerical occupations	532	1	4	21	51	7	34	59	319	21	2	1	12
4b Secretarial occupations	199	1	2	16	35	5	29	15	87	5	1	-	3
5a Skilled construction trades	165	-	-	5	1	-	2	3	90	39	10	3	12
5b Skilled engineering trades	278	-	-	-	3	-	3	1	226	31	7	2	5
5c Other skilled trades	374	-	-	4	6	-	16	9	247	55	18	7	12
6a Protective service occupations	117	-	-	3	1	-	1	6	54	24	7	7	14
6b Personal service occupations	360	1	28	48	64	15	44	16	100	26	5	2	11
7a Buyers, brokers and sales representatives	101	-	3	5	1	1	7	4	53	14	9	1	3
7b Other sales occupations	327	1	16	110	66	8	33	11	65	7	2	2	6
8a Industrial plant and machine operators, assemblers	448	2	-	12	13	1	10	12	349	20	9	6	14
8b Drivers and mobile machinery operators	159	2	1	5	2	-	2	3	86	23	19	10	6
9a Other occupations in agriculture, forestry and fishing	12	-	1	-	-	-	2	-	6	1	1	-	1
9b Other elementary occupations	371	4	12	66	49	5	27	18	127	42	14	2	5
Occupation not stated or inadequately described	45	1	-	3	-	-	2	2	14	4	1	-	18
Working outside district of usual residence	2,360	4	16	69	106	20	89	144	1,491	261	77	36	47

78. Residents aged 16 and over, employees and self-employed

Standard Occupational Classification Sub-major Groups	TOTAL PERSONS	Hours worked weekly											Not stated
		3 and under	4 - 7	8 - 15	16 - 21	22 - 23	24 - 30	31 - 35	36 - 40	41 - 50	51 - 60	61 and over	
a	b	c	d	e	f	g	h	i	j	k	l	m	n
New Forest													
ALL OCCUPATIONS	6,894	26	147	530	469	58	381	537	3,167	901	290	172	216
1a Corporate managers and administrators	735	1	6	13	9	2	18	79	368	170	41	15	13
1b Managers/proprietors in agriculture and services	502	-	3	14	16	1	16	22	149	101	83	73	24
2a Science and engineering professionals	192	-	-	2	7	1	2	10	141	20	5	1	3
2b Health professionals	53	-	-	4	2	-	6	2	14	9	6	9	1
2c Teaching professionals	199	6	4	20	13	4	20	20	45	41	14	4	8
2d Other professional occupations	121	-	-	2	4	1	8	12	47	28	8	8	3
3a Science and engineering associate professionals	222	-	2	2	1	1	5	15	169	19	4	-	4
3b Health associate professionals	152	1	2	17	18	6	26	10	59	5	1	4	3
3c Other associate professional occupations	292	-	4	8	13	-	14	37	147	32	14	10	13
4a Clerical occupations	715	1	16	53	80	9	32	142	331	26	3	1	21
4b Secretarial occupations	382	4	17	33	63	7	32	48	154	15	2	-	7
5a Skilled construction trades	199	-	1	-	2	-	6	2	115	51	9	4	9
5b Skilled engineering trades	282	1	-	2	-	1	-	10	219	37	8	2	3
5c Other skilled trades	452	1	-	13	10	1	14	14	300	72	13	5	9
6a Protective service occupations	124	-	-	2	1	-	1	3	52	30	10	6	19
6b Personal service occupations	556	5	44	104	77	12	89	26	117	43	9	9	21
7a Buyers, brokers and sales representatives	139	-	-	4	7	-	4	19	62	31	9	1	2
7b Other sales occupations	415	-	19	129	69	8	33	20	112	13	5	2	5
8a Industrial plant and machine operators, assemblers	361	1	1	4	9	-	9	13	251	54	10	4	5
8b Drivers and mobile machinery operators	219	-	2	4	7	-	4	5	118	42	23	9	5
9a Other occupations in agriculture, forestry and fishing	73	-	-	3	2	1	2	3	37	18	3	3	1
9b Other elementary occupations	457	6	25	97	59	3	36	24	148	41	6	1	11
Occupation not stated or inadequately described	52	-	1	-	-	-	4	1	12	3	4	1	26
Working outside district of usual residence	2,495	2	22	100	107	11	99	288	1,297	376	98	34	61

Table 78 Occupation and hours worked (10% sample) – continued

(10% sample)

78. Residents aged 16 and over, employees and self-employed

Portsmouth

Standard Occupational Classification Sub-major Groups	TOTAL PERSONS	Hours worked weekly											
		3 and under	4 - 7	8 - 15	16 - 21	22 - 23	24 - 30	31 - 35	36 - 40	41 - 50	51 - 60	61 and over	Not stated
a	b	c	d	e	f	g	h	i	j	k	l	m	n
ALL OCCUPATIONS	7,563	18	116	447	477	90	382	449	4,030	785	267	187	315
1a Corporate managers and administrators	603	1	1	2	8	3	15	59	363	100	31	10	10
1b Managers/proprietors in agriculture and services	398	1	1	10	5	-	12	19	146	68	48	59	29
2a Science and engineering professionals	228	-	-	1	3	-	1	4	190	22	6	-	1
2b Health professionals	27	-	-	1	1	-	-	2	5	6	1	10	1
2c Teaching professionals	192	-	4	16	8	1	27	37	45	25	9	2	18
2d Other professional occupations	99	-	-	1	6	-	2	11	59	10	3	3	4
3a Science and engineering associate professionals	240	-	-	1	4	-	4	13	199	16	-	-	3
3b Health associate professionals	191	-	-	8	19	3	27	12	115	2	-	2	3
3c Other associate professional occupations	258	2	3	8	11	-	6	23	154	20	12	4	15
4a Clerical occupations	858	1	8	38	76	15	37	93	529	42	4	1	14
4b Secretarial occupations	276	1	6	20	31	6	21	43	133	13	-	1	1
5a Skilled construction trades	228	-	-	1	1	-	3	10	143	47	10	2	12
5b Skilled engineering trades	362	-	-	2	1	-	4	8	294	31	11	2	9
5c Other skilled trades	495	-	-	4	10	2	22	11	349	61	19	3	14
6a Protective service occupations	450	-	-	7	1	3	5	20	192	76	37	39	70
6b Personal service occupations	608	4	44	74	74	21	79	36	190	45	11	14	16
7a Buyers, brokers and sales representatives	109	-	1	1	4	2	2	8	54	19	10	2	6
7b Other sales occupations	490	2	28	109	96	17	43	10	143	22	6	3	11
8a Industrial plant and machine operators, assemblers	413	-	-	9	13	2	7	4	320	28	16	-	14
8b Drivers and mobile machinery operators	279	-	-	4	9	-	9	1	150	55	18	23	10
9a Other occupations in agriculture, forestry and fishing	9	-	-	2	-	-	-	-	4	2	-	1	-
9b Other elementary occupations	689	6	20	128	94	15	55	24	236	71	12	4	24
Occupation not stated or inadequately described	61	-	-	1	2	-	1	1	17	4	3	2	30
Working outside district of usual residence	1,591	-	8	33	36	8	45	97	1,062	181	64	22	35

78. Residents aged 16 and over, employees and self-employed (10% sample)

Rushmoor

Standard Occupational Classification Sub-major Groups	TOTAL PERSONS	Hours worked weekly											
		3 and under	4 - 7	8 - 15	16 - 21	22 - 23	24 - 30	31 - 35	36 - 40	41 - 50	51 - 60	61 and over	Not stated
a	b	c	d	e	f	g	h	i	j	k	l	m	n
ALL OCCUPATIONS	4,333	15	53	231	230	45	202	320	2,195	614	141	93	194
1a Corporate managers and administrators	494	-	-	5	6	1	10	50	272	108	24	10	8
1b Managers/proprietors in agriculture and services	165	-	-	2	4	1	11	7	60	39	16	21	4
2a Science and engineering professionals	180	-	-	-	-	1	1	6	150	17	-	1	4
2b Health professionals	9	-	-	-	-	-	-	1	6	1	1	-	-
2c Teaching professionals	80	2	4	10	6	1	13	7	17	12	6	-	2
2d Other professional occupations	51	-	-	1	1	-	1	10	29	5	2	2	-
3a Science and engineering associate professionals	149	-	-	-	2	-	2	20	108	11	1	-	5
3b Health associate professionals	74	1	1	10	13	-	11	4	28	2	1	1	2
3c Other associate professional occupations	163	-	-	4	11	-	7	20	91	16	4	3	7
4a Clerical occupations	549	1	2	23	48	2	33	114	290	26	4	-	6
4b Secretarial occupations	205	2	-	12	24	5	18	31	101	7	-	-	5
5a Skilled construction trades	105	-	-	1	-	-	-	5	54	31	10	-	4
5b Skilled engineering trades	197	-	-	1	1	-	-	1	148	32	6	4	4
5c Other skilled trades	219	-	1	3	3	-	5	4	131	56	7	1	8
6a Protective service occupations	468	6	1	3	-	-	1	3	181	118	27	44	84
6b Personal service occupations	282	-	16	36	31	7	38	14	105	21	4	-	10
7a Buyers, brokers and sales representatives	87	1	1	6	3	-	1	6	40	19	5	2	3
7b Other sales occupations	195	-	6	43	34	15	16	3	61	13	1	-	3
8a Industrial plant and machine operators, assemblers	191	-	-	3	3	6	6	7	140	12	5	3	6
8b Drivers and mobile machinery operators	117	-	-	2	1	-	2	2	72	27	5	1	5
9a Other occupations in agriculture, forestry and fishing	4	-	-	-	-	-	1	-	1	-	2	-	-
9b Other elementary occupations	326	2	21	66	38	6	25	5	107	40	8	-	8
Occupation not stated or inadequately described	23	-	-	-	1	-	-	-	3	1	2	-	16
Working outside district of usual residence	1,744	5	15	62	55	16	64	160	1,020	239	59	21	28

Table 78 Occupation and hours worked (10% sample) – continued

County, districts

(10% sample)

78. Residents aged 16 and over, employees and self-employed

Southampton

Standard Occupational Classification Sub-major Groups	TOTAL PERSONS	Hours worked weekly											
		3 and under	4 - 7	8 - 15	16 - 21	22 - 23	24 - 30	31 - 35	36 - 40	41 - 50	51 - 60	61 and over	Not stated
a	b	c	d	e	f	g	h	i	j	k	l	m	n
ALL OCCUPATIONS	8,320	19	125	555	559	66	458	657	4,299	864	273	174	271
1a Corporate managers and administrators	611	1	2	12	12	-	16	66	328	126	30	10	8
1b Managers/proprietors in agriculture and services	413	-	2	9	9	1	16	19	153	80	46	66	12
2a Science and engineering professionals	196	-	-	3	-	1	-	16	147	19	4	1	5
2b Health professionals	49	-	-	1	1	1	1	4	13	6	5	14	3
2c Teaching professionals	269	1	1	18	13	-	34	39	83	49	18	2	11
2d Other professional occupations	161	-	1	6	8	-	2	19	94	16	6	4	5
3a Science and engineering associate professionals	301	-	1	4	2	1	6	31	228	17	3	-	8
3b Health associate professionals	220	1	1	15	18	7	22	16	129	5	-	1	5
3c Other associate professional occupations	283	1	5	9	17	3	19	36	138	27	7	8	13
4a Clerical occupations	1,001	2	7	38	93	8	47	169	577	30	8	3	19
4b Secretarial occupations	374	-	4	22	47	9	37	62	158	28	1	-	6
5a Skilled construction trades	271	-	-	3	-	-	2	8	178	45	13	5	17
5b Skilled engineering trades	402	-	-	3	-	-	3	8	328	35	11	3	11
5c Other skilled trades	571	1	2	9	13	1	12	17	409	60	24	9	14
6a Protective service occupations	126	-	-	10	3	3	2	4	61	16	7	7	13
6b Personal service occupations	645	5	49	81	93	13	87	24	201	48	11	9	24
7a Buyers, brokers and sales representatives	149	-	-	3	2	-	1	20	82	29	7	1	4
7b Other sales occupations	563	1	25	148	112	8	47	23	154	21	9	3	12
8a Industrial plant and machine operators, assemblers	447	-	1	5	12	1	13	26	328	37	10	2	12
8b Drivers and mobile machinery operators	385	1	-	5	7	1	10	8	219	58	37	20	19
9a Other occupations in agriculture, forestry and fishing	10	-	-	1	-	-	-	-	5	-	1	-	1
9b Other elementary occupations	807	5	24	147	96	8	77	39	265	106	13	4	23
Occupation not stated or inadequately described	66	-	-	3	1	-	2	3	21	6	2	2	26
Working outside district of usual residence	2,303	3	11	100	68	9	89	157	1,426	246	84	49	61

78. Residents aged 16 and over, employees and self-employed — (10% sample)

Test Valley

Standard Occupational Classification Sub-major Groups	TOTAL PERSONS	Hours worked weekly											
		3 and under	4 - 7	8 - 15	16 - 21	22 - 23	24 - 30	31 - 35	36 - 40	41 - 50	51 - 60	61 and over	Not stated
a	b	c	d	e	f	g	h	i	j	k	l	m	n
ALL OCCUPATIONS	5,030	15	107	310	260	51	281	457	2,389	673	214	123	150
1a Corporate managers and administrators	631	-	2	7	7	1	9	86	338	126	36	10	9
1b Managers/proprietors in agriculture and services	337	1	2	8	11	-	12	12	109	75	45	44	18
2a Science and engineering professionals	128	-	-	-	1	2	3	4	95	18	2	-	3
2b Health professionals	38	-	1	1	1	-	3	1	9	6	6	10	-
2c Teaching professionals	171	4	7	20	5	3	15	35	41	29	6	1	5
2d Other professional occupations	119	-	-	1	3	-	3	13	57	24	10	6	2
3a Science and engineering associate professionals	171	-	-	-	5	2	10	24	110	14	2	-	4
3b Health associate professionals	88	-	1	12	17	1	13	6	28	1	3	1	5
3c Other associate professional occupations	170	2	6	5	4	1	13	18	78	19	10	7	7
4a Clerical occupations	594	1	14	37	39	12	46	122	281	30	3	-	9
4b Secretarial occupations	227	-	4	18	29	4	17	51	87	9	-	-	8
5a Skilled construction trades	122	-	-	-	-	-	2	4	70	31	6	4	5
5b Skilled engineering trades	192	-	-	-	1	-	1	5	146	27	9	-	3
5c Other skilled trades	314	-	1	8	4	2	8	4	199	64	12	4	8
6a Protective service occupations	206	-	-	5	-	-	2	4	120	39	12	6	18
6b Personal service occupations	309	2	29	41	40	6	44	25	86	16	4	8	8
7a Buyers, brokers and sales representatives	108	1	1	2	2	2	1	13	52	19	8	1	1
7b Other sales occupations	205	2	11	53	37	7	20	8	47	6	4	3	7
8a Industrial plant and machine operators, assemblers	296	-	2	11	8	1	19	7	208	28	6	3	3
8b Drivers and mobile machinery operators	156	1	1	4	-	1	3	-	84	33	17	8	4
9a Other occupations in agriculture, forestry and fishing	65	-	1	1	2	-	2	3	30	18	5	2	1
9b Other elementary occupations	344	1	23	74	37	6	33	11	103	38	7	3	8
Occupation not stated or inadequately described	39	-	1	2	2	-	2	1	11	3	1	2	14
Working outside district of usual residence	1,711	4	18	63	72	12	73	166	938	233	76	28	28

113

Table 78 Occupation and hours worked (10% sample) – continued

78. Residents aged 16 and over, employees and self-employed

(10% sample)

Winchester

Standard Occupational Classification Sub-major Groups	TOTAL PERSONS	Hours worked weekly											Not stated
		3 and under	4 - 7	8 - 15	16 - 21	22 - 23	24 - 30	31 - 35	36 - 40	41 - 50	51 - 60	61 and over	
a	b	c	d	e	f	g	h	i	j	k	l	m	n
ALL OCCUPATIONS	4,521	26	97	277	271	36	279	282	2,104	686	194	128	141
1a Corporate managers and administrators	637	1	3	10	9	4	13	45	341	133	45	16	17
1b Managers/proprietors in agriculture and services	358	2	5	9	11	1	18	10	108	87	39	51	17
2a Science and engineering professionals	183	-	1	2	2	-	1	7	129	28	8	2	3
2b Health professionals	40	-	1	1	3	-	4	3	10	3	10	5	-
2c Teaching professionals	224	9	19	19	18	1	13	27	46	46	15	3	8
2d Other professional occupations	168	-	1	5	6	1	7	13	91	31	6	4	3
3a Science and engineering associate professionals	142	-	1	3	5	2	3	13	101	9	4	-	1
3b Health associate professionals	99	-	2	14	10	2	9	6	51	2	-	2	1
3c Other associate professional occupations	195	-	1	5	10	1	13	15	94	35	9	6	6
4a Clerical occupations	441	3	10	24	40	5	30	55	243	24	1	3	3
4b Secretarial occupations	203	-	3	19	26	4	24	22	95	5	-	1	4
5a Skilled construction trades	109	1	-	-	1	-	1	4	63	29	2	1	7
5b Skilled engineering trades	97	-	-	-	-	-	2	2	66	18	3	2	4
5c Other skilled trades	246	-	1	8	8	1	6	8	139	47	11	4	13
6a Protective service occupations	164	-	-	3	-	1	2	8	74	43	12	10	11
6b Personal service occupations	325	3	20	50	40	3	62	20	86	29	4	2	6
7a Buyers, brokers and sales representatives	60	-	-	1	2	-	3	6	28	14	3	-	3
7b Other sales occupations	194	2	10	44	26	4	16	7	68	8	1	-	8
8a Industrial plant and machine operators, assemblers	121	-	1	3	6	1	2	1	81	22	2	1	1
8b Drivers and mobile machinery operators	116	-	1	3	3	-	2	1	62	20	10	10	4
9a Other occupations in agriculture, forestry and fishing	76	-	-	3	1	-	5	-	41	17	4	3	1
9b Other elementary occupations	291	5	17	50	44	5	42	7	76	31	5	1	8
Occupation not stated or inadequately described	32	-	-	1	-	-	1	2	11	5	-	1	11
Working outside district of usual residence	1,556	3	13	39	48	11	49	131	845	280	83	25	29

Table 79 Industry and employment status (10% sample)

79. Residents aged 16 and over, employees and self-employed

(10% sample)

HAMPSHIRE

Employment status	TOTAL PERSONS	Agriculture	Forestry and fishing	Energy and water	Mining	Industry Manufacturing metal etc	Other manufacturing	Construction	Distribution and catering	Transport	Banking and finance etc	Other services	Not stated, inadequately described or workplace outside UK
a	b	c	d	e	f	g	h	i	j	k	l	m	n
Males	**40,790**	**796**	**73**	**781**	**808**	**6,376**	**2,303**	**5,146**	**6,741**	**3,127**	**4,572**	**9,737**	**330**
Self-employed	**6,744**	**325**	**33**	**1**	**19**	**252**	**273**	**2,556**	**1,274**	**391**	**903**	**609**	**108**
With employees	1,911	94	5	-	8	84	83	432	546	55	343	228	33
Without employees	4,833	231	28	1	11	168	190	2,124	728	336	560	381	75
Employees	**32,995**	**467**	**40**	**768**	**773**	**6,027**	**2,001**	**2,527**	**5,344**	**2,654**	**3,614**	**8,631**	**149**
Working 31 or more hours per week	31,494	422	40	764	764	5,959	1,946	2,483	4,768	2,599	3,511	8,097	141
Working 30 or fewer hours per week	1,501	45	-	4	9	68	55	44	576	55	103	534	8
Economically active students (included above)	*373*	*10*	*-*	*-*	*1*	*4*	*5*	*5*	*261*	*7*	*12*	*66*	*2*
Females	**31,083**	**245**	**8**	**207**	**473**	**2,029**	**1,346**	**541**	**7,720**	**1,001**	**4,520**	**12,811**	**182**
Self-employed	**1,913**	**64**	**1**	**-**	**13**	**15**	**89**	**57**	**501**	**49**	**336**	**744**	**44**
With employees	618	24	1	-	3	9	16	24	257	17	59	197	11
Without employees	1,295	40	-	-	10	6	73	33	244	32	277	547	33
Employees	**28,544**	**174**	**7**	**202**	**452**	**1,985**	**1,237**	**480**	**7,102**	**927**	**4,104**	**11,798**	**76**
Working 31 or more hours per week	16,278	76	3	166	360	1,669	856	283	3,003	703	3,087	6,032	40
Working 30 or fewer hours per week	12,266	98	4	36	92	316	381	197	4,099	224	1,017	5,766	36
Economically active students (included above)	*474*	*1*	*-*	*1*	*-*	*5*	*4*	*2*	*329*	*3*	*15*	*112*	*2*

Table 79 Industry and employment status (10% sample) – **continued**

79. Residents aged 16 and over, employees and self-employed

(10% sample)

Basingstoke & Deane

Employment status	TOTAL PERSONS	Industry												Not stated, inadequately described or workplace outside UK
		Agriculture	Forestry and fishing	Energy and water	Mining	Manufacturing metal etc	Other manufacturing	Construction	Distribution and catering	Transport	Banking and finance etc	Other services		
a	b	c	d	e	f	g	h	i	j	k	l	m	n	
Males	4,237	109	3	40	106	617	273	519	801	277	629	838	25
Self-employed	**651**	**37**	**2**	**1**	**1**	**25**	**17**	**266**	**92**	**28**	**118**	**55**	**9**
With employees	179	9	-	-	-	9	4	52	37	2	41	23	2
Without employees	472	28	2	1	1	16	13	214	55	26	77	32	7
Employees	**3,516**	**72**	**1**	**37**	**102**	**588**	**255**	**247**	**696**	**239**	**504**	**765**	**10**
Working 31 or more hours per week	3,378	63	1	37	102	580	252	245	635	236	490	727	10
Working 30 or fewer hours per week	138	9	-	-	-	8	3	2	61	3	14	38	-
Economically active students (included above)	*35*	*2*	*-*	*-*	*-*	*1*	*-*	*-*	*27*	*-*	*1*	*4*	*-*
Females	3,235	19	1	28	77	219	144	58	783	71	560	1,256	19
Self-employed	**171**	**5**	**-**	**-**	**2**	**2**	**7**	**7**	**32**	**3**	**46**	**63**	**4**
With employees	44	1	-	-	-	1	2	5	13	2	8	11	1
Without employees	127	4	-	-	2	1	5	2	19	1	38	52	3
Employees	**3,016**	**14**	**1**	**28**	**75**	**216**	**137**	**51**	**743**	**66**	**504**	**1,171**	**10**
Working 31 or more hours per week	1,861	4	1	26	67	181	105	30	374	45	397	626	5
Working 30 or fewer hours per week	1,155	10	-	2	8	35	32	21	369	21	107	545	5
Economically active students (included above)	*45*	*-*	*-*	*-*	*-*	*2*	*1*	*-*	*29*	*-*	*-*	*13*	*-*

79. Residents aged 16 and over, employees and self-employed

(10% sample)

East Hampshire

Employment status	TOTAL PERSONS	Agriculture	Forestry and fishing	Energy and water	Mining	Industry Manufacturing metal etc	Other manufacturing	Construction	Distribution and catering	Transport	Banking and finance etc	Other services	Not stated, inadequately described or workplace outside UK
a	b	c	d	e	f	g	h	i	j	k	l	m	n
Males	**2,821**	**121**	**15**	**49**	**53**	**341**	**191**	**365**	**479**	**160**	**395**	**635**	**17**
Self-employed	**606**	**53**	**5**	**-**	**-**	**17**	**36**	**209**	**117**	**25**	**84**	**57**	**3**
With employees	176	17	-	-	-	4	13	41	50	4	28	18	1
Without employees	430	36	5	-	-	13	23	168	67	21	56	39	2
Employees	**2,157**	**66**	**10**	**45**	**52**	**317**	**154**	**154**	**355**	**131**	**309**	**552**	**12**
Working 31 or more hours per week	2,058	61	10	44	52	313	148	153	324	126	299	517	11
Working 30 or fewer hours per week	99	5	-	1	-	4	6	1	31	5	10	35	1
Economically active students (included above)	*26*	*1*	*-*	*-*	*-*	*-*	*-*	*-*	*13*	*-*	*-*	*12*	*-*
Females	**2,135**	**39**	**1**	**9**	**34**	**119**	**96**	**40**	**470**	**77**	**323**	**914**	**13**
Self-employed	**195**	**14**	**-**	**-**	**-**	**2**	**10**	**5**	**55**	**4**	**34**	**67**	**4**
With employees	57	4	-	-	-	1	3	1	30	-	4	12	2
Without employees	138	10	-	-	-	1	7	4	25	4	30	55	2
Employees	**1,894**	**24**	**1**	**9**	**33**	**117**	**86**	**35**	**407**	**69**	**281**	**826**	**6**
Working 31 or more hours per week	1,068	14	-	8	31	94	57	16	182	54	214	397	1
Working 30 or fewer hours per week	826	10	1	1	2	23	29	19	225	15	67	429	5
Economically active students (included above)	*23*	*1*	*-*	*-*	*-*	*-*	*-*	*-*	*16*	*-*	*-*	*6*	*-*

Table 79 Industry and employment status (10% sample) – **continued**

79. Residents aged 16 and over, employees and self-employed

County, districts

(10% sample)

Eastleigh

Employment status	TOTAL PERSONS	Agriculture	Forestry and fishing	Energy and water	Mining	Manufacturing metal etc	Other manufacturing	Construction	Distribution and catering	Transport	Banking and finance etc	Other services	Not stated, inadequately described or workplace outside UK
a	b	c	d	e	f	g	h	i	j	k	l	m	n
Males	**2,945**	39	2	59	46	610	172	397	502	271	335	492	20
Self-employed	**449**	**16**	**1**	**-**	**2**	**20**	**26**	**179**	**86**	**27**	**51**	**33**	**8**
With employees	126	4	-	-	2	7	7	34	34	3	18	13	4
Without employees	323	12	1	-	-	13	19	145	52	24	33	20	4
Employees	**2,446**	**23**	**1**	**58**	**44**	**581**	**143**	**214**	**408**	**240**	**281**	**445**	**8**
Working 31 or more hours per week	2,324	20	1	58	42	574	138	212	357	234	276	404	8
Working 30 or fewer hours per week	122	3	-	-	2	7	5	2	51	6	5	41	-
Economically active students (included above)	*31*	-	-	-	-	*1*	-	-	*27*	-	-	*3*	-
Females	**2,260**	14	-	27	20	130	87	61	593	92	357	870	9
Self-employed	**114**	**2**	**-**	**-**	**1**	**-**	**6**	**7**	**24**	**3**	**20**	**48**	**3**
With employees	32	-	-	-	-	-	1	2	14	2	2	11	-
Without employees	82	2	-	-	1	-	5	5	10	1	18	37	3
Employees	**2,106**	**12**	**-**	**27**	**19**	**130**	**77**	**54**	**566**	**87**	**328**	**804**	**2**
Working 31 or more hours per week	1,169	5	-	21	17	97	50	42	229	60	245	402	1
Working 30 or fewer hours per week	937	7	-	6	2	33	27	12	337	27	83	402	1
Economically active students (included above)	*32*	-	-	*1*	-	*1*	-	-	*23*	-	*2*	*5*	-

Table 79 Industry and employment status (10% sample) – continued

(10% sample)

79. Residents aged 16 and over, employees and self-employed

Fareham

Employment status	TOTAL PERSONS	Agriculture	Forestry and fishing	Energy and water	Mining	Manufacturing metal etc	Other manufacturing	Construction	Distribution and catering	Transport	Banking and finance etc	Other services	Not stated, inadequately described or workplace outside UK
a	b	c	d	e	f	g	h	i	j	k	l	m	n
Males	**2,698**	**33**	**-**	**41**	**55**	**523**	**130**	**320**	**357**	**165**	**263**	**783**	**28**
Self-employed	**416**	**16**	**-**	**-**	**1**	**22**	**24**	**166**	**70**	**16**	**55**	**37**	**9**
With employees	119	1	-	-	-	9	4	30	30	1	19	20	5
Without employees	297	15	-	-	1	13	20	136	40	15	36	17	4
Employees	**2,223**	**16**	**-**	**40**	**54**	**493**	**104**	**153**	**282**	**145**	**202**	**721**	**13**
Working 31 or more hours per week	2,129	12	-	40	53	488	99	152	244	144	193	692	12
Working 30 or fewer hours per week	94	4	-	-	1	5	5	1	38	1	9	29	1
Economically active students (included above)	*25*	*3*	*-*	*-*	*-*	*-*	*-*	*-*	*18*	*1*	*-*	*3*	*-*
Females	**2,092**	**12**	**-**	**10**	**37**	**151**	**79**	**45**	**451**	**66**	**299**	**934**	**8**
Self-employed	**132**	**2**	**-**	**-**	**-**	**1**	**6**	**3**	**31**	**6**	**16**	**65**	**2**
With employees	45	-	-	-	-	1	2	1	12	2	2	25	-
Without employees	87	2	-	-	-	-	4	2	19	4	14	40	2
Employees	**1,922**	**10**	**-**	**10**	**36**	**147**	**70**	**42**	**415**	**60**	**280**	**850**	**2**
Working 31 or more hours per week	1,097	4	-	9	30	123	44	30	160	47	214	434	2
Working 30 or fewer hours per week	825	6	-	1	6	24	26	12	255	13	66	416	-
Economically active students (included above)	*34*	*-*	*-*	*-*	*-*	*1*	*1*	*-*	*18*	*-*	*3*	*11*	*-*

Industry

Table 79 Industry and employment status (10% sample) – **continued**

79. Residents aged 16 and over, employees and self-employed

(10% sample)

Gosport

Employment status	TOTAL PERSONS	Agriculture	Forestry and fishing	Energy and water	Mining	Manufacturing metal etc	Other manufacturing	Construction	Distribution and catering	Transport	Banking and finance etc	Other services	Not stated, inadequately described or workplace outside UK
a	b	c	d	e	f	g	h	i	j	k	l	m	n
Males	**1,931**	**17**	**1**	**17**	**49**	**318**	**87**	**186**	**240**	**90**	**110**	**801**	**15**
Self-employed	**204**	**3**	**1**	**-**	**-**	**10**	**6**	**88**	**42**	**10**	**16**	**23**	**5**
With employees	55	-	-	-	-	2	3	7	21	1	11	10	-
Without employees	149	3	1	-	-	8	3	81	21	9	5	13	5
Employees	**1,638**	**14**	**-**	**17**	**47**	**301**	**80**	**96**	**192**	**80**	**94**	**712**	**5**
Working 31 or more hours per week	1,577	13	-	17	47	297	79	95	176	78	91	680	4
Working 30 or fewer hours per week	61	1	-	-	-	4	1	1	16	2	3	32	1
Economically active students (included above)	*11*	*1*	*-*	*-*	*-*	*-*	*-*	*-*	*9*	*-*	*1*	*1*	*-*
Females	**1,459**	**2**	**-**	**4**	**77**	**100**	**49**	**15**	**366**	**27**	**150**	**660**	**9**
Self-employed	**56**	**-**	**-**	**-**	**-**	**-**	**-**	**2**	**16**	**3**	**5**	**28**	**2**
With employees	15	-	-	-	-	-	-	1	5	2	1	6	-
Without employees	41	-	-	-	-	-	-	1	11	1	4	22	2
Employees	**1,371**	**2**	**-**	**4**	**76**	**98**	**49**	**13**	**347**	**23**	**141**	**614**	**4**
Working 31 or more hours per week	746	-	-	4	58	93	35	6	112	15	107	314	2
Working 30 or fewer hours per week	625	2	-	-	18	5	14	7	235	8	34	300	2
Economically active students (included above)	*25*	*-*	*-*	*-*	*-*	*-*	*-*	*-*	*19*	*-*	*-*	*5*	*1*

Industry

Table 79 Industry and employment status (10% sample) – **continued**

79. Residents aged 16 and over, employees and self-employed

(10% sample)

Hart

Employment status	TOTAL PERSONS	Agriculture	Forestry and fishing	Energy and water	Mining	Manufacturing metal etc	Other manufacturing	Construction	Distribution and catering	Transport	Banking and finance etc	Other services	Not stated, inadequately described or workplace outside UK
a	b	c	d	e	f	g	h	i	j	k	l	m	n
Males	**2,485**	48	4	37	50	294	133	232	389	216	438	627	17
Self-employed	**400**	**21**	**3**	**-**	**2**	**10**	**25**	**114**	**73**	**23**	**97**	**26**	**6**
With employees	122	7	-	-	1	2	4	27	32	1	32	14	2
Without employees	278	14	3	-	1	8	21	87	41	22	65	12	4
Employees	**2,049**	**27**	**1**	**37**	**48**	**281**	**107**	**114**	**313**	**185**	**339**	**586**	**11**
Working 31 or more hours per week	1,959	27	1	37	47	278	103	110	276	179	325	566	10
Working 30 or fewer hours per week	90	-	-	-	1	3	4	4	37	6	14	20	1
Economically active students (included above)	*35*	*-*	*-*	*-*	*1*	*1*	*1*	*-*	*21*	*-*	*3*	*8*	*-*
Females	**1,737**	16	-	9	26	104	48	32	437	60	359	633	13
Self-employed	**130**	**4**	**-**	**-**	**1**	**-**	**8**	**5**	**20**	**5**	**39**	**42**	**6**
With employees	30	2	-	-	-	-	-	1	12	1	5	7	2
Without employees	100	2	-	-	1	-	8	4	8	4	34	35	4
Employees	**1,574**	**12**	**-**	**9**	**24**	**104**	**39**	**26**	**410**	**54**	**313**	**578**	**5**
Working 31 or more hours per week	899	8	-	7	21	81	27	11	198	45	208	291	2
Working 30 or fewer hours per week	675	4	-	2	3	23	12	15	212	9	105	287	3
Economically active students (included above)	*32*	*-*	*-*	*-*	*-*	*-*	*1*	*1*	*19*	*-*	*2*	*9*	*-*

Industry

Table 79 Industry and employment status (10% sample) – **continued**

County, districts

79. Residents aged 16 and over, employees and self-employed

(10% sample)

County, districts — Havant

Employment status	TOTAL PERSONS	Agriculture	Forestry and fishing	Energy and water	Mining	Manufacturing metal etc	Other manufacturing	Construction	Distribution and catering	Transport	Banking and finance etc	Other services	Not stated, inadequately described or workplace outside UK
a	b	c	d	e	f	g	h	i	j	k	l	m	n
Males	2,918	22	6	48	55	677	184	439	442	179	240	609	17
Self-employed	513	10	4	-	2	27	19	229	91	34	48	43	6
With employees	138	5	1	-	1	12	6	39	35	6	19	12	2
Without employees	375	5	3	-	1	15	13	190	56	28	29	31	4
Employees	2,337	12	2	48	52	644	162	205	339	139	188	539	7
Working 31 or more hours per week	2,241	11	2	48	52	640	158	200	302	136	180	505	7
Working 30 or fewer hours per week	96	1	-	-	-	4	4	5	37	3	8	34	-
Economically active students (included above)	*22*	*-*	*-*	*-*	*-*	*-*	*-*	*1*	*13*	*1*	*3*	*4*	*-*
Females	2,259	9	-	23	52	317	130	40	550	59	246	816	17
Self-employed	119	1	-	-	1	3	12	7	32	2	21	36	4
With employees	44	-	-	-	1	2	3	4	18	-	5	10	1
Without employees	75	1	-	-	-	1	9	3	14	2	16	26	3
Employees	2,092	8	-	22	49	308	116	32	509	55	217	768	8
Working 31 or more hours per week	1,143	3	-	17	34	274	77	19	181	39	133	361	5
Working 30 or fewer hours per week	949	5	-	5	15	34	39	13	328	16	84	407	3
Economically active students (included above)	*38*	*-*	*-*	*-*	*-*	*-*	*-*	*-*	*31*	*1*	*-*	*6*	*-*

Industry

Table 79 Industry and employment status (10% sample) – continued

79. Residents aged 16 and over, employees and self-employed

Employment status	TOTAL PERSONS	Industry											Not stated, inadequately described or workplace outside UK
		Agriculture	Forestry and fishing	Energy and water	Mining	Manufacturing metal etc	Other manufacturing	Construction	Distribution and catering	Transport	Banking and finance etc	Other services	
a	b	c	d	e	f	g	h	i	j	k	l	m	n
New Forest													
Males	3,847	111	23	199	161	515	225	506	694	323	456	586	48
Self-employed	**787**	**56**	**8**	**-**	**3**	**33**	**22**	**259**	**167**	**41**	**102**	**81**	**15**
With employees	245	11	1	-	1	11	7	47	78	12	42	33	2
Without employees	542	45	7	-	2	22	15	212	89	29	60	48	13
Employees	**2,967**	**55**	**15**	**197**	**155**	**476**	**199**	**244**	**512**	**276**	**346**	**471**	**21**
Working 31 or more hours per week	2,806	48	15	196	155	472	193	239	446	270	336	416	20
Working 30 or fewer hours per week	161	7	-	1	-	4	6	5	66	6	10	55	1
Economically active students (included above)	*46*	*1*	*-*	*-*	*-*	*-*	*-*	*2*	*35*	*2*	*2*	*4*	*-*
Females	3,047	36	4	24	19	156	120	66	856	123	463	1,158	22
Self-employed	**248**	**13**	**-**	**-**	**5**	**-**	**10**	**4**	**83**	**2**	**49**	**78**	**4**
With employees	94	7	-	-	1	-	1	1	46	-	15	22	1
Without employees	154	6	-	-	4	-	9	3	37	2	34	56	3
Employees	**2,736**	**22**	**4**	**23**	**14**	**154**	**107**	**62**	**754**	**119**	**408**	**1,056**	**13**
Working 31 or more hours per week	1,448	8	1	18	9	125	68	34	314	90	310	466	5
Working 30 or fewer hours per week	1,288	14	3	5	5	29	39	28	440	29	98	590	8
Economically active students (included above)	*44*	*-*	*-*	*-*	*-*	*-*	*1*	*-*	*34*	*-*	*-*	*9*	*-*

Table 79 Industry and employment status (10% sample) – continued

79. Residents aged 16 and over, employees and self-employed

Portsmouth

Employment status	TOTAL PERSONS	Agriculture	Forestry and fishing	Energy and water	Mining	Manufacturing metal etc	Other manufacturing	Construction	Distribution and catering	Transport	Banking and finance etc	Other services	Not stated, inadequately described or workplace outside UK
a	b	c	d	e	f	g	h	i	j	k	l	m	n
Males	**4,288**	**13**	**3**	**70**	**45**	**638**	**228**	**556**	**702**	**377**	**306**	**1,305**	**45**
Self-employed	**649**	**4**	**2**	**-**	**5**	**11**	**21**	**273**	**152**	**64**	**50**	**56**	**11**
With employees	160	1	-	-	2	6	6	44	65	10	13	13	-
Without employees	489	3	2	-	3	5	15	229	87	54	37	43	11
Employees	**3,467**	**9**	**1**	**69**	**39**	**612**	**202**	**274**	**535**	**303**	**249**	**1,152**	**22**
Working 31 or more hours per week	3,311	8	1	69	37	606	196	270	476	296	244	1,087	21
Working 30 or fewer hours per week	156	1	-	-	2	6	6	4	59	7	5	65	1
Economically active students (included above)	*32*	*-*	*-*	*-*	*-*	*-*	*-*	*-*	*22*	*-*	*-*	*10*	*-*
Females	**3,275**	**2**	**-**	**25**	**32**	**227**	**200**	**38**	**852**	**115**	**370**	**1,394**	**20**
Self-employed	**179**	**-**	**-**	**-**	**2**	**-**	**6**	**5**	**58**	**8**	**19**	**78**	**3**
With employees	66	-	-	-	1	-	1	2	32	4	1	25	-
Without employees	113	-	-	-	1	-	5	3	26	4	18	53	3
Employees	**3,028**	**1**	**-**	**24**	**29**	**225**	**190**	**32**	**778**	**106**	**349**	**1,288**	**6**
Working 31 or more hours per week	1,762	-	-	20	27	200	140	21	300	84	266	701	3
Working 30 or fewer hours per week	1,266	1	-	4	2	25	50	11	478	22	83	587	3
Economically active students (included above)	*53*	*-*	*-*	*-*	*-*	*-*	*-*	*-*	*37*	*-*	*-*	*16*	*-*

Industry

Table 79 Industry and employment status (10% sample) – **continued**

79. Residents aged 16 and over, employees and self-employed

(10% sample)

Rushmoor

Employment status	TOTAL PERSONS	Agriculture	Forestry and fishing	Energy and water	Mining	Manufacturing metal etc	Other manufacturing	Construction	Distribution and catering	Transport	Banking and finance etc	Other services	Not stated, inadequately described or workplace outside UK
a	b	c	d	e	f	g	h	i	j	k	l	m	n
Males	**2,464**	**7**	**-**	**41**	**29**	**287**	**82**	**283**	**381**	**207**	**273**	**856**	**18**
Self-employed	**299**	**1**	**-**	**-**	**-**	**14**	**16**	**145**	**43**	**17**	**33**	**24**	**6**
With employees	59	-	-	-	-	4	6	13	14	4	9	5	4
Without employees	240	1	-	-	-	10	10	132	29	13	24	19	2
Employees	**2,038**	**6**	**-**	**41**	**29**	**270**	**65**	**136**	**330**	**183**	**236**	**735**	**7**
Working 31 or more hours per week	1,959	6	-	41	29	267	64	133	300	182	232	698	7
Working 30 or fewer hours per week	79	-	-	-	-	3	1	3	30	1	4	37	-
Economically active students (included above)	*12*	-	-	-	-	-	-	-	*10*	-	-	*2*	-
Females	**1,869**	**3**	**1**	**6**	**38**	**141**	**62**	**17**	**439**	**86**	**323**	**743**	**10**
Self-employed	**68**	**-**	**-**	**-**	**-**	**3**	**2**	**-**	**16**	**1**	**11**	**35**	**-**
With employees	21	-	-	-	-	-	-	-	10	1	-	10	-
Without employees	47	-	-	-	-	3	2	-	6	-	11	25	-
Employees	**1,762**	**3**	**1**	**6**	**38**	**135**	**60**	**17**	**416**	**81**	**306**	**694**	**5**
Working 31 or more hours per week	1,109	1	1	6	19	115	48	9	185	64	252	406	3
Working 30 or fewer hours per week	653	2	-	-	19	20	12	8	231	17	54	288	2
Economically active students (included above)	*26*	-	-	-	-	-	-	-	*18*	*1*	*3*	*4*	-

Table 79 Industry and employment status (10% sample) – continued

79. Residents aged 16 and over, employees and self-employed

(10% sample)

Southampton

Employment status	TOTAL PERSONS	Agriculture	Forestry and fishing	Energy and water	Mining	Manufacturing metal etc	Other manufacturing	Construction	Distribution and catering	Transport	Banking and finance etc	Other services	Not stated, inadequately described or workplace outside UK
a	b	c	d	e	f	g	h	i	j	k	l	m	n
Males	4,643	15	3	101	68	780	273	670	878	556	408	856	35
Self-employed	720	7	2	-	2	28	28	293	149	61	62	79	9
With employees	151	-	1	-	-	6	9	35	48	5	20	24	3
Without employees	569	7	1	-	2	22	19	258	101	56	42	55	6
Employees	3,806	8	1	100	62	734	240	365	713	480	338	751	14
Working 31 or more hours per week	3,624	8	1	100	61	724	233	358	642	471	328	685	13
Working 30 or fewer hours per week	182	-	-	-	1	10	7	7	71	9	10	66	1
Economically active students (included above)	*45*	*1*	*-*	*-*	*-*	*-*	*2*	*1*	*28*	*3*	*2*	*8*	*-*
Females	3,677	5	-	29	29	176	144	51	1,015	143	481	1,583	21
Self-employed	180	1	-	-	-	2	10	5	51	6	22	81	2
With employees	50	-	-	-	-	2	-	2	22	1	3	20	-
Without employees	130	1	-	-	-	-	10	3	29	5	19	61	2
Employees	3,409	4	-	27	28	170	133	45	946	133	453	1,460	10
Working 31 or more hours per week	1,934	2	-	20	23	148	85	28	400	105	353	762	8
Working 30 or fewer hours per week	1,475	2	-	7	5	22	48	17	546	28	100	698	2
Economically active students (included above)	*46*	*-*	*-*	*-*	*-*	*-*	*-*	*1*	*31*	*-*	*2*	*12*	*-*

Table 79 Industry and employment status (10% sample) – **continued**

79. Residents aged 16 and over, employees and self-employed

(10% sample)

Test Valley

Employment status	TOTAL PERSONS	Industry												Not stated, inadequately described or workplace outside UK
		Agriculture	Forestry and fishing	Energy and water	Mining	Manufacturing metal etc	Other manufacturing	Construction	Distribution and catering	Transport	Banking and finance etc	Other services	
a	b	c	d	e	f	g	h	i	j	k	l	m	n
Males	2,915	122	4	41	59	437	220	350	484	179	343	651	25
Self-employed	531	41	1	-	1	16	14	186	108	23	87	45	9
With employees	182	14	1	-	1	7	7	33	50	2	43	21	3
Without employees	349	27	-	-	-	9	7	153	58	21	44	24	6
Employees	2,329	80	3	41	57	417	205	159	368	152	256	579	12
Working 31 or more hours per week	2,225	73	3	39	56	411	201	156	326	149	253	547	11
Working 30 or fewer hours per week	104	7	-	2	1	6	4	3	42	3	3	32	1
Economically active students (included above)	*28*	*1*	*-*	*-*	*-*	*1*	*1*	*1*	*20*	*-*	*-*	*3*	*1*
Females	2,115	42	-	9	17	112	118	35	503	40	336	890	13
Self-employed	137	9	-	-	-	2	4	5	36	1	23	54	3
With employees	52	3	-	-	-	2	1	4	16	-	5	20	1
Without employees	85	6	-	-	-	-	3	1	20	1	18	34	2
Employees	1,926	31	-	9	17	106	112	30	459	39	308	811	4
Working 31 or more hours per week	1,091	14	-	6	13	78	76	16	208	28	236	414	2
Working 30 or fewer hours per week	835	17	-	3	4	28	36	14	251	11	72	397	2
Economically active students (included above)	*42*	*-*	*-*	*-*	*-*	*-*	*-*	*-*	*35*	*-*	*-*	*6*	*1*

Table 79 Industry and employment status (10% sample) – continued

79. Residents aged 16 and over, employees and self-employed

(10% sample)

Winchester

Employment status	TOTAL PERSONS	Agriculture	Forestry and fishing	Energy and water	Mining	Manufacturing metal etc	Other manufacturing	Construction	Distribution and catering	Transport	Banking and finance etc	Other services	Not stated, inadequately described or workplace outside UK
a	b	c	d	e	f	g	h	i	j	k	l	m	n
Males	**2,598**	**139**	**9**	**38**	**32**	**339**	**105**	**323**	**392**	**127**	**376**	**698**	**20**
Self-employed	**519**	**60**	**4**	**-**	**-**	**19**	**19**	**149**	**84**	**22**	**100**	**50**	**12**
With employees	199	25	1	-	-	5	7	30	52	4	48	22	5
Without employees	320	35	3	-	-	14	12	119	32	18	52	28	7
Employees	**2,022**	**79**	**5**	**38**	**32**	**313**	**85**	**166**	**301**	**101**	**272**	**623**	**7**
Working 31 or more hours per week	1,903	72	5	38	31	309	82	160	264	98	264	573	7
Working 30 or fewer hours per week	119	7	-	-	1	4	3	6	37	3	8	50	-
Economically active students (included above)	*25*	*-*	*-*	*-*	*-*	*-*	*1*	*-*	*18*	*-*	*1*	*4*	*1*
Females	**1,923**	**46**	**1**	**4**	**15**	**77**	**69**	**43**	**405**	**42**	**253**	**960**	**8**
Self-employed	**184**	**13**	**1**	**-**	**1**	**-**	**8**	**2**	**47**	**5**	**31**	**69**	**7**
With employees	68	7	1	-	-	-	2	-	27	2	8	18	3
Without employees	116	6	-	-	1	-	6	2	20	3	23	51	4
Employees	**1,708**	**31**	**-**	**4**	**14**	**75**	**61**	**41**	**352**	**35**	**216**	**878**	**1**
Working 31 or more hours per week	951	13	-	4	11	60	44	21	160	27	152	458	1
Working 30 or fewer hours per week	757	18	-	-	3	15	17	20	192	8	64	420	-
Economically active students (included above)	*34*	*-*	*-*	*-*	*-*	*1*	*-*	*-*	*19*	*1*	*3*	*10*	*-*

Table 80 Working parents: hours worked (10% sample)

80. Women in couple families and lone parents in employment

(10% sample)

a	Age of youngest dependent child in family (b)	TOTAL PERSONS (c)	Hours worked weekly											Not stated
			3 and under (d)	4 - 7 (e)	8 - 15 (f)	16 - 21 (g)	22 - 23 (h)	24 - 30 (i)	31 - 35 (j)	36 - 40 (k)	41 - 50 (l)	51 - 60 (m)	61 and over (n)	(o)
HAMPSHIRE														
Women in couple families in employment		21,909	162	824	3,271	3,479	553	2,552	2,030	7,143	963	225	219	488
No dependent child in family		12,715	61	293	1,238	1,576	283	1,269	1,425	5,417	634	142	131	246
1 or more dependent child(ren)	0 - 4	2,707	50	211	842	561	76	260	124	405	72	13	26	67
	5 - 10	3,181	38	219	728	718	92	490	194	448	113	30	26	85
	11 - 18	3,306	13	101	463	624	102	533	287	873	144	40	36	90
Male lone parents in employment		419	1	-	12	7	2	12	16	250	69	25	7	18
No dependent child in family		216	1	-	3	6	2	2	5	137	34	13	4	9
1 or more dependent child(ren)	0 - 4	35	-	-	2	-	-	-	1	21	8	1	1	1
	5 - 10	63	-	-	4	1	-	4	1	31	10	4	1	7
	11 - 18	105	-	-	3	-	-	6	9	61	17	7	1	1
Female lone parents in employment		1,730	17	127	194	186	27	269	169	590	75	18	14	44
No dependent child in family		629	2	12	60	70	6	82	66	264	32	8	7	20
1 or more dependent child(ren)	0 - 4	233	4	34	32	31	3	27	22	66	5	2	1	6
	5 - 10	410	7	62	59	49	10	75	33	89	12	2	1	11
	11 - 18	458	4	19	43	36	8	85	48	171	26	6	5	7
Basingstoke & Deane														
Women in couple families in employment		2,349	12	73	311	334	49	270	229	907	105	20	8	31
No dependent child in family		1,390	4	31	110	145	21	137	156	687	64	14	5	16
1 or more dependent child(ren)	0 - 4	302	3	16	100	56	13	23	22	50	10	1	1	7
	5 - 10	327	5	20	64	82	5	55	18	56	14	3	2	3
	11 - 18	330	-	6	37	51	10	55	33	114	17	2	-	5
Male lone parents in employment		52	-	-	2	1	-	2	4	32	5	2	2	2
No dependent child in family		30	-	-	1	1	-	-	2	22	2	-	1	1
1 or more dependent child(ren)	0 - 4	4	-	-	-	-	-	-	-	1	3	-	-	-
	5 - 10	4	-	-	-	-	-	1	-	3	-	-	-	-
	11 - 18	14	-	-	1	-	-	1	2	6	-	2	1	1
Female lone parents in employment		163	3	6	18	20	2	27	14	59	6	4	-	4
No dependent child in family		60	-	1	2	7	-	6	9	29	3	-	-	3
1 or more dependent child(ren)	0 - 4	27	1	2	5	4	1	5	-	8	1	-	-	-
	5 - 10	35	-	3	4	7	1	8	2	8	1	-	-	-
	11 - 18	41	2	-	7	2	-	8	3	14	4	-	1	1

Table 80 Working parents: hours worked (10% sample) – continued

80. Women in couple families and lone parents in employment

	Age of youngest dependent child in family	TOTAL PERSONS	Hours worked weekly											Not stated
			3 and under	4 - 7	8 - 15	16 - 21	22 - 23	24 - 30	31 - 35	36 - 40	41 - 50	51 - 60	61 and over	
a	b	c	d	e	f	g	h	i	j	k	l	m	n	o
East Hampshire														
Women in couple families in employment		1,532	18	78	213	203	37	184	148	443	106	31	21	50
No dependent child in family		854	6	34	83	84	20	85	99	320	67	17	11	28
1 or more dependent child(ren)	0 - 4	193	6	17	58	33	5	20	5	33	9	1	3	3
	5 - 10	225	5	20	33	48	6	41	15	29	11	6	4	7
	11 - 18	260	1	7	39	38	6	38	29	61	19	7	3	12
Male lone parents in employment		20	-	-	-	-	-	-	1	12	5	2	-	-
No dependent child in family		9	-	-	-	-	-	-	-	5	2	2	-	-
1 or more dependent child(ren)	0 - 4	1	-	-	-	-	-	-	-	-	1	-	-	-
	5 - 10	-	-	-	-	-	-	-	-	-	-	-	-	-
	11 - 18	10	-	-	-	-	-	-	1	7	2	-	-	-
Female lone parents in employment		123	1	13	14	11	3	21	12	33	6	1	2	6
No dependent child in family		46	-	2	5	4	-	8	7	11	5	1	1	2
1 or more dependent child(ren)	0 - 4	15	-	4	2	1	1	1	1	3	-	-	-	2
	5 - 10	24	-	6	3	2	2	4	2	4	-	-	-	1
	11 - 18	38	1	1	4	4	-	8	2	15	1	-	1	1
Eastleigh														
Women in couple families in employment		1,691	10	67	272	255	54	195	188	512	68	20	13	37
No dependent child in family		963	5	11	90	107	24	101	142	396	49	11	8	19
1 or more dependent child(ren)	0 - 4	215	3	29	74	43	8	14	8	22	5	3	1	5
	5 - 10	271	1	17	75	57	10	41	17	37	7	1	1	7
	11 - 18	242	1	10	33	48	12	39	21	57	7	5	3	6
Male lone parents in employment		31	-	-	2	-	-	2	1	18	5	1	-	2
No dependent child in family		9	-	-	-	-	-	-	-	5	1	1	-	2
1 or more dependent child(ren)	0 - 4	3	-	-	-	-	-	-	-	3	-	-	-	-
	5 - 10	6	-	-	1	-	-	1	-	4	-	-	-	-
	11 - 18	13	-	-	1	-	-	1	1	6	4	-	-	-
Female lone parents in employment		109	1	12	13	12	1	18	10	35	3	1	2	1
No dependent child in family		39	-	-	4	4	1	5	4	17	2	1	1	-
1 or more dependent child(ren)	0 - 4	12	-	3	1	3	-	1	-	3	1	-	-	-
	5 - 10	28	1	7	3	2	-	7	2	5	-	-	-	1
	11 - 18	30	-	2	5	3	-	5	4	10	-	-	1	-

Table 80 Working parents: hours worked (10% sample) – continued

80. Women in couple families and lone parents in employment

a	b Age of youngest dependent child in family	c TOTAL PERSONS	Hours worked weekly											
			d 3 and under	e 4 - 7	f 8 - 15	g 16 - 21	h 22 - 23	i 24 - 30	j 31 - 35	k 36 - 40	l 41 - 50	m 51 - 60	n 61 and over	o Not stated
Fareham														
Women in couple families in employment		**1,541**	**13**	**62**	**212**	**253**	**37**	**176**	**142**	**519**	**69**	**15**	**13**	**30**
No dependent child in family		915	4	24	81	117	21	97	91	395	50	9	9	17
1 or more dependent child(ren)	0 - 4	194	3	13	58	42	6	19	13	29	1	2	2	6
	5 - 10	204	5	17	47	40	6	27	16	34	4	3	1	4
	11 - 18	228	1	8	26	54	4	33	22	61	14	1	1	3
Male lone parents in employment		**25**	-	-	-	-	-	-	**2**	**15**	**6**	**2**	-	-
No dependent child in family		15	-	-	-	-	-	-	2	9	3	1	-	-
1 or more dependent child(ren)	0 - 4	2	-	-	-	-	-	-	-	2	-	-	-	-
	5 - 10	3	-	-	-	-	-	-	-	2	1	-	-	-
	11 - 18	5	-	-	-	-	-	-	-	2	2	1	-	-
Female lone parents in employment		**116**	**2**	**5**	**10**	**13**	**2**	**14**	**10**	**51**	**4**	-	**2**	**3**
No dependent child in family		43	-	-	2	7	-	4	5	20	2	-	-	3
1 or more dependent child(ren)	0 - 4	9	-	-	1	3	-	3	-	2	-	-	-	-
	5 - 10	29	1	4	7	2	1	3	2	7	1	-	1	-
	11 - 18	35	1	1	-	1	1	4	3	22	1	-	1	-
Gosport														
Women in couple families in employment		**1,043**	**6**	**37**	**167**	**188**	**22**	**100**	**102**	**341**	**44**	**5**	**9**	**22**
No dependent child in family		561	2	13	54	70	12	45	66	252	26	5	6	10
1 or more dependent child(ren)	0 - 4	158	2	7	45	47	2	15	13	21	2	-	2	2
	5 - 10	176	1	15	43	34	6	25	9	26	10	-	1	6
	11 - 18	148	1	2	25	37	2	15	14	42	6	-	-	4
Male lone parents in employment		**26**	**1**	-	**2**	**1**	**1**	**2**	-	**13**	**4**	**1**	-	**1**
No dependent child in family		10	1	-	1	1	1	-	-	3	2	-	-	1
1 or more dependent child(ren)	0 - 4	4	-	-	1	-	-	-	-	2	1	-	-	-
	5 - 10	5	-	-	-	-	-	2	-	3	-	-	-	-
	11 - 18	7	-	-	-	-	-	-	-	5	1	1	-	-
Female lone parents in employment		**96**	-	**6**	**14**	**14**	-	**20**	**10**	**28**	**3**	-	**1**	-
No dependent child in family		30	-	2	2	7	-	4	2	11	1	-	1	-
1 or more dependent child(ren)	0 - 4	7	-	-	1	-	-	2	3	1	-	-	-	-
	5 - 10	27	-	2	4	6	-	6	2	7	-	-	-	-
	11 - 18	32	-	2	7	1	-	8	3	9	2	-	-	-

Table 80 Working parents: hours worked (10% sample) – continued

80. Women in couple families and lone parents in employment
(10% sample)

	Age of youngest dependent child in family	TOTAL PERSONS	Hours worked weekly 3 and under	4 - 7	8 - 15	16 - 21	22 - 23	24 - 30	31 - 35	36 - 40	41 - 50	51 - 60	61 and over	Not stated
a	b	c	d	e	f	g	h	i	j	k	l	m	n	o
Hart														
Women in couple families in employment	-	1,278	14	47	203	197	43	145	131	383	64	19	9	23
No dependent child in family	-	718	4	7	73	75	21	71	90	297	48	14	8	10
1 or more dependent child(ren)	0 - 4	152	5	22	49	27	3	11	6	22	4	1	-	2
	5 - 10	195	5	10	48	56	10	28	12	17	6	1	-	2
	11 - 18	213	-	8	33	39	9	35	23	47	6	3	1	9
Male lone parents in employment	-	19	-	-	-	-	-	-	1	7	7	3	1	-
No dependent child in family	-	11	-	-	-	-	-	-	-	6	3	1	1	-
1 or more dependent child(ren)	0 - 4	1	-	-	-	-	-	-	-	-	1	-	-	-
	5 - 10	3	-	-	-	-	-	-	-	-	1	2	-	-
	11 - 18	4	-	-	-	-	-	-	1	1	2	-	-	-
Female lone parents in employment	-	73	-	3	9	9	1	7	6	27	6	1	2	2
No dependent child in family	-	28	-	1	6	3	1	3	-	11	1	-	1	1
1 or more dependent child(ren)	0 - 4	6	-	-	1	1	-	1	-	2	-	1	-	-
	5 - 10	12	-	2	-	2	-	-	1	5	1	-	1	-
	11 - 18	27	-	-	2	3	-	3	5	9	4	-	-	1
Havant														
Women in couple families in employment	-	1,602	8	59	227	295	50	194	94	547	59	16	16	37
No dependent child in family	-	974	6	29	100	143	26	111	69	411	40	10	11	18
1 or more dependent child(ren)	0 - 4	172	-	9	45	48	6	19	4	32	3	1	1	4
	5 - 10	213	-	15	53	58	5	28	8	33	4	2	1	6
	11 - 18	243	2	6	29	46	13	36	13	71	12	3	3	9
Male lone parents in employment	-	33	-	-	2	-	-	2	-	21	5	-	1	2
No dependent child in family	-	14	-	-	-	-	-	-	-	11	1	-	1	1
1 or more dependent child(ren)	0 - 4	2	-	-	-	-	-	-	-	2	-	-	-	-
	5 - 10	6	-	-	1	-	-	1	-	3	1	-	-	-
	11 - 18	11	-	-	1	-	-	1	-	5	3	-	-	1
Female lone parents in employment	-	127	1	12	20	14	-	16	8	52	1	-	1	2
No dependent child in family	-	39	-	-	8	2	-	3	4	19	1	-	1	1
1 or more dependent child(ren)	0 - 4	10	1	1	-	3	-	1	-	4	-	-	-	-
	5 - 10	36	-	7	5	5	-	7	3	9	-	-	-	-
	11 - 18	42	-	4	7	4	-	5	1	20	-	-	-	1

Table 80 Working parents: hours worked (10% sample) – continued

80. Women in couple families and lone parents in employment

(10% sample)

	Age of youngest dependent child in family	TOTAL PERSONS	Hours worked weekly											Not stated
			3 and under	4 - 7	8 - 15	16 - 21	22 - 23	24 - 30	31 - 35	36 - 40	41 - 50	51 - 60	61 and over	
a	b	c	d	e	f	g	h	i	j	k	l	m	n	o
New Forest														
Women in couple families in employment		**2,162**	**19**	**96**	**380**	**360**	**41**	**246**	**188**	**610**	**102**	**35**	**31**	**54**
No dependent child in family		1,237	11	39	153	152	21	119	134	473	66	24	17	28
1 or more dependent child(ren)	0 - 4	241	3	21	88	49	1	33	5	17	9	2	4	9
	5 - 10	324	5	24	84	79	9	47	15	31	11	3	5	11
	11 - 18	360	-	12	55	80	10	47	34	89	16	6	5	6
Male lone parents in employment		**22**	-	-	-	-	-	-	-	**19**	**1**	**2**	-	-
No dependent child in family		13	-	-	-	-	-	-	-	10	1	2	-	-
1 or more dependent child(ren)	0 - 4	1	-	-	-	-	-	-	-	1	-	-	-	-
	5 - 10	2	-	-	-	-	-	-	-	2	-	-	-	-
	11 - 18	6	-	-	-	-	-	-	-	6	-	-	-	-
Female lone parents in employment		**160**	**2**	**15**	**21**	**23**	**5**	**27**	**12**	**39**	**9**	-	**1**	**6**
No dependent child in family		59	-	2	7	9	-	8	5	19	4	-	1	4
1 or more dependent child(ren)	0 - 4	13	1	3	4	1	-	-	2	1	1	-	-	-
	5 - 10	42	1	9	7	8	3	5	2	4	1	-	-	2
	11 - 18	46	-	1	3	5	2	14	3	15	3	-	-	-
Portsmouth														
Women in couple families in employment		**2,153**	**13**	**66**	**313**	**345**	**67**	**235**	**177**	**766**	**83**	**17**	**19**	**52**
No dependent child in family		1,283	3	28	110	163	41	114	131	593	55	9	11	25
1 or more dependent child(ren)	0 - 4	293	8	12	80	62	8	35	12	60	9	1	1	6
	5 - 10	296	-	18	71	67	6	43	19	44	10	4	7	13
	11 - 18	281	2	8	52	53	12	43	15	69	9	3	7	8
Male lone parents in employment		**59**	-	-	**1**	**3**	-	**2**	**2**	**35**	**8**	**3**	**1**	**4**
No dependent child in family		33	-	-	-	2	-	2	-	20	5	2	-	2
1 or more dependent child(ren)	0 - 4	7	-	-	1	-	-	-	1	4	-	1	1	1
	5 - 10	11	-	-	-	1	-	-	1	4	3	-	1	1
	11 - 18	8	-	-	-	-	-	-	-	7	-	-	-	-
Female lone parents in employment		**230**	**1**	**21**	**27**	**26**	**4**	**26**	**19**	**86**	**6**	**5**	**2**	**7**
No dependent child in family		76	-	1	7	9	3	10	3	35	1	2	1	4
1 or more dependent child(ren)	0 - 4	42	-	6	7	5	1	2	4	16	-	-	1	-
	5 - 10	67	1	13	10	8	-	9	7	14	3	1	-	1
	11 - 18	45	-	1	3	4	-	5	5	21	2	2	-	2

Table 80 Working parents: hours worked (10% sample) – **continued**

80. Women in couple families and lone parents in employment

a	b	TOTAL PERSONS	Hours worked weekly											
	Age of youngest dependent child in family		3 and under	4 - 7	8 - 15	16 - 21	22 - 23	24 - 30	31 - 35	36 - 40	41 - 50	51 - 60	61 and over	Not stated
		c	d	e	f	g	h	i	j	k	l	m	n	o
Rushmoor														
Women in couple families in employment		**1,266**	**10**	**27**	**155**	**191**	**39**	**138**	**129**	**483**	**56**	**5**	**9**	**24**
No dependent child in family		738	2	5	50	82	20	63	93	365	35	5	6	12
1 or more dependent child(ren)	0 - 4	168	5	11	55	36	5	17	6	23	6	-	-	4
	5 - 10	178	3	7	33	43	7	31	14	31	6	-	1	2
	11 - 18	182	-	4	17	30	7	27	16	64	9	-	2	6
Male lone parents in employment		**23**	**-**	**-**	**1**	**-**	**-**	**-**	**-**	**13**	**2**	**3**	**-**	**4**
No dependent child in family		14	-	-	1	-	-	-	-	8	2	1	-	2
1 or more dependent child(ren)	0 - 4	1	-	-	-	-	-	-	-	1	-	-	-	-
	5 - 10	2	-	-	-	-	-	-	-	-	-	2	-	-
	11 - 18	6	-	-	-	-	-	-	-	4	-	-	-	2
Female lone parents in employment		**110**	**-**	**5**	**9**	**5**	**2**	**16**	**13**	**48**	**9**	**1**	**-**	**2**
No dependent child in family		42	-	1	3	2	-	7	7	20	2	-	-	-
1 or more dependent child(ren)	0 - 4	18	-	2	2	-	-	1	-	9	2	-	-	2
	5 - 10	23	-	1	4	-	2	4	2	8	1	1	-	-
	11 - 18	27	-	1	-	3	-	4	4	11	4	-	-	-
Southampton														
Women in couple families in employment		**2,411**	**11**	**71**	**397**	**439**	**48**	**281**	**230**	**741**	**79**	**21**	**30**	**63**
No dependent child in family		1,441	4	26	164	229	22	141	161	574	56	14	17	33
1 or more dependent child(ren)	0 - 4	310	4	16	99	70	14	30	12	43	7	-	7	8
	5 - 10	334	2	20	90	81	8	39	25	44	5	3	4	13
	11 - 18	326	1	9	44	59	4	71	32	80	11	4	2	9
Male lone parents in employment		**53**	**-**	**-**	**1**	**1**	**-**	**-**	**2**	**33**	**11**	**3**	**-**	**2**
No dependent child in family		29	-	-	-	1	-	-	1	19	6	1	-	1
1 or more dependent child(ren)	0 - 4	4	-	-	-	-	-	-	-	3	1	-	-	-
	5 - 10	9	-	-	1	-	-	-	-	4	2	1	-	-
	11 - 18	11	-	-	-	-	-	-	1	7	2	1	-	1
Female lone parents in employment		**241**	**4**	**19**	**24**	**23**	**7**	**43**	**29**	**72**	**12**	**4**	**-**	**4**
No dependent child in family		98	-	1	8	11	1	15	12	39	7	4	-	-
1 or more dependent child(ren)	0 - 4	46	2	10	5	4	-	7	6	11	-	-	-	1
	5 - 10	51	2	5	8	5	1	13	5	9	1	-	-	2
	11 - 18	46	-	3	3	3	5	8	6	13	4	-	-	1

Table 80 Working parents: hours worked (10% sample) – continued

(10% sample)

80. Women in couple families and lone parents in employment

a	b (Age of youngest dependent child in family)	c TOTAL PERSONS	Hours worked weekly — 3 and under (d)	4 - 7 (e)	8 - 15 (f)	16 - 21 (g)	22 - 23 (h)	24 - 30 (i)	31 - 35 (j)	36 - 40 (k)	41 - 50 (l)	51 - 60 (m)	61 and over (n)	Not stated (o)
Test Valley														
Women in couple families in employment	-	**1,534**	**8**	**78**	**220**	**212**	**41**	**202**	**174**	**465**	**62**	**10**	**24**	**38**
No dependent child in family	-	864	2	23	84	107	19	87	129	332	41	6	13	21
1 or more dependent child(ren)	0 - 4	186	3	27	57	27	2	21	12	24	3	-	4	6
	5 - 10	248	2	16	50	39	12	52	12	44	10	3	4	4
	11 - 18	236	1	12	29	39	8	42	21	65	8	1	3	7
Male lone parents in employment	-	**30**	-	-	**1**	**1**	-	-	**2**	**18**	**6**	**1**	**1**	-
No dependent child in family	-	16	-	-	1	1	-	-	-	10	4	1	1	-
1 or more dependent child(ren)	0 - 4	4	-	-	-	-	-	-	1	1	1	-	-	-
	5 - 10	5	-	-	1	-	-	-	-	3	1	-	-	-
	11 - 18	5	-	-	-	-	-	-	1	4	-	-	-	-
Female lone parents in employment	-	**104**	-	**6**	**9**	**11**	-	**19**	**16**	**34**	**6**	-	-	**3**
No dependent child in family	-	40	-	1	3	4	-	6	5	18	2	-	-	1
1 or more dependent child(ren)	0 - 4	16	-	2	1	5	-	1	4	2	-	-	-	1
	5 - 10	23	-	2	4	1	-	6	1	7	1	-	-	1
	11 - 18	25	-	1	1	1	-	6	6	7	3	-	-	-
Winchester														
Women in couple families in employment	-	**1,347**	**20**	**63**	**201**	**207**	**25**	**186**	**98**	**426**	**66**	**11**	**17**	**27**
No dependent child in family	-	777	8	23	86	102	15	98	64	322	37	4	9	9
1 or more dependent child(ren)	0 - 4	123	5	11	34	21	3	3	6	29	4	1	1	5
	5 - 10	190	4	20	37	34	2	33	14	22	15	1	1	7
	11 - 18	257	3	9	44	50	5	52	14	53	10	5	6	6
Male lone parents in employment	-	**26**	-	-	-	-	**1**	**2**	**1**	**14**	**4**	**1**	**1**	**2**
No dependent child in family	-	13	-	-	-	-	1	-	-	9	2	1	1	1
1 or more dependent child(ren)	0 - 4	1	-	-	-	-	-	-	-	1	-	-	-	-
	5 - 10	7	-	-	-	-	-	-	-	3	1	-	-	2
	11 - 18	5	-	-	-	-	-	2	1	1	1	-	-	-
Female lone parents in employment	-	**78**	**2**	**4**	**6**	**5**	-	**15**	**10**	**26**	**4**	**1**	**1**	**4**
No dependent child in family	-	29	2	-	3	1	-	3	3	15	1	1	-	1
1 or more dependent child(ren)	0 - 4	12	-	1	2	1	-	2	1	4	-	-	-	-
	5 - 10	13	-	1	-	1	-	3	3	2	2	-	-	1
	11 - 18	24	-	2	1	2	-	7	3	5	1	-	1	2

Table 81 Occupation and employment status (10% sample)

County, districts

(10% sample)

81. Residents aged 16 and over, employees and self-employed

Employment status	TOTAL PERSONS	Managers and administrators	Professional	Associate professional	Clerical and secretarial	Craft and related	Personal and protective service	Sales	Plant and machine operatives	Other occupations	Not stated or inadequately described
a	b	c	d	e	f	g	h	i	j	k	l

HAMPSHIRE

	b	c	d	e	f	g	h	i	j	k	l
Males	40,790	8,259	4,233	3,784	2,533	8,791	3,766	1,847	4,568	2,697	312
Self-employed	6,744	1,332	623	508	50	2,786	71	248	574	414	138
With employees	1,911	756	321	112	8	464	25	39	95	47	44
Without employees	4,833	576	302	396	42	2,322	46	209	479	367	94
Employees	32,995	6,787	3,542	3,209	2,438	5,890	3,339	1,562	3,904	2,225	99
Working 31 or more hours per week	31,494	6,682	3,358	3,132	2,322	5,772	3,136	1,292	3,782	1,926	92
Working 30 or fewer hours per week	1,501	105	184	77	116	118	203	270	122	299	7
Economically active students (included above)	*373*	*5*	*7*	*13*	*21*	*13*	*45*	*156*	*11*	*99*	*3*
Females	31,083	3,911	2,256	3,023	9,042	698	4,193	3,450	1,424	2,902	184
Self-employed	1,913	742	187	290	170	98	181	72	45	74	54
With employees	618	363	65	70	24	18	24	10	11	14	19
Without employees	1,295	379	122	220	146	80	157	62	34	60	35
Employees	28,544	3,101	2,005	2,679	8,742	585	3,894	3,337	1,353	2,784	64
Working 31 or more hours per week	16,278	2,625	1,332	1,811	5,889	404	1,467	1,097	1,045	568	40
Working 30 or fewer hours per week	12,266	476	673	868	2,853	181	2,427	2,240	308	2,216	24
Economically active students (included above)	*474*	*5*	*6*	*16*	*34*	*3*	*95*	*231*	*6*	*75*	*3*

Standard Occupational Classification Major Groups

Table 81 Occupation and employment status (10% sample) – continued

81. Residents aged 16 and over, employees and self-employed

(10% sample)

Employment status	TOTAL PERSONS	Standard Occupational Classification Major Groups									
		Managers and administrators	Professional	Associate professional	Clerical and secretarial	Craft and related	Personal and protective service	Sales	Plant and machine operatives	Other occupations	Not stated or inadequately described
a	b	c	d	e	f	g	h	i	j	k	l
Basingstoke & Deane											
Males	**4,237**	**901**	**461**	**421**	**335**	**874**	**232**	**187**	**518**	**275**	**33**
Self-employed	**651**	**104**	**65**	**55**	**4**	**274**	**9**	**24**	**57**	**41**	**18**
With employees	179	58	32	9	-	50	5	7	10	3	5
Without employees	472	46	33	46	4	224	4	17	47	38	13
Employees	**3,516**	**787**	**392**	**360**	**327**	**591**	**214**	**158**	**448**	**230**	**9**
Working 31 or more hours per week	3,378	778	382	354	315	581	202	132	432	196	6
Working 30 or fewer hours per week	138	9	10	6	12	10	12	26	16	34	3
Economically active students (included above)	*35*	*-*	*-*	*-*	*2*	*1*	*1*	*15*	*2*	*14*	*-*
Females	**3,235**	**440**	**216**	**306**	**1,134**	**45**	**323**	**305**	**149**	**301**	**16**
Self-employed	**171**	**53**	**17**	**30**	**21**	**7**	**18**	**8**	**4**	**8**	**5**
With employees	44	20	3	3	6	1	4	2	2	2	1
Without employees	127	33	14	27	15	6	14	6	2	6	4
Employees	**3,016**	**381**	**198**	**267**	**1,100**	**38**	**299**	**294**	**145**	**288**	**6**
Working 31 or more hours per week	1,861	321	130	195	777	24	117	119	116	59	3
Working 30 or fewer hours per week	1,155	60	68	72	323	14	182	175	29	229	3
Economically active students (included above)	*45*	*1*	*-*	*-*	*2*	*-*	*8*	*22*	*1*	*11*	*-*

Table 81 Occupation and employment status (10% sample) – continued

81. Residents aged 16 and over, employees and self-employed

(10% sample)

East Hampshire

Employment status	TOTAL PERSONS	Standard Occupational Classification Major Groups									
		Managers and administrators	Professional	Associate professional	Clerical and secretarial	Craft and related	Personal and protective service	Sales	Plant and machine operatives	Other occupations	Not stated or inadequately described
a	b	c	d	e	f	g	h	i	j	k	l
Males	**2,821**	**744**	**329**	**244**	**127**	**572**	**235**	**126**	**244**	**186**	**14**
Self-employed	**606**	**126**	**66**	**51**	**1**	**249**	**5**	**26**	**41**	**34**	**7**
With employees	176	70	32	11	-	43	-	5	6	6	3
Without employees	430	56	34	40	1	206	5	21	35	28	4
Employees	**2,157**	**608**	**256**	**189**	**123**	**313**	**215**	**99**	**200**	**149**	**5**
Working 31 or more hours per week	2,058	595	241	183	116	303	211	85	192	127	5
Working 30 or fewer hours per week	99	13	15	6	7	10	4	14	8	22	-
Economically active students (included above)	*26*	*-*	*-*	*1*	*-*	*-*	*6*	*8*	*1*	*10*	*-*
Females	**2,135**	**286**	**219**	**213**	**594**	**58**	**304**	**184**	**83**	**181**	**13**
Self-employed	**195**	**72**	**17**	**35**	**20**	**13**	**16**	**5**	**3**	**10**	**4**
With employees	57	33	7	3	2	3	2	1	-	3	3
Without employees	138	39	10	32	18	10	14	4	3	7	1
Employees	**1,894**	**204**	**195**	**173**	**568**	**44**	**277**	**178**	**80**	**169**	**6**
Working 31 or more hours per week	1,068	175	122	111	377	24	98	60	56	41	4
Working 30 or fewer hours per week	826	29	73	62	191	20	179	118	24	128	2
Economically active students (included above)	*23*	*-*	*-*	*1*	*-*	*1*	*5*	*12*	*-*	*4*	*-*

Table 81 Occupation and employment status (10% sample) – continued

(10% sample)

81. Residents aged 16 and over, employees and self-employed

Employment status	TOTAL PERSONS	Managers and administrators	Professional	Associate professional	Clerical and secretarial	Craft and related	Personal and protective service	Sales	Plant and machine operatives	Other occupations	Not stated or inadequately described
a	b	c	d	e	f	g	h	i	j	k	l

Standard Occupational Classification Major Groups

Eastleigh

	b	c	d	e	f	g	h	i	j	k	l
Males	2,945	582	314	306	188	695	141	172	364	170	13
Self-employed	449	81	33	26	3	211	5	20	35	27	8
With employees	126	44	15	7	1	42	-	-	7	5	5
Without employees	323	37	18	19	2	169	5	20	28	22	3
Employees	2,446	492	279	273	182	476	128	152	320	142	2
Working 31 or more hours per week	2,324	485	259	263	174	466	121	126	310	119	1
Working 30 or fewer hours per week	122	7	20	10	8	10	7	26	10	23	1
Economically active students (included above)	*31*	*-*	*1*	*-*	*-*	*3*	*2*	*16*	*-*	*9*	*-*
Females	2,260	291	153	222	753	34	267	289	86	155	10
Self-employed	114	43	15	11	16	7	11	1	2	5	3
With employees	32	22	5	1	-	-	2	-	-	1	1
Without employees	82	21	10	10	16	7	9	1	2	4	2
Employees	2,106	242	132	207	728	27	249	288	84	146	3
Working 31 or more hours per week	1,169	208	82	139	472	19	75	102	53	17	2
Working 30 or fewer hours per week	937	34	50	68	256	8	174	186	31	129	1
Economically active students (included above)	*32*	*-*	*-*	*1*	*5*	*1*	*4*	*16*	*1*	*4*	*-*

Table 81 Occupation and employment status (10% sample) – **continued**

County, districts

(10% sample)

81. Residents aged 16 and over, employees and self-employed

Employment status	TOTAL PERSONS	Standard Occupational Classification Major Groups									
		Managers and administrators	Professional	Associate professional	Clerical and secretarial	Craft and related	Personal and protective service	Sales	Plant and machine operatives	Other occupations	Not stated or inadequately described
a	b	c	d	e	f	g	h	i	j	k	l
Fareham											
Males	**2,698**	**628**	**310**	**293**	**131**	**560**	**289**	**104**	**230**	**134**	**19**
Self-employed	**416**	**79**	**41**	**34**	**2**	**184**	**4**	**12**	**32**	**22**	**6**
With employees	119	47	19	8	-	30	4	1	3	3	4
Without employees	297	32	22	26	2	154	-	11	29	19	2
Employees	**2,223**	**539**	**264**	**254**	**126**	**372**	**269**	**89**	**191**	**111**	**8**
Working 31 or more hours per week	2,129	533	244	249	122	361	260	75	188	90	7
Working 30 or fewer hours per week	94	6	20	5	4	11	9	14	3	21	1
Economically active students (included above)	*25*	*-*	*-*	*1*	*1*	*1*	*2*	*10*	*-*	*9*	*1*
Females	**2,092**	**260**	**183**	**234**	**632**	**40**	**260**	**225**	**73**	**175**	**10**
Self-employed	**132**	**56**	**10**	**22**	**14**	**5**	**12**	**4**	**3**	**4**	**2**
With employees	45	23	2	12	1	1	2	-	2	1	1
Without employees	87	33	8	10	13	4	10	4	1	3	1
Employees	**1,922**	**198**	**169**	**207**	**612**	**34**	**242**	**220**	**69**	**168**	**3**
Working 31 or more hours per week	1,097	174	106	132	421	20	90	67	58	28	1
Working 30 or fewer hours per week	825	24	63	75	191	14	152	153	11	140	2
Economically active students (included above)	*34*	*-*	*-*	*1*	*3*	*-*	*6*	*15*	*-*	*9*	*-*

Table 81 Occupation and employment status (10% sample) – **continued**

County, districts

81. Residents aged 16 and over, employees and self-employed

(10% sample)

Gosport

Employment status	TOTAL PERSONS	Standard Occupational Classification Major Groups										
		Managers and administrators	Professional	Associate professional	Clerical and secretarial	Craft and related	Personal and protective service	Sales	Plant and machine operatives	Other occupations	Not stated or inadequately described
a	b	c	d	e	f	g	h	i	j	k	l
Males	**1,931**	**260**	**111**	**143**	**100**	**460**	**453**	**64**	**217**	**107**	**16**
Self-employed	**204**	**32**	**15**	**12**	**1**	**96**	**3**	**5**	**21**	**14**	**5**
With employees	55	23	11	4	-	14	1	1	1	14	-
Without employees	149	9	4	8	1	82	2	4	20	14	5
Employees	**1,638**	**218**	**93**	**130**	**96**	**356**	**398**	**59**	**192**	**90**	**6**
Working 31 or more hours per week	1,577	215	83	128	93	350	387	50	190	75	6
Working 30 or fewer hours per week	61	3	10	2	3	6	11	9	2	15	-
Economically active students (included above)	*11*	*-*	*-*	*-*	*-*	*1*	*1*	*5*	*-*	*4*	*-*
Females	**1,459**	**151**	**52**	**121**	**385**	**31**	**262**	**186**	**103**	**157**	**11**
Self-employed	**56**	**23**	**5**	**4**	**4**	**1**	**8**	**4**	**2**	**4**	**1**
With employees	15	12	-	-	-	-	2	-	1	-	-
Without employees	41	11	5	4	4	1	6	4	1	4	1
Employees	**1,371**	**128**	**45**	**116**	**373**	**29**	**242**	**180**	**99**	**153**	**6**
Working 31 or more hours per week	746	107	33	74	260	22	102	41	79	25	3
Working 30 or fewer hours per week	625	21	12	42	113	7	140	139	20	128	3
Economically active students (included above)	*25*	*1*	*-*	*1*	*1*	*-*	*4*	*14*	*-*	*3*	*1*

141

Table 81 Occupation and employment status (10% sample) – continued

81. Residents aged 16 and over, employees and self-employed

(10% sample)

Standard Occupational Classification Major Groups

Hart

Employment status	TOTAL PERSONS	Managers and administrators	Professional	Associate professional	Clerical and secretarial	Craft and related	Personal and protective service	Sales	Plant and machine operatives	Other occupations	Not stated or inadequately described
a	b	c	d	e	f	g	h	i	j	k	l
Males	**2,485**	**697**	**343**	**231**	**106**	**413**	**267**	**128**	**179**	**106**	**15**
Self-employed	**400**	**80**	**53**	**41**	**5**	**152**	**3**	**16**	**30**	**14**	**6**
With employees	122	44	22	10	2	27	1	5	7	2	2
Without employees	278	36	31	31	3	125	2	11	23	12	4
Employees	**2,049**	**605**	**288**	**190**	**101**	**256**	**255**	**111**	**147**	**88**	**8**
Working 31 or more hours per week	1,959	593	282	183	96	253	239	94	143	68	8
Working 30 or fewer hours per week	90	12	6	7	5	3	16	17	4	20	-
Economically active students (included above)	*35*	*-*	*2*	*1*	*1*	*-*	*6*	*11*	*2*	*12*	*-*
Females	**1,737**	**270**	**179**	**192**	**534**	**27**	**186**	**185**	**38**	**118**	**8**
Self-employed	**130**	**35**	**18**	**27**	**21**	**7**	**8**	**3**	**3**	**4**	**4**
With employees	30	17	4	2	2	1	1	1	1	-	1
Without employees	100	18	14	25	19	6	7	2	2	4	3
Employees	**1,574**	**230**	**157**	**161**	**506**	**20**	**171**	**180**	**35**	**113**	**1**
Working 31 or more hours per week	899	196	105	101	306	14	59	60	27	31	-
Working 30 or fewer hours per week	675	34	52	60	200	6	112	120	8	82	1
Economically active students (included above)	*32*	*1*	*-*	*2*	*5*	*-*	*5*	*17*	*1*	*1*	*-*

Table 81 Occupation and employment status (10% sample) – continued

(10% sample)

81. Residents aged 16 and over, employees and self-employed

Havant

Employment status	TOTAL PERSONS	Standard Occupational Classification Major Groups									
		Managers and administrators	Professional	Associate professional	Clerical and secretarial	Craft and related	Personal and protective service	Sales	Plant and machine operatives	Other occupations	Not stated or inadequately described
a	b	c	d	e	f	g	h	i	j	k	l
Males	**2,918**	**520**	**304**	**284**	**185**	**730**	**180**	**121**	**380**	**187**	**27**
Self-employed	**513**	**84**	**37**	**31**	**10**	**238**	**6**	**15**	**55**	**27**	**10**
With employees	138	53	17	6	1	40	3	4	9	3	2
Without employees	375	31	20	25	9	198	3	11	46	24	8
Employees	**2,337**	**424**	**265**	**250**	**173**	**478**	**158**	**102**	**319**	**156**	**12**
Working 31 or more hours per week	2,241	414	251	246	167	470	143	83	309	146	12
Working 30 or fewer hours per week	96	10	14	4	6	8	15	19	10	10	-
Economically active students (included above)	*22*	*-*	*-*	*2*	*1*	*2*	*3*	*11*	*1*	*2*	*-*
Females	**2,259**	**256**	**138**	**187**	**546**	**87**	**297**	**307**	**227**	**196**	**18**
Self-employed	**119**	**47**	**9**	**8**	**8**	**14**	**11**	**8**	**5**	**5**	**4**
With employees	44	28	2	2	-	3	3	2	1	2	1
Without employees	75	19	7	6	8	11	8	6	4	3	3
Employees	**2,092**	**206**	**123**	**178**	**526**	**73**	**278**	**296**	**215**	**190**	**7**
Working 31 or more hours per week	1,143	162	84	117	335	57	96	70	180	38	4
Working 30 or fewer hours per week	949	44	39	61	191	16	182	226	35	152	3
Economically active students (included above)	*38*	*-*	*-*	*-*	*1*	*-*	*13*	*22*	*-*	*2*	*-*

Table 81 Occupation and employment status (10% sample) – **continued**

County, districts

81. Residents aged 16 and over, employees and self-employed

(10% sample)

		Standard Occupational Classification Major Groups									
Employment status	TOTAL PERSONS	Managers and administrators	Professional	Associate professional	Clerical and secretarial	Craft and related	Personal and protective service	Sales	Plant and machine operatives	Other occupations	Not stated or inadequately described
a	b	c	d	e	f	g	h	i	j	k	l
New Forest											
Males	3,847	827	372	391	211	857	207	191	489	268	34
Self-employed	**787**	**183**	**78**	**68**	**5**	**287**	**7**	**26**	**60**	**58**	**15**
With employees	245	98	49	15	1	56	1	3	15	6	1
Without employees	542	85	29	53	4	231	6	23	45	52	14
Employees	**2,967**	**629**	**287**	**312**	**198**	**565**	**176**	**162**	**424**	**205**	**9**
Working 31 or more hours per week	2,806	621	268	302	175	555	149	133	414	180	9
Working 30 or fewer hours per week	161	8	19	10	23	10	27	29	10	25	-
Economically active students (included above)	*46*	*1*	*-*	*3*	*6*	*1*	*11*	*18*	*-*	*6*	*-*
Females	3,047	410	193	275	886	76	473	363	91	262	18
Self-employed	**248**	**115**	**19**	**34**	**17**	**13**	**14**	**15**	**2**	**11**	**8**
With employees	94	62	13	8	2	2	-	1	-	4	2
Without employees	154	53	6	26	15	11	14	14	2	7	6
Employees	**2,736**	**288**	**169**	**238**	**851**	**61**	**443**	**345**	**87**	**248**	**6**
Working 31 or more hours per week	1,448	237	106	152	537	39	148	112	64	50	3
Working 30 or fewer hours per week	1,288	51	63	86	314	22	295	233	23	198	3
Economically active students (included above)	*44*	*-*	*1*	*1*	*1*	*1*	*12*	*19*	*2*	*7*	*-*

Table 81 Occupation and employment status (10% sample) – continued

(10% sample)

81. Residents aged 16 and over, employees and self-employed

Portsmouth

Employment status	TOTAL PERSONS	Standard Occupational Classification Major Groups									
		Managers and administrators	Professional	Associate professional	Clerical and secretarial	Craft and related	Personal and protective service	Sales	Plant and machine operatives	Other occupations	Not stated or inadequately described
a	b	c	d	e	f	g	h	i	j	k	l
Males	**4,288**	**627**	**365**	**374**	**281**	**976**	**574**	**194**	**517**	**339**	**41**
Self-employed	**649**	**125**	**39**	**40**	**9**	**262**	**6**	**28**	**76**	**50**	**14**
With employees	160	69	16	9	-	41	3	5	12	1	4
Without employees	489	56	23	31	9	221	3	23	64	49	10
Employees	**3,467**	**488**	**315**	**327**	**267**	**701**	**493**	**161**	**427**	**275**	**13**
Working 31 or more hours per week	3,311	484	298	325	258	692	460	129	410	242	13
Working 30 or fewer hours per week	156	4	17	2	9	9	33	32	17	33	-
Economically active students (included above)	*32*	*1*	*1*	*-*	*2*	*1*	*4*	*11*	*-*	*12*	*-*
Females	**3,275**	**374**	**181**	**315**	**853**	**109**	**484**	**405**	**175**	**359**	**20**
Self-employed	**179**	**73**	**17**	**25**	**9**	**8**	**22**	**5**	**9**	**4**	**7**
With employees	66	36	5	10	2	3	2	2	4	-	2
Without employees	113	37	12	15	7	5	20	3	5	4	5
Employees	**3,028**	**295**	**155**	**288**	**834**	**97**	**452**	**393**	**161**	**348**	**5**
Working 31 or more hours per week	1,762	261	114	210	592	73	182	126	132	67	5
Working 30 or fewer hours per week	1,266	34	41	78	242	24	270	267	29	281	-
Economically active students (included above)	*53*	*1*	*3*	*3*	*4*	*-*	*14*	*22*	*-*	*6*	*-*

Table 81 Occupation and employment status (10% sample) – **continued**

81. Residents aged 16 and over, employees and self-employed

County, districts

(10% sample)

Rushmoor

Employment status	TOTAL PERSONS	Standard Occupational Classification Major Groups									
		Managers and administrators	Professional	Associate professional	Clerical and secretarial	Craft and related	Personal and protective service	Sales	Plant and machine operatives	Other occupations	Not stated or inadequately described
a	b	c	d	e	f	g	h	i	j	k	l
Males	**2,464**	**436**	**219**	**217**	**158**	**484**	**471**	**105**	**214**	**144**	**16**
Self-employed	**299**	**43**	**9**	**24**	**2**	**149**	**6**	**8**	**27**	**23**	**8**
With employees	59	19	6	4	-	16	2	1	6	2	3
Without employees	240	24	3	20	2	133	4	7	21	21	5
Employees	**2,038**	**384**	**206**	**187**	**152**	**329**	**382**	**96**	**183**	**118**	**1**
Working 31 or more hours per week	1,959	380	201	184	144	325	367	83	177	97	1
Working 30 or fewer hours per week	79	4	5	3	8	4	15	13	6	21	-
Economically active students *(included above)*	12	-	-	-	1	-	1	7	-	3	-
Females	**1,869**	**223**	**101**	**169**	**596**	**37**	**279**	**177**	**94**	**186**	**7**
Self-employed	**68**	**21**	**11**	**13**	**4**	**2**	**8**	**4**	**2**	**3**	**-**
With employees	21	11	5	5	-	-	-	-	-	-	-
Without employees	47	10	6	8	4	2	8	4	2	3	-
Employees	**1,762**	**201**	**89**	**151**	**585**	**33**	**264**	**169**	**89**	**180**	**1**
Working 31 or more hours per week	1,109	172	63	101	426	25	144	57	75	46	-
Working 30 or fewer hours per week	653	29	26	50	159	8	120	112	14	134	1
Economically active students *(included above)*	26	-	-	-	3	-	3	12	-	8	-

146

Table 81 Occupation and employment status (10% sample) – **continued**

County, districts

(10% sample)

81. Residents aged 16 and over, employees and self-employed

Employment status	TOTAL PERSONS	Standard Occupational Classification Major Groups									
		Managers and administrators	Professional	Associate professional	Clerical and secretarial	Craft and related	Personal and protective service	Sales	Plant and machine operatives	Other occupations	Not stated or inadequately described
a	b	c	d	e	f	g	h	i	j	k	l
Southampton											
Males	4,643	633	447	403	389	1,173	253	226	677	401	41
Self-employed	720	114	43	52	-	331	6	31	74	50	19
With employees	151	62	19	8	-	43	1	-	6	6	6
Without employees	569	52	24	44	-	288	5	31	68	44	13
Employees	3,806	510	393	340	382	827	229	188	586	340	11
Working 31 or more hours per week	3,624	503	366	331	367	810	203	154	569	310	11
Working 30 or fewer hours per week	182	7	27	9	15	17	26	34	17	30	-
Economically active students (included above)	*45*	*2*	*3*	*1*	*4*	*1*	*3*	*22*	*3*	*6*	*-*
Females	3,677	391	228	401	986	71	518	486	155	416	25
Self-employed	180	76	14	29	12	7	23	5	6	5	3
With employees	50	34	5	7	2	-	1	-	-	1	-
Without employees	130	42	9	22	10	7	22	5	6	4	3
Employees	3,409	310	205	364	957	61	478	473	145	405	11
Working 31 or more hours per week	1,934	262	151	271	665	44	168	167	111	86	9
Working 30 or fewer hours per week	1,475	48	54	93	292	17	310	306	34	319	2
Economically active students (included above)	*46*	*-*	*-*	*3*	*7*	*-*	*6*	*22*	*-*	*8*	*-*

Table 81 Occupation and employment status (10% sample) – **continued**

81. Residents aged 16 and over, employees and self-employed

(10% sample)

Employment status	TOTAL PERSONS	Managers and administrators	Professional	Associate professional	Clerical and secretarial	Craft and related	Personal and protective service	Sales	Plant and machine operatives	Other occupations	Not stated or inadequately described
a	b	c	d	e	f	g	h	i	j	k	l
Test Valley											
Males	2,915	704	279	234	177	583	248	129	340	200	21
Self-employed	**531**	**132**	**60**	**36**	**3**	**188**	**7**	**26**	**42**	**28**	**9**
With employees	182	73	37	11	-	33	3	6	9	6	4
Without employees	349	59	23	25	3	155	4	20	33	22	5
Employees	**2,329**	**565**	**216**	**195**	**172**	**387**	**222**	**100**	**295**	**169**	**8**
Working 31 or more hours per week	2,225	554	205	189	167	380	212	82	283	147	6
Working 30 or fewer hours per week	104	11	11	6	5	7	10	18	12	22	2
Economically active students (included above)	*28*	*-*	*-*	*2*	*2*	*2*	*3*	*11*	*1*	*6*	*1*
Females	2,115	264	177	195	644	45	267	184	112	209	18
Self-employed	**137**	**51**	**16**	**22**	**12**	**7**	**12**	**8**	**2**	**3**	**4**
With employees	52	26	7	6	6	2	2	1	-	-	2
Without employees	85	25	9	16	6	5	10	7	2	3	2
Employees	**1,926**	**208**	**156**	**166**	**620**	**38**	**248**	**172**	**109**	**201**	**8**
Working 31 or more hours per week	1,091	182	105	97	412	24	95	53	72	46	5
Working 30 or fewer hours per week	835	26	51	69	208	14	153	119	37	155	3
Economically active students (included above)	*42*	*-*	*-*	*2*	*1*	*-*	*8*	*22*	*1*	*6*	*2*

Standard Occupational Classification Major Groups

Table 81 Occupation and employment status (10% sample) – continued

81. Residents aged 16 and over, employees and self-employed

(10% sample)

Winchester

Employment status	TOTAL PERSONS	Standard Occupational Classification Major Groups									
		Managers and administrators	Professional	Associate professional	Clerical and secretarial	Craft and related	Personal and protective service	Sales	Plant and machine operatives	Other occupations	Not stated or inadequately described
a	b	c	d	e	f	g	h	i	j	k	l
Males	2,598	700	379	243	145	414	216	100	199	180	22
Self-employed	519	149	84	38	5	165	4	11	24	26	13
With employees	199	96	46	10	3	29	1	1	4	4	5
Without employees	320	53	38	28	2	136	3	10	20	22	8
Employees	2,022	538	288	202	139	239	200	85	172	152	7
Working 31 or more hours per week	1,903	527	278	195	128	226	182	66	165	129	7
Working 30 or fewer hours per week	119	11	10	7	11	13	18	19	7	23	-
Economically active students (included above)	*25*	*1*	*-*	*2*	*1*	*-*	*2*	*11*	*1*	*6*	*1*
Females	1,923	295	236	193	499	38	273	154	38	187	10
Self-employed	184	77	19	30	12	7	18	2	2	8	9
With employees	68	39	7	11	1	2	3	-	-	-	5
Without employees	116	38	12	19	11	5	15	2	2	8	4
Employees	1,708	210	212	163	482	30	251	149	35	175	1
Working 31 or more hours per week	951	168	131	111	309	19	93	63	22	34	1
Working 30 or fewer hours per week	757	42	81	52	173	11	158	86	13	141	-
Economically active students (included above)	*34*	*1*	*2*	*1*	*1*	*-*	*7*	*16*	*-*	*6*	*-*

Table 82 Travel to work and SEG (10% sample)

82. Residents aged 16 and over, employees and self-employed

(10% sample)

HAMPSHIRE

Socio-economic group (SEG)	TOTAL PERSONS	Means of transport to work											Not stated	Working outside district of usual residence
		British Rail train	Other rail	Bus	Car		Motor cycle	Pedal cycle	On foot	Other	Works at home			
					Driver	Passenger								
a	b	c	d	e	f	g	h	i	j	k	l	m	n
TOTAL PERSONS	**71,873**	**2,160**	**46**	**4,042**	**42,858**	**5,110**	**1,541**	**3,515**	**7,739**	**383**	**3,406**	**1,073**	**26,966**
Total males	**40,790**	**1,501**	**28**	**1,227**	**26,761**	**1,931**	**1,263**	**2,301**	**3,105**	**298**	**1,727**	**648**	**17,018**
Total females	**31,083**	**659**	**18**	**2,815**	**16,097**	**3,179**	**278**	**1,214**	**4,634**	**85**	**1,679**	**425**	**9,948**
1,2 Employers and managers	11,864	557	8	278	8,709	476	95	157	576	69	817	122	6,208
3,4 Professional workers	4,122	251	5	53	2,978	108	68	197	164	16	251	31	2,355
5 Intermediate non-manual workers	9,891	381	7	359	6,867	573	146	369	611	21	485	72	4,609
6 Junior non-manual workers	15,254	475	4	1,577	8,326	1,459	185	542	2,147	29	359	151	5,620
8,9,12 Manual workers (foremen, supervisors, skilled and own account)	13,744	242	6	391	9,260	975	463	640	644	70	855	198	4,435
7,10 Personal service and semi-skilled manual workers	9,802	143	5	904	4,413	954	371	819	1,764	58	217	154	2,831
11 Unskilled manual workers	3,334	40	-	381	998	418	108	368	886	16	45	74	701
13,14,15 Farmers and agricultural workers	838	1	-	10	283	30	22	41	135	14	286	16	102
16,17 Members of armed forces and inadequately described and not stated occupations	3,024	70	11	89	1,024	117	83	382	812	90	91	255	105
Working outside district of usual residence	26,966	1,851	28	1,137	20,321	1,736	631	559	372	136	27	168	
Employed and self-employed persons resident in households with:													
No car	5,790	308	3	1,324	335	643	282	841	1,751	32	144	127	1,154
1 car	29,473	976	14	1,884	15,534	2,871	846	1,900	3,583	166	1,245	454	9,941
2 cars	26,655	654	24	633	20,187	1,159	310	592	1,346	74	1,342	334	12,090
3 or more cars	8,776	218	4	176	6,721	416	98	158	372	32	483	98	3,728

Table 82 Travel to work and SEG (10% sample) – **continued**

82. Residents aged 16 and over, employees and self-employed

(10% sample)

Basingstoke & Deane

Socio-economic group (SEG)	TOTAL PERSONS	British Rail train	Other rail	Bus	Car Driver	Car Passenger	Motor cycle	Pedal cycle	On foot	Other	Works at home	Not stated	Working outside district of usual residence
a	b	c	d	e	f	g	h	i	j	k	l	m	n
TOTAL PERSONS	**7,472**	**271**	**2**	**412**	**4,569**	**613**	**108**	**225**	**814**	**22**	**345**	**91**	**2,237**
Total males	**4,237**	**189**	**2**	**111**	**2,874**	**209**	**98**	**159**	**343**	**15**	**189**	**48**	**1,566**
Total females	**3,235**	**82**	**-**	**301**	**1,695**	**404**	**10**	**66**	**471**	**7**	**156**	**43**	**671**
1,2 Employers and managers	1,360	84	-	31	1,016	58	7	12	63	4	73	12	606
3,4 Professional workers	492	36	-	5	349	19	6	22	22	-	31	2	269
5 Intermediate non-manual workers	1,019	48	-	38	710	63	10	24	67	2	55	2	348
6 Junior non-manual workers	1,715	67	-	183	914	206	9	40	241	3	32	20	432
8,9,12 Manual workers (foremen, supervisors, skilled and own account)	1,411	24	2	37	966	106	41	52	74	7	85	17	332
7,10 Personal service and semi-skilled manual workers	968	7	-	80	443	104	22	53	225	2	21	11	177
11 Unskilled manual workers	327	4	-	35	92	53	7	20	97	3	7	9	56
13,14,15 Farmers and agricultural workers	97	-	-	-	32	2	1	1	22	1	37	1	9
16,17 Members of armed forces and inadequately described and not stated occupations	83	1	-	3	47	2	5	1	3	-	4	17	8
Working outside district of usual residence	2,237	233	1	42	1,672	121	40	52	50	10	3	13	
Employed and self-employed persons resident in households with:													
No car	541	34	-	122	29	55	19	58	198	-	12	14	72
1 car	2,989	105	1	193	1,605	376	58	107	383	13	105	43	759
2 cars	2,904	90	1	75	2,189	132	22	37	169	6	157	26	1,055
3 or more cars	993	42	-	20	738	49	9	22	45	3	58	7	338

Means of transport to work

Table 82 Travel to work and SEG (10% sample) – **continued**

82. Residents aged 16 and over, employees and self-employed   (10% sample)

East Hampshire

Socio-economic group (SEG)	TOTAL PERSONS	Means of transport to work											Not stated	Working outside district of usual residence
		British Rail train	Other rail	Bus	Car		Motor cycle	Pedal cycle	On foot	Other	Works at home			
					Driver	Passenger								
a	b	c	d	e	f	g	h	i	j	k	l	m	n
TOTAL PERSONS	**4,956**	**230**	**4**	**113**	**3,076**	**304**	**80**	**111**	**579**	**35**	**365**	**59**	**2,043**
Total males	**2,821**	**176**	**4**	**40**	**1,868**	**117**	**67**	**73**	**245**	**26**	**177**	**28**	**1,245**
Total females	**2,135**	**54**	**-**	**73**	**1,208**	**187**	**13**	**38**	**334**	**9**	**188**	**31**	**798**
1,2 Employers and managers	989	72	1	8	729	24	8	5	50	7	77	8	617
3,4 Professional workers	314	36	1	1	234	6	-	5	3	-	26	2	192
5 Intermediate non-manual workers	715	36	-	11	514	41	3	9	42	-	53	6	379
6 Junior non-manual workers	920	44	-	31	553	73	10	19	143	-	43	4	395
8,9,12 Manual workers (foremen, supervisors, skilled and own account)	908	26	1	10	600	64	30	21	44	9	89	14	240
7,10 Personal service and semi-skilled manual workers	566	10	-	24	266	57	12	20	138	11	20	8	153
11 Unskilled manual workers	195	-	-	17	63	26	7	12	56	4	3	7	42
13,14,15 Farmers and agricultural workers	140	-	-	1	48	5	7	5	19	1	51	3	15
16,17 Members of armed forces and inadequately described and not stated occupations	209	6	1	10	69	8	3	15	84	3	3	7	10
Working outside district of usual residence	2,043	201	3	57	1,567	118	40	19	22	8	2	6	
Employed and self-employed persons resident in households with:													
No car	225	19	-	24	15	27	16	17	92	-	8	7	52
1 car	1,766	92	1	64	930	157	42	60	265	14	115	26	634
2 cars	2,106	93	2	14	1,583	84	15	26	115	6	152	16	1,040
3 or more cars	764	26	1	8	546	33	6	7	31	10	86	10	316

Table 82 Travel to work and SEG (10% sample) – **continued**

82. Residents aged 16 and over, employees and self-employed

(10% sample)

Socio-economic group (SEG)	TOTAL PERSONS	British Rail train	Other rail	Bus	Car		Motor cycle	Pedal cycle	On foot	Other	Works at home	Not stated	Working outside district of usual residence
					Driver	Passenger							
a	b	c	d	e	f	g	h	i	j	k	l	m	n
Eastleigh													
TOTAL PERSONS	**5,205**	**120**	**1**	**268**	**3,533**	**331**	**132**	**171**	**394**	**21**	**181**	**53**	**2,760**
Total males	**2,945**	**76**	**-**	**64**	**2,182**	**116**	**116**	**113**	**133**	**19**	**97**	**29**	**1,616**
Total females	**2,260**	**44**	**1**	**204**	**1,351**	**215**	**16**	**58**	**261**	**2**	**84**	**24**	**1,144**
1,2 Employers and managers	894	30	1	17	730	29	3	4	25	6	44	5	557
3,4 Professional workers	273	5	-	6	218	5	5	8	12	3	11	-	201
5 Intermediate non-manual workers	800	31	-	31	604	42	12	14	34	2	29	1	531
6 Junior non-manual workers	1,290	29	-	131	817	110	20	30	120	-	21	12	721
8,9,12 Manual workers (foremen, supervisors, skilled and own account)	1,045	9	-	20	743	61	40	45	53	3	60	11	424
7,10 Personal service and semi-skilled manual workers	627	12	-	41	294	58	41	50	103	5	9	14	246
11 Unskilled manual workers	194	2	-	19	75	22	8	19	44	1	1	3	57
13,14,15 Farmers and agricultural workers	27	-	-	1	14	4	1	-	1	-	6	-	12
16,17 Members of armed forces and inadequately described and not stated occupations	55	2	-	2	38	-	2	1	2	1	-	7	11
Working outside district of usual residence	2,760	106	1	171	2,152	187	67	42	20	5	1	8	
Employed and self-employed persons resident in households with:													
No car	244	22	-	48	27	25	22	21	72	1	3	3	89
1 car	2,002	51	1	135	1,144	184	73	102	214	6	72	20	984
2 cars	2,271	37	-	69	1,811	88	29	38	85	10	82	22	1,314
3 or more cars	685	10	-	16	550	34	8	10	23	4	23	7	372

Means of transport to work

Table 82 Travel to work and SEG (10% sample) – **continued**

82. Residents aged 16 and over, employees and self-employed

(10% sample)

Fareham

Socio-economic group (SEG)	TOTAL PERSONS	Means of transport to work											Not stated	Working outside district of usual residence
		British Rail train	Other rail	Bus	Car		Motor cycle	Pedal cycle	On foot	Other	Works at home			
					Driver	Passenger								
a	b	c	d	e	f	g	h	i	j	k	l	m	n
TOTAL PERSONS	**4,790**	**131**	**8**	**174**	**3,196**	**355**	**139**	**218**	**295**	**32**	**193**	**49**	**2,392**
Total males	**2,698**	**89**	**5**	**49**	**1,923**	**124**	**116**	**134**	**97**	**28**	**107**	**26**	**1,455**
Total females	**2,092**	**42**	**3**	**125**	**1,273**	**231**	**23**	**84**	**198**	**4**	**86**	**23**	**937**
1,2 Employers and managers	858	21	-	7	691	44	8	9	28	10	34	4	552
3,4 Professional workers	297	8	2	1	234	11	9	10	6	4	14	-	212
5 Intermediate non-manual workers	751	20	1	12	586	51	15	21	20	1	20	4	476
6 Junior non-manual workers	1,020	37	2	82	631	105	15	25	92	1	19	11	489
8,9,12 Manual workers (foremen, supervisors, skilled and own account)	844	21	-	14	585	55	40	35	23	7	54	10	372
7,10 Personal service and semi-skilled manual workers	502	11	-	38	257	45	26	47	63	4	4	7	224
11 Unskilled manual workers	205	2	-	16	58	33	9	43	36	1	4	3	52
13,14,15 Farmers and agricultural workers	28	-	-	-	12	1	2	3	2	1	6	1	2
16,17 Members of armed forces and inadequately described and not stated occupations	285	11	3	4	142	10	15	25	25	3	38	9	13
Working outside district of usual residence	2,392	105	5	76	1,863	165	71	50	24	22	1	10	
Employed and self-employed persons resident in households with:													
No car	216	20	-	47	12	38	17	35	39	2	3	3	80
1 car	1,813	72	2	85	1,004	197	87	128	147	17	52	22	852
2 cars	2,052	30	5	35	1,640	85	28	42	82	11	74	20	1,144
3 or more cars	664	9	1	7	538	35	7	13	25	2	23	4	314

Table 82 Travel to work and SEG (10% sample) – **continued**

82. Residents aged 16 and over, employees and self-employed (10% sample)

Gosport

Socio-economic group (SEG)	TOTAL PERSONS	British Rail train	Other rail	Bus	Car		Motor cycle	Pedal cycle	On foot	Other	Works at home	Not stated	Working outside district of usual residence
					Driver	Passenger							
a	b	c	d	e	f	g	h	i	j	k	l	m	n
TOTAL PERSONS	**3,390**	**47**	**4**	**271**	**1,671**	**247**	**143**	**490**	**352**	**28**	**68**	**69**	**1,290**
Total males	**1,931**	**34**	**3**	**80**	**1,018**	**101**	**114**	**337**	**152**	**18**	**30**	**44**	**787**
Total females	**1,459**	**13**	**1**	**191**	**653**	**146**	**29**	**153**	**200**	**10**	**38**	**25**	**503**
1,2 Employers and managers	362	5	1	33	219	19	7	22	24	5	19	8	204
3,4 Professional workers	98	2	-	1	64	3	9	11	1	-	4	3	53
5 Intermediate non-manual workers	380	8	-	21	246	24	11	34	20	3	8	5	189
6 Junior non-manual workers	678	9	-	100	339	67	15	61	68	5	10	4	301
8,9,12 Manual workers (foremen, supervisors, skilled and own account)	658	7	-	21	422	38	31	82	27	3	18	9	288
7,10 Personal service and semi-skilled manual workers	566	4	-	53	208	52	41	110	80	2	5	11	187
11 Unskilled manual workers	178	4	-	23	37	15	9	45	41	1	1	2	56
13,14,15 Farmers and agricultural workers	12	-	-	1	5	3	1	1	1	-	-	-	8
16,17 Members of armed forces and inadequately described and not stated occupations	458	8	3	18	131	26	19	124	90	9	3	27	4
Working outside district of usual residence	1,290	34	1	131	828	90	72	87	27	13	-	7	
Employed and self-employed persons resident in households with:													
No car	427	13	-	99	13	38	39	130	80	2	7	6	116
1 car	1,851	27	3	137	892	166	79	293	169	20	32	33	697
2 cars	831	6	1	29	606	34	16	57	40	2	20	20	386
3 or more cars	210	1	-	6	159	7	9	8	6	1	6	7	91

Means of transport to work

Table 82 Travel to work and SEG (10% sample) – **continued**

82. Residents aged 16 and over, employees and self-employed

(10% sample)

Hart

Socio-economic group (SEG)	TOTAL PERSONS	Means of transport to work											Working outside district of usual residence
		British Rail train	Other rail	Bus	Car		Motor cycle	Pedal cycle	On foot	Other	Works at home	Not stated	
					Driver	Passenger							
a	b	c	d	e	f	g	h	i	j	k	l	m	n
TOTAL PERSONS	**4,222**	**255**	**5**	**67**	**2,820**	**202**	**66**	**130**	**339**	**18**	**262**	**58**	**2,484**
Total males	**2,485**	**178**	**1**	**13**	**1,711**	**76**	**53**	**82**	**195**	**14**	**122**	**40**	**1,531**
Total females	**1,737**	**77**	**4**	**54**	**1,109**	**126**	**13**	**48**	**144**	**4**	**140**	**18**	**953**
1,2 Employers and managers	954	104	1	4	730	33	2	2	18	3	49	8	701
3,4 Professional workers	364	43	3	1	264	6	6	5	4	2	26	4	275
5 Intermediate non-manual workers	606	35	-	7	453	21	8	7	17	-	51	7	399
6 Junior non-manual workers	862	50	-	28	580	63	5	22	73	-	31	10	557
8,9,12 Manual workers (foremen, supervisors, skilled and own account)	633	7	-	2	469	28	17	14	15	3	63	15	314
7,10 Personal service and semi-skilled manual workers	386	4	1	16	210	24	12	34	53	2	23	7	174
11 Unskilled manual workers	122	2	-	6	46	17	8	17	23	1	2	-	49
13,14,15 Farmers and agricultural workers	41	-	-	-	12	2	-	3	10	1	13	-	8
16,17 Members of armed forces and inadequately described and not stated occupations	254	10	-	3	56	8	8	26	126	6	4	7	7
Working outside district of usual residence	2,484	234	5	40	1,967	111	36	38	25	2	4	22	
Employed and self-employed persons resident in households with:													
No car	86	5	-	9	7	11	8	19	18	-	8	1	30
1 car	1,172	94	-	30	642	94	22	69	127	7	73	14	639
2 cars	2,074	117	4	23	1,593	60	26	27	61	3	134	26	1,349
3 or more cars	750	39	1	4	574	33	10	13	19	3	40	14	466

Table 82 Travel to work and SEG (10% sample) – **continued**

82. Residents aged 16 and over, employees and self-employed

(10% sample)

Havant

Socio-economic group (SEG)	TOTAL PERSONS	British Rail train	Other rail	Bus	Car		Motor cycle	Pedal cycle	On foot	Other	Works at home	Not stated	Working outside district of usual residence
					Driver	Passenger							
a	b	c	d	e	f	g	h	i	j	k	l	m	n
TOTAL PERSONS	**5,177**	**155**	**-**	**244**	**3,255**	**469**	**109**	**229**	**442**	**19**	**184**	**71**	**2,360**
Total males	**2,918**	**106**	**-**	**76**	**2,087**	**170**	**83**	**121**	**129**	**11**	**95**	**40**	**1,493**
Total females	**2,259**	**49**	**-**	**168**	**1,168**	**299**	**26**	**108**	**313**	**8**	**89**	**31**	**867**
1,2 Employers and managers	794	23	-	13	604	35	8	9	39	3	50	10	425
3,4 Professional workers	287	16	-	1	225	6	3	12	8	1	12	3	180
5 Intermediate non-manual workers	683	26	-	19	505	53	11	24	24	2	15	4	400
6 Junior non-manual workers	1,052	34	-	76	581	120	9	26	170	2	22	12	449
8,9,12 Manual workers (foremen, supervisors, skilled and own account)	1,092	30	-	31	765	87	32	43	34	4	53	13	472
7,10 Personal service and semi-skilled manual workers	876	15	-	75	410	120	36	76	107	4	22	11	346
11 Unskilled manual workers	241	7	-	19	77	38	4	33	52	1	3	7	66
13,14,15 Farmers and agricultural workers	24	1	-	4	13	-	1	-	1	-	3	1	11
16,17 Members of armed forces and inadequately described and not stated occupations	128	3	-	6	75	10	5	6	7	2	4	10	11
Working outside district of usual residence	2,360	132	-	134	1,740	198	61	46	24	6	3	16	
Employed and self-employed persons resident in households with:													
No car	401	22	-	85	24	76	22	59	98	1	7	7	132
1 car	2,261	90	-	116	1,279	256	61	118	222	15	69	35	994
2 cars	1,875	35	-	35	1,448	109	21	42	94	2	68	21	917
3 or more cars	615	8	-	8	504	27	5	10	27	-	20	6	316

Means of transport to work

157

Table 82 Travel to work and SEG (10% sample) – continued

82. Residents aged 16 and over, employees and self-employed

County, districts

(10% sample)

New Forest

Socio-economic group (SEG)	TOTAL PERSONS	Means of transport to work												Working outside district of usual residence
		British Rail train	Other rail	Bus	Car		Motor cycle	Pedal cycle	On foot	Other	Works at home	Not stated	
					Driver	Passenger							
a	b	c	d	e	f	g	h	i	j	k	l	m	n
TOTAL PERSONS	**6,894**	**103**	**2**	**226**	**4,523**	**381**	**169**	**407**	**477**	**40**	**440**	**126**	**2,495**
Total males	**3,847**	**76**	**2**	**70**	**2,717**	**127**	**135**	**243**	**172**	**24**	**211**	**70**	**1,534**
Total females	**3,047**	**27**	**-**	**156**	**1,806**	**254**	**34**	**164**	**305**	**16**	**229**	**56**	**961**
1,2 Employers and managers	1,242	30	1	8	951	28	10	20	49	5	122	18	603
3,4 Professional workers	348	9	-	2	267	6	7	11	6	2	37	1	186
5 Intermediate non-manual workers	923	24	-	19	670	46	18	45	32	3	52	14	395
6 Junior non-manual workers	1,522	15	-	97	978	113	18	80	139	14	50	18	634
8,9,12 Manual workers (foremen, supervisors, skilled and own account)	1,365	13	-	35	953	77	53	75	38	6	97	18	376
7,10 Personal service and semi-skilled manual workers	926	7	1	48	488	70	36	111	111	5	29	20	229
11 Unskilled manual workers	306	1	-	16	115	33	19	38	70	1	4	9	56
13,14,15 Farmers and agricultural workers	147	-	-	-	60	4	4	14	14	3	43	5	5
16,17 Members of armed forces and inadequately described and not stated occupations	115	4	-	1	41	4	4	13	18	1	6	23	11
Working outside district of usual residence	2,495	83	1	115	1,963	139	67	51	24	23	2	27	
Employed and self-employed persons resident in households with:													
No car	306	10	-	35	23	36	20	72	81	4	15	10	64
1 car	2,524	45	1	115	1,382	198	100	212	232	21	158	60	806
2 cars	3,008	36	1	57	2,316	112	38	97	107	8	188	48	1,245
3 or more cars	993	11	-	17	796	32	9	25	34	4	58	7	375

Table 82 Travel to work and SEG (10% sample) – continued

82. Residents aged 16 and over, employees and self-employed

(10% sample)

Portsmouth

Socio-economic group (SEG)	TOTAL PERSONS	Means of transport to work											Working outside district of usual residence
		British Rail train	Other rail	Bus	Car		Motor cycle	Pedal cycle	On foot	Other	Works at home	Not stated	
					Driver	Passenger							
a	b	c	d	e	f	g	h	i	j	k	l	m	n
TOTAL PERSONS	**7,563**	**182**	**6**	**680**	**3,615**	**566**	**191**	**657**	**1,138**	**73**	**300**	**155**	**1,591**
Total males	**4,288**	**125**	**3**	**232**	**2,369**	**235**	**155**	**434**	**416**	**65**	**152**	**102**	**1,077**
Total females	**3,275**	**57**	**3**	**448**	**1,246**	**331**	**36**	**223**	**722**	**8**	**148**	**53**	**514**
1,2 Employers and managers	954	24	-	56	600	58	12	26	78	9	76	15	288
3,4 Professional workers	340	10	1	11	211	15	10	36	25	1	16	4	120
5 Intermediate non-manual workers	1,014	30	-	68	596	64	17	90	97	-	45	7	270
6 Junior non-manual workers	1,542	42	1	218	620	146	27	95	345	1	30	17	252
8,9,12 Manual workers (foremen, supervisors, skilled and own account)	1,565	29	2	67	913	133	63	136	103	6	90	23	354
7,10 Personal service and semi-skilled manual workers	1,241	39	1	173	436	95	44	134	266	9	24	20	258
11 Unskilled manual workers	450	4	-	63	100	34	9	70	156	1	5	8	46
13,14,15 Farmers and agricultural workers	9	-	-	1	4	1	-	2	-	-	1	-	1
16,17 Members of armed forces and inadequately described and not stated occupations	448	4	1	23	135	20	9	68	68	46	13	61	2
Working outside district of usual residence	1,591	134	4	97	1,086	123	39	48	29	14	3	14	
Employed and self-employed persons resident in households with:													
No car	1,420	70	2	316	63	132	55	241	463	8	37	33	166
1 car	3,698	75	1	281	1,880	321	98	320	487	14	157	64	796
2 cars	1,797	26	2	63	1,302	88	32	81	103	6	63	31	487
3 or more cars	477	10	-	12	351	24	5	12	34	1	21	7	134

Table 82 Travel to work and SEG (10% sample) – **continued**

County, districts

82. Residents aged 16 and over, employees and self-employed

(10% sample)

Rushmoor

Socio-economic group (SEG)	TOTAL PERSONS	British Rail train	Other rail	Bus	Car Driver	Car Passenger	Motor cycle	Pedal cycle	On foot	Other	Works at home	Not stated	Working outside district of usual residence
a	b	c	d	e	f	g	h	i	j	k	l	m	n
TOTAL PERSONS	**4,333**	**213**	**2**	**177**	**2,440**	**306**	**71**	**228**	**700**	**17**	**105**	**74**	**1,744**
Total males	**2,464**	**120**	**1**	**38**	**1,497**	**106**	**59**	**175**	**353**	**14**	**48**	**53**	**1,035**
Total females	**1,869**	**93**	**1**	**139**	**943**	**200**	**12**	**53**	**347**	**3**	**57**	**21**	**709**
1,2 Employers and managers	636	54	-	16	455	34	6	8	36	-	23	4	390
3,4 Professional workers	228	23	-	5	160	5	2	13	12	-	6	2	138
5 Intermediate non-manual workers	520	37	1	14	340	30	12	18	44	-	20	4	278
6 Junior non-manual workers	936	70	-	69	492	92	11	34	145	1	16	6	395
8,9,12 Manual workers (foremen, supervisors, skilled and own account)	751	15	1	15	529	49	23	23	55	2	31	8	270
7,10 Personal service and semi-skilled manual workers	591	8	-	39	292	58	9	49	126	1	4	5	216
11 Unskilled manual workers	197	1	-	14	64	30	2	15	61	1	1	8	49
13,14,15 Farmers and agricultural workers	7	-	-	-	4	-	-	1	1	-	1	-	3
16,17 Members of armed forces and inadequately described and not stated occupations	467	5	-	5	104	8	6	67	220	12	3	37	5
Working outside district of usual residence	1,744	197	2	57	1,273	114	27	28	29	3	3	11	
Employed and self-employed persons resident in households with:													
No car	328	19	-	52	24	25	10	45	138	2	6	7	84
1 car	1,880	119	1	80	958	188	45	142	268	2	50	27	733
2 cars	1,359	56	1	32	1,044	71	7	26	79	2	32	9	693
3 or more cars	502	19	-	8	399	18	9	10	25	-	8	6	228

Table 82 Travel to work and SEG (10% sample) – **continued**

82. Residents aged 16 and over, employees and self-employed

(10% sample)

Southampton

Socio-economic group (SEG)	TOTAL PERSONS	British Rail train	Other rail	Bus	Car Driver	Car Passenger	Motor cycle	Pedal cycle	On foot	Other	Works at home	Not stated	Working outside district of usual residence
a	b	c	d	e	f	g	h	i	j	k	l	m	n
TOTAL PERSONS	**8,320**	**193**	**5**	**1,087**	**4,455**	**653**	**170**	**358**	**948**	**31**	**285**	**135**	**2,303**
Total males	**4,643**	**133**	**4**	**350**	**2,925**	**293**	**143**	**251**	**291**	**26**	**137**	**90**	**1,557**
Total females	**3,677**	**60**	**1**	**737**	**1,530**	**360**	**27**	**107**	**657**	**5**	**148**	**45**	**746**
1,2 Employers and managers	1,031	30	-	64	689	51	10	26	67	5	73	16	363
3,4 Professional workers	444	19	-	13	278	12	7	49	38	3	20	5	164
5 Intermediate non-manual workers	1,133	33	2	97	674	77	13	59	113	2	55	8	324
6 Junior non-manual workers	1,870	45	1	436	800	158	22	59	308	-	26	15	407
8,9,12 Manual workers (foremen, supervisors, skilled and own account)	1,853	35	-	106	1,241	152	52	68	70	11	86	32	560
7,10 Personal service and semi-skilled manual workers	1,386	19	1	255	580	135	49	72	224	7	18	26	358
11 Unskilled manual workers	499	11	-	107	149	61	15	22	121	1	2	10	112
13,14,15 Farmers and agricultural workers	12	-	-	1	6	2	-	-	1	-	2	-	6
16,17 Members of armed forces and inadequately described and not stated occupations	92	1	1	8	38	5	2	3	6	2	3	23	9
Working outside district of usual residence	2,303	164	1	137	1,593	187	67	63	52	17	2	20	
Employed and self-employed persons resident in households with:													
No car	1,087	58	1	408	56	112	39	97	270	3	15	28	212
1 car	3,994	92	1	498	2,084	366	82	183	474	21	126	67	1,109
2 cars	2,478	31	2	128	1,793	131	41	62	161	5	90	34	761
3 or more cars	723	11	1	52	515	44	7	13	37	2	35	6	215

Table 82 Travel to work and SEG (10% sample) – **continued**

82. Residents aged 16 and over, employees and self-employed (10% sample)

Socio-economic group (SEG)	TOTAL PERSONS	Means of transport to work											Working outside district of usual residence
		British Rail train	Other rail	Bus	Car Driver	Car Passenger	Motor cycle	Pedal cycle	On foot	Other	Works at home	Not stated	
a	b	c	d	e	f	g	h	i	j	k	l	m	n
Test Valley													
TOTAL PERSONS	**5,030**	**95**	**1**	**157**	**3,058**	**400**	**107**	**186**	**649**	**25**	**293**	**59**	**1,711**
Total males	**2,915**	**74**	**-**	**47**	**1,905**	**177**	**82**	**115**	**305**	**19**	**152**	**39**	**1,069**
Total females	**2,115**	**21**	**1**	**110**	**1,153**	**223**	**25**	**71**	**344**	**6**	**141**	**20**	**642**
1,2 Employers and managers	895	26	-	11	664	31	10	9	47	7	88	2	435
3,4 Professional workers	268	19	-	3	206	10	1	6	7	-	15	1	159
5 Intermediate non-manual workers	640	17	1	12	471	33	11	13	41	2	36	3	327
6 Junior non-manual workers	1,002	15	-	55	584	117	14	29	149	2	30	7	348
8,9,12 Manual workers (foremen, supervisors, skilled and own account)	957	7	-	20	640	88	26	34	64	5	59	14	234
7,10 Personal service and semi-skilled manual workers	660	1	-	33	293	82	30	44	149	5	15	8	148
11 Unskilled manual workers	229	1	-	20	77	26	7	19	71	-	4	4	43
13,14,15 Farmers and agricultural workers	131	-	-	-	41	2	5	8	28	3	41	3	10
16,17 Members of armed forces and inadequately described and not stated occupations	248	9	-	3	82	11	3	24	93	1	5	17	7
Working outside district of usual residence	1,711	79	1	58	1,378	105	27	23	27	6	2	5	
Employed and self-employed persons resident in households with:													
No car	275	4	-	44	23	41	12	30	105	4	8	4	23
1 car	1,944	45	-	73	981	230	62	112	304	10	101	26	515
2 cars	1,995	33	1	30	1,509	80	25	28	128	5	136	20	889
3 or more cars	707	12	-	10	538	47	8	12	35	2	37	6	275

Table 82 Travel to work and SEG (10% sample) – **continued**

82. Residents aged 16 and over, employees and self-employed

(10% sample)

Winchester

Socio-economic group (SEG)	TOTAL PERSONS	British Rail train	Other rail	Bus	Car		Motor cycle	Pedal cycle	On foot	Other	Works at home	Not stated	Working outside district of usual residence
					Driver	Passenger							
a	b	c	d	e	f	g	h	i	j	k	l	m	n
TOTAL PERSONS	**4,521**	**165**	**6**	**166**	**2,647**	**283**	**56**	**105**	**612**	**22**	**385**	**74**	**1,556**
Total males	**2,598**	**125**	**3**	**57**	**1,685**	**80**	**42**	**64**	**274**	**19**	**210**	**39**	**1,053**
Total females	**1,923**	**40**	**3**	**109**	**962**	**203**	**14**	**41**	**338**	**3**	**175**	**35**	**503**
1,2 Employers and managers	895	54	1	10	631	32	4	5	52	5	89	12	467
3,4 Professional workers	369	25	-	3	268	4	3	9	20	-	33	4	206
5 Intermediate non-manual workers	707	36	2	10	498	28	5	11	60	4	46	7	293
6 Junior non-manual workers	845	18	-	71	437	89	10	22	154	-	29	15	240
8,9,12 Manual workers (foremen, supervisors, skilled and own account)	662	19	-	13	434	37	15	12	44	4	70	14	199
7,10 Personal service and semi-skilled manual workers	507	6	1	29	236	54	13	19	119	1	23	6	115
11 Unskilled manual workers	191	1	-	26	45	30	4	15	58	-	8	4	17
13,14,15 Farmers and agricultural workers	163	-	-	1	32	4	-	3	35	4	82	2	12
16,17 Members of armed forces and inadequately described and not stated occupations	182	6	2	3	66	5	2	9	70	4	5	10	7
Working outside district of usual residence	1,556	149	3	22	1,239	78	17	12	19	7	1	9	
Employed and self-employed persons resident in households with:													
No car	234	12	-	35	19	27	3	17	97	5	15	4	34
1 car	1,579	69	2	77	753	138	37	54	291	6	135	17	423
2 cars	1,905	64	4	43	1,353	85	10	29	122	8	146	41	810
3 or more cars	693	20	-	8	513	33	6	3	31	-	68	11	288

Table 83 Travel to work and car availability (10% sample)

83. Households with residents aged 16 and over, employees and self-employed

(10% sample)

Households with the following number of resident employees or self-employed aged 16 and over and means of transport to work

Cars available	1			2									3 or more			
	Car	Public transport	Other	Both car	Both public transport	1 car and 1 public transport	1 car and 1 other	1 public transport and 1 other	Others	All car	All public transport	Any car and any public transport with or without other(s)	Any car and any other(s) - no public transport	Any public transport and any other(s) - no car	Others
a	b	c	d	e	f	g	h	i	j	k	l	m	n	o	p
HAMPSHIRE															
TOTAL HOUSEHOLDS	11,202	1,676	3,977	9,780	255	1,841	4,793	599	1,591	1,588	27	1,079	1,901	150	206
No car	450	843	1,499	60	124	91	172	265	418	6	13	35	57	65	53
1 car	7,071	599	1,956	2,741	91	1,244	3,043	262	794	112	10	366	474	59	81
2 or more cars	3,681	234	522	6,979	40	506	1,578	72	379	1,470	4	678	1,370	26	72
Basingstoke & Deane															
TOTAL HOUSEHOLDS	1,096	166	323	1,106	28	204	424	69	140	180	1	127	231	20	19
No car	28	73	121	4	9	10	17	28	38	-	1	6	8	11	6
1 car	698	52	141	332	12	130	263	26	57	17	-	45	71	4	6
2 or more cars	370	41	61	770	7	64	144	15	45	163	-	76	152	5	7
East Hampshire															
TOTAL HOUSEHOLDS	780	109	232	715	9	110	331	44	115	127	-	47	138	6	22
No car	24	24	63	1	2	2	6	12	14	1	-	-	3	1	7
1 car	440	48	128	157	2	61	172	24	61	10	-	16	31	1	5
2 or more cars	316	37	41	557	5	47	153	8	40	116	-	31	104	4	10
Eastleigh															
TOTAL HOUSEHOLDS	839	85	207	870	9	134	339	27	67	132	1	97	117	8	9
No car	27	40	68	2	4	5	7	7	14	1	1	3	2	2	1
1 car	525	37	109	213	4	94	205	18	41	6	-	21	24	3	5
2 or more cars	287	8	30	655	1	35	127	2	12	125	-	73	91	3	3
Fareham															
TOTAL HOUSEHOLDS	792	77	202	765	11	113	318	21	72	141	1	58	124	7	3
No car	19	35	43	3	7	4	11	8	12	-	-	1	5	3	-
1 car	473	35	127	197	4	76	188	11	39	6	-	15	20	4	1
2 or more cars	300	7	32	565	-	33	119	2	21	135	1	42	99	-	2

Table 83 Travel to work and car availability (10% sample) – continued

83. Households with residents aged 16 and over, employees and self-employed

Households with the following number of resident employees or self-employed aged 16 and over and means of transport to work

Cars available	1			2						3 or more					
	Car	Public transport	Other	Both car	Both public transport	1 car and 1 public transport	1 car and 1 other	1 public transport and 1 other	Others	All car	All public transport	Any car and any public transport with or without other(s)	Any car and any other(s) - no public transport	Any public transport and any other(s) - no car	Others
a	b	c	d	e	f	g	h	i	j	k	l	m	n	o	p
Gosport															
TOTAL HOUSEHOLDS	448	86	277	360	14	90	327	40	112	40	1	44	78	15	17
No car	21	50	120	7	12	5	10	22	38	-	-	-	1	7	7
1 car	327	31	137	152	2	78	250	14	64	7	1	22	31	7	7
2 or more cars	100	5	20	201	-	7	67	4	10	33	-	22	46	1	3
Hart															
TOTAL HOUSEHOLDS	633	85	139	654	15	109	258	23	60	123	1	58	102	6	10
No car	12	7	29	1	1	-	2	3	6	-	-	1	1	-	2
1 car	319	39	77	101	5	49	119	11	29	1	-	8	20	3	2
2 or more cars	302	39	33	552	9	60	137	9	25	122	1	49	81	3	6
Havant															
TOTAL HOUSEHOLDS	971	112	222	738	19	116	337	32	92	136	2	74	136	7	7
No car	45	59	97	7	9	7	19	16	23	-	-	2	7	3	-
1 car	622	44	98	241	9	82	214	14	50	15	2	32	29	3	6
2 or more cars	304	9	27	490	1	27	104	2	19	121	-	40	100	1	1
New Forest															
TOTAL HOUSEHOLDS	1,180	78	409	1,046	11	113	478	28	157	163	-	69	204	5	23
No car	22	23	109	6	5	3	15	8	22	1	-	-	3	1	5
1 car	674	41	232	225	3	72	272	15	75	7	-	17	43	3	11
2 or more cars	484	14	68	815	3	38	191	5	60	155	-	52	158	1	7
Portsmouth															
TOTAL HOUSEHOLDS	1,067	259	654	725	37	217	618	103	246	95	4	123	179	34	32
No car	83	195	370	11	24	19	45	71	122	1	3	9	8	23	14
1 car	770	56	246	303	13	163	466	30	97	8	1	57	67	7	12
2 or more cars	214	8	38	411	-	35	107	2	27	86	-	57	104	4	6

Table 83 Travel to work and car availability (10% sample) – **continued**

(10% sample)

83. Households with residents aged 16 and over, employees and self-employed

Households with the following number of resident employees or self-employed aged 16 and over and means of transport to work

Cars available	1			2						3 or more					
	Car	Public transport	Other	Both car	Both public transport	1 car and 1 public transport	1 car and 1 other	1 public transport and 1 other	Others	All car	All public transport	Any car and any public transport with or without other(s)	Any car and any other(s) - no public transport	Any public transport and any other(s) - no car	Others
a	b	c	d	e	f	g	h	i	j	k	l	m	n	o	p
Rushmoor															
TOTAL HOUSEHOLDS	578	93	220	550	12	117	272	45	101	95	2	81	105	5	10
No car	27	35	85	3	1	5	6	19	37	-	1	1	4	3	3
1 car	402	48	122	180	10	76	213	22	56	8	1	26	20	1	5
2 or more cars	149	10	13	367	1	36	53	4	8	87	-	54	81	1	2
Southampton															
TOTAL HOUSEHOLDS	1,360	365	536	933	69	341	491	117	167	124	7	192	174	29	16
No car	94	250	250	5	45	23	20	59	46	1	4	10	4	10	2
1 car	980	101	243	341	20	256	346	50	85	12	3	74	36	16	7
2 or more cars	286	14	43	587	4	62	125	8	36	111	-	108	134	3	7
Test Valley															
TOTAL HOUSEHOLDS	749	65	275	721	8	83	332	24	115	131	4	47	183	4	17
No car	28	23	82	7	3	4	7	6	24	1	2	2	5	1	2
1 car	448	27	140	184	4	56	193	12	65	11	-	12	58	3	9
2 or more cars	273	15	53	530	1	23	132	6	26	119	2	33	120	-	6
Winchester															
TOTAL HOUSEHOLDS	709	96	281	597	13	94	268	26	147	101	3	62	130	4	21
No car	20	29	62	3	2	4	7	6	22	-	1	-	6	-	4
1 car	393	40	156	115	3	51	142	15	75	4	1	21	24	4	5
2 or more cars	296	27	63	479	8	39	119	5	50	97	1	41	100	-	12

Table 84 Qualified manpower (10% sample)

County, districts

84. Residents aged 18 and over (10% sample)

Level of highest qualification, age and economic position	TOTAL PERSONS	Males	Females	Level of highest qualification, age and economic position	TOTAL PERSONS	Males	Females
a	b	c	d	a	b	c	d

HAMPSHIRE / East Hampshire

Level of highest qualification, age and economic position	TOTAL PERSONS	Males	Females	Level of highest qualification, age and economic position	TOTAL PERSONS	Males	Females
ALL PERSONS AGED 18 AND OVER	118,052	56,772	61,280	**ALL PERSONS AGED 18 AND OVER**	7,787	3,723	4,064
All persons qualified	17,115	10,087	7,028	All persons qualified	1,414	819	595
Level a (higher degree)	1,047	835	212	**Level a (higher degree)**	98	73	25
18 - 29	126	97	29	18 - 29	9	7	2
30 - 44	522	404	118	30 - 44	50	35	15
45 up to pensionable age	315	275	40	45 up to pensionable age	27	23	4
Pensionable age and over	84	59	25	Pensionable age and over	12	8	4
Level b (degree)	7,904	5,242	2,662	**Level b (degree)**	707	456	251
18 - 29	1,808	986	822	18 - 29	117	58	59
30 - 44	3,307	2,092	1,215	30 - 44	304	181	123
45 up to pensionable age	1,935	1,529	406	45 up to pensionable age	206	158	48
Pensionable age and over	854	635	219	Pensionable age and over	80	59	21
Level c (diploma etc)	8,164	4,010	4,154	**Level c (diploma etc)**	609	290	319
18 - 29	1,464	752	712	18 - 29	81	45	36
30 - 44	3,072	1,571	1,501	30 - 44	227	110	117
45 up to pensionable age	2,462	1,312	1,150	45 up to pensionable age	197	98	99
Pensionable age and over	1,166	375	791	Pensionable age and over	104	37	67
All persons qualified at level a, b or c aged 18 up to pensionable age	15,011	9,018	5,993	**All persons qualified at level a, b or c aged 18 up to pensionable age**	1,218	715	503
Employees or self-employed	12,918	8,193	4,725	Employees or self-employed	1,061	657	404
On a Government scheme	41	23	18	On a Government scheme	3	2	1
Unemployed	411	282	129	Unemployed	31	24	7

Basingstoke & Deane / Eastleigh

Level of highest qualification, age and economic position	TOTAL PERSONS	Males	Females	Level of highest qualification, age and economic position	TOTAL PERSONS	Males	Females
ALL PERSONS AGED 18 AND OVER	10,916	5,399	5,517	**ALL PERSONS AGED 18 AND OVER**	8,054	3,901	4,153
All persons qualified	1,693	1,050	643	All persons qualified	1,144	674	470
Level a (higher degree)	97	81	16	**Level a (higher degree)**	52	46	6
18 - 29	16	13	3	18 - 29	6	5	1
30 - 44	56	47	9	30 - 44	27	22	5
45 up to pensionable age	23	20	3	45 up to pensionable age	17	17	-
Pensionable age and over	2	1	1	Pensionable age and over	2	2	-
Level b (degree)	801	524	277	**Level b (degree)**	492	313	179
18 - 29	225	128	97	18 - 29	123	63	60
30 - 44	362	223	139	30 - 44	221	140	81
45 up to pensionable age	170	141	29	45 up to pensionable age	122	92	30
Pensionable age and over	44	32	12	Pensionable age and over	26	18	8
Level c (diploma etc)	795	445	350	**Level c (diploma etc)**	600	315	285
18 - 29	175	98	77	18 - 29	112	58	54
30 - 44	318	178	140	30 - 44	256	142	114
45 up to pensionable age	239	141	98	45 up to pensionable age	165	91	74
Pensionable age and over	63	28	35	Pensionable age and over	67	24	43
All persons qualified at level a, b or c aged 18 up to pensionable age	1,584	989	595	**All persons qualified at level a, b or c aged 18 up to pensionable age**	1,049	630	419
Employees or self-employed	1,405	922	483	Employees or self-employed	922	587	335
On a Government scheme	4	2	2	On a Government scheme	-	-	-
Unemployed	26	16	10	Unemployed	26	18	8

Table 84   Qualified manpower (10% sample) – **continued**

County, districts

84. Residents aged 18 and over   (10% sample)

Level of highest qualification, age and economic position	TOTAL PERSONS	Males	Females	Level of highest qualification, age and economic position	TOTAL PERSONS	Males	Females
a	b	c	d	a	b	c	d
Fareham				**Hart**			
ALL PERSONS AGED 18 AND OVER	7,698	3,657	4,041	**ALL PERSONS AGED 18 AND OVER**	6,090	3,033	3,057
All persons qualified	1,238	742	496	**All persons qualified**	1,358	843	515
Level a (higher degree)	51	43	8	**Level a (higher degree)**	111	94	17
18 - 29	3	2	1	18 - 29	10	7	3
30 - 44	24	22	2	30 - 44	55	45	10
45 up to pensionable age	20	16	4	45 up to pensionable age	42	39	3
Pensionable age and over	4	3	1	Pensionable age and over	4	3	1
Level b (degree)	498	344	154	**Level b (degree)**	664	459	205
18 - 29	88	49	39	18 - 29	117	61	56
30 - 44	224	146	78	30 - 44	320	215	105
45 up to pensionable age	133	107	26	45 up to pensionable age	176	143	33
Pensionable age and over	53	42	11	Pensionable age and over	51	40	11
Level c (diploma etc)	689	355	334	**Level c (diploma etc)**	583	290	293
18 - 29	104	50	54	18 - 29	91	58	33
30 - 44	285	159	126	30 - 44	240	114	126
45 up to pensionable age	216	122	94	45 up to pensionable age	192	104	88
Pensionable age and over	84	24	60	Pensionable age and over	60	14	46
All persons qualified at level a, b or c aged 18 up to pensionable age	1,097	673	424	**All persons qualified at level a, b or c aged 18 up to pensionable age**	1,243	786	457
Employees or self-employed	943	611	332	Employees or self-employed	1,083	734	349
On a Government scheme	4	3	1	On a Government scheme	1	1	-
Unemployed	32	25	7	Unemployed	31	21	10
Gosport				**Havant**			
ALL PERSONS AGED 18 AND OVER	5,578	2,622	2,956	**ALL PERSONS AGED 18 AND OVER**	9,063	4,306	4,757
All persons qualified	575	317	258	**All persons qualified**	1,106	687	419
Level a (higher degree)	21	15	6	**Level a (higher degree)**	50	43	7
18 - 29	3	2	1	18 - 29	2	2	-
30 - 44	9	5	4	30 - 44	20	17	3
45 up to pensionable age	8	7	1	45 up to pensionable age	22	19	3
Pensionable age and over	1	1	-	Pensionable age and over	6	5	1
Level b (degree)	192	137	55	**Level b (degree)**	518	365	153
18 - 29	39	22	17	18 - 29	78	49	29
30 - 44	71	49	22	30 - 44	207	131	76
45 up to pensionable age	48	40	8	45 up to pensionable age	163	129	34
Pensionable age and over	34	26	8	Pensionable age and over	70	56	14
Level c (diploma etc)	362	165	197	**Level c (diploma etc)**	538	279	259
18 - 29	80	37	43	18 - 29	88	44	44
30 - 44	126	63	63	30 - 44	153	83	70
45 up to pensionable age	101	50	51	45 up to pensionable age	199	117	82
Pensionable age and over	55	15	40	Pensionable age and over	98	35	63
All persons qualified at level a, b or c aged 18 up to pensionable age	485	275	210	**All persons qualified at level a, b or c aged 18 up to pensionable age**	932	591	341
Employees or self-employed	403	244	159	Employees or self-employed	776	518	258
On a Government scheme	6	4	2	On a Government scheme	2	1	1
Unemployed	20	13	7	Unemployed	33	28	5

Table 84 Qualified manpower (10% sample) – **continued**　　　　　　　　　　　　　　　County, districts

84. Residents aged 18 and over　　　　　　　　　　　　　　　　　　　　　　　　　　　　　　　　　　　(10% sample)

Level of highest qualification, age and economic position	TOTAL PERSONS	Males	Females	Level of highest qualification, age and economic position	TOTAL PERSONS	Males	Females
a	b	c	d	a	b	c	d
New Forest				**Rushmoor**			
ALL PERSONS AGED 18 AND OVER	12,573	5,885	6,688	**ALL PERSONS AGED 18 AND OVER**	6,243	3,057	3,186
All persons qualified	1,793	1,071	722	**All persons qualified**	781	484	297
Level a (higher degree)	70	55	15	**Level a (higher degree)**	42	28	14
18 - 29	3	3	-	18 - 29	5	4	1
30 - 44	26	18	8	30 - 44	21	14	7
45 up to pensionable age	27	24	3	45 up to pensionable age	13	9	4
Pensionable age and over	14	10	4	Pensionable age and over	3	1	2
Level b (degree)	809	567	242	**Level b (degree)**	334	233	101
18 - 29	116	63	53	18 - 29	100	67	33
30 - 44	310	189	121	30 - 44	147	98	49
45 up to pensionable age	199	170	29	45 up to pensionable age	56	43	13
Pensionable age and over	184	145	39	Pensionable age and over	31	25	6
Level c (diploma etc)	914	449	465	**Level c (diploma etc)**	405	223	182
18 - 29	110	63	47	18 - 29	105	53	52
30 - 44	303	159	144	30 - 44	170	98	72
45 up to pensionable age	295	154	141	45 up to pensionable age	105	66	39
Pensionable age and over	206	73	133	Pensionable age and over	25	6	19
All persons qualified at level a, b or c aged 18 up to pensionable age	1,389	843	546	**All persons qualified at level a, b or c aged 18 up to pensionable age**	722	452	270
Employees or self-employed	1,170	743	427	Employees or self-employed	643	425	218
On a Government scheme	4	1	3	On a Government scheme	1	1	-
Unemployed	36	26	10	Unemployed	15	10	5
Portsmouth				**Southampton**			
ALL PERSONS AGED 18 AND OVER	13,704	6,597	7,107	**ALL PERSONS AGED 18 AND OVER**	15,091	7,251	7,840
All persons qualified	1,448	810	638	**All persons qualified**	1,683	939	744
Level a (higher degree)	74	57	17	**Level a (higher degree)**	178	142	36
18 - 29	18	13	5	18 - 29	33	28	5
30 - 44	39	29	10	30 - 44	100	78	22
45 up to pensionable age	11	10	1	45 up to pensionable age	39	32	7
Pensionable age and over	6	5	1	Pensionable age and over	6	4	2
Level b (degree)	641	398	243	**Level b (degree)**	790	487	303
18 - 29	256	135	121	18 - 29	306	173	133
30 - 44	231	150	81	30 - 44	294	180	114
45 up to pensionable age	99	72	27	45 up to pensionable age	127	92	35
Pensionable age and over	55	41	14	Pensionable age and over	63	42	21
Level c (diploma etc)	733	355	378	**Level c (diploma etc)**	715	310	405
18 - 29	189	90	99	18 - 29	182	86	96
30 - 44	256	131	125	30 - 44	270	114	156
45 up to pensionable age	181	99	82	45 up to pensionable age	168	84	84
Pensionable age and over	107	35	72	Pensionable age and over	95	26	69
All persons qualified at level a, b or c aged 18 up to pensionable age	1,280	729	551	**All persons qualified at level a, b or c aged 18 up to pensionable age**	1,519	867	652
Employees or self-employed	1,084	638	446	Employees or self-employed	1,268	745	523
On a Government scheme	6	3	3	On a Government scheme	3	2	1
Unemployed	50	31	19	Unemployed	53	38	15

Table 84 Qualified manpower (10% sample) – **continued**   County, districts

84. Residents aged 18 and over   (10% sample)

Level of highest qualification, age and economic position	TOTAL PERSONS	Males	Females	Level of highest qualification, age and economic position	TOTAL PERSONS	Males	Females
a	b	c	d	a	b	c	d
Test Valley				**Winchester**			
ALL PERSONS AGED 18 AND OVER	7,730	3,779	3,951	**ALL PERSONS AGED 18 AND OVER**	7,525	3,562	3,963
All persons qualified	1,242	732	510	**All persons qualified**	1,640	919	721
Level a (higher degree)	83	68	15	**Level a (higher degree)**	120	90	30
18 - 29	7	4	3	18 - 29	11	7	4
30 - 44	44	34	10	30 - 44	51	38	13
45 up to pensionable age	25	24	1	45 up to pensionable age	41	35	6
Pensionable age and over	7	6	1	Pensionable age and over	17	10	7
Level b (degree)	580	394	186	**Level b (degree)**	878	565	313
18 - 29	102	54	48	18 - 29	141	64	77
30 - 44	255	163	92	30 - 44	361	227	134
45 up to pensionable age	170	143	27	45 up to pensionable age	266	199	67
Pensionable age and over	53	34	19	Pensionable age and over	110	75	35
Level c (diploma etc)	579	270	309	**Level c (diploma etc)**	642	264	378
18 - 29	78	39	39	18 - 29	69	31	38
30 - 44	251	129	122	30 - 44	217	91	126
45 up to pensionable age	180	79	101	45 up to pensionable age	224	107	117
Pensionable age and over	70	23	47	Pensionable age and over	132	35	97
All persons qualified at level a, b or c aged 18 up to pensionable age	1,112	669	443	**All persons qualified at level a, b or c aged 18 up to pensionable age**	1,381	799	582
Employees or self-employed	965	630	335	Employees or self-employed	1,195	739	456
On a Government scheme	5	2	3	On a Government scheme	2	1	1
Unemployed	20	10	10	Unemployed	38	22	16

Table 85 Ethnic group of qualified manpower (10% sample)

85. Residents aged 18 and over

(10% sample)

Qualified persons: age and economic position	TOTAL PERSONS	White	Ethnic group Black Caribbean	Black African	Black other	Indian	Pakistani	Bangladeshi	Chinese	Other groups Asian	Other	Persons born in Ireland
a	b	c	d	e	f	g	h	i	j	k	l	m
HAMPSHIRE												
ALL PERSONS AGED 18 AND OVER	118,052	116,144	207	99	102	546	82	117	265	249	241	1,783
All persons qualified at levels a, b or c	17,115	16,726	32	32	17	106	23	4	56	50	69	317
18 - 29	3,398	3,278	4	10	3	34	11	1	23	11	23	65
30 - 44	6,901	6,732	12	12	10	44	3	2	28	30	28	112
45 up to pensionable age	4,712	4,617	15	10	4	27	9	1	5	9	15	81
Pensionable age and over	2,104	2,099	1	-	-	1	-	-	-	-	3	59
All persons qualified at level a, b or c aged 18 - pensionable age	15,011	14,627	31	32	17	105	23	4	56	50	66	258
Employees or self-employed	12,918	12,604	30	24	16	89	18	2	45	39	51	219
On a Government scheme	41	39	-	1	-	-	-	-	-	-	1	1
Unemployed	411	398	-	2	-	5	1	-	2	1	2	7
Basingstoke & Deane												
ALL PERSONS AGED 18 AND OVER	10,916	10,719	33	14	9	64	14	6	15	17	25	207
All persons qualified at levels a, b or c	1,693	1,627	6	3	2	25	8	-	2	7	13	31
18 - 29	416	398	1	-	-	7	5	-	1	-	4	8
30 - 44	736	708	1	1	2	11	1	-	1	5	6	10
45 up to pensionable age	432	413	3	2	-	7	2	-	-	2	3	9
Pensionable age and over	109	108	1	-	-	-	-	-	-	-	-	4
All persons qualified at level a, b or c aged 18 - pensionable age	1,584	1,519	5	3	2	25	8	-	2	7	13	27
Employees or self-employed	1,405	1,346	5	3	2	22	8	-	2	7	10	26
On a Government scheme	4	3	-	-	-	-	-	-	-	-	1	-
Unemployed	26	24	-	-	-	1	-	-	-	-	1	-

Table 85 Ethnic group of qualified manpower (10% sample) – **continued**

85. Residents aged 18 and over

(10% sample)

Qualified persons: age and economic position	TOTAL PERSONS	Ethnic group								Other groups		Persons born in Ireland
		White	Black Caribbean	Black African	Black other	Indian	Pakistani	Bangladeshi	Chinese	Asian	Other	
a	b	c	d	e	f	g	h	i	j	k	l	m
East Hampshire												
ALL PERSONS AGED 18 AND OVER	**7,787**	**7,728**	**3**	**5**	**9**	**16**	**-**	**3**	**6**	**6**	**11**	**119**
All persons qualified at levels a, b or c	**1,414**	**1,396**	**-**	**1**	**-**	**4**	**-**	**1**	**3**	**3**	**6**	**32**
18 - 29	207	200	-	-	-	1	-	1	1	1	3	7
30 - 44	581	572	-	1	-	3	-	-	1	1	3	11
45 up to pensionable age	430	428	-	-	-	-	-	-	1	1	-	8
Pensionable age and over	196	196	-	-	-	-	-	-	-	-	-	6
All persons qualified at level a, b or c aged 18 - pensionable age	**1,218**	**1,200**	**-**	**1**	**-**	**4**	**-**	**1**	**3**	**3**	**6**	**26**
Employees or self-employed	1,061	1,045	-	1	-	4	-	-	2	3	6	20
On a Government scheme	3	3	-	-	-	-	-	-	-	-	-	-
Unemployed	31	31	-	-	-	-	-	-	-	-	-	2
Eastleigh												
ALL PERSONS AGED 18 AND OVER	**8,054**	**7,933**	**11**	**3**	**4**	**58**	**-**	**17**	**11**	**8**	**9**	**94**
All persons qualified at levels a, b or c	**1,144**	**1,122**	**2**	**2**	**-**	**8**	**-**	**-**	**6**	**1**	**3**	**18**
18 - 29	241	236	1	-	-	2	-	-	2	-	-	4
30 - 44	504	493	1	1	-	3	-	-	4	-	2	6
45 up to pensionable age	304	298	-	1	-	3	-	-	-	1	1	7
Pensionable age and over	95	95	-	-	-	-	-	-	-	-	-	1
All persons qualified at level a, b or c aged 18 - pensionable age	**1,049**	**1,027**	**2**	**2**	**-**	**8**	**-**	**-**	**6**	**1**	**3**	**17**
Employees or self-employed	922	903	2	1	-	7	-	-	5	1	3	16
On a Government scheme	-	-	-	-	-	-	-	-	-	-	-	-
Unemployed	26	25	-	-	-	1	-	-	-	-	-	-

Table 85 Ethnic group of qualified manpower (10% sample) – continued

85. Residents aged 18 and over

(10% sample)

Qualified persons: age and economic position	TOTAL PERSONS	Ethnic group								Other groups		Persons born in Ireland
		White	Black Caribbean	Black African	Black other	Indian	Pakistani	Bangladeshi	Chinese	Asian	Other	
a	b	c	d	e	f	g	h	i	j	k	l	m

Fareham

a	b	c	d	e	f	g	h	i	j	k	l	m
ALL PERSONS AGED 18 AND OVER	7,698	7,643	6	2	4	9	2	2	14	13	3	86
All persons qualified at levels a, b or c	1,238	1,217	2	1	2	3	2	-	5	6	-	17
18 - 29	195	194	1	-	-	-	-	-	-	-	-	4
30 - 44	533	519	-	1	1	2	1	-	5	4	-	5
45 up to pensionable age	369	363	1	-	1	1	1	-	-	2	-	5
Pensionable age and over	141	141	-	-	-	-	-	-	-	-	-	3
All persons qualified at level a, b or c aged 18 - pensionable age	1,097	1,076	2	1	2	3	2	-	5	6	-	14
Employees or self-employed	943	926	2	-	2	2	2	-	5	4	-	13
On a Government scheme	4	4	-	-	-	-	-	-	-	-	-	-
Unemployed	32	31	-	-	-	1	-	-	-	-	-	-

Gosport

a	b	c	d	e	f	g	h	i	j	k	l	m
ALL PERSONS AGED 18 AND OVER	5,578	5,535	3	3	5	4	-	2	11	3	11	88
All persons qualified at levels a, b or c	575	566	2	2	3	1	-	-	1	-	2	16
18 - 29	122	118	1	1	1	-	-	-	-	-	2	3
30 - 44	206	204	1	1	1	-	-	-	-	-	-	5
45 up to pensionable age	157	155	-	-	1	-	-	-	1	-	-	5
Pensionable age and over	90	89	-	-	-	1	-	-	-	-	-	3
All persons qualified at level a, b or c aged 18 - pensionable age	485	477	2	2	3	-	-	-	1	-	2	13
Employees or self-employed	403	397	-	-	3	-	-	-	1	-	2	10
On a Government scheme	6	5	1	1	1	-	-	-	-	-	-	-
Unemployed	20	19	1	1	-	-	-	-	-	-	-	-

Table 85 Ethnic group of qualified manpower (10% sample) – **continued**

85. Residents aged 18 and over (10% sample)

Qualified persons: age and economic position	TOTAL PERSONS	Ethnic group White	Black Caribbean	Black African	Black other	Indian	Pakistani	Bangladeshi	Chinese	Other groups Asian	Other	Persons born in Ireland
a	b	c	d	e	f	g	h	i	j	k	l	m
Hart												
ALL PERSONS AGED 18 AND OVER	6,090	5,950	6	6	2	20	3	-	18	76	9	121
All persons qualified at levels a, b or c	1,358	1,339	2	4	2	4	1	-	1	2	3	31
18 - 29	218	214	-	2	-	1	-	-	-	-	1	4
30 - 44	615	607	-	1	2	2	1	-	-	2	-	19
45 up to pensionable age	410	403	2	1	-	1	-	-	1	-	2	3
Pensionable age and over	115	115	-	-	-	-	-	-	-	-	-	5
All persons qualified at level a, b or c aged 18 - pensionable age	1,243	1,224	2	4	2	4	1	-	1	2	3	26
Employees or self-employed	1,083	1,066	2	3	1	4	1	-	1	2	3	22
On a Government scheme	1	1	-	-	-	-	-	-	-	-	-	-
Unemployed	31	31	-	-	-	-	-	-	-	-	-	-
Havant												
ALL PERSONS AGED 18 AND OVER	9,063	8,990	8	6	8	10	3	7	13	6	12	98
All persons qualified at levels a, b or c	1,106	1,090	3	2	1	2	2	-	2	1	3	14
18 - 29	168	163	-	-	-	1	-	-	2	1	1	-
30 - 44	380	376	2	1	-	1	-	-	-	-	-	4
45 up to pensionable age	384	377	1	1	1	1	2	-	-	-	2	6
Pensionable age and over	174	174	-	-	-	-	-	-	-	-	-	4
All persons qualified at level a, b or c aged 18 - pensionable age	932	916	3	2	1	2	2	-	2	1	3	10
Employees or self-employed	776	763	3	2	1	2	1	-	1	1	2	6
On a Government scheme	2	2	-	-	-	-	-	-	-	-	-	-
Unemployed	33	32	-	-	-	-	-	-	1	-	-	2

Table 85 Ethnic group of qualified manpower (10% sample) – **continued**

County, districts

85. Residents aged 18 and over

(10% sample)

Qualified persons: age and economic position	TOTAL PERSONS	Ethnic group								Other groups		Persons born in Ireland
		White	Black Caribbean	Black African	Black other	Indian	Pakistani	Bangladeshi	Chinese	Asian	Other	
a	b	c	d	e	f	g	h	i	j	k	l	m
New Forest												
ALL PERSONS AGED 18 AND OVER	12,573	12,515	6	6	1	9	1	4	11	9	11	161
All persons qualified at levels a, b or c	1,793	1,778	1	1	-	3	1	-	3	4	2	28
18 - 29	229	228	-	-	-	1	-	-	-	-	-	4
30 - 44	639	630	1	1	-	1	-	-	2	4	1	7
45 up to pensionable age	521	516	-	1	-	1	1	-	1	-	1	6
Pensionable age and over	404	404	-	-	-	-	-	-	-	-	-	11
All persons qualified at level a, b or c aged 18 - pensionable age	1,389	1,374	1	1	-	3	1	-	3	4	2	17
Employees or self-employed	1,170	1,159	1	1	-	3	-	-	3	2	1	13
On a Government scheme	4	4	-	-	-	-	-	-	-	-	-	-
Unemployed	36	36	-	-	-	-	-	-	-	-	1	1
Portsmouth												
ALL PERSONS AGED 18 AND OVER	13,704	13,453	12	14	17	35	3	53	57	31	29	164
All persons qualified at levels a, b or c	1,448	1,400	2	6	1	15	2	1	7	8	6	26
18 - 29	463	441	1	4	-	6	-	-	4	5	2	7
30 - 44	526	508	1	1	1	7	-	1	3	3	1	10
45 up to pensionable age	291	284	-	1	-	2	2	-	-	-	2	6
Pensionable age and over	168	167	-	-	-	-	-	-	-	-	1	3
All persons qualified at level a, b or c aged 18 - pensionable age	1,280	1,233	2	6	1	15	2	1	7	8	5	23
Employees or self-employed	1,084	1,052	2	5	1	9	1	1	4	5	4	21
On a Government scheme	6	6	-	-	-	-	-	-	-	-	-	-
Unemployed	50	47	-	1	-	2	-	-	-	-	-	1

Table 85 Ethnic group of qualified manpower (10% sample) – continued

County, districts

85. Residents aged 18 and over

(10% sample)

Qualified persons: age and economic position	TOTAL PERSONS	Ethnic group								Other groups		Persons born in Ireland
		White	Black Caribbean	Black African	Black other	Indian	Pakistani	Bangladeshi	Chinese	Asian	Other	
a	b	c	d	e	f	g	h	i	j	k	l	m
Rushmoor												
ALL PERSONS AGED 18 AND OVER	6,243	6,095	25	7	6	31	5	3	19	29	23	142
All persons qualified at levels a, b or c	**781**	**757**	**2**	**3**	**1**	**5**	**-**	**-**	**2**	**5**	**6**	**18**
18 - 29	210	206	-	-	1	2	-	-	-	1	-	3
30 - 44	338	326	1	-	-	3	-	-	2	3	3	6
45 up to pensionable age	174	167	1	3	-	-	-	-	-	1	2	5
Pensionable age and over	59	58	-	-	-	-	-	-	-	-	1	4
All persons qualified at level a, b or c aged 18 - pensionable age	**722**	**699**	**2**	**3**	**1**	**5**	**-**	**-**	**2**	**5**	**5**	**14**
Employees or self-employed	643	621	2	3	1	5	-	-	2	4	5	11
On a Government scheme	1	1	-	-	-	-	-	-	-	-	-	-
Unemployed	15	14	-	-	-	-	-	-	-	1	-	-
Southampton												
ALL PERSONS AGED 18 AND OVER	15,091	14,467	81	24	28	260	46	15	61	40	69	303
All persons qualified at levels a, b or c	**1,683**	**1,581**	**7**	**6**	**4**	**31**	**4**	**1**	**18**	**11**	**20**	**45**
18 - 29	521	483	-	3	1	11	3	-	10	3	7	16
30 - 44	664	619	3	3	3	10	-	1	8	5	12	12
45 up to pensionable age	334	316	4	-	-	10	1	-	-	3	-	9
Pensionable age and over	164	163	-	-	-	-	-	-	-	-	1	8
All persons qualified at level a, b or c aged 18 - pensionable age	**1,519**	**1,418**	**7**	**6**	**4**	**31**	**4**	**1**	**18**	**11**	**19**	**37**
Employees or self-employed	1,268	1,191	7	4	4	26	2	-	13	8	13	30
On a Government scheme	3	3	-	-	-	-	-	-	-	-	-	1
Unemployed	53	50	-	-	-	1	1	-	1	-	1	1

Table 85 Ethnic group of qualified manpower (10% sample) – **continued**

(10% sample)

85. Residents aged 18 and over

Qualified persons: age and economic position	TOTAL PERSONS	Ethnic group										Persons born in Ireland
		White	Black Caribbean	Black African	Black other	Indian	Pakistani	Bangladeshi	Chinese	Other groups		
										Asian	Other	
a	b	c	d	e	f	g	h	i	j	k	l	m
Test Valley												
ALL PERSONS AGED 18 AND OVER	7,730	7,654	9	5	5	18	4	-	17	5	13	96
All persons qualified at levels a, b or c	1,242	1,224	4	-	-	4	3	-	4	1	2	17
18 - 29	187	179	-	-	-	1	3	-	2	-	2	1
30 - 44	550	545	2	-	-	1	-	-	1	1	-	6
45 up to pensionable age	375	370	2	-	-	2	-	-	1	-	-	8
Pensionable age and over	130	130	-	-	-	-	-	-	-	-	-	2
All persons qualified at level a, b or c aged 18 - pensionable age	1,112	1,094	4	-	-	4	3	-	4	1	2	15
Employees or self-employed	965	949	3	-	-	4	3	-	4	1	1	14
On a Government scheme	5	5	-	-	-	-	-	-	-	-	-	-
Unemployed	20	20	-	-	-	-	-	-	-	-	-	-
Winchester												
ALL PERSONS AGED 18 AND OVER	7,525	7,462	3	4	4	12	1	5	12	6	16	104
All persons qualified at levels a, b or c	1,640	1,629	1	1	1	1	-	1	2	1	3	24
18 - 29	221	218	1	-	-	1	-	-	1	1	-	4
30 - 44	629	625	-	1	1	-	-	-	1	1	1	11
45 up to pensionable age	531	527	-	-	1	-	-	1	-	-	2	4
Pensionable age and over	259	259	-	-	-	-	-	-	-	-	-	5
All persons qualified at level a, b or c aged 18 - pensionable age	1,381	1,370	1	1	1	1	-	1	2	1	3	19
Employees or self-employed	1,195	1,186	1	1	1	1	-	1	2	1	1	17
On a Government scheme	2	2	-	-	-	-	-	-	-	-	-	-
Unemployed	38	38	-	-	-	-	-	-	-	-	-	-

Table 86 SEG of households and families (10% sample)

86. Households with residents; residents in households; families of resident persons

Socio-economic group	TOTAL HOUSE-HOLDS	Households				
		Tenure of households in permanent buildings				
		Owner occupied		Rented privately	Rented from a housing association	Rented from a local authority or new town
		Owned outright	Buying			
a	b	c	d	e	f	g

HAMPSHIRE

By socio-economic group of economically active head of household

TOTAL		**59,458**	**14,552**	**28,675**	**4,030**	**1,179**	**9,266**
1	Employers and managers in large establishments	2,885	215	2,480	96	6	61
2	Employers and managers in small establishments	5,504	570	4,265	304	20	156
3	Professional workers - self-employed	598	85	479	24	1	2
4	Professional workers - employees	2,682	245	2,193	151	7	24
5.1	Ancillary workers and artists	4,584	521	3,472	295	22	184
5.2	Foremen and supervisors - non-manual	311	28	237	16	3	22
6	Junior non-manual workers	4,345	574	2,833	371	57	417
7	Personal service workers	820	102	321	111	17	220
8	Foremen and supervisors - manual	1,021	117	711	44	12	126
9	Skilled manual workers	5,430	604	3,499	330	60	849
10	Semi-skilled manual workers	3,453	452	1,732	250	62	849
11	Unskilled manual workers	1,329	209	420	147	29	493
12	Own account workers (other than professional)	3,623	450	2,580	240	23	296
13	Farmers - employers and managers	134	46	35	7	-	-
14	Farmers - own account	95	53	25	5	-	2
15	Agricultural workers	283	37	49	24	1	24
16	Members of armed forces	1,482	29	760	126	-	15
17	Inadequately described and not stated occupations	293	59	154	36	9	27
	Economically inactive head	20,239	10,127	2,370	1,391	833	5,323
TOTAL PERSONS		**149,450**	**27,808**	**84,278**	**8,143**	**2,074**	**22,175**
	Persons economically active	76,735	9,344	51,311	4,611	595	8,048
	Dependent children	32,772	1,363	22,536	1,201	355	5,888

Basingstoke & Deane

By socio-economic group of economically active head of household

TOTAL		**5,369**	**904**	**2,914**	**240**	**128**	**988**
1	Employers and managers in large establishments	361	22	317	6	2	12
2	Employers and managers in small establishments	599	53	491	30	3	12
3	Professional workers - self-employed	62	6	54	1	-	-
4	Professional workers - employees	313	20	265	14	1	3
5.1	Ancillary workers and artists	468	35	361	29	-	31
5.2	Foremen and supervisors - non-manual	39	1	33	1	1	2
6	Junior non-manual workers	465	42	308	27	10	62
7	Personal service workers	57	5	16	6	5	18
8	Foremen and supervisors - manual	118	7	85	3	2	16
9	Skilled manual workers	552	42	344	19	18	105
10	Semi-skilled manual workers	363	36	160	12	5	131
11	Unskilled manual workers	103	13	30	5	1	47
12	Own account workers (other than professional)	323	27	231	19	1	39
13	Farmers - employers and managers	13	4	2	-	-	-
14	Farmers - own account	10	5	2	2	-	1
15	Agricultural workers	49	2	7	2	-	4
16	Members of armed forces	27	-	21	1	-	1
17	Inadequately described and not stated occupations	22	1	11	3	2	3
	Economically inactive head	1,403	580	173	58	75	489
TOTAL PERSONS		**14,167**	**1,822**	**8,565**	**508**	**265**	**2,477**
	Persons economically active	7,936	697	5,408	333	101	1,076
	Dependent children	3,241	117	2,276	64	53	607

(10% sample)

Households		Persons				Families		Socio-economic group
Migrant head of household	No car	TOTAL PERSONS	Persons econom- ically active	Dependent children	Adults with limiting long-term illness	TOTAL FAMILIES	Lone parent with dependent child(ren)	
h	i	j	k	l	m	n	o	a

		By socio-economic group of economically active head of household				By socio-economic group of economically active head of family		
6,060	14,294	149,450	76,735	32,772	14,296	43,919	2,791	**TOTAL**
300	89	8,632	5,338	2,278	231	2,526	50	1 Employers and managers in large establishments
654	210	16,525	10,266	4,612	475	4,784	112	2 Employers and managers in small establishments
56	2	1,866	1,059	569	39	524	3	3 Professional workers - self-employed
367	88	7,604	4,786	1,982	211	2,175	23	4 Professional workers - employees
588	303	12,417	8,174	3,077	447	3,548	208	5.1 Ancillary workers and artists
46	24	851	581	210	35	254	11	5.2 Foremen and supervisors - non-manual
646	664	10,861	7,591	2,524	408	3,200	413	6 Junior non-manual workers
140	307	2,095	1,399	562	86	596	174	7 Personal service workers
77	97	3,144	2,071	752	104	938	10	8 Foremen and supervisors - manual
573	597	16,064	10,553	3,942	614	4,794	61	9 Skilled manual workers
382	784	9,686	6,525	2,160	500	2,898	123	10 Semi-skilled manual workers
142	514	3,469	2,339	766	243	1,018	100	11 Unskilled manual workers
361	173	11,164	6,902	3,047	361	3,235	68	12 Own account workers (other than professional)
12	-	395	256	78	14	120	1	13 Farmers - employers and managers
1	4	260	173	48	16	76	-	14 Farmers - own account
44	32	771	522	158	32	228	3	15 Agricultural workers
432	141	4,776	2,617	1,646	93	1,385	13	16 Members of armed forces
								17 Inadequately described and not stated
36	46	838	514	209	61	239	12	occupations
1,150	10,002	37,085	4,545	3,867	10,227	11,142	1,359	Economically inactive head
14,668	**25,255**					**128,310**	**7,728**	**TOTAL PERSONS**
8,405	7,485					66,769	1,776	Persons economically active
3,620	4,347					32,772	4,553	Dependent children

		By socio-economic group of economically active head of household				By socio-economic group of economically active head of family		
492	1,041	14,167	7,936	3,241	1,051	4,165	238	**TOTAL**
30	19	1,027	686	243	24	303	4	1 Employers and managers in large establishments
71	15	1,894	1,131	575	50	522	7	2 Employers and managers in small establishments
8	-	186	106	57	-	53	1	3 Professional workers - self-employed
46	5	870	552	230	19	249	1	4 Professional workers - employees
62	31	1,320	851	355	45	355	17	5.1 Ancillary workers and artists
5	3	103	74	20	5	32	-	5.2 Foremen and supervisors - non-manual
57	65	1,154	828	265	31	360	46	6 Junior non-manual workers
14	18	144	101	36	6	40	12	7 Personal service workers
3	9	339	240	67	12	110	2	8 Foremen and supervisors - manual
59	55	1,650	1,144	378	42	501	8	9 Skilled manual workers
28	72	1,052	738	230	49	316	19	10 Semi-skilled manual workers
6	33	295	215	56	16	85	8	11 Unskilled manual workers
27	11	1,001	614	289	31	288	9	12 Own account workers (other than professional)
1	-	39	21	11	3	12	-	13 Farmers - employers and managers
-	1	33	17	11	4	8	-	14 Farmers - own account
6	1	158	95	42	6	43	-	15 Agricultural workers
5	-	95	49	32	2	26	-	16 Members of armed forces
								17 Inadequately described and not stated
2	1	73	47	17	3	19	-	occupations
61	689	2,687	395	319	700	830	103	Economically inactive head
1,178	**1,943**					**12,455**	**668**	**TOTAL PERSONS**
749	633					6,956	167	Persons economically active
277	383					3,241	397	Dependent children

Table 86   SEG of households and families (10% sample) – **continued**

86. Households with residents; residents in households; families of resident persons

Socio-economic group	TOTAL HOUSE-HOLDS	Households				
		Tenure of households in permanent buildings				
		Owner occupied		Rented privately	Rented from a housing association	Rented from a local authority or new town
		Owned outright	Buying			
a	b	c	d	e	f	g

East Hampshire

By socio-economic group of economically active head of household

TOTAL	**3,873**	**1,054**	**1,951**	**228**	**33**	**443**
1 Employers and managers in large establishments	222	21	194	3	-	2
2 Employers and managers in small establishments	517	53	412	26	-	12
3 Professional workers - self-employed	61	6	52	1	-	-
4 Professional workers - employees	183	20	148	6	-	2
5.1 Ancillary workers and artists	330	50	243	14	1	8
5.2 Foremen and supervisors - non-manual	14	1	11	2	-	-
6 Junior non-manual workers	270	42	181	16	2	23
7 Personal service workers	59	12	23	6	-	15
8 Foremen and supervisors - manual	54	6	38	3	-	6
9 Skilled manual workers	269	38	168	16	3	40
10 Semi-skilled manual workers	161	21	81	5	3	37
11 Unskilled manual workers	57	11	14	3	1	24
12 Own account workers (other than professional)	291	53	195	24	1	16
13 Farmers - employers and managers	22	10	4	2	-	-
14 Farmers - own account	12	4	6	1	-	1
15 Agricultural workers	43	8	6	3	1	2
16 Members of armed forces	96	2	31	11	-	1
17 Inadequately described and not stated occupations	14	3	7	2	-	2
Economically inactive head	1,186	692	135	83	21	244
TOTAL PERSONS	**9,915**	**2,022**	**5,820**	**490**	**55**	**1,066**
Persons economically active	5,142	730	3,427	274	17	414
Dependent children	2,265	111	1,679	72	7	270

Eastleigh

By socio-economic group of economically active head of household

TOTAL	**4,073**	**957**	**2,372**	**173**	**79**	**457**
1 Employers and managers in large establishments	195	12	174	4	-	3
2 Employers and managers in small establishments	445	30	386	8	2	9
3 Professional workers - self-employed	32	4	26	2	-	-
4 Professional workers - employees	190	21	159	6	-	1
5.1 Ancillary workers and artists	350	30	296	15	1	7
5.2 Foremen and supervisors - non-manual	32	1	29	-	-	2
6 Junior non-manual workers	368	40	291	15	1	19
7 Personal service workers	55	7	32	4	1	8
8 Foremen and supervisors - manual	74	10	59	-	-	5
9 Skilled manual workers	445	57	314	22	5	46
10 Semi-skilled manual workers	229	36	137	9	3	40
11 Unskilled manual workers	72	10	37	5	1	19
12 Own account workers (other than professional)	277	34	222	11	2	7
13 Farmers - employers and managers	3	-	2	1	-	-
14 Farmers - own account	3	1	1	-	-	-
15 Agricultural workers	7	1	5	-	-	-
16 Members of armed forces	22	1	19	1	-	1
17 Inadequately described and not stated occupations	12	2	9	1	-	-
Economically inactive head	1,251	660	172	68	63	283
TOTAL PERSONS	**10,435**	**1,842**	**6,989**	**349**	**128**	**1,034**
Persons economically active	5,516	637	4,268	187	29	338
Dependent children	2,369	80	1,966	47	16	238

(10% sample)

Households		Persons				Families		
Migrant head of household	No car	TOTAL PERSONS	Persons economically active	Dependent children	Adults with limiting long-term illness	TOTAL FAMILIES	Lone parent with dependent child(ren)	Socio-economic group
h	i	j	k	l	m	n	o	a

		By socio-economic group of economically active head of household				By socio-economic group of economically active head of family		
409	606	9,915	5,142	2,265	805	2,952	154	**TOTAL**
27	1	682	401	188	10	204	-	1 Employers and managers in large establishments
68	7	1,637	952	518	33	457	12	2 Employers and managers in small establishments
2	-	190	110	62	5	53	-	3 Professional workers - self-employed
23	-	520	316	138	18	160	2	4 Professional workers - employees
36	14	870	568	211	21	253	12	5.1 Ancillary workers and artists
2	-	39	27	8	3	13	1	5.2 Foremen and supervisors - non-manual
36	24	670	470	149	26	196	29	6 Junior non-manual workers
8	16	143	92	44	3	47	18	7 Personal service workers
4	3	173	110	45	6	50	-	8 Foremen and supervisors - manual
24	21	805	531	197	25	248	2	9 Skilled manual workers
19	27	456	315	94	24	142	5	10 Semi-skilled manual workers
7	16	133	92	26	12	43	5	11 Unskilled manual workers
28	6	885	555	234	29	259	4	12 Own account workers (other than professional)
1	-	71	42	15	4	20	-	13 Farmers - employers and managers
-	-	40	27	10	1	12	-	14 Farmers - own account
9	7	103	71	19	2	30	-	15 Agricultural workers
39	3	299	175	97	6	92	1	16 Members of armed forces
2	2	35	27	8	2	10	1	17 Inadequately described and not stated occupations
71	454	2,136	240	200	572	652	62	Economically inactive head
1,029	977					8,679	428	**TOTAL PERSONS**
580	267					4,569	106	Persons economically active
260	125					2,265	257	Dependent children

		By socio-economic group of economically active head of household				By socio-economic group of economically active head of family		
390	752	10,435	5,516	2,369	892	3,134	163	**TOTAL**
15	2	601	368	166	15	181	6	1 Employers and managers in large establishments
54	14	1,312	810	381	37	385	9	2 Employers and managers in small establishments
2	-	98	57	29	2	29	-	3 Professional workers - self-employed
24	1	560	352	159	11	162	-	4 Professional workers - employees
44	13	982	628	280	21	279	15	5.1 Ancillary workers and artists
2	1	98	66	27	4	26	1	5.2 Foremen and supervisors - non-manual
55	28	934	644	229	29	283	30	6 Junior non-manual workers
7	20	145	94	44	7	42	11	7 Personal service workers
4	3	235	153	58	10	67	1	8 Foremen and supervisors - manual
46	33	1,331	858	342	44	400	1	9 Skilled manual workers
23	29	644	437	142	32	198	8	10 Semi-skilled manual workers
5	15	188	129	37	11	60	5	11 Unskilled manual workers
37	10	883	544	243	34	260	10	12 Own account workers (other than professional)
-	-	9	5	2	-	1	-	13 Farmers - employers and managers
-	-	8	6	2	2	3	-	14 Farmers - own account
3	-	18	15	1	2	7	-	15 Agricultural workers
3	-	67	43	19	1	21	-	16 Members of armed forces
2	3	33	20	8	5	10	-	17 Inadequately described and not stated occupations
62	571	2,249	262	191	620	711	64	Economically inactive head
914	1,232					9,182	446	**TOTAL PERSONS**
566	300					4,916	125	Persons economically active
206	168					2,369	256	Dependent children

181

Table 86 SEG of households and families (10% sample) – continued

86. Households with residents; residents in households; families of resident persons

Socio-economic group	TOTAL HOUSE-HOLDS	Households				
		Tenure of households in permanent buildings				
		Owner occupied		Rented privately	Rented from a housing association	Rented from a local authority or new town
		Owned outright	Buying			
a	b	c	d	e	f	g

Fareham

By socio-economic group of economically active head of household

TOTAL	**3,810**	**1,133**	**2,153**	**143**	**25**	**301**
1 Employers and managers in large establishments	240	20	213	4	-	1
2 Employers and managers in small establishments	374	31	313	18	1	4
3 Professional workers - self-employed	43	8	34	1	-	-
4 Professional workers - employees	213	25	174	10	-	1
5.1 Ancillary workers and artists	361	52	286	13	-	7
5.2 Foremen and supervisors - non-manual	24	2	19	2	-	-
6 Junior non-manual workers	275	42	201	10	1	19
7 Personal service workers	29	5	16	1	-	6
8 Foremen and supervisors - manual	64	13	48	2	-	1
9 Skilled manual workers	316	50	227	11	1	24
10 Semi-skilled manual workers	139	29	81	3	1	23
11 Unskilled manual workers	66	14	34	2	-	16
12 Own account workers (other than professional)	221	33	167	11	-	10
13 Farmers - employers and managers	3	1	1	-	-	-
14 Farmers - own account	4	2	1	1	-	-
15 Agricultural workers	3	-	2	-	-	-
16 Members of armed forces	193	5	159	6	-	-
17 Inadequately described and not stated occupations	19	7	12	-	-	-
Economically inactive head	1,214	793	161	48	21	185
TOTAL PERSONS	**9,737**	**2,151**	**6,368**	**323**	**31**	**692**
Persons economically active	5,040	701	3,858	163	4	231
Dependent children	2,139	88	1,731	74	1	189

Gosport

By socio-economic group of economically active head of household

TOTAL	**2,899**	**651**	**1,399**	**162**	**61**	**489**
1 Employers and managers in large establishments	92	11	70	3	-	7
2 Employers and managers in small establishments	160	13	127	7	-	7
3 Professional workers - self-employed	13	1	11	1	-	-
4 Professional workers - employees	64	9	48	4	-	-
5.1 Ancillary workers and artists	176	16	135	6	-	15
5.2 Foremen and supervisors - non-manual	11	2	7	-	1	-
6 Junior non-manual workers	201	18	133	15	2	26
7 Personal service workers	47	5	26	5	-	7
8 Foremen and supervisors - manual	51	5	35	2	-	9
9 Skilled manual workers	340	36	234	13	2	53
10 Semi-skilled manual workers	182	14	118	7	1	38
11 Unskilled manual workers	72	11	23	6	-	31
12 Own account workers (other than professional)	136	15	95	12	-	14
13 Farmers - employers and managers	1	-	1	-	-	-
14 Farmers - own account	1	-	1	-	-	-
15 Agricultural workers	4	1	2	-	-	1
16 Members of armed forces	320	3	206	28	-	2
17 Inadequately described and not stated occupations	19	4	8	4	1	2
Economically inactive head	993	485	114	49	54	269
TOTAL PERSONS	**7,288**	**1,159**	**4,048**	**363**	**103**	**1,190**
Persons economically active	3,636	338	2,483	198	15	407
Dependent children	1,755	33	1,099	87	21	357

(10% sample)

Households		Persons				Families		Socio-economic group
Migrant head of household	No car	TOTAL PERSONS	Persons economically active	Dependent children	Adults with limiting long-term illness	TOTAL FAMILIES	Lone parent with dependent child(ren)	
h	i	j	k	l	m	n	o	a

By socio-economic group of economically active head of household (columns j, k, l) / **By socio-economic group of economically active head of family** (columns n, o)

h	i	j	k	l	m	n	o	a
319	662	9,737	5,040	2,139	858	2,985	131	**TOTAL**
15	2	725	443	196	20	214	3	1 Employers and managers in large establishments
45	10	1,117	698	307	30	342	3	2 Employers and managers in small establishments
2	-	150	78	49	5	37	-	3 Professional workers - self-employed
30	3	630	395	165	13	184	3	4 Professional workers - employees
27	9	1,016	676	241	32	315	12	5.1 Ancillary workers and artists
3	3	70	46	22	3	20	2	5.2 Foremen and supervisors - non-manual
50	31	710	485	173	25	218	34	6 Junior non-manual workers
5	8	72	54	15	-	21	4	7 Personal service workers
1	5	201	138	39	4	60	-	8 Foremen and supervisors - manual
25	15	919	595	222	42	286	1	9 Skilled manual workers
10	24	376	251	85	20	124	7	10 Semi-skilled manual workers
3	18	189	123	49	11	59	8	11 Unskilled manual workers
19	5	663	426	172	18	204	5	12 Own account workers (other than professional)
-	-	11	9	1	-	3	-	13 Farmers - employers and managers
-	-	8	5	-	-	4	-	14 Farmers - own account
-	-	11	9	2	-	3	-	15 Agricultural workers
32	9	634	338	223	12	183	2	16 Members of armed forces
1	-	48	30	11	3	18	1	17 Inadequately described and not stated occupations
50	516	2,163	228	161	620	683	46	Economically inactive head
824	1,097					8,666	373	**TOTAL PERSONS**
458	260					4,597	102	Persons economically active
228	162					2,139	222	Dependent children

By socio-economic group of economically active head of household (columns j, k, l) / **By socio-economic group of economically active head of family** (columns n, o)

h	i	j	k	l	m	n	o	a
322	871	7,288	3,636	1,755	696	2,149	176	**TOTAL**
8	12	261	166	73	11	77	4	1 Employers and managers in large establishments
17	9	479	311	119	21	136	5	2 Employers and managers in small establishments
3	-	38	23	9	1	12	-	3 Professional workers - self-employed
10	1	186	121	37	10	58	-	4 Professional workers - employees
16	13	499	326	123	30	150	10	5.1 Ancillary workers and artists
2	3	31	23	8	-	11	-	5.2 Foremen and supervisors - non-manual
29	43	500	325	139	12	154	27	6 Junior non-manual workers
3	19	132	78	44	4	38	10	7 Personal service workers
4	8	159	96	47	7	44	1	8 Foremen and supervisors - manual
45	44	978	634	252	36	292	5	9 Skilled manual workers
20	44	520	350	122	32	154	5	10 Semi-skilled manual workers
8	38	179	117	45	12	55	7	11 Unskilled manual workers
13	14	424	249	125	15	124	3	12 Own account workers (other than professional)
-	-	1	1	-	-	1	1	13 Farmers - employers and managers
-	-	2	2	-	-	1	-	14 Farmers - own account
1	2	12	6	4	1	5	-	15 Agricultural workers
82	38	1,016	569	343	21	297	6	16 Members of armed forces
3	8	50	34	8	9	13	1	17 Inadequately described and not stated occupations
56	565	1,782	186	244	467	514	87	Economically inactive head
815	1,647					6,309	494	**TOTAL PERSONS**
471	522					3,220	114	Persons economically active
213	357					1,755	292	Dependent children

Table 86 SEG of households and families (10% sample) – **continued**

86. Households with residents; residents in households; families of resident persons

Socio-economic group	TOTAL HOUSE-HOLDS	Households				
		Tenure of households in permanent buildings				
		Owner occupied		Rented privately	Rented from a housing association	Rented from a local authority or new town
		Owned outright	Buying			
a	b	c	d	e	f	g

Hart

By socio-economic group of economically active head of household

TOTAL		**2,875**	**586**	**1,733**	**169**	**27**	**241**
1	Employers and managers in large establishments	245	17	218	9	-	-
2	Employers and managers in small establishments	437	37	370	18	-	1
3	Professional workers - self-employed	55	7	46	2	-	-
4	Professional workers - employees	243	18	208	11	-	3
5.1	Ancillary workers and artists	260	28	198	20	4	5
5.2	Foremen and supervisors - non-manual	12	2	7	-	-	3
6	Junior non-manual workers	189	25	136	13	1	10
7	Personal service workers	28	4	13	3	-	3
8	Foremen and supervisors - manual	42	4	33	-	-	4
9	Skilled manual workers	225	20	158	12	1	26
10	Semi-skilled manual workers	94	14	42	12	1	19
11	Unskilled manual workers	43	9	17	3	-	13
12	Own account workers (other than professional)	180	18	139	13	2	7
13	Farmers - employers and managers	6	2	3	-	-	-
14	Farmers - own account	3	1	1	-	-	-
15	Agricultural workers	14	2	2	2	-	2
16	Members of armed forces	92	-	24	9	-	-
17	Inadequately described and not stated occupations	15	2	11	1	-	-
	Economically inactive head	681	375	102	41	18	140
TOTAL PERSONS		**7,848**	**1,170**	**5,292**	**398**	**43**	**574**
	Persons economically active	4,301	457	3,168	233	13	228
	Dependent children	1,890	77	1,473	81	5	129

Havant

By socio-economic group of economically active head of household

TOTAL		**4,562**	**1,184**	**2,182**	**180**	**39**	**938**
1	Employers and managers in large establishments	213	19	181	7	-	4
2	Employers and managers in small establishments	345	43	254	16	2	20
3	Professional workers - self-employed	35	6	25	2	-	1
4	Professional workers - employees	196	25	164	6	-	-
5.1	Ancillary workers and artists	337	51	253	13	1	19
5.2	Foremen and supervisors - non-manual	26	5	17	1	-	3
6	Junior non-manual workers	282	42	183	16	1	38
7	Personal service workers	41	4	11	2	-	22
8	Foremen and supervisors - manual	76	11	52	2	-	11
9	Skilled manual workers	452	41	306	20	2	83
10	Semi-skilled manual workers	329	44	165	16	2	99
11	Unskilled manual workers	97	13	32	5	2	44
12	Own account workers (other than professional)	306	30	233	8	-	32
13	Farmers - employers and managers	6	4	2	-	-	-
14	Farmers - own account	1	1	-	-	-	-
15	Agricultural workers	9	2	3	1	-	3
16	Members of armed forces	67	5	51	4	-	1
17	Inadequately described and not stated occupations	25	5	15	-	1	4
	Economically inactive head	1,686	832	231	59	24	532
TOTAL PERSONS		**11,581**	**2,243**	**6,447**	**387**	**79**	**2,310**
	Persons economically active	5,712	709	3,872	224	25	820
	Dependent children	2,533	99	1,667	55	16	658

(10% sample)

Households		Persons				Families		Socio-economic group
Migrant head of household	No car	TOTAL PERSONS	Persons economically active	Dependent children	Adults with limiting long-term illness	TOTAL FAMILIES	Lone parent with dependent child(ren)	
h	i	j	k	l	m	n	o	a

		By socio-economic group of economically active head of household				By socio-economic group of economically active head of family		
309	310	7,848	4,301	1,890	502	2,283	95	**TOTAL**
25	-	765	468	209	16	224	5	1 Employers and managers in large establishments
52	5	1,335	819	381	22	386	5	2 Employers and managers in small establishments
10	-	176	96	54	4	52	-	3 Professional workers - self-employed
31	2	724	453	192	25	197	-	4 Professional workers - employees
37	8	743	468	195	18	213	11	5.1 Ancillary workers and artists
-	1	35	20	11	5	7	1	5.2 Foremen and supervisors - non-manual
22	7	506	354	116	18	149	14	6 Junior non-manual workers
3	5	70	50	15	3	20	5	7 Personal service workers
1	-	134	92	29	4	40	-	8 Foremen and supervisors - manual
19	4	710	444	199	26	196	1	9 Skilled manual workers
9	10	246	179	38	15	78	1	10 Semi-skilled manual workers
3	8	114	81	25	8	31	4	11 Unskilled manual workers
20	3	547	330	147	14	164	4	12 Own account workers (other than professional)
-	-	15	13	1	2	4	-	13 Farmers - employers and managers
-	-	5	4	-	-	2	-	14 Farmers - own account
2	-	46	29	14	1	13	1	15 Agricultural workers
34	1	317	155	120	6	92	1	16 Members of armed forces
1	-	45	29	13	2	14	1	17 Inadequately described and not stated occupations
39	253	1,273	192	119	311	389	39	Economically inactive head
805	480					7,005	266	**TOTAL PERSONS**
463	103					3,833	71	Persons economically active
217	61					1,890	154	Dependent children

		By socio-economic group of economically active head of household				By socio-economic group of economically active head of family		
369	1,110	11,581	5,712	2,533	1,287	3,468	248	**TOTAL**
20	1	630	385	154	13	182	5	1 Employers and managers in large establishments
29	14	1,009	613	281	41	299	11	2 Employers and managers in small establishments
3	-	111	66	26	1	32	-	3 Professional workers - self-employed
18	1	556	361	143	9	168	5	4 Professional workers - employees
32	12	908	579	224	48	263	15	5.1 Ancillary workers and artists
4	2	76	46	22	3	21	1	5.2 Foremen and supervisors - non-manual
31	34	717	490	179	31	212	35	6 Junior non-manual workers
4	18	111	67	40	7	34	15	7 Personal service workers
6	15	229	153	52	7	72	-	8 Foremen and supervisors - manual
41	48	1,383	888	358	54	407	4	9 Skilled manual workers
30	75	921	645	187	50	286	11	10 Semi-skilled manual workers
13	47	274	164	72	22	80	10	11 Unskilled manual workers
23	13	984	584	288	29	271	5	12 Own account workers (other than professional)
-	-	16	11	3	1	5	-	13 Farmers - employers and managers
-	-	1	1	-	-	-	-	14 Farmers - own account
1	2	19	14	2	1	7	-	15 Agricultural workers
12	2	237	125	85	3	64	-	16 Members of armed forces
4	3	78	41	19	11	25	1	17 Inadequately described and not stated occupations
93	803	3,220	431	355	948	1,020	125	Economically inactive head
936	2,061					10,099	688	**TOTAL PERSONS**
473	554					5,040	162	Persons economically active
261	416					2,533	396	Dependent children

185

Table 86 SEG of households and families (10% sample) – **continued**

86. Households with residents; residents in households; families of resident persons

			Households				
			Tenure of households in permanent buildings				
		TOTAL HOUSE-HOLDS	Owner occupied		Rented privately	Rented from a housing association	Rented from a local authority or new town
Socio-economic group			Owned outright	Buying			
a		b	c	d	e	f	g

New Forest

By socio-economic group of economically active head of household

TOTAL		**6,429**	**2,345**	**2,833**	**386**	**84**	**617**
1	Employers and managers in large establishments	272	20	237	6	-	2
2	Employers and managers in small establishments	613	92	448	37	2	9
3	Professional workers - self-employed	78	12	61	3	-	-
4	Professional workers - employees	205	19	168	11	-	3
5.1	Ancillary workers and artists	449	61	341	22	3	11
5.2	Foremen and supervisors - non-manual	26	5	18	1	-	1
6	Junior non-manual workers	430	87	285	27	1	17
7	Personal service workers	77	15	30	8	1	19
8	Foremen and supervisors - manual	123	20	84	7	1	10
9	Skilled manual workers	472	63	329	26	3	44
10	Semi-skilled manual workers	319	55	190	23	2	40
11	Unskilled manual workers	119	20	44	14	-	36
12	Own account workers (other than professional)	382	62	272	29	1	15
13	Farmers - employers and managers	18	1	6	1	-	-
14	Farmers - own account	20	15	2	-	-	-
15	Agricultural workers	49	13	9	3	-	4
16	Members of armed forces	36	-	16	6	-	2
17	Inadequately described and not stated occupations	34	9	14	7	1	2
	Economically inactive head	2,687	1,773	276	154	68	390
TOTAL PERSONS		**15,492**	**4,348**	**8,334**	**805**	**156**	**1,433**
	Persons economically active	7,355	1,190	4,975	424	28	482
	Dependent children	3,071	199	2,282	127	27	341

Portsmouth

By socio-economic group of economically active head of household

TOTAL		**7,101**	**1,742**	**3,025**	**785**	**227**	**1,172**
1	Employers and managers in large establishments	190	14	148	21	-	5
2	Employers and managers in small establishments	452	64	304	47	1	12
3	Professional workers - self-employed	33	7	23	2	-	-
4	Professional workers - employees	226	23	172	25	2	1
5.1	Ancillary workers and artists	504	43	374	55	7	19
5.2	Foremen and supervisors - non-manual	29	2	21	4	-	2
6	Junior non-manual workers	512	59	309	76	13	43
7	Personal service workers	130	11	58	25	6	26
8	Foremen and supervisors - manual	105	13	67	5	2	18
9	Skilled manual workers	672	85	444	62	8	71
10	Semi-skilled manual workers	484	66	239	71	12	87
11	Unskilled manual workers	221	35	64	37	10	74
12	Own account workers (other than professional)	391	43	280	25	5	37
13	Farmers - employers and managers	-	-	-	-	-	-
14	Farmers - own account	-	-	-	-	-	-
15	Agricultural workers	6	3	1	2	-	-
16	Members of armed forces	223	7	124	23	-	2
17	Inadequately described and not stated occupations	42	8	23	3	2	5
	Economically inactive head	2,804	1,254	366	282	154	731
TOTAL PERSONS		**16,868**	**3,277**	**8,571**	**1,459**	**378**	**2,749**
	Persons economically active	8,391	1,106	5,224	842	110	892
	Dependent children	3,439	135	2,162	170	71	756

(10% sample)

Households		Persons				Families		
Migrant head of household	No car	TOTAL PERSONS	Persons economically active	Dependent children	Adults with limiting long-term illness	TOTAL FAMILIES	Lone parent with dependent child(ren)	Socio-economic group
h	i	j	k	l	m	n	o	a

		By socio-economic group of economically active head of household				By socio-economic group of economically active head of family		
557	1,194	15,492	7,355	3,071	1,661	4,688	215	**TOTAL**
27	3	878	499	275	25	247	7	1 Employers and managers in large establishments
69	11	1,812	1,118	508	61	532	8	2 Employers and managers in small establishments
5	-	241	146	72	7	69	-	3 Professional workers - self-employed
25	2	615	365	174	19	174	3	4 Professional workers - employees
42	20	1,258	813	325	53	362	24	5.1 Ancillary workers and artists
5	-	70	54	11	-	24	-	5.2 Foremen and supervisors - non-manual
49	36	1,059	746	244	45	318	34	6 Junior non-manual workers
8	22	187	118	59	3	56	18	7 Personal service workers
9	4	390	248	105	9	118	2	8 Foremen and supervisors - manual
56	20	1,369	915	313	48	430	4	9 Skilled manual workers
31	41	903	595	216	44	266	5	10 Semi-skilled manual workers
15	35	298	209	61	15	93	8	11 Unskilled manual workers
36	7	1,117	711	289	34	337	5	12 Own account workers (other than professional)
5	-	44	33	5	-	16	-	13 Farmers - employers and managers
-	1	55	39	9	2	14	-	14 Farmers - own account
3	7	125	91	23	3	41	-	15 Agricultural workers
17	7	112	63	36	3	30	-	16 Members of armed forces
6	4	93	51	26	8	23	1	17 Inadequately described and not stated occupations
147	961	4,802	510	299	1,278	1,520	95	Economically inactive head
1,342	1,870					13,275	592	**TOTAL PERSONS**
700	414					6,524	149	Persons economically active
332	225					3,071	344	Dependent children

		By socio-economic group of economically active head of household				By socio-economic group of economically active head of family		
804	2,871	16,868	8,391	3,439	2,077	4,774	457	**TOTAL**
29	22	514	338	111	25	146	4	1 Employers and managers in large establishments
63	48	1,274	872	296	49	371	13	2 Employers and managers in small establishments
4	2	87	56	18	1	26	-	3 Professional workers - self-employed
34	28	583	390	134	16	160	2	4 Professional workers - employees
90	73	1,253	886	265	41	357	31	5.1 Ancillary workers and artists
4	7	75	51	20	3	21	1	5.2 Foremen and supervisors - non-manual
95	164	1,204	874	265	45	347	57	6 Junior non-manual workers
28	67	350	229	94	22	93	29	7 Personal service workers
11	16	304	207	65	13	85	2	8 Foremen and supervisors - manual
76	143	1,945	1,270	472	93	570	15	9 Skilled manual workers
78	199	1,308	885	281	68	368	20	10 Semi-skilled manual workers
23	130	568	359	141	36	163	13	11 Unskilled manual workers
44	42	1,204	747	325	54	348	6	12 Own account workers (other than professional)
-	-	-	-	-	-	-	-	13 Farmers - employers and managers
-	-	-	-	-	-	-	-	14 Farmers - own account
1	2	14	11	1	1	5	-	15 Agricultural workers
57	44	694	385	235	15	192	1	16 Members of armed forces
2	11	123	78	29	12	31	4	17 Inadequately described and not stated occupations
153	1,817	5,150	652	601	1,563	1,435	244	Economically inactive head
1,850	5,412					13,558	1,241	**TOTAL PERSONS**
1,105	1,865					6,817	261	Persons economically active
417	958					3,439	734	Dependent children

187

Table 86 SEG of households and families (10% sample) – **continued**

86. Households with residents; residents in households; families of resident persons

			Households					
				Tenure of households in permanent buildings				
		TOTAL HOUSE-HOLDS	Owner occupied		Rented privately	Rented from a housing association	Rented from a local authority or new town		
Socio-economic group			Owned outright	Buying				
a		b	c	d	e	f	g

Rushmoor

By socio-economic group of economically active head of household

TOTAL		**3,008**	**495**	**1,531**	**216**	**64**	**487**
1	Employers and managers in large establishments	166	12	140	8	-	5
2	Employers and managers in small establishments	260	17	203	18	1	14
3	Professional workers - self-employed	10	1	9	-	-	-
4	Professional workers - employees	176	14	146	8	-	1
5.1	Ancillary workers and artists	208	19	165	9	1	8
5.2	Foremen and supervisors - non-manual	22	-	20	1	-	1
6	Junior non-manual workers	251	28	157	27	1	28
7	Personal service workers	54	4	29	4	-	14
8	Foremen and supervisors - manual	58	5	39	8	2	4
9	Skilled manual workers	296	24	202	21	3	35
10	Semi-skilled manual workers	193	22	105	14	4	41
11	Unskilled manual workers	87	15	24	15	2	28
12	Own account workers (other than professional)	191	18	142	12	2	15
13	Farmers - employers and managers	-	-	-	-	-	-
14	Farmers - own account	1	-	1	-	-	-
15	Agricultural workers	2	-	2	-	-	-
16	Members of armed forces	200	1	26	19	-	3
17	Inadequately described and not stated occupations	12	2	7	2	-	1
	Economically inactive head	812	313	110	49	48	286
TOTAL PERSONS		**7,815**	**984**	**4,428**	**464**	**110**	**1,177**
	Persons economically active	4,353	392	2,843	296	31	428
	Dependent children	1,818	49	1,112	79	21	332

Southampton

By socio-economic group of economically active head of household

TOTAL		**7,955**	**1,724**	**3,135**	**849**	**271**	**1,885**
1	Employers and managers in large establishments	209	15	174	8	2	9
2	Employers and managers in small establishments	493	44	351	34	6	31
3	Professional workers - self-employed	37	4	28	3	1	1
4	Professional workers - employees	285	22	212	35	2	6
5.1	Ancillary workers and artists	537	66	374	60	1	33
5.2	Foremen and supervisors - non-manual	37	3	27	2	1	3
6	Junior non-manual workers	603	84	334	90	15	79
7	Personal service workers	159	19	47	33	3	54
8	Foremen and supervisors - manual	151	17	105	5	3	21
9	Skilled manual workers	823	84	473	72	6	181
10	Semi-skilled manual workers	613	79	286	47	20	173
11	Unskilled manual workers	266	42	74	41	10	97
12	Own account workers (other than professional)	489	50	318	41	5	67
13	Farmers - employers and managers	-	-	-	-	-	-
14	Farmers - own account	-	-	-	-	-	-
15	Agricultural workers	6	1	1	2	-	2
16	Members of armed forces	16	-	14	2	-	-
17	Inadequately described and not stated occupations	40	6	18	7	2	7
	Economically inactive head	3,092	1,180	285	337	189	1,079
TOTAL PERSONS		**19,108**	**3,323**	**9,020**	**1,507**	**477**	**4,569**
	Persons economically active	9,437	1,175	5,566	827	139	1,597
	Dependent children	4,069	163	2,309	155	82	1,321

(10% sample)

Households		Persons				Families		Socio-economic group
Migrant head of household	No car	TOTAL PERSONS	Persons economically active	Dependent children	Adults with limiting long-term illness	TOTAL FAMILIES	Lone parent with dependent child(ren)	
h	i	j	k	l	m	n	o	a

		By socio-economic group of economically active head of household				By socio-economic group of economically active head of family		
395	662	7,815	4,353	1,818	642	2,298	162	**TOTAL**
19	6	494	323	125	16	147	3	1 Employers and managers in large establishments
34	11	769	517	192	22	232	5	2 Employers and managers in small establishments
-	-	35	20	12	-	9	-	3 Professional workers - self-employed
24	9	506	310	143	17	143	3	4 Professional workers - employees
29	13	541	380	121	26	156	12	5.1 Ancillary workers and artists
5	1	54	37	14	3	18	1	5.2 Foremen and supervisors - non-manual
46	34	663	456	162	25	182	19	6 Junior non-manual workers
11	14	134	81	37	4	36	10	7 Personal service workers
6	7	179	122	41	1	52	-	8 Foremen and supervisors - manual
37	31	851	582	194	28	257	3	9 Skilled manual workers
28	36	533	370	113	39	162	7	10 Semi-skilled manual workers
15	30	202	149	39	13	56	8	11 Unskilled manual workers
19	5	582	380	154	15	165	6	12 Own account workers (other than professional)
-	-	-	-	-	-	-	-	13 Farmers - employers and managers
-	-	2	2	-	-	-	-	14 Farmers - own account
-	1	6	2	2	2	2	-	15 Agricultural workers
73	28	641	362	227	10	193	2	16 Members of armed forces
3	1	37	23	11	1	10	-	17 Inadequately described and not stated occupations
46	433	1,556	222	222	415	470	81	Economically inactive head
985	1,246					6,808	449	**TOTAL PERSONS**
611	397					3,782	95	Persons economically active
247	267					1,818	270	Dependent children

		By socio-economic group of economically active head of household				By socio-economic group of economically active head of family		
904	2,800	19,108	9,437	4,069	2,161	5,400	494	**TOTAL**
31	14	573	382	133	15	169	3	1 Employers and managers in large establishments
69	46	1,417	902	370	36	401	11	2 Employers and managers in small establishments
4	-	110	62	34	3	28	-	3 Professional workers - self-employed
58	31	729	489	158	28	193	3	4 Professional workers - employees
96	68	1,361	950	291	63	372	25	5.1 Ancillary workers and artists
7	2	98	64	24	2	29	1	5.2 Foremen and supervisors - non-manual
102	144	1,417	991	320	64	389	52	6 Junior non-manual workers
34	78	389	271	87	15	107	27	7 Personal service workers
11	14	471	293	127	19	139	1	8 Foremen and supervisors - manual
78	136	2,419	1,556	624	109	705	13	9 Skilled manual workers
72	165	1,767	1,109	452	78	503	25	10 Semi-skilled manual workers
31	102	682	474	124	62	193	12	11 Unskilled manual workers
49	43	1,521	925	414	52	424	3	12 Own account workers (other than professional)
-	-	-	-	-	-	-	-	13 Farmers - employers and managers
-	-	-	-	-	-	-	-	14 Farmers - own account
3	3	11	8	2	-	3	-	15 Agricultural workers
3	2	36	26	7	2	13	-	16 Members of armed forces
6	9	119	73	36	4	32	2	17 Inadequately described and not stated occupations
231	1,876	5,749	713	810	1,577	1,646	304	Economically inactive head
1,994	4,991					15,579	1,359	**TOTAL PERSONS**
1,136	1,550					7,722	240	Persons economically active
424	900					4,069	810	Dependent children

Table 86　SEG of households and families (10% sample) – **continued**

86. Households with residents; residents in households; families of resident persons

Socio-economic group	TOTAL HOUSE-HOLDS	Households				
		Tenure of households in permanent buildings				
		Owner occupied		Rented privately	Rented from a housing association	Rented from a local authority or new town
		Owned outright	Buying			
a	b	c	d	e	f	g

Test Valley

By socio-economic group of economically active head of household

TOTAL	**3,781**	**821**	**1,828**	**248**	**59**	**635**
1　Employers and managers in large establishments	241	14	208	9	2	8
2　Employers and managers in small establishments	408	54	300	21	1	12
3　Professional workers - self-employed	59	11	47	1	-	-
4　Professional workers - employees	161	12	139	5	-	1
5.1　Ancillary workers and artists	288	30	222	18	1	9
5.2　Foremen and supervisors - non-manual	23	2	16	2	-	3
6　Junior non-manual workers	261	19	172	21	4	38
7　Personal service workers	45	5	9	8	-	17
8　Foremen and supervisors - manual	71	6	47	3	1	14
9　Skilled manual workers	346	31	195	25	3	80
10　Semi-skilled manual workers	200	23	89	13	4	61
11　Unskilled manual workers	65	9	16	5	1	31
12　Own account workers (other than professional)	252	39	175	18	2	15
13　Farmers - employers and managers	25	8	8	-	-	-
14　Farmers - own account	19	11	6	1	-	-
15　Agricultural workers	41	1	7	3	-	4
16　Members of armed forces	113	2	35	11	-	2
17　Inadequately described and not stated occupations	21	4	11	4	-	1
Economically inactive head	1,124	538	122	78	40	329
TOTAL PERSONS	**9,921**	**1,630**	**5,570**	**550**	**107**	**1,527**
Persons economically active	5,228	606	3,327	306	36	620
Dependent children	2,261	99	1,521	109	13	383

Winchester

By socio-economic group of economically active head of household

TOTAL	**3,723**	**956**	**1,619**	**251**	**82**	**613**
1　Employers and managers in large establishments	239	18	206	8	-	3
2　Employers and managers in small establishments	401	39	306	24	1	13
3　Professional workers - self-employed	80	12	63	5	-	-
4　Professional workers - employees	227	17	190	10	2	2
5.1　Ancillary workers and artists	316	40	224	21	2	12
5.2　Foremen and supervisors - non-manual	16	2	12	-	-	2
6　Junior non-manual workers	238	46	143	18	5	15
7　Personal service workers	39	6	11	6	1	11
8　Foremen and supervisors - manual	34	-	19	4	1	7
9　Skilled manual workers	222	33	105	11	5	61
10　Semi-skilled manual workers	147	13	39	18	4	60
11　Unskilled manual workers	61	7	11	6	1	33
12　Own account workers (other than professional)	184	28	111	17	2	22
13　Farmers - employers and managers	37	16	6	3	-	-
14　Farmers - own account	21	13	4	-	-	-
15　Agricultural workers	50	3	2	6	-	2
16　Members of armed forces	77	3	34	5	-	-
17　Inadequately described and not stated occupations	18	6	8	2	-	-
Economically inactive head	1,306	652	123	85	58	366
TOTAL PERSONS	**9,275**	**1,837**	**4,826**	**540**	**142**	**1,377**
Persons economically active	4,688	606	2,892	304	47	515
Dependent children	1,922	113	1,259	81	22	307

County, districts

(10% sample)

Households		Persons				Families		Socio-economic group
Migrant head of household	No car	TOTAL PERSONS	Persons economically active	Dependent children	Adults with limiting long-term illness	TOTAL FAMILIES	Lone parent with dependent child(ren)	
h	i	j	k	l	m	n	o	a

		By socio-economic group of economically active head of household				By socio-economic group of economically active head of family		
430	698	9,921	5,228	2,261	834	2,914	135	TOTAL
28	2	746	449	208	20	217	3	1 Employers and managers in large establishments
44	10	1,260	785	345	40	368	8	2 Employers and managers in small establishments
7	-	191	99	70	2	54	2	3 Professional workers - self-employed
18	2	495	290	150	12	139	-	4 Professional workers - employees
31	11	796	492	221	24	235	14	5.1 Ancillary workers and artists
7	-	67	45	18	3	21	2	5.2 Foremen and supervisors - non-manual
50	30	706	481	173	25	204	22	6 Junior non-manual workers
8	16	114	84	26	7	34	10	7 Personal service workers
12	10	228	151	48	9	68	-	8 Foremen and supervisors - manual
46	32	1,032	685	242	39	307	4	9 Skilled manual workers
20	32	562	373	122	36	174	6	10 Semi-skilled manual workers
7	20	171	113	42	15	50	6	11 Unskilled manual workers
30	8	802	493	227	18	233	4	12 Own account workers (other than professional)
2	-	79	50	18	2	26	-	13 Farmers - employers and managers
-	-	52	34	8	-	16	-	14 Farmers - own account
6	3	114	80	17	5	32	-	15 Agricultural workers
48	6	368	202	128	7	107	-	16 Members of armed forces
3	3	51	36	6	1	18	-	17 Inadequately described and not stated occupations
58	503	2,038	262	175	562	600	51	Economically inactive head
1,109	1,176					8,754	370	TOTAL PERSONS
626	342					4,691	102	Persons economically active
310	178					2,261	213	Dependent children

		By socio-economic group of economically active head of household				By socio-economic group of economically active head of family		
360	717	9,275	4,688	1,922	830	2,709	123	TOTAL
26	5	736	430	197	21	215	3	1 Employers and managers in large establishments
39	10	1,210	738	339	33	353	15	2 Employers and managers in small establishments
6	-	253	140	77	8	70	-	3 Professional workers - self-employed
26	3	630	392	159	14	188	1	4 Professional workers - employees
46	18	870	557	225	25	238	10	5.1 Ancillary workers and artists
-	1	35	28	5	1	11	-	5.2 Foremen and supervisors - non-manual
24	24	621	447	110	32	188	14	6 Junior non-manual workers
7	6	104	80	21	5	28	5	7 Personal service workers
5	3	102	68	29	3	33	1	8 Foremen and supervisors - manual
21	15	672	451	149	28	195	-	9 Skilled manual workers
14	30	398	278	78	13	127	4	10 Semi-skilled manual workers
6	22	176	114	49	10	50	6	11 Unskilled manual workers
16	6	551	344	140	18	158	4	12 Own account workers (other than professional)
3	-	110	71	22	2	32	-	13 Farmers - employers and managers
1	2	54	36	8	7	16	-	14 Farmers - own account
9	4	134	91	29	8	37	2	15 Agricultural workers
27	1	260	125	94	5	75	-	16 Members of armed forces
1	1	53	25	17	-	16	-	17 Inadequately described and not stated occupations
83	561	2,280	252	171	594	672	58	Economically inactive head
887	1,123					7,941	354	TOTAL PERSONS
467	278					4,102	82	Persons economically active
228	147					1,922	208	Dependent children

Table 87 Family type and tenure (10% sample)

County, districts

87. Households with residents; residents in households

(10% sample)

HAMPSHIRE

Household composition	TOTAL HOUSE-HOLDS	Tenure of households in permanent buildings					Migrant head of household	No car	2 or more cars	Persons	
		Owner occupied		Rented privately	Rented from a housing association	Rented from a local authority or new town				TOTAL PERSONS	Dependent children 0 - 18
		Owned outright	Buying								
a	b	c	d	e	f	g	h	i	j	k	l
TOTAL HOUSEHOLDS	59,458	14,552	28,675	4,030	1,179	9,266	6,060	14,294	18,561	149,450	32,772
Households with no families	16,043	5,498	4,133	2,051	709	3,335	1,857	8,386	1,026	18,588	
One person	14,066	5,001	3,424	1,611	677	3,091	1,489	7,832	388	14,066	
Two or more persons	1,977	497	709	440	32	244	368	554	638	4,522	
Households with one family	42,924	8,961	24,290	1,956	463	5,826	4,168	5,840	17,287	128,235	32,105
Married couple family	34,905	8,016	20,364	1,174	318	3,739	2,645	3,635	14,924	106,871	26,167
with no children	15,779	6,265	6,482	629	209	1,709	1,125	2,421	4,430	32,308	
with dependent child(ren)	14,194	617	10,893	437	91	1,462	1,386	874	7,136	57,760	26,167
with non-dependent child(ren) only	4,932	1,134	2,989	108	18	568	134	340	3,358	16,803	
Cohabiting couple family	3,615	162	2,356	497	42	497	1,039	419	1,611	9,511	1,712
with no children	2,411	124	1,707	406	22	118	788	234	1,123	5,005	
with dependent child(ren)	1,036	18	550	86	18	342	236	169	382	3,944	1,712
with non-dependent child(ren) only	168	20	99	5	2	37	15	16	106	562	
Lone parent family	4,404	783	1,570	285	103	1,590	484	1,786	752	11,853	4,226
with dependent child(ren)	2,521	161	944	189	79	1,102	419	1,239	229	7,437	4,226
with non-dependent child(ren) only	1,883	622	626	96	24	488	65	547	523	4,416	
Households with two or more families	491	93	252	23	7	105	35	68	248	2,627	667
Total dependent children aged 0 - 17 in lone parent families	4,486	285	1,646	293	141	2,039	685	2,223	452		

Table 87 Family type and tenure (10% sample) – continued

(10% sample)

87. Households with residents; residents in households

Basingstoke & Deane

Household composition	TOTAL HOUSE-HOLDS	Tenure of households in permanent buildings					Migrant head of household	No car	2 or more cars	Persons	
		Owner occupied		Rented privately	Rented from a housing association	Rented from a local authority or new town				TOTAL PERSONS	Dependent children 0 -18
		Owned outright	Buying								
a	b	c	d	e	f	g	h	i	j	k	l
TOTAL HOUSEHOLDS	5,369	904	2,914	240	128	988	492	1,041	1,983	14,167	3,241
Households with no families	1,256	296	424	114	63	313	157	555	107	1,465	
One person	1,097	276	353	79	58	291	130	533	34	1,097	
Two or more persons	159	20	71	35	5	22	27	22	73	368	
Households with one family	4,061	599	2,465	125	65	659	331	480	1,848	12,425	3,169
Married couple family	3,329	523	2,067	82	52	477	209	304	1,595	10,466	2,653
with no children	1,379	388	647	46	29	221	83	206	415	2,822	
with dependent child(ren)	1,414	45	1,102	28	18	163	114	64	816	5,801	2,653
with non-dependent child(ren) only	536	90	318	8	5	93	12	34	364	1,843	
Cohabiting couple family	366	19	260	32	5	40	95	33	181	960	152
with no children	248	11	192	26	2	12	77	18	125	513	
with dependent child(ren)	93	3	52	6	3	25	16	13	40	359	152
with non-dependent child(ren) only	25	5	16	-	-	3	2	2	16	88	
Lone parent family	366	57	138	11	8	142	27	143	72	999	364
with dependent child(ren)	211	17	79	7	6	97	24	102	25	634	364
with non-dependent child(ren) only	155	40	59	4	2	45	3	41	47	365	
Households with two or more families	52	9	25	1	-	16	4	6	28	277	72
Total dependent children aged 0 - 17 in lone parent families	391	32	136	8	11	198	42	204	38		

Table 87 Family type and tenure (10% sample) – continued

87. Households with residents; residents in households

(10% sample)

East Hampshire

Household composition	TOTAL HOUSE-HOLDS	Tenure of households in permanent buildings					Migrant head of household	No car	2 or more cars	Persons	
		Owner occupied		Rented privately	Rented from a housing association	Rented from a local authority or new town				TOTAL PERSONS	Dependent children 0 - 18
		Owned outright	Buying								
a	b	c	d	e	f	g	h	i	j	k	l
TOTAL HOUSEHOLDS	3,873	1,054	1,951	228	33	443	409	606	1,559	9,915	2,265
Households with no families	950	408	245	97	22	149	95	402	75	1,085	75
One person	844	371	217	76	22	134	78	371	37	844	
Two or more persons	106	37	28	21	-	15	17	31	38	241	
Households with one family	2,895	642	1,688	130	10	291	312	203	1,462	8,679	2,225
Married couple family	2,406	568	1,432	88	6	190	217	131	1,269	7,373	1,869
with no children	1,083	441	457	49	5	82	93	95	401	2,216	
with dependent child(ren)	1,016	50	803	25	1	75	114	20	652	4,120	1,869
with non-dependent child(ren) only	307	77	172	14	-	33	10	16	216	1,037	
Cohabiting couple family	239	16	171	23	1	22	62	10	143	631	118
with no children	158	11	119	19	-	4	52	6	96	327	
with dependent child(ren)	74	4	48	3	1	17	10	3	43	281	118
with non-dependent child(ren) only	7	1	4	1	-	1	-	1	4	23	
Lone parent family	250	58	85	19	3	79	33	62	50	675	238
with dependent child(ren)	140	10	57	11	3	55	29	42	12	414	238
with non-dependent child(ren) only	110	48	28	8	-	24	4	20	38	261	
Households with two or more families	28	4	18	1	1	3	2	1	22	151	40
Total dependent children aged 0 - 17 in lone parent families	252	19	101	23	5	99	50	82	27		

Table 87 Family type and tenure (10% sample) – **continued**

87. Households with residents; residents in households

(10% sample)

Household composition	Households										Persons	
	TOTAL HOUSE-HOLDS	Tenure of households in permanent buildings					Migrant head of household	No car	2 or more cars		TOTAL PERSONS	Dependent children 0 - 18
		Owner occupied		Rented privately	Rented from a housing association	Rented from a local authority or new town						
		Owned outright	Buying									
a	b	c	d	e	f	g	h	i	j		k	l
Eastleigh												
TOTAL HOUSEHOLDS	4,073	957	2,372	173	79	457	390	752	1,501		10,435	2,369
Households with no families	966	342	320	81	45	165	102	467	67		1,104	
One person	853	309	277	64	44	149	87	440	24		853	
Two or more persons	113	33	43	17	1	16	15	27	43		251	
Households with one family	3,080	608	2,038	91	33	289	287	281	1,419		9,191	2,331
Married couple family	2,543	549	1,693	68	22	195	180	190	1,206		7,831	1,991
with no children	1,095	431	495	43	16	104	88	139	338		2,239	
with dependent child(ren)	1,087	35	954	22	5	64	84	34	595		4,360	1,991
with non-dependent child(ren) only	361	83	244	3	1	27	8	17	273		1,232	
Cohabiting couple family	274	8	223	13	3	24	78	15	152		676	101
with no children	199	8	171	11	2	5	61	7	122		408	
with dependent child(ren)	64	-	41	2	1	19	16	8	21		233	101
with non-dependent child(ren) only	11	-	11	-	-	-	1	-	9		35	
Lone parent family	263	51	122	10	8	70	29	76	61		684	239
with dependent child(ren)	148	6	81	7	7	46	23	50	25		425	239
with non-dependent child(ren) only	115	45	41	3	1	24	6	26	36		259	
Households with two or more families	27	7	14	1	1	3	1	4	15		140	38
Total dependent children aged 0 - 17 in lone parent families	249	11	141	11	8	77	32	82	47			

Table 87 Family type and tenure (10% sample) – continued

87. Households with residents; residents in households

(10% sample)

Fareham

Household composition	TOTAL HOUSE-HOLDS	Tenure of households in permanent buildings					Migrant head of household	No car	2 or more cars	TOTAL PERSONS	Dependent children 0 - 18
		Owner occupied		Rented privately	Rented from a housing association	Rented from a local authority or new town					
		Owned outright	Buying								
a	b	c	d	e	f	g	h	i	j	k	l
TOTAL HOUSEHOLDS	3,810	1,133	2,153	143	25	301	319	662	1,421	9,737	2,139
Households with no families	853	400	251	53	20	122	72	421	46	951	
One person	764	368	213	43	20	115	63	399	18	764	
Two or more persons	89	32	38	10	-	7	9	22	28	187	
Households with one family	2,929	725	1,887	89	5	176	245	237	1,357	8,643	2,103
Married couple family	2,493	658	1,622	58	4	110	176	167	1,191	7,495	1,803
with no children	1,155	537	522	25	4	55	67	120	384	2,355	
with dependent child(ren)	998	43	857	30	-	43	96	32	547	4,003	1,803
with non-dependent child(ren) only	340	78	243	3	-	12	13	15	260	1,137	
Cohabiting couple family	207	14	156	17	1	15	49	11	113	536	97
with no children	141	9	116	13	-	2	39	5	80	286	
with dependent child(ren)	58	2	35	4	1	13	8	6	28	226	97
with non-dependent child(ren) only	8	3	5	-	-	-	2	-	5	24	
Lone parent family	229	53	109	14	-	51	20	59	53	612	203
with dependent child(ren)	115	8	67	7	-	33	15	39	11	344	203
with non-dependent child(ren) only	114	45	42	7	-	18	5	20	42	268	
Households with two or more families	28	8	15	1	-	3	2	4	18	143	36
Total dependent children aged 0 - 17 in lone parent families	215	14	127	12	-	61	23	76	25		

Table 87 Family type and tenure (10% sample) – continued

87. Households with residents; residents in households

(10% sample)

Gosport

Household composition	TOTAL HOUSE-HOLDS	Tenure of households in permanent buildings					Migrant head of household	No car	2 or more cars	TOTAL PERSONS	Dependent children 0 - 18
		Owner occupied		Rented privately	Rented from a housing association	Rented from a local authority or new town					
		Owned outright	Buying								
a	b	c	d	e	f	g	h	i	j	k	l
TOTAL HOUSEHOLDS	2,899	651	1,399	162	61	489	322	871	544	7,288	1,755
Households with no families	764	272	208	64	42	168	70	450	32	857	
One person	686	252	174	54	41	157	58	420	19	686	
Two or more persons	78	20	34	10	1	11	12	30	13	171	
Households with one family	2,121	379	1,183	98	19	315	251	420	509	6,361	1,742
Married couple family	1,699	351	979	50	15	193	163	253	430	5,217	1,365
with no children	747	288	305	17	11	84	68	151	124	1,518	
with dependent child(ren)	747	19	540	29	4	88	86	82	193	3,016	1,365
with non-dependent child(ren) only	205	44	134	4	-	21	9	20	113	683	
Cohabiting couple family	169	3	111	30	1	21	58	28	59	451	91
with no children	110	3	76	26	-	4	44	20	35	227	
with dependent child(ren)	54	-	32	4	1	15	14	8	21	208	91
with non-dependent child(ren) only	5	-	3	-	-	2	-	-	3	16	
Lone parent family	253	25	93	18	3	101	30	139	20	693	286
with dependent child(ren)	170	5	63	15	2	74	25	103	8	499	286
with non-dependent child(ren) only	83	20	30	3	1	27	5	36	12	194	
Households with two or more families	14	-	8	-	-	6	1	1	3	70	13
Total dependent children aged 0 - 17 in lone parent families	290	7	98	26	4	134	37	177	9		

Table 87 Family type and tenure (10% sample) – continued

(10% sample)

87. Households with residents; residents in households

Hart

Household composition	TOTAL HOUSE-HOLDS	Tenure of households in permanent buildings					Migrant head of household	No car	2 or more cars	Persons	
		Owner occupied		Rented privately	Rented from a housing association	Rented from a local authority or new town				TOTAL PERSONS	Dependent children 0 - 18
		Owned outright	Buying								
a	b	c	d	e	f	g	h	i	j	k	l
TOTAL HOUSEHOLDS	2,875	586	1,733	169	27	241	309	310	1,482	7,848	1,890
Households with no families	618	219	220	70	16	83	80	214	75	723	
One person	535	197	190	48	15	79	62	207	26	535	
Two or more persons	83	22	30	22	1	4	18	7	49	188	
Households with one family	2,233	361	1,502	96	11	155	226	96	1,389	6,992	1,858
Married couple family	1,900	328	1,308	54	9	103	154	62	1,232	6,129	1,652
with no children	724	231	380	23	7	50	58	44	354	1,484	
with dependent child(ren)	883	34	729	28	2	32	89	11	628	3,618	1,652
with non-dependent child(ren) only	293	63	199	3	-	21	7	7	250	1,027	
Cohabiting couple family	180	7	132	27	1	10	58	5	113	447	65
with no children	131	6	100	18	1	4	41	2	87	270	
with dependent child(ren)	41	1	27	9	-	4	15	1	21	152	65
with non-dependent child(ren) only	8	-	5	-	-	2	2	2	5	25	
Lone parent family	153	26	62	15	1	42	14	29	44	416	141
with dependent child(ren)	83	12	32	7	1	26	12	18	15	253	141
with non-dependent child(ren) only	70	14	30	8	-	16	2	11	29	163	
Households with two or more families	24	6	11	3	-	3	3	-	18	133	32
Total dependent children aged 0 - 17 in lone parent families	151	20	56	14	2	50	21	38	34		

Table 87 Family type and tenure (10% sample) – **continued**

County, districts

(10% sample)

87. Households with residents; residents in households

Havant

Household composition	TOTAL HOUSE-HOLDS	Tenure of households in permanent buildings					Migrant head of household	No car	2 or more cars	TOTAL PERSONS	Dependent children 0 - 18
		Owner occupied		Rented privately	Rented from a housing association	Rented from a local authority or new town					
		Owned outright	Buying								
a	b	c	d	e	f	g	h	i	j	k	l
TOTAL HOUSEHOLDS	4,562	1,184	2,182	180	39	938	369	1,110	1,317	11,581	2,533
Households with no families	1,139	407	289	77	20	337	116	606	60	1,293	
One person	1,011	374	245	53	19	312	97	574	20	1,011	
Two or more persons	128	33	44	24	1	25	19	32	40	282	
Households with one family	3,380	771	1,877	103	17	583	247	497	1,236	10,051	2,453
Married couple family	2,760	698	1,614	55	14	355	156	310	1,084	8,349	1,944
with no children	1,301	581	525	31	9	149	51	203	314	2,653	
with dependent child(ren)	1,031	45	797	19	5	150	92	79	485	4,236	1,944
with non-dependent child(ren) only	428	72	292	5	-	56	13	28	285	1,460	
Cohabiting couple family	261	15	147	33	2	62	60	32	101	731	156
with no children	152	12	101	21	1	15	40	15	59	321	
with dependent child(ren)	90	-	39	11	1	39	19	16	29	345	156
with non-dependent child(ren) only	19	3	7	1	-	8	1	1	13	65	
Lone parent family	359	58	116	15	1	166	31	155	51	971	353
with dependent child(ren)	214	13	69	11	1	118	30	109	22	636	353
with non-dependent child(ren) only	145	45	47	4	-	48	1	46	29	335	
Households with two or more families	43	6	16	-	2	18	6	7	21	237	80
Total dependent children aged 0 - 17 in lone parent families	387	19	115	13	3	232	50	199	44		

Households

Persons

Table 87 Family type and tenure (10% sample) – continued

County, districts

87. Households with residents; residents in households

(10% sample)

New Forest

Household composition	TOTAL HOUSE-HOLDS	Tenure of households in permanent buildings					Migrant head of household	No car	2 or more cars	TOTAL PERSONS	Dependent children 0 - 18
		Owner occupied		Rented privately	Rented from a housing association	Rented from a local authority or new town					
		Owned outright	Buying								
a	b	c	d	e	f	g	h	i	j	k	l
TOTAL HOUSEHOLDS	6,429	2,345	2,833	386	84	617	557	1,194	2,249	15,492	3,071
Households with no families	1,778	916	371	166	44	239	144	792	119	2,005	
One person	1,580	833	322	136	41	215	119	752	45	1,580	
Two or more persons	198	83	49	30	3	24	25	40	74	425	
Households with one family	4,615	1,420	2,441	220	40	372	412	401	2,107	13,287	3,026
Married couple family	3,928	1,282	2,112	163	25	239	279	269	1,846	11,503	2,564
with no children	2,016	1,049	698	89	17	114	146	202	607	4,119	
with dependent child(ren)	1,408	94	1,127	54	6	82	122	41	857	5,683	2,564
with non-dependent child(ren) only	504	139	287	20	2	43	11	26	382	1,701	
Cohabiting couple family	297	29	191	33	6	28	91	21	163	761	135
with no children	212	24	145	28	4	6	64	12	123	432	
with dependent child(ren)	77	3	41	5	2	21	26	8	34	302	135
with non-dependent child(ren) only	8	2	5	-	-	1	1	1	6	27	
Lone parent family	390	109	138	24	9	105	42	111	98	1,023	327
with dependent child(ren)	201	24	87	13	7	67	36	71	26	580	327
with non-dependent child(ren) only	189	85	51	11	2	38	6	40	72	443	
Households with two or more families	36	9	21	-	-	6	1	1	23	200	45
Total dependent children aged 0 - 17 in lone parent families	340	41	154	21	10	110	54	122	47		

Table 87 Family type and tenure (10% sample) – **continued**

87. Households with residents; residents in households

(10% sample)

Portsmouth

Household composition	TOTAL HOUSE-HOLDS	Tenure of households in permanent buildings					Migrant head of household	No car	2 or more cars	TOTAL PERSONS	Dependent children 0 - 18
		Owner occupied		Rented privately	Rented from a housing association	Rented from a local authority or new town					
		Owned outright	Buying								
a	b	c	d	e	f	g	h	i	j	k	l
TOTAL HOUSEHOLDS	7,101	1,742	3,025	785	227	1,172	804	2,871	1,154	16,868	3,439
Households with no families	2,409	740	567	467	144	460	321	1,576	125	2,919	
One person	2,044	653	433	373	135	423	236	1,415	46	2,044	
Two or more persons	365	87	134	94	9	37	85	161	79	875	
Households with one family	4,616	987	2,412	313	83	702	479	1,274	1,010	13,532	3,337
Married couple family	3,405	862	1,865	146	43	383	247	770	799	10,272	2,403
with no children	1,634	669	642	85	31	171	110	480	225	3,362	
with dependent child(ren)	1,321	56	974	53	12	159	129	210	365	5,371	2,403
with non-dependent child(ren) only	450	137	249	8	-	53	8	80	209	1,539	
Cohabiting couple family	526	17	304	109	8	84	150	120	150	1,408	265
with no children	341	12	210	91	4	21	115	68	100	722	
with dependent child(ren)	162	3	83	17	4	54	34	46	36	611	265
with non-dependent child(ren) only	23	2	11	1	-	9	1	6	14	75	
Lone parent family	685	108	243	58	32	235	82	384	61	1,852	669
with dependent child(ren)	405	20	151	43	25	160	76	249	17	1,185	669
with non-dependent child(ren) only	280	88	92	15	7	75	6	135	44	667	
Households with two or more families	76	15	46	5	-	10	4	21	19	417	102
Total dependent children aged 0 - 17 in lone parent families	730	44	273	66	40	295	127	451	46		

Table 87 Family type and tenure (10% sample) – **continued**

County, districts

(10% sample)

87. Households with residents; residents in households

Rushmoor

Household composition	TOTAL HOUSE-HOLDS	Tenure of households in permanent buildings					Migrant head of household	No car	2 or more cars	TOTAL PERSONS	Dependent children 0 - 18
		Owner occupied		Rented privately	Rented from a housing association	Rented from a local authority or new town					
		Owned outright	Buying								
a	b	c	d	e	f	g	h	i	j	k	l
TOTAL HOUSEHOLDS	3,008	495	1,531	216	64	487	395	662	890	7,815	1,818
Households with no families	734	180	233	96	45	161	88	357	53	875	
One person	624	157	180	75	44	151	71	335	21	624	
Two or more persons	110	23	53	21	1	10	17	22	32	251	
Households with one family	2,250	308	1,285	120	19	322	307	303	825	6,816	1,795
Married couple family	1,762	275	1,026	68	11	194	190	177	676	5,529	1,445
with no children	723	203	337	32	5	84	77	101	195	1,474	
with dependent child(ren)	802	25	534	35	5	80	104	66	314	3,239	1,445
with non-dependent child(ren) only	237	47	155	1	1	30	9	10	167	816	
Cohabiting couple family	231	2	162	36	2	27	80	23	110	597	94
with no children	163	2	127	29	1	4	66	14	86	348	
with dependent child(ren)	58	-	26	6	1	23	14	9	18	216	94
with non-dependent child(ren) only	10	-	9	1	-	-	-	-	6	33	
Lone parent family	257	31	97	16	6	101	37	103	39	690	256
with dependent child(ren)	148	3	53	11	3	73	31	79	10	442	256
with non-dependent child(ren) only	109	28	44	5	3	28	6	24	29	248	
Households with two or more families	24	7	13	-	-	4	-	2	12	124	23
Total dependent children aged 0 - 17 in lone parent families	265	6	99	13	8	130	46	132	18		

Table 87 Family type and tenure (10% sample) – continued

87. Households with residents; residents in households

(10% sample)

Southampton

Household composition	TOTAL HOUSE-HOLDS	Tenure of households in permanent buildings					Migrant head of household	No car	2 or more cars	Persons	
		Owner occupied		Rented privately	Rented from a housing association	Rented from a local authority or new town				TOTAL PERSONS	Dependent children 0 - 18
		Owned outright	Buying								
a	b	c	d	e	f	g	h	i	j	k	l
TOTAL HOUSEHOLDS	7,955	1,724	3,135	849	271	1,885	904	2,800	1,617	19,108	4,069
Households with no families	2,635	658	578	533	165	673	400	1,625	123	3,089	
One person	2,307	610	449	438	161	625	315	1,510	40	2,307	
Two or more persons	328	48	129	95	4	48	85	115	83	782	
Households with one family	5,241	1,053	2,522	308	103	1,194	495	1,161	1,460	15,595	3,954
Married couple family	3,967	917	2,030	158	74	738	264	670	1,209	12,187	2,938
with no children	1,848	693	664	105	48	311	125	446	344	3,819	
with dependent child(ren)	1,552	75	1,082	39	21	318	127	165	550	6,418	2,938
with non-dependent child(ren) only	567	149	284	14	5	109	12	59	315	1,950	
Cohabiting couple family	510	14	283	91	7	108	145	94	155	1,346	250
with no children	341	12	210	83	5	27	110	55	106	715	
with dependent child(ren)	154	1	66	8	1	76	33	37	44	580	250
with non-dependent child(ren) only	15	1	7	-	1	5	2	2	5	51	
Lone parent family	764	122	209	59	22	348	86	397	96	2,062	766
with dependent child(ren)	456	23	117	42	17	256	71	284	28	1,341	766
with non-dependent child(ren) only	308	99	92	17	5	92	15	113	68	721	
Households with two or more families	79	13	35	8	3	18	9	14	34	424	115
Total dependent children aged 0 - 17 in lone parent families	803	36	192	65	39	469	131	496	61		

Table 87 Family type and tenure (10% sample) – continued

County, districts

(10% sample)

87. Households with residents; residents in households

Test Valley

Household composition	TOTAL HOUSE-HOLDS	Owner occupied Owned outright	Owner occupied Buying	Rented privately	Rented from a housing association	Rented from a local authority or new town	Migrant head of household	No car	2 or more cars	TOTAL PERSONS	Dependent children 0-18
a	b	c	d	e	f	g	h	i	j	k	l
TOTAL HOUSEHOLDS	3,781	821	1,828	248	59	635	430	698	1,408	9,921	2,261
Households with no families	900	290	213	110	33	224	99	434	54	1,020	
One person	803	266	184	88	30	208	83	413	24	803	
Two or more persons	97	24	29	22	3	16	16	21	30	217	
Households with one family	2,848	524	1,600	135	26	405	330	261	1,333	8,728	2,222
Married couple family	2,414	473	1,391	97	20	282	229	170	1,196	7,547	1,914
with no children	1,023	353	427	42	15	131	86	117	361	2,097	
with dependent child(ren)	1,034	43	755	42	2	116	129	40	577	4,239	1,914
with non-dependent child(ren) only	357	77	209	13	3	35	14	13	258	1,211	
Cohabiting couple family	202	9	126	27	2	35	68	14	87	553	111
with no children	120	8	77	22	1	12	48	6	48	243	
with dependent child(ren)	66	-	41	5	-	19	19	7	28	255	111
with non-dependent child(ren) only	16	1	8	-	1	4	1	1	11	55	
Lone parent family	232	42	83	11	4	88	33	77	50	628	197
with dependent child(ren)	122	9	45	7	4	55	29	53	14	356	197
with non-dependent child(ren) only	110	33	38	4	-	33	4	24	36	272	
Households with two or more families	33	7	15	3	-	6	1	3	21	173	39
Total dependent children aged 0 - 17 in lone parent families	209	18	72	12	6	97	49	86	29		

204

Table 87 Family type and tenure (10% sample) – **continued**

87. Households with residents; residents in households

(10% sample)

Household composition	TOTAL HOUSE-HOLDS	Tenure of households in permanent buildings					Migrant head of household	No car	2 or more cars	Persons	
		Owner occupied		Rented privately	Rented from a housing association	Rented from a local authority or new town				TOTAL PERSONS	Dependent children 0 - 18
		Owned outright	Buying								
a	b	c	d	e	f	g	h	i	j	k	l
Winchester											
TOTAL HOUSEHOLDS	3,723	956	1,619	251	82	613	360	717	1,436	9,275	1,922
Households with no families	1,041	370	214	123	50	241	113	487	90	1,202	
One person	918	335	187	84	47	232	90	463	34	918	
Two or more persons	123	35	27	39	3	9	23	24	56	284	
Households with one family	2,655	584	1,390	128	32	363	246	226	1,332	7,935	1,890
Married couple family	2,299	532	1,225	87	23	280	181	162	1,191	6,973	1,626
with no children	1,051	401	383	42	12	153	73	117	368	2,150	
with dependent child(ren)	901	53	639	33	10	92	100	30	557	3,656	1,626
with non-dependent child(ren) only	347	78	203	12	1	35	8	15	266	1,167	
Cohabiting couple family	153	9	90	26	3	21	45	13	84	414	77
with no children	95	6	63	19	1	2	31	6	56	193	
with dependent child(ren)	45	1	19	6	2	17	12	7	19	176	77
with non-dependent child(ren) only	13	2	8	1	-	2	2	-	9	45	
Lone parent family	203	43	75	15	6	62	20	51	57	548	187
with dependent child(ren)	108	11	43	8	3	42	18	40	16	328	187
with non-dependent child(ren) only	95	32	32	7	3	20	2	11	41	220	
Households with two or more families	27	2	15	-	-	9	1	4	14	138	32
Total dependent children aged 0 - 17 in lone parent families	204	18	82	9	5	87	23	78	27		

Table 88 'Concealed' families (10% sample)

County, districts

88. Families of resident persons (10% sample)

Family composition	All 16 and over	16 - 29	30 - 44	45 up to pensionable age	Pensionable age - 69	70 - 74	75 - 84	85 and over
a	b	c	d	e	f	g	h	i

HAMPSHIRE

Age of head of household

TOTAL FAMILIES	43,919	6,040	14,888	14,997	3,166	2,222	2,302	304
'Concealed' families	765	74	131	338	88	58	66	10
Lone parent families	391	30	71	182	52	29	24	3
with dependent child(ren)	331	28	60	172	41	23	7	-
with non-dependent child(ren) only	60	2	11	10	11	6	17	3
Couple families	374	44	60	156	36	29	42	7
with no children	211	32	41	88	13	11	20	6
with dependent child(ren)	152	10	17	68	23	17	16	1
with non-dependent child(ren) only	11	2	2	-	-	1	6	-
'Unconcealed' families	43,154	5,966	14,757	14,659	3,078	2,164	2,236	294
with no children	18,335	2,875	2,526	6,584	2,399	1,813	1,919	219
with dependent child(ren)	17,752	3,060	11,232	3,383	43	19	12	3
with non-dependent child(ren) only	7,067	31	999	4,692	636	332	305	72

Age of head of family

TOTAL FAMILIES	43,919	6,341	14,985	14,747	3,095	2,178	2,273	300
'Concealed' families	765	375	228	88	17	14	37	6
Lone parent families	391	230	112	31	4	2	10	2
with dependent child(ren)	331	230	96	5	-	-	-	-
with non-dependent child(ren) only	60	-	16	26	4	2	10	2
Couple families	374	145	116	57	13	12	27	4
with no children	211	73	43	40	13	11	27	4
with dependent child(ren)	152	72	68	11	-	1	-	-
with non-dependent child(ren) only	11	-	5	6	-	-	-	-

Basingstoke & Deane

Age of head of household

TOTAL FAMILIES	4,165	597	1,516	1,468	245	161	170	8
'Concealed' families	77	7	12	42	6	2	8	-
Lone parent families	43	2	7	25	4	2	3	-
with dependent child(ren)	35	1	6	24	2	2	-	-
with non-dependent child(ren) only	8	1	1	1	2	-	3	-
Couple families	34	5	5	17	2	-	5	-
with no children	15	3	3	6	1	-	2	-
with dependent child(ren)	19	2	2	11	1	-	3	-
with non-dependent child(ren) only	-	-	-	-	-	-	-	-
'Unconcealed' families	4,088	590	1,504	1,426	239	159	162	8
with no children	1,647	326	257	606	179	135	138	6
with dependent child(ren)	1,715	261	1,126	320	5	2	1	-
with non-dependent child(ren) only	726	3	121	500	55	22	23	2

Age of head of family

TOTAL FAMILIES	4,165	630	1,528	1,432	239	159	167	10
'Concealed' families	77	40	24	6	-	-	5	2
Lone parent families	43	24	15	2	-	-	1	1
with dependent child(ren)	35	24	11	-	-	-	-	-
with non-dependent child(ren) only	8	-	4	2	-	-	1	1
Couple families	34	16	9	4	-	-	4	1
with no children	15	5	3	2	-	-	4	1
with dependent child(ren)	19	11	6	2	-	-	-	-
with non-dependent child(ren) only	-	-	-	-	-	-	-	-

Table 88 'Concealed' families (10% sample) – **continued**　　　　　　　　County, districts

88. Families of resident persons　　　　　　　　　　　　　　　　　　　　　　　　　　　(10% sample)

Family composition	All 16 and over	16 - 29	30 - 44	45 up to pensionable age	Pensionable age - 69	70 - 74	75 - 84	85 and over
a	b	c	d	e	f	g	h	i

East Hampshire

Age of head of household

TOTAL FAMILIES	2,952	342	1,045	1,044	208	140	152	21
'Concealed' families	52	4	12	21	4	4	5	2
Lone parent families	23	2	5	11	1	3	1	-
with dependent child(ren)	19	2	4	10	1	2	-	-
with non-dependent child(ren) only	4	-	1	1	-	1	1	-
Couple families	29	2	7	10	3	1	4	2
with no children	22	2	6	8	2	-	2	2
with dependent child(ren)	5	-	-	2	1	1	1	-
with non-dependent child(ren) only	2	-	1	-	-	-	1	-
'Unconcealed' families	2,900	338	1,033	1,023	204	136	147	19
with no children	1,242	177	218	433	162	111	127	14
with dependent child(ren)	1,231	161	777	289	3	-	1	-
with non-dependent child(ren) only	427	-	38	301	39	25	19	5

Age of head of family

TOTAL FAMILIES	2,952	357	1,050	1,030	205	140	150	20
'Concealed' families	52	19	17	7	1	4	3	1
Lone parent families	23	14	6	2	1	-	-	-
with dependent child(ren)	19	14	5	-	-	-	-	-
with non-dependent child(ren) only	4	-	1	2	1	-	-	-
Couple families	29	5	11	5	-	4	3	1
with no children	22	4	7	3	-	4	3	1
with dependent child(ren)	5	1	4	-	-	-	-	-
with non-dependent child(ren) only	2	-	-	2	-	-	-	-

Eastleigh

Age of head of household

TOTAL FAMILIES	3,134	428	1,154	1,023	216	162	126	25
'Concealed' families	35	3	8	14	6	3	1	-
Lone parent families	15	-	3	6	3	2	1	-
with dependent child(ren)	13	-	3	6	3	1	-	-
with non-dependent child(ren) only	2	-	-	-	-	1	1	-
Couple families	20	3	5	8	3	1	-	-
with no children	10	2	2	5	-	1	-	-
with dependent child(ren)	9	-	3	3	3	-	-	-
with non-dependent child(ren) only	1	1	-	-	-	-	-	-
'Unconcealed' families	3,099	425	1,146	1,009	210	159	125	25
with no children	1,306	234	201	440	170	140	101	20
with dependent child(ren)	1,303	189	883	229	2	-	-	-
with non-dependent child(ren) only	490	2	62	340	38	19	24	5

Age of head of family

TOTAL FAMILIES	3,134	448	1,151	1,013	211	159	127	25
'Concealed' families	35	23	5	4	1	-	2	-
Lone parent families	15	12	1	1	-	-	1	-
with dependent child(ren)	13	12	1	-	-	-	-	-
with non-dependent child(ren) only	2	-	-	1	-	-	1	-
Couple families	20	11	4	3	1	-	1	-
with no children	10	6	-	2	1	-	1	-
with dependent child(ren)	9	5	3	1	-	-	-	-
with non-dependent child(ren) only	1	-	1	-	-	-	-	-

Table 88 'Concealed' families (10% sample) – **continued**   County, districts

88. Families of resident persons   (10% sample)

Family composition	All 16 and over	16 - 29	30 - 44	45 up to pensionable age	Pensionable age - 69	70 - 74	75 - 84	85 and over
a	b	c	d	e	f	g	h	i

Fareham

Age of head of household

TOTAL FAMILIES	**2,985**	**302**	**1,038**	**1,127**	**212**	**122**	**169**	**15**
'Concealed' families	**37**	**3**	**6**	**16**	**2**	**6**	**4**	**-**
Lone parent families	**18**	**1**	**4**	**7**	**-**	**3**	**3**	**-**
with dependent child(ren)	16	1	4	7	-	3	1	-
with non-dependent child(ren) only	2	-	-	-	-	-	2	-
Couple families	**19**	**2**	**2**	**9**	**2**	**3**	**1**	**-**
with no children	6	1	1	3	-	1	-	-
with dependent child(ren)	13	1	1	6	2	2	1	-
with non-dependent child(ren) only	-	-	-	-	-	-	-	-
'Unconcealed' families	**2,948**	**299**	**1,032**	**1,111**	**210**	**116**	**165**	**15**
with no children	1,309	149	188	537	174	104	146	11
with dependent child(ren)	1,172	148	782	235	5	1	1	-
with non-dependent child(ren) only	467	2	62	339	31	11	18	4

Age of head of family

TOTAL FAMILIES	**2,985**	**318**	**1,047**	**1,113**	**210**	**116**	**166**	**15**
'Concealed' families	**37**	**19**	**15**	**2**	**-**	**-**	**1**	**-**
Lone parent families	**18**	**11**	**5**	**2**	**-**	**-**	**-**	**-**
with dependent child(ren)	16	11	5	-	-	-	-	-
with non-dependent child(ren) only	2	-	-	2	-	-	-	-
Couple families	**19**	**8**	**10**	**-**	**-**	**-**	**1**	**-**
with no children	6	2	3	-	-	-	1	-
with dependent child(ren)	13	6	7	-	-	-	-	-
with non-dependent child(ren) only	-	-	-	-	-	-	-	-

Gosport

Age of head of household

TOTAL FAMILIES	**2,149**	**419**	**774**	**626**	**133**	**92**	**95**	**10**
'Concealed' families	**22**	**4**	**5**	**9**	**1**	**1**	**-**	**2**
Lone parent families	**10**	**-**	**3**	**5**	**1**	**-**	**-**	**1**
with dependent child(ren)	8	-	3	4	1	-	-	-
with non-dependent child(ren) only	2	-	-	1	-	-	-	1
Couple families	**12**	**4**	**2**	**4**	**-**	**1**	**-**	**1**
with no children	11	4	1	4	-	1	-	1
with dependent child(ren)	1	-	1	-	-	-	-	-
with non-dependent child(ren) only	-	-	-	-	-	-	-	-
'Unconcealed' families	**2,127**	**415**	**769**	**617**	**132**	**91**	**95**	**8**
with no children	856	173	115	303	100	77	85	3
with dependent child(ren)	973	241	607	119	4	1	-	1
with non-dependent child(ren) only	298	1	47	195	28	13	10	4

Age of head of family

TOTAL FAMILIES	**2,149**	**423**	**774**	**622**	**134**	**91**	**97**	**8**
'Concealed' families	**22**	**8**	**5**	**5**	**2**	**-**	**2**	**-**
Lone parent families	**10**	**5**	**3**	**1**	**-**	**-**	**1**	**-**
with dependent child(ren)	8	5	3	-	-	-	-	-
with non-dependent child(ren) only	2	-	-	1	-	-	1	-
Couple families	**12**	**3**	**2**	**4**	**2**	**-**	**1**	**-**
with no children	11	2	2	4	2	-	1	-
with dependent child(ren)	1	1	-	-	-	-	-	-
with non-dependent child(ren) only	-	-	-	-	-	-	-	-

Table 88 'Concealed' families (10% sample) – **continued** County, districts

88. Families of resident persons (10% sample)

Family composition	All 16 and over	16 - 29	30 - 44	45 up to pensionable age	Pensionable age - 69	70 - 74	75 - 84	85 and over
a	b	c	d	e	f	g	h	i

Hart

Age of head of household

Family composition	All 16 and over	16 - 29	30 - 44	45 up to pensionable age	Pensionable age - 69	70 - 74	75 - 84	85 and over
TOTAL FAMILIES	2,283	246	859	903	106	89	68	12
'Concealed' families	35	1	11	19	1	2	1	-
Lone parent families	17	-	4	10	1	1	1	-
with dependent child(ren)	17	-	4	10	1	1	1	-
with non-dependent child(ren) only	-	-	-	-	-	-	-	-
Couple families	18	1	7	9	-	1	-	-
with no children	10	-	4	6	-	-	-	-
with dependent child(ren)	8	1	3	3	-	1	-	-
with non-dependent child(ren) only	-	-	-	-	-	-	-	-
'Unconcealed' families	2,248	245	848	884	105	87	67	12
with no children	860	143	143	361	82	63	60	8
with dependent child(ren)	1,009	101	664	242	-	2	-	-
with non-dependent child(ren) only	379	1	41	281	23	22	7	4

Age of head of family

Family composition	All 16 and over	16 - 29	30 - 44	45 up to pensionable age	Pensionable age - 69	70 - 74	75 - 84	85 and over
TOTAL FAMILIES	2,283	261	861	888	106	87	68	12
'Concealed' families	35	16	13	4	1	-	1	-
Lone parent families	17	9	6	2	-	-	-	-
with dependent child(ren)	17	9	6	2	-	-	-	-
with non-dependent child(ren) only	-	-	-	-	-	-	-	-
Couple families	18	7	7	2	1	-	1	-
with no children	10	3	4	1	1	-	1	-
with dependent child(ren)	8	4	3	1	-	-	-	-
with non-dependent child(ren) only	-	-	-	-	-	-	-	-

Havant

Age of head of household

Family composition	All 16 and over	16 - 29	30 - 44	45 up to pensionable age	Pensionable age - 69	70 - 74	75 - 84	85 and over
TOTAL FAMILIES	3,468	409	1,085	1,303	285	180	182	24
'Concealed' families	61	7	13	30	9	1	1	-
Lone parent families	37	5	10	17	5	-	-	-
with dependent child(ren)	35	5	9	17	4	-	-	-
with non-dependent child(ren) only	2	-	1	-	1	-	-	-
Couple families	24	2	3	13	4	1	1	-
with no children	13	2	2	7	1	-	1	-
with dependent child(ren)	11	-	1	6	3	1	-	-
with non-dependent child(ren) only	-	-	-	-	-	-	-	-
'Unconcealed' families	3,407	402	1,072	1,273	276	179	181	24
with no children	1,469	160	152	611	217	156	160	13
with dependent child(ren)	1,342	239	833	265	3	1	1	-
with non-dependent child(ren) only	596	3	87	397	56	22	20	11

Age of head of family

Family composition	All 16 and over	16 - 29	30 - 44	45 up to pensionable age	Pensionable age - 69	70 - 74	75 - 84	85 and over
TOTAL FAMILIES	3,468	441	1,085	1,280	276	179	182	25
'Concealed' families	61	39	13	7	-	-	1	1
Lone parent families	37	26	9	2	-	-	-	-
with dependent child(ren)	35	26	8	1	-	-	-	-
with non-dependent child(ren) only	2	-	1	1	-	-	-	-
Couple families	24	13	4	5	-	-	1	1
with no children	13	5	1	5	-	-	1	1
with dependent child(ren)	11	8	3	-	-	-	-	-
with non-dependent child(ren) only	-	-	-	-	-	-	-	-

Table 88 'Concealed' families (10% sample) – **continued**　　　　　　　　County, districts

88. Families of resident persons　　　　　　　　　　　　　　　　　　　　　　(10% sample)

Family composition	All 16 and over	16 - 29	30 - 44	45 up to pensionable age	Pensionable age - 69	70 - 74	75 - 84	85 and over
a	b	c	d	e	f	g	h	i

New Forest

Age of head of household

TOTAL FAMILIES	4,688	471	1,444	1,556	454	330	372	61
'Concealed' families	60	3	9	23	5	7	12	1
Lone parent families	27	1	5	11	4	1	5	-
with dependent child(ren)	18	1	4	9	3	-	1	-
with non-dependent child(ren) only	9	-	1	2	1	1	4	-
Couple families	33	2	4	12	1	6	7	1
with no children	15	1	2	7	-	2	2	1
with dependent child(ren)	18	1	2	5	1	4	5	-
with non-dependent child(ren) only	-	-	-	-	-	-	-	-
'Unconcealed' families	4,628	468	1,435	1,533	449	323	360	60
with no children	2,235	266	238	708	371	286	312	54
with dependent child(ren)	1,685	198	1,110	364	7	2	4	-
with non-dependent child(ren) only	708	4	87	461	71	35	44	6

Age of head of family

TOTAL FAMILIES	4,688	493	1,452	1,542	452	324	364	61
'Concealed' families	60	25	17	9	3	1	4	1
Lone parent families	27	15	6	3	1	-	1	1
with dependent child(ren)	18	15	3	-	-	-	-	-
with non-dependent child(ren) only	9	-	3	3	1	-	1	1
Couple families	33	10	11	6	2	1	3	-
with no children	15	3	2	4	2	1	3	-
with dependent child(ren)	18	7	9	2	-	-	-	-
with non-dependent child(ren) only	-	-	-	-	-	-	-	-

Portsmouth

Age of head of household

TOTAL FAMILIES	4,774	882	1,498	1,406	383	272	293	40
'Concealed' families	136	14	17	53	23	12	15	2
Lone parent families	75	5	9	35	17	5	3	1
with dependent child(ren)	67	5	8	34	15	4	1	-
with non-dependent child(ren) only	8	-	1	1	2	1	2	1
Couple families	61	9	8	18	6	7	12	1
with no children	36	6	7	9	2	2	9	1
with dependent child(ren)	22	2	1	9	4	5	1	-
with non-dependent child(ren) only	3	1	-	-	-	-	2	-
'Unconcealed' families	4,638	868	1,481	1,353	360	260	278	38
with no children	1,999	377	271	618	262	212	228	31
with dependent child(ren)	1,873	486	1,096	287	1	2	1	-
with non-dependent child(ren) only	766	5	114	448	97	46	49	7

Age of head of family

TOTAL FAMILIES	4,774	933	1,521	1,371	365	263	282	39
'Concealed' families	136	65	40	18	5	3	4	1
Lone parent families	75	45	22	5	1	-	2	-
with dependent child(ren)	67	45	21	1	-	-	-	-
with non-dependent child(ren) only	8	-	1	4	1	-	2	-
Couple families	61	20	18	13	4	3	2	1
with no children	36	11	6	10	4	2	2	1
with dependent child(ren)	22	9	10	2	-	1	-	-
with non-dependent child(ren) only	3	-	2	1	-	-	-	-

Table 88 'Concealed' families (10% sample) – **continued**　　　　　　　　　　　　　　　　County, districts

88. Families of resident persons　　　　　　　　　　　　　　　　　　　　　　　　　　　　　　　　　(10% sample)

Family composition	All 16 and over	16 - 29	30 - 44	45 up to pensionable age	Pensionable age - 69	70 - 74	75 - 84	85 and over
a	b	c	d	e	f	g	h	i

Rushmoor

Age of head of household

TOTAL FAMILIES	2,298	457	827	705	123	80	92	14
'Concealed' families	35	5	5	14	3	5	3	-
Lone parent families	22	2	5	7	3	3	2	-
with dependent child(ren)	20	2	5	7	1	3	2	-
with non-dependent child(ren) only	2	-	-	-	2	-	-	-
Couple families	13	3	-	7	-	2	1	-
with no children	9	3	-	4	-	2	-	-
with dependent child(ren)	4	-	-	3	-	-	1	-
with non-dependent child(ren) only	-	-	-	-	-	-	-	-
'Unconcealed' families	2,263	452	822	691	120	75	89	14
with no children	895	220	153	296	88	57	72	9
with dependent child(ren)	1,004	231	603	165	1	2	2	-
with non-dependent child(ren) only	364	1	66	230	31	16	15	5

Age of head of family

TOTAL FAMILIES	2,298	470	834	693	120	76	91	14
'Concealed' families	35	18	12	2	-	1	2	-
Lone parent families	22	13	7	-	-	1	1	-
with dependent child(ren)	20	13	7	-	-	-	-	-
with non-dependent child(ren) only	2	-	-	-	-	1	1	-
Couple families	13	5	5	2	-	-	1	-
with no children	9	5	2	1	-	-	1	-
with dependent child(ren)	4	-	3	1	-	-	-	-
with non-dependent child(ren) only	-	-	-	-	-	-	-	-

Southampton

Age of head of household

TOTAL FAMILIES	5,400	922	1,726	1,723	406	290	292	41
'Concealed' families	129	15	18	57	19	9	11	-
Lone parent families	62	7	7	28	11	6	3	-
with dependent child(ren)	53	7	5	27	9	4	1	-
with non-dependent child(ren) only	9	-	2	1	2	2	2	-
Couple families	67	8	11	29	8	3	8	-
with no children	34	6	7	13	5	-	3	-
with dependent child(ren)	29	2	3	16	3	2	3	-
with non-dependent child(ren) only	4	-	1	-	-	1	2	-
'Unconcealed' families	5,271	907	1,708	1,666	387	281	281	41
with no children	2,212	387	272	778	281	225	241	28
with dependent child(ren)	2,159	516	1,298	334	6	3	-	2
with non-dependent child(ren) only	900	4	138	554	100	53	40	11

Age of head of family

TOTAL FAMILIES	5,400	970	1,752	1,680	390	282	285	41
'Concealed' families	129	63	44	14	3	1	4	-
Lone parent families	62	36	20	5	-	-	1	-
with dependent child(ren)	53	36	16	1	-	-	-	-
with non-dependent child(ren) only	9	-	4	4	-	-	1	-
Couple families	67	27	24	9	3	1	3	-
with no children	34	11	10	6	3	1	3	-
with dependent child(ren)	29	16	12	1	-	-	-	-
with non-dependent child(ren) only	4	-	2	2	-	-	-	-

Table 88 'Concealed' families (10% sample) – **continued**   County, districts

88. Families of resident persons   (10% sample)

Family composition	All 16 and over	16 - 29	30 - 44	45 up to pensionable age	Pensionable age - 69	70 - 74	75 - 84	85 and over
a	b	c	d	e	f	g	h	i

Test Valley

Age of head of household

TOTAL FAMILIES	2,914	349	1,036	1,068	180	144	118	19
'Concealed' families	43	4	10	17	6	3	-	3
Lone parent families	20	3	6	8	1	1	-	1
with dependent child(ren)	12	2	2	7	-	1	-	-
with non-dependent child(ren) only	8	1	4	1	1	-	-	1
Couple families	23	1	4	9	5	2	-	2
with no children	16	-	4	8	2	1	-	1
with dependent child(ren)	7	1	-	1	3	1	-	1
with non-dependent child(ren) only	-	-	-	-	-	-	-	-
'Unconcealed' families	2,871	345	1,026	1,051	174	141	118	16
with no children	1,153	165	152	462	141	119	103	11
with dependent child(ren)	1,231	178	801	250	1	1	-	-
with non-dependent child(ren) only	487	2	73	339	32	21	15	5

Age of head of family

TOTAL FAMILIES	2,914	360	1,040	1,056	174	144	124	16
'Concealed' families	43	15	14	5	-	3	6	-
Lone parent families	20	7	7	3	-	1	2	-
with dependent child(ren)	12	7	5	-	-	-	-	-
with non-dependent child(ren) only	8	-	2	3	-	1	2	-
Couple families	23	8	7	2	-	2	4	-
with no children	16	6	2	2	-	2	4	-
with dependent child(ren)	7	2	5	-	-	-	-	-
with non-dependent child(ren) only	-	-	-	-	-	-	-	-

Winchester

Age of head of household

TOTAL FAMILIES	2,709	216	886	1,045	215	160	173	14
'Concealed' families	43	4	5	23	3	3	5	-
Lone parent families	22	2	3	12	1	2	2	-
with dependent child(ren)	18	2	3	10	1	2	-	-
with non-dependent child(ren) only	4	-	-	2	-	-	2	-
Couple families	21	2	2	11	2	1	3	-
with no children	14	2	2	8	-	1	1	-
with dependent child(ren)	6	-	-	3	2	-	1	-
with non-dependent child(ren) only	1	-	-	-	-	-	1	-
'Unconcealed' families	2,666	212	881	1,022	212	157	168	14
with no children	1,152	98	166	431	172	128	146	11
with dependent child(ren)	1,055	111	652	284	5	2	1	-
with non-dependent child(ren) only	459	3	63	307	35	27	21	3

Age of head of family

TOTAL FAMILIES	2,709	237	890	1,027	213	158	170	14
'Concealed' families	43	25	9	5	1	1	2	-
Lone parent families	22	13	5	3	1	-	-	-
with dependent child(ren)	18	13	5	-	-	-	-	-
with non-dependent child(ren) only	4	-	-	3	1	-	-	-
Couple families	21	12	4	2	-	1	2	-
with no children	14	10	1	-	-	1	2	-
with dependent child(ren)	6	2	3	1	-	-	-	-
with non-dependent child(ren) only	1	-	-	1	-	-	-	-

Table 89   Family composition (10% sample)

89. Families of resident persons   (10% sample)

Family composition	TOTAL FAMILIES	Type of family		
		Married couple	Cohabiting couple	Lone parent
a	b	c	d	e

HAMPSHIRE

TOTAL FAMILIES	43,919	35,501	3,683	4,735
No children	18,546	16,095	2,451	
With dependent child(ren)	18,235	14,381	1,063	2,791
With non-dependent child(ren) only	7,138	5,025	169	1,944
In households with two or more families	995	596	68	331

Basingstoke & Deane

TOTAL FAMILIES	4,165	3,392	371	402
No children	1,662	1,411	251	
With dependent child(ren)	1,769	1,436	95	238
With non-dependent child(ren) only	734	545	25	164
In households with two or more families	104	63	5	36

East Hampshire

TOTAL FAMILIES	2,952	2,444	241	267
No children	1,264	1,104	160	
With dependent child(ren)	1,255	1,027	74	154
With non-dependent child(ren) only	433	313	7	113
In households with two or more families	57	38	2	17

Eastleigh

TOTAL FAMILIES	3,134	2,577	278	279
No children	1,316	1,115	201	
With dependent child(ren)	1,325	1,096	66	163
With non-dependent child(ren) only	493	366	11	116
In households with two or more families	54	34	4	16

Fareham

TOTAL FAMILIES	2,985	2,525	213	247
No children	1,315	1,171	144	
With dependent child(ren)	1,201	1,009	61	131
With non-dependent child(ren) only	469	345	8	116
In households with two or more families	56	32	6	18

Gosport

TOTAL FAMILIES	2,149	1,716	172	261
No children	867	756	111	
With dependent child(ren)	982	750	56	176
With non-dependent child(ren) only	300	210	5	85
In households with two or more families	28	17	3	8

Hart

TOTAL FAMILIES	2,283	1,932	181	170
No children	870	739	131	
With dependent child(ren)	1,034	897	42	95
With non-dependent child(ren) only	379	296	8	75
In households with two or more families	50	32	1	17

Table 89 Family composition (10% sample) – **continued**   County, districts

89. Families of resident persons   (10% sample)

Family composition	TOTAL FAMILIES	Type of family		
		Married couple	Cohabiting couple	Lone parent
a	b	c	d	e

Havant

TOTAL FAMILIES	**3,468**	**2,804**	**270**	**394**
No children	1,482	1,325	157	
With dependent child(ren)	1,388	1,047	93	248
With non-dependent child(ren) only	598	432	20	146
In households with two or more families	88	44	9	35

New Forest

TOTAL FAMILIES	**4,688**	**3,973**	**305**	**410**
No children	2,250	2,035	215	
With dependent child(ren)	1,721	1,424	82	215
With non-dependent child(ren) only	717	514	8	195
In households with two or more families	73	45	8	20

Portsmouth

TOTAL FAMILIES	**4,774**	**3,496**	**533**	**745**
No children	2,035	1,687	348	
With dependent child(ren)	1,962	1,343	162	457
With non-dependent child(ren) only	777	466	23	288
In households with two or more families	158	91	7	60

Rushmoor

TOTAL FAMILIES	**2,298**	**1,793**	**232**	**273**
No children	904	740	164	
With dependent child(ren)	1,028	808	58	162
With non-dependent child(ren) only	366	245	10	111
In households with two or more families	48	31	1	16

Southampton

TOTAL FAMILIES	**5,400**	**4,062**	**525**	**813**
No children	2,246	1,899	347	
With dependent child(ren)	2,241	1,584	163	494
With non-dependent child(ren) only	913	579	15	319
In households with two or more families	159	95	15	49

Test Valley

TOTAL FAMILIES	**2,914**	**2,456**	**206**	**252**
No children	1,169	1,045	124	
With dependent child(ren)	1,250	1,049	66	135
With non-dependent child(ren) only	495	362	16	117
In households with two or more families	66	42	4	20

Winchester

TOTAL FAMILIES	**2,709**	**2,331**	**156**	**222**
No children	1,166	1,068	98	
With dependent child(ren)	1,079	911	45	123
With non-dependent child(ren) only	464	352	13	99
In households with two or more families	54	32	3	19

Table 90 Social class of households (10% sample)

County, districts

Note: * Females in married or cohabiting couples

90. Households with residents; residents in households (10% sample)

Social class based on occupation of household head	TOTAL HOUSEHOLDS	TOTAL PERSONS	Persons aged 0 - 15	Persons of pensionable age	Females in couples*
a	b	c	d	e	f

HAMPSHIRE

Economically active heads

Total	**39,215**	**112,357**	**26,671**	**3,736**	**30,280**
I Professional etc occupations	3,282	9,489	2,279	254	2,655
II Managerial and technical	12,763	36,618	8,645	1,096	10,016
III(N) Skilled occupations - non-manual	5,113	13,117	2,895	518	3,159
III(M) Skilled occupations - manual	9,463	28,562	6,818	785	8,107
IV Partly skilled occupations	4,751	13,407	3,005	657	3,494
V Unskilled occupations	1,613	4,320	967	309	1,041
Armed forces	1,445	4,667	1,506	25	1,334
On a Government scheme	159	417	104	13	92
Occupation inadequately described or not stated	292	837	191	51	217

Economically inactive heads

Retired	14,424	24,070	210	19,818	7,127
Other inactive	5,815	13,015	3,478	2,715	1,777

Basingstoke & Deane

Economically active heads

Total	**3,966**	**11,480**	**2,719**	**356**	**3,091**
I Professional etc occupations	376	1,060	268	24	298
II Managerial and technical	1,393	4,121	1,032	93	1,088
III(N) Skilled occupations - non-manual	536	1,368	305	49	344
III(M) Skilled occupations - manual	950	2,846	655	61	825
IV Partly skilled occupations	501	1,480	327	97	385
V Unskilled occupations	127	360	67	24	92
Armed forces	25	86	30	2	23
On a Government scheme	14	39	11	1	8
Occupation inadequately described or not stated	22	73	16	3	19

Economically inactive heads

Retired	1,031	1,767	12	1,402	542
Other inactive	372	920	297	143	130

East Hampshire

Economically active heads

Total	**2,687**	**7,779**	**1,880**	**322**	**2,147**
I Professional etc occupations	245	714	179	30	211
II Managerial and technical	1,075	3,158	786	114	877
III(N) Skilled occupations - non-manual	323	821	175	52	196
III(M) Skilled occupations - manual	567	1,740	423	58	498
IV Partly skilled occupations	271	766	171	44	209
V Unskilled occupations	78	203	43	17	45
Armed forces	89	279	84	2	84
On a Government scheme	12	33	9	-	10
Occupation inadequately described or not stated	14	35	8	1	10

Economically inactive heads

Retired	859	1,439	19	1,202	439
Other inactive	327	697	180	197	99

Note: * Females in married or cohabiting couples

90. Households with residents; residents in households   (10% sample)

Social class based on occupation of household head	TOTAL HOUSEHOLDS	TOTAL PERSONS	Persons aged 0 - 15	Persons of pensionable age	Females in couples*
a	b	c	d	e	f

Eastleigh

Economically active heads

Total	**2,822**	**8,186**	**1,998**	**207**	**2,268**
I Professional etc occupations	222	658	166	8	191
II Managerial and technical	958	2,782	711	47	773
III(N) Skilled occupations - non-manual	444	1,190	283	31	302
III(M) Skilled occupations - manual	750	2,295	561	62	663
IV Partly skilled occupations	301	853	189	34	232
V Unskilled occupations	98	258	56	20	68
Armed forces	22	67	16	-	21
On a Government scheme	5	15	6	-	4
Occupation inadequately described or not stated	12	33	6	4	8

Economically inactive heads

Retired	904	1,524	9	1,270	477
Other inactive	347	725	174	193	110

Fareham

Economically active heads

Total	**2,595**	**7,573**	**1,821**	**223**	**2,146**
I Professional etc occupations	255	779	197	18	215
II Managerial and technical	948	2,744	643	74	803
III(N) Skilled occupations - non-manual	318	836	185	22	205
III(M) Skilled occupations - manual	553	1,668	392	56	495
IV Partly skilled occupations	207	570	120	32	154
V Unskilled occupations	83	245	57	9	65
Armed forces	189	628	206	2	179
On a Government scheme	14	30	6	1	8
Occupation inadequately described or not stated	19	48	9	6	17

Economically inactive heads

Retired	915	1,550	15	1,257	504
Other inactive	299	613	137	169	88

Gosport

Economically active heads

Total	**1,905**	**5,503**	**1,411**	**138**	**1,501**
I Professional etc occupations	77	224	40	14	70
II Managerial and technical	406	1,157	259	24	315
III(N) Skilled occupations - non-manual	226	571	149	8	143
III(M) Skilled occupations - manual	511	1,522	393	42	429
IV Partly skilled occupations	244	700	174	26	186
V Unskilled occupations	82	213	51	12	49
Armed forces	312	996	317	8	283
On a Government scheme	15	36	8	1	9
Occupation inadequately described or not stated	18	49	7	2	11

Economically inactive heads

Retired	681	1,066	4	912	294
Other inactive	312	716	235	139	93

Note: * Females in married or cohabiting couples

90. Households with residents; residents in households (10% sample)

Social class based on occupation of household head	TOTAL HOUSEHOLDS	TOTAL PERSONS	Persons aged 0 - 15	Persons of pensionable age	Females in couples*
a	b	c	d	e	f

Hart

Economically active heads

Total	**2,194**	**6,575**	**1,601**	**199**	**1,795**
I Professional etc occupations	300	909	217	20	249
II Managerial and technical	926	2,770	674	81	770
III(N) Skilled occupations - non-manual	228	642	150	25	159
III(M) Skilled occupations - manual	420	1,299	320	37	367
IV Partly skilled occupations	148	407	77	25	106
V Unskilled occupations	52	140	29	7	33
Armed forces	90	310	108	2	88
On a Government scheme	4	11	3	-	3
Occupation inadequately described or not stated	15	45	11	2	10

Economically inactive heads

Retired	494	861	8	646	257
Other inactive	187	412	101	100	61

Havant

Economically active heads

Total	**2,876**	**8,361**	**2,001**	**274**	**2,254**
I Professional etc occupations	231	667	142	17	193
II Managerial and technical	865	2,440	541	87	670
III(N) Skilled occupations - non-manual	348	918	220	36	216
III(M) Skilled occupations - manual	770	2,383	600	54	672
IV Partly skilled occupations	415	1,194	268	50	321
V Unskilled occupations	114	325	92	23	76
Armed forces	66	233	75	1	63
On a Government scheme	9	19	4	-	5
Occupation inadequately described or not stated	25	78	19	5	23

Economically inactive heads

Retired	1,143	1,944	19	1,606	620
Other inactive	543	1,276	325	249	200

New Forest

Economically active heads

Total	**3,741**	**10,688**	**2,529**	**397**	**2,951**
I Professional etc occupations	284	861	220	32	237
II Managerial and technical	1,325	3,885	975	137	1,073
III(N) Skilled occupations - non-manual	514	1,287	254	62	329
III(M) Skilled occupations - manual	906	2,684	608	76	791
IV Partly skilled occupations	463	1,283	301	55	347
V Unskilled occupations	154	404	87	29	105
Armed forces	36	112	35	-	31
On a Government scheme	6	17	5	1	3
Occupation inadequately described or not stated	34	93	24	4	21

Economically inactive heads

Retired	2,045	3,537	31	2,956	1,156
Other inactive	642	1,265	240	404	171

Note: * Females in married or cohabiting couples

90. Households with residents; residents in households   (10% sample)

Social class based on occupation of household head	TOTAL HOUSEHOLDS	TOTAL PERSONS	Persons aged 0 - 15	Persons of pensionable age	Females in couples*
a	b	c	d	e	f

Portsmouth

Economically active heads

Total	**4,297**	**11,718**	**2,674**	**402**	**2,977**
I Professional etc occupations	258	669	143	17	182
II Managerial and technical	1,112	2,890	555	93	764
III(N) Skilled occupations - non-manual	588	1,435	310	64	319
III(M) Skilled occupations - manual	1,097	3,247	768	83	879
IV Partly skilled occupations	618	1,701	382	80	407
V Unskilled occupations	256	680	173	46	162
Armed forces	221	689	223	5	187
On a Government scheme	33	78	17	5	16
Occupation inadequately described or not stated	42	123	27	5	26

Economically inactive heads

Retired	1,982	3,224	38	2,656	822
Other inactive	822	1,926	538	294	230

Rushmoor

Economically active heads

Total	**2,196**	**6,259**	**1,486**	**166**	**1,683**
I Professional etc occupations	187	542	143	11	149
II Managerial and technical	624	1,757	396	36	476
III(N) Skilled occupations - non-manual	289	767	173	21	180
III(M) Skilled occupations - manual	524	1,550	345	39	439
IV Partly skilled occupations	241	665	149	34	182
V Unskilled occupations	102	243	44	20	48
Armed forces	195	623	205	-	186
On a Government scheme	14	48	12	3	10
Occupation inadequately described or not stated	12	37	10	2	9

Economically inactive heads

Retired	573	965	11	773	264
Other inactive	239	591	204	80	78

Southampton

Economically active heads

Total	**4,863**	**13,359**	**3,046**	**459**	**3,392**
I Professional etc occupations	320	835	166	16	213
II Managerial and technical	1,207	3,239	699	103	840
III(N) Skilled occupations - non-manual	694	1,680	368	78	370
III(M) Skilled occupations - manual	1,374	4,138	1,027	111	1,147
IV Partly skilled occupations	790	2,227	522	87	542
V Unskilled occupations	309	815	168	50	194
Armed forces	15	35	7	-	13
On a Government scheme	18	37	5	-	5
Occupation inadequately described or not stated	40	119	33	6	29

Economically inactive heads

Retired	2,015	3,223	26	2,706	860
Other inactive	1,077	2,526	747	379	335

Note: * Females in married or cohabiting couples

90. Households with residents; residents in households					(10% sample)
Social class based on occupation of household head	TOTAL HOUSEHOLDS	TOTAL PERSONS	Persons aged 0 - 15	Persons of pensionable age	Females in couples*
a	b	c	d	e	f

Test Valley

Economically active heads

Total	**2,656**	**7,881**	**1,931**	**252**	**2,161**
I Professional etc occupations	220	686	201	11	190
II Managerial and technical	944	2,814	693	92	786
III(N) Skilled occupations - non-manual	333	917	218	23	225
III(M) Skilled occupations - manual	616	1,902	435	55	541
IV Partly skilled occupations	305	865	188	41	232
V Unskilled occupations	83	216	48	22	51
Armed forces	109	352	111	1	103
On a Government scheme	8	29	13	-	6
Occupation inadequately described or not stated	21	51	6	5	18

Economically inactive heads

Retired	819	1,392	9	1,121	419
Other inactive	305	646	154	165	82

Winchester

Economically active heads

Total	**2,417**	**6,995**	**1,574**	**341**	**1,914**
I Professional etc occupations	307	885	197	36	257
II Managerial and technical	980	2,861	681	115	781
III(N) Skilled occupations - non-manual	272	685	105	47	171
III(M) Skilled occupations - manual	425	1,288	291	51	361
IV Partly skilled occupations	247	696	137	52	191
V Unskilled occupations	75	218	52	30	53
Armed forces	76	257	89	2	73
On a Government scheme	7	25	5	1	5
Occupation inadequately described or not stated	18	53	15	6	16

Economically inactive heads

Retired	963	1,578	9	1,311	473
Other inactive	343	702	146	203	100

Table 91 Social class and economic position (10% sample)

County, districts

Note: * Females in married or cohabiting couples

91. Residents aged 16 and over in households (10% sample)

Social class based on occupation	TOTAL PERSONS			Economic position					
				In employment			Unemployed		
	Males	Females		Males	Females		Males	Females	
		Total	In a couple*		Total	In a couple*		Total	In a couple*
a	b	c	d	e	f	g	h	i	j

HAMPSHIRE

Economically active

Total	**44,044**	**32,691**	**26,031**	**40,252**	**31,065**	**25,037**	**3,792**	**1,626**	**994**
I Professional etc occupations	3,594	616	460	3,498	606	453	96	10	7
II Managerial and technical	12,530	9,004	7,093	11,992	8,770	6,934	538	234	159
III(N) Skilled occupations - non-manual	4,524	13,014	10,730	4,259	12,514	10,393	265	500	337
III(M) Skilled occupations - manual	12,316	1,932	1,522	11,242	1,842	1,457	1,074	90	65
IV Partly skilled occupations	5,926	5,052	3,947	5,268	4,751	3,776	658	301	171
V Unskilled occupations	2,099	2,149	1,697	1,682	2,056	1,646	417	93	51
Armed forces	1,666	98	73	1,627	90	65	39	8	8
On a Government scheme	371	252	172	371	252	172			
Occupation inadequately described or not stated	374	202	152	306	181	138	68	21	14

Economically inactive

Retired	9,387	11,142	4,890						
Other inactive	3,929	17,894	13,354						

Basingstoke & Deane

Economically active

Total	**4,547**	**3,389**	**2,777**	**4,239**	**3,245**	**2,680**	**308**	**144**	**97**
I Professional etc occupations	412	82	62	405	82	62	7	-	-
II Managerial and technical	1,387	924	728	1,343	899	710	44	25	18
III(N) Skilled occupations - non-manual	477	1,463	1,239	450	1,412	1,204	27	51	35
III(M) Skilled occupations - manual	1,280	191	152	1,192	179	142	88	12	10
IV Partly skilled occupations	660	449	369	590	425	354	70	24	15
V Unskilled occupations	191	212	180	164	204	175	27	8	5
Armed forces	34	2	2	32	2	2	2	-	-
On a Government scheme	31	26	17	31	26	17			
Occupation inadequately described or not stated	38	18	16	32	16	14	6	2	2

Economically inactive

Retired	682	809	378						
Other inactive	296	1,416	1,114						

East Hampshire

Economically active

Total	**2,936**	**2,206**	**1,773**	**2,771**	**2,128**	**1,721**	**165**	**78**	**52**
I Professional etc occupations	276	47	41	268	47	41	8	-	-
II Managerial and technical	1,049	710	580	1,004	697	573	45	13	7
III(N) Skilled occupations - non-manual	267	804	648	256	777	626	11	27	22
III(M) Skilled occupations - manual	730	141	112	689	136	107	41	5	5
IV Partly skilled occupations	337	323	252	315	310	246	22	13	6
V Unskilled occupations	113	133	103	99	128	100	14	5	3
Armed forces	101	5	5	101	5	5	-	-	-
On a Government scheme	23	15	13	23	15	13			
Occupation inadequately described or not stated	16	13	10	14	13	10	2	-	-

Economically inactive

Retired	603	619	270						
Other inactive	217	1,255	997						

Note: * Females in married or cohabiting couples

91. Residents aged 16 and over in households   (10% sample)

	TOTAL PERSONS			Economic position					
				In employment			Unemployed		
Social class based on occupation	Males	Females Total	Females In a couple*	Males	Females Total	Females In a couple*	Males	Females Total	Females In a couple*
a	b	c	d	e	f	g	h	i	j

Eastleigh

Economically active

Total	**3,162**	**2,354**	**1,959**	**2,961**	**2,275**	**1,905**	**201**	**79**	**54**
I Professional etc occupations	244	34	27	239	34	27	5	-	-
II Managerial and technical	957	674	557	927	658	546	30	16	11
III(N) Skilled occupations - non-manual	393	1,072	917	379	1,046	896	14	26	21
III(M) Skilled occupations - manual	965	110	88	889	106	85	76	4	3
IV Partly skilled occupations	386	300	248	356	290	242	30	10	6
V Unskilled occupations	128	115	93	110	114	92	18	1	1
Armed forces	32	2	2	30	2	2	2	-	-
On a Government scheme	19	15	9	19	15	9			
Occupation inadequately described or not stated	15	10	6	12	10	6	3	-	-

Economically inactive

Retired	603	718	351
Other inactive	251	1,166	881

Fareham

Economically active

Total	**2,867**	**2,173**	**1,837**	**2,694**	**2,097**	**1,777**	**173**	**76**	**60**
I Professional etc occupations	264	47	36	251	46	35	13	1	1
II Managerial and technical	933	656	558	892	639	545	41	17	13
III(N) Skilled occupations - non-manual	275	890	751	262	863	729	13	27	22
III(M) Skilled occupations - manual	727	83	72	684	79	68	43	4	4
IV Partly skilled occupations	272	318	265	243	305	254	29	13	11
V Unskilled occupations	115	130	115	105	127	113	10	3	2
Armed forces	206	14	12	204	14	12	2	-	-
On a Government scheme	33	13	11	33	13	11			
Occupation inadequately described or not stated	21	10	9	19	10	9	2	-	-

Economically inactive

Retired	611	720	357
Other inactive	222	1,170	911

Gosport

Economically active

Total	**2,073**	**1,563**	**1,260**	**1,899**	**1,462**	**1,185**	**174**	**101**	**75**
I Professional etc occupations	90	11	8	87	11	8	3	-	-
II Managerial and technical	381	336	272	363	322	260	18	14	12
III(N) Skilled occupations - non-manual	175	598	502	165	574	483	10	24	19
III(M) Skilled occupations - manual	614	87	62	562	84	59	52	3	3
IV Partly skilled occupations	296	314	253	268	292	237	28	22	16
V Unskilled occupations	86	132	100	72	120	92	14	12	8
Armed forces	353	31	23	344	27	19	9	4	4
On a Government scheme	21	21	18	21	21	18			
Occupation inadequately described or not stated	19	13	11	16	11	9	3	2	2

Economically inactive

Retired	411	539	220
Other inactive	166	885	643

Note: * Females in married or cohabiting couples

91. Residents aged 16 and over in households　　　　　　　　　　　　　　　　　　　　　　　　　　　(10% sample)

	TOTAL PERSONS			Economic position					
				In employment			Unemployed		
Social class based on occupation	Males	Females		Males	Females		Males	Females	
		Total	In a couple*		Total	In a couple*		Total	In a couple*
a	b	c	d	e	f	g	h	i	j

Hart

Economically active

Total	**2,496**	**1,805**	**1,522**	**2,365**	**1,736**	**1,477**	**131**	**69**	**45**
I　Professional etc occupations	320	62	51	307	60	49	13	2	2
II　Managerial and technical	955	606	494	925	587	483	30	19	11
III(N)　Skilled occupations - non-manual	237	751	667	223	725	647	14	26	20
III(M)　Skilled occupations - manual	553	90	75	524	87	73	29	3	2
IV　Partly skilled occupations	213	187	155	202	182	151	11	5	4
V　Unskilled occupations	68	80	63	59	76	61	9	4	2
Armed forces	97	3	3	97	3	3	-	-	-
On a Government scheme	13	6	4	13	6	4			
Occupation inadequately described or not stated	21	8	4	15	8	4	6	-	-

Economically inactive

Retired	337	379	161
Other inactive	198	923	768

Havant

Economically active

Total	**3,309**	**2,403**	**1,923**	**2,944**	**2,266**	**1,851**	**365**	**137**	**72**
I　Professional etc occupations	262	31	23	256	31	23	6	-	-
II　Managerial and technical	847	591	458	800	578	449	47	13	9
III(N)　Skilled occupations - non-manual	335	894	745	313	853	722	22	41	23
III(M)　Skilled occupations - manual	966	167	135	861	164	135	105	3	-
IV　Partly skilled occupations	513	495	397	436	463	379	77	32	18
V　Unskilled occupations	172	148	115	131	140	111	41	8	4
Armed forces	85	2	2	81	1	1	4	1	1
On a Government scheme	38	20	17	38	20	17			
Occupation inadequately described or not stated	35	17	14	27	16	14	8	1	-

Economically inactive

Retired	754	894	421
Other inactive	346	1,530	1,140

New Forest

Economically active

Total	**4,177**	**3,178**	**2,581**	**3,825**	**3,044**	**2,494**	**352**	**134**	**87**
I　Professional etc occupations	312	45	34	305	44	33	7	1	1
II　Managerial and technical	1,294	893	711	1,230	872	699	64	21	12
III(N)　Skilled occupations - non-manual	441	1,319	1,111	423	1,267	1,073	18	52	38
III(M)　Skilled occupations - manual	1,185	206	162	1,084	200	158	101	6	4
IV　Partly skilled occupations	574	454	366	519	437	358	55	17	8
V　Unskilled occupations	212	188	147	169	182	144	43	6	3
Armed forces	47	4	1	44	4	1	3	-	-
On a Government scheme	17	21	15	17	21	15			
Occupation inadequately described or not stated	43	20	14	34	17	13	9	3	1

Economically inactive

Retired	1,442	1,480	733
Other inactive	365	2,049	1,527

Note: * Females in married or cohabiting couples

91. Residents aged 16 and over in households　　　　　　　　　　　　　　　　　　　　　　　　　　(10% sample)

	TOTAL PERSONS			Economic position					
				In employment			Unemployed		
Social class based on occupation	Males	Females		Males	Females		Males	Females	
		Total	In a couple*		Total	In a couple*		Total	In a couple*
a	b	c	d	e	f	g	h	i	j

Portsmouth

Economically active

Total	4,830	3,561	2,563	4,223	3,277	2,423	607	284	140
I Professional etc occupations	296	42	29	288	42	29	8	-	-
II Managerial and technical	1,043	869	625	987	836	608	56	33	17
III(N) Skilled occupations - non-manual	472	1,330	1,008	430	1,259	969	42	71	39
III(M) Skilled occupations - manual	1,443	234	166	1,274	221	157	169	13	9
IV Partly skilled occupations	740	650	448	628	588	421	112	62	27
V Unskilled occupations	317	269	202	248	253	194	69	16	8
Armed forces	270	17	10	260	17	10	10	-	-
On a Government scheme	67	41	22	67	41	22			
Occupation inadequately described or not stated	50	23	15	41	20	13	9	3	2

Economically inactive

Retired	1,210	1,562	598						
Other inactive	507	1,948	1,303						

Rushmoor

Economically active

Total	2,438	1,915	1,527	2,274	1,828	1,462	164	87	65
I Professional etc occupations	203	33	22	196	33	22	7	-	-
II Managerial and technical	634	480	381	606	468	372	28	12	9
III(N) Skilled occupations - non-manual	283	771	637	272	738	609	11	33	28
III(M) Skilled occupations - manual	660	130	104	613	122	98	47	8	6
IV Partly skilled occupations	285	319	257	258	306	245	27	13	12
V Unskilled occupations	112	131	93	94	129	92	18	2	1
Armed forces	207	12	11	205	9	8	2	3	3
On a Government scheme	17	16	10	17	16	10			
Occupation inadequately described or not stated	15	10	7	13	7	6	2	3	1

Economically inactive

Retired	350	452	179						
Other inactive	156	803	608						

Southampton

Economically active

Total	5,481	3,956	2,885	4,674	3,690	2,747	807	266	138
I Professional etc occupations	369	83	51	359	80	50	10	3	1
II Managerial and technical	1,137	980	690	1,068	960	676	69	20	14
III(N) Skilled occupations - non-manual	602	1,559	1,199	549	1,487	1,155	53	72	44
III(M) Skilled occupations - manual	1,800	234	177	1,565	221	169	235	13	8
IV Partly skilled occupations	929	638	447	776	577	419	153	61	28
V Unskilled occupations	360	320	247	247	302	240	113	18	7
Armed forces	24	3	-	23	3	-	1	-	-
On a Government scheme	47	35	19	47	35	19			
Occupation inadequately described or not stated	55	30	24	40	25	19	15	5	5

Economically inactive

Retired	1,220	1,610	630						
Other inactive	694	2,328	1,583						

Note: * Females in married or cohabiting couples

91. Residents aged 16 and over in households   (10% sample)

	TOTAL PERSONS			Economic position					
				In employment			Unemployed		
Social class based on occupation	Males	Females		Males	Females		Males	Females	
		Total	In a couple*		Total	In a couple*		Total	In a couple*
a	b	c	d	e	f	g	h	i	j

Test Valley

Economically active

Total	**3,022**	**2,206**	**1,826**	**2,839**	**2,118**	**1,776**	**183**	**88**	**50**
I Professional etc occupations	228	44	35	226	42	34	2	2	1
II Managerial and technical	941	602	493	911	589	482	30	13	11
III(N) Skilled occupations - non-manual	300	873	747	285	844	733	15	29	14
III(M) Skilled occupations - manual	825	142	120	777	136	117	48	6	3
IV Partly skilled occupations	395	337	272	374	322	261	21	15	11
V Unskilled occupations	125	156	127	100	152	125	25	4	2
Armed forces	125	2	1	121	2	1	4	-	-
On a Government scheme	23	13	10	23	13	10			
Occupation inadequately described or not stated	24	19	13	21	18	13	3	1	-

Economically inactive

Retired	548	632	287						
Other inactive	243	1,175	924						

Winchester

Economically active

Total	**2,706**	**1,982**	**1,598**	**2,544**	**1,899**	**1,539**	**162**	**83**	**59**
I Professional etc occupations	318	55	41	311	54	40	7	1	1
II Managerial and technical	972	683	546	936	665	531	36	18	15
III(N) Skilled occupations - non-manual	267	690	559	252	669	547	15	21	12
III(M) Skilled occupations - manual	568	117	97	528	107	89	40	10	8
IV Partly skilled occupations	326	268	218	303	254	209	23	14	9
V Unskilled occupations	100	135	112	84	129	107	16	6	5
Armed forces	85	1	1	85	1	1	-	-	-
On a Government scheme	22	10	7	22	10	7			
Occupation inadequately described or not stated	22	11	9	22	10	8	-	1	1

Economically inactive

Retired	616	728	305						
Other inactive	268	1,246	955						

Table 92   SEG and economic position (10% sample)   **County, districts**

92. Economically active residents   (10% sample)

Socio-economic group	TOTAL PERSONS		Economic position				Persons with different address 1 year before census (migrants)	
			In employment		Unemployed			
	Males	Females	Males	Females	Males	Females	Males	Females
a	b	c	d	e	f	g	h	i

HAMPSHIRE

Socio-economic group	Males	Females	Males	Females	Males	Females	Males	Females
TOTAL PERSONS	45,053	32,980	41,184	31,337	3,869	1,643	6,200	4,375
1.1 Employers in large establishments	10	5	10	5	-	-	1	-
1.2 Managers in large establishments	2,855	1,170	2,813	1,152	42	18	299	170
2.1 Employers in small establishments	1,437	484	1,433	483	4	1	111	39
2.2 Managers in small establishments	4,248	2,144	3,930	2,038	318	106	586	369
3 Professional workers - self-employed	614	98	613	98	1	-	61	10
4 Professional workers - employees	2,990	526	2,895	516	95	10	453	123
5.1 Ancillary workers and artists	4,236	5,181	4,068	5,073	168	108	583	708
5.2 Foremen and supervisors - non-manual	290	489	277	473	13	16	41	72
6 Junior non-manual workers	3,768	12,218	3,525	11,729	243	489	500	1,585
7 Personal service workers	673	2,808	583	2,686	90	122	153	351
8 Foremen and supervisors - manual	1,124	244	1,068	237	56	7	98	16
9 Skilled manual workers	7,607	632	6,823	593	784	39	868	90
10 Semi-skilled manual workers	4,602	2,703	4,038	2,495	564	208	572	335
11 Unskilled manual workers	1,737	2,097	1,329	2,005	408	92	218	187
12 Own account workers (other than professional)	4,399	935	4,099	924	300	11	499	80
13 Farmers - employers and managers	155	34	152	32	3	2	14	3
14 Farmers - own account	116	26	116	26	-	-	1	-
15 Agricultural workers	382	164	358	154	24	10	54	31
16 Members of armed forces	2,387	188	2,348	180	39	8	869	84
17 Inadequately described and not stated occupations	380	205	312	184	68	21	59	22
On a Government scheme	394	254	394	254			64	35

Basingstoke & Deane

Socio-economic group	Males	Females	Males	Females	Males	Females	Males	Females
TOTAL PERSONS	4,587	3,405	4,268	3,261	319	144	560	372
1.1 Employers in large establishments	-	-	-	-	-	-	-	-
1.2 Managers in large establishments	346	177	342	176	4	1	27	24
2.1 Employers in small establishments	133	36	133	36	-	-	9	3
2.2 Managers in small establishments	486	225	459	214	27	11	69	37
3 Professional workers - self-employed	63	11	63	11	-	-	9	1
4 Professional workers - employees	354	71	347	71	7	-	62	11
5.1 Ancillary workers and artists	466	494	453	481	13	13	74	55
5.2 Foremen and supervisors - non-manual	37	51	35	50	2	1	3	6
6 Junior non-manual workers	399	1,390	374	1,341	25	49	53	148
7 Personal service workers	71	260	64	249	7	11	16	24
8 Foremen and supervisors - manual	127	31	124	30	3	1	6	-
9 Skilled manual workers	801	68	731	62	70	6	92	8
10 Semi-skilled manual workers	508	221	450	205	58	16	56	19
11 Unskilled manual workers	157	207	128	199	29	8	15	18
12 Own account workers (other than professional)	404	82	383	81	21	1	37	4
13 Farmers - employers and managers	16	2	16	1	-	1	2	1
14 Farmers - own account	13	1	13	1	-	-	-	-
15 Agricultural workers	59	10	57	9	2	1	6	4
16 Members of armed forces	34	2	32	2	2	-	8	-
17 Inadequately described and not stated occupations	39	18	33	16	6	2	5	4
On a Government scheme	31	26	31	26			3	2

92. Economically active residents (10% sample)

Socio-economic group	TOTAL PERSONS		Economic position				Persons with different address 1 year before census (migrants)	
			In employment		Unemployed			
	Males	Females	Males	Females	Males	Females	Males	Females
a	b	c	d	e	f	g	h	i

East Hampshire

TOTAL PERSONS		3,010	2,228	2,845	2,150	165	78	430	302
1.1	Employers in large establishments	-	-	-	-	-	-	-	-
1.2	Managers in large establishments	236	55	231	55	5	-	31	8
2.1	Employers in small establishments	126	43	125	42	1	1	9	5
2.2	Managers in small establishments	407	166	375	161	32	5	55	24
3	Professional workers - self-employed	62	11	62	11	-	-	1	2
4	Professional workers - employees	213	36	205	36	8	-	26	7
5.1	Ancillary workers and artists	277	414	270	406	7	8	34	55
5.2	Foremen and supervisors - non-manual	13	27	13	26	-	1	4	1
6	Junior non-manual workers	209	748	198	722	11	26	26	109
7	Personal service workers	36	180	32	177	4	3	9	25
8	Foremen and supervisors - manual	65	21	64	21	1	-	3	1
9	Skilled manual workers	380	38	354	36	26	2	34	3
10	Semi-skilled manual workers	209	173	195	162	14	11	23	21
11	Unskilled manual workers	84	129	71	124	13	5	15	11
12	Own account workers (other than professional)	359	88	345	88	14	-	45	7
13	Farmers - employers and managers	24	5	24	5	-	-	-	1
14	Farmers - own account	16	11	16	11	-	-	-	-
15	Agricultural workers	62	28	57	27	5	1	7	7
16	Members of armed forces	170	12	170	12	-	-	97	10
17	Inadequately described and not stated occupations	16	13	14	13	2	-	3	3
	On a Government scheme	24	15	24	15			5	1

Eastleigh

TOTAL PERSONS		3,165	2,356	2,964	2,275	201	81	381	304
1.1	Employers in large establishments	2	1	2	1	-	-	1	-
1.2	Managers in large establishments	193	80	187	79	6	1	19	10
2.1	Employers in small establishments	102	24	102	24	-	-	3	2
2.2	Managers in small establishments	343	181	325	174	18	7	49	33
3	Professional workers - self-employed	32	7	32	7	-	-	3	-
4	Professional workers - employees	212	27	207	27	5	-	29	8
5.1	Ancillary workers and artists	351	382	345	376	6	6	53	47
5.2	Foremen and supervisors - non-manual	25	54	25	54	-	-	1	12
6	Junior non-manual workers	335	996	321	969	14	27	39	130
7	Personal service workers	40	179	34	174	6	5	3	22
8	Foremen and supervisors - manual	82	11	79	10	3	1	6	1
9	Skilled manual workers	614	44	561	44	53	-	72	5
10	Semi-skilled manual workers	310	140	287	132	23	8	34	17
11	Unskilled manual workers	102	110	85	109	17	1	10	4
12	Own account workers (other than professional)	311	63	289	62	22	1	42	5
13	Farmers - employers and managers	4	1	4	-	-	1	-	-
14	Farmers - own account	4	1	4	1	-	-	-	-
15	Agricultural workers	13	5	13	5	-	-	3	2
16	Members of armed forces	32	2	30	2	2	-	4	-
17	Inadequately described and not stated occupations	16	10	13	10	3	-	5	2
	On a Government scheme	19	15	19	15			2	2

92. Economically active residents

(10% sample)

Socio-economic group	TOTAL PERSONS		Economic position				Persons with different address 1 year before census (migrants)	
			In employment		Unemployed			
	Males	Females	Males	Females	Males	Females	Males	Females
a	b	c	d	e	f	g	h	i

Fareham

TOTAL PERSONS	**2,906**	**2,181**	**2,732**	**2,105**	**174**	**76**	**350**	**235**
1.1 Employers in large establishments	1	1	1	1	-	-	-	-
1.2 Managers in large establishments	243	75	240	73	3	2	18	4
2.1 Employers in small establishments	94	39	94	39	-	-	10	2
2.2 Managers in small establishments	303	136	280	130	23	6	41	23
3 Professional workers - self-employed	44	5	43	5	1	-	2	2
4 Professional workers - employees	220	42	208	41	12	1	32	9
5.1 Ancillary workers and artists	318	408	303	400	15	8	30	49
5.2 Foremen and supervisors - non-manual	23	27	22	26	1	1	2	7
6 Junior non-manual workers	224	833	214	806	10	27	38	86
7 Personal service workers	23	162	20	160	3	2	6	15
8 Foremen and supervisors - manual	71	14	70	13	1	1	1	-
9 Skilled manual workers	445	25	415	22	30	3	41	4
10 Semi-skilled manual workers	199	155	176	146	23	9	17	12
11 Unskilled manual workers	91	126	82	123	9	3	9	8
12 Own account workers (other than professional)	275	69	256	68	19	1	35	4
13 Farmers - employers and managers	4	2	4	2	-	-	-	-
14 Farmers - own account	5	1	5	1	-	-	-	-
15 Agricultural workers	9	8	9	7	-	1	1	-
16 Members of armed forces	239	19	237	19	2	-	60	7
17 Inadequately described and not stated occupations	21	10	19	10	2	-	1	-
On a Government scheme	34	13	34	13			3	2

Gosport

TOTAL PERSONS	**2,130**	**1,581**	**1,954**	**1,480**	**176**	**101**	**347**	**238**
1.1 Employers in large establishments	-	1	-	1	-	-	-	-
1.2 Managers in large establishments	83	47	82	47	1	-	9	9
2.1 Employers in small establishments	41	14	41	14	-	-	3	2
2.2 Managers in small establishments	118	75	106	71	12	4	13	15
3 Professional workers - self-employed	15	3	15	3	-	-	3	-
4 Professional workers - employees	75	8	72	8	3	-	15	2
5.1 Ancillary workers and artists	157	206	152	197	5	9	15	32
5.2 Foremen and supervisors - non-manual	10	22	10	21	-	1	2	2
6 Junior non-manual workers	152	560	141	537	11	23	17	64
7 Personal service workers	33	144	29	136	4	8	7	15
8 Foremen and supervisors - manual	54	12	51	12	3	-	3	3
9 Skilled manual workers	428	26	394	26	34	-	69	6
10 Semi-skilled manual workers	238	204	214	187	24	17	28	34
11 Unskilled manual workers	74	129	61	117	13	12	9	15
12 Own account workers (other than professional)	160	32	144	31	16	1	14	4
13 Farmers - employers and managers	2	-	2	-	-	-	-	-
14 Farmers - own account	1	-	1	-	-	-	-	-
15 Agricultural workers	6	4	5	4	1	-	1	1
16 Members of armed forces	404	40	395	36	9	4	124	19
17 Inadequately described and not stated occupations	19	13	16	11	3	2	3	2
On a Government scheme	23	21	23	21			5	6

92. Economically active residents　　　　　　　　　　　　　　　　　　　　　　　　　　　　　(10% sample)

Socio-economic group	TOTAL PERSONS		Economic position				Persons with different address 1 year before census (migrants)	
			In employment		Unemployed			
	Males	Females	Males	Females	Males	Females	Males	Females
a	b	c	d	e	f	g	h	i

Hart

	Males	Females	Males	Females	Males	Females	Males	Females
TOTAL PERSONS	**2,630**	**1,812**	**2,499**	**1,743**	**131**	**69**	**351**	**242**
1.1 Employers in large establishments	-	-	-	-	-	-	-	-
1.2 Managers in large establishments	250	91	246	90	4	1	28	16
2.1 Employers in small establishments	90	22	90	22	-	-	7	2
2.2 Managers in small establishments	369	163	354	152	15	11	52	32
3 Professional workers - self-employed	56	10	56	10	-	-	11	2
4 Professional workers - employees	261	52	248	50	13	2	34	13
5.1 Ancillary workers and artists	268	324	257	317	11	7	39	41
5.2 Foremen and supervisors - non-manual	13	23	11	21	2	2	2	5
6 Junior non-manual workers	196	701	185	677	11	24	16	86
7 Personal service workers	39	144	38	143	1	1	7	13
8 Foremen and supervisors - manual	46	11	45	11	1	-	2	1
9 Skilled manual workers	313	20	290	18	23	2	25	3
10 Semi-skilled manual workers	151	67	143	62	8	5	16	6
11 Unskilled manual workers	58	77	49	73	9	4	8	9
12 Own account workers (other than professional)	216	61	208	61	8	-	24	5
13 Farmers - employers and managers	8	4	8	4	-	-	1	-
14 Farmers - own account	3	-	3	-	-	-	-	-
15 Agricultural workers	17	9	17	9	-	-	2	1
16 Members of armed forces	222	9	222	9	-	-	72	2
17 Inadequately described and not stated occupations	21	8	15	8	6	-	2	-
On a Government scheme	14	6	14	6			1	1

Havant

	Males	Females	Males	Females	Males	Females	Males	Females
TOTAL PERSONS	**3,325**	**2,417**	**2,957**	**2,280**	**368**	**137**	**364**	**254**
1.1 Employers in large establishments	2	1	2	1	-	-	-	-
1.2 Managers in large establishments	215	74	212	71	3	3	17	12
2.1 Employers in small establishments	112	39	112	39	-	-	9	3
2.2 Managers in small establishments	237	148	215	142	22	6	22	16
3 Professional workers - self-employed	36	5	36	5	-	-	4	-
4 Professional workers - employees	226	26	220	26	6	-	24	2
5.1 Ancillary workers and artists	315	338	295	334	20	4	29	39
5.2 Foremen and supervisors - non-manual	25	34	23	31	2	3	3	5
6 Junior non-manual workers	267	842	248	804	19	38	35	87
7 Personal service workers	36	192	30	186	6	6	10	26
8 Foremen and supervisors - manual	80	18	76	18	4	-	7	1
9 Skilled manual workers	599	69	522	67	77	2	60	4
10 Semi-skilled manual workers	420	338	349	311	71	27	48	34
11 Unskilled manual workers	147	143	106	135	41	8	18	13
12 Own account workers (other than professional)	373	62	347	62	26	-	40	4
13 Farmers - employers and managers	8	1	7	1	1	-	1	-
14 Farmers - own account	1	-	1	-	-	-	-	-
15 Agricultural workers	10	7	8	7	2	-	1	1
16 Members of armed forces	86	2	82	1	4	1	20	-
17 Inadequately described and not stated occupations	35	19	27	18	8	1	5	2
On a Government scheme	39	21	39	21			4	1

92. Economically active residents   (10% sample)

Socio-economic group	TOTAL PERSONS		Economic position				Persons with different address 1 year before census (migrants)	
			In employment		Unemployed			
	Males	Females	Males	Females	Males	Females	Males	Females
a	b	c	d	e	f	g	h	i

New Forest

TOTAL PERSONS	4,218	3,203	3,864	3,068	354	135	491	357
1.1 Employers in large establishments	2	-	2	-	-	-	-	-
1.2 Managers in large establishments	272	91	269	90	3	1	25	12
2.1 Employers in small establishments	176	68	176	68	-	-	17	4
2.2 Managers in small establishments	456	235	413	224	43	11	55	38
3 Professional workers - self-employed	79	10	79	10	-	-	5	1
4 Professional workers - employees	232	35	225	34	7	1	33	6
5.1 Ancillary workers and artists	396	489	381	479	15	10	40	50
5.2 Foremen and supervisors - non-manual	24	39	24	39	-	-	5	3
6 Junior non-manual workers	357	1,232	342	1,180	15	52	32	130
7 Personal service workers	70	276	66	268	4	8	10	35
8 Foremen and supervisors - manual	129	17	121	17	8	-	11	-
9 Skilled manual workers	692	62	618	59	74	3	84	10
10 Semi-skilled manual workers	414	234	367	225	47	9	47	21
11 Unskilled manual workers	168	182	129	177	39	5	19	19
12 Own account workers (other than professional)	467	116	436	114	31	2	54	14
13 Farmers - employers and managers	20	5	19	5	1	-	5	1
14 Farmers - own account	26	4	26	4	-	-	-	-
15 Agricultural workers	65	33	62	31	3	2	5	6
16 Members of armed forces	61	5	58	5	3	-	30	2
17 Inadequately described and not stated occupations	43	21	34	18	9	3	9	1
On a Government scheme	17	21	17	21			2	2

Portsmouth

TOTAL PERSONS	4,993	3,606	4,361	3,316	632	290	833	557
1.1 Employers in large establishments	2	-	2	-	-	-	-	-
1.2 Managers in large establishments	178	124	175	119	3	5	29	24
2.1 Employers in small establishments	142	57	141	57	1	-	10	6
2.2 Managers in small establishments	326	175	298	162	28	13	63	41
3 Professional workers - self-employed	36	4	36	4	-	-	4	-
4 Professional workers - employees	265	43	257	43	8	-	42	14
5.1 Ancillary workers and artists	447	530	424	515	23	15	84	85
5.2 Foremen and supervisors - non-manual	33	45	31	44	2	1	5	7
6 Junior non-manual workers	388	1,265	348	1,194	40	71	64	191
7 Personal service workers	95	321	78	302	17	19	34	44
8 Foremen and supervisors - manual	118	39	109	38	9	1	18	2
9 Skilled manual workers	932	85	810	79	122	6	120	14
10 Semi-skilled manual workers	624	392	521	340	103	52	103	67
11 Unskilled manual workers	276	265	201	249	75	16	33	20
12 Own account workers (other than professional)	492	85	445	84	47	1	57	11
13 Farmers - employers and managers	-	-	-	-	-	-	-	-
14 Farmers - own account	-	-	-	-	-	-	-	-
15 Agricultural workers	9	2	7	2	2	-	3	-
16 Members of armed forces	374	23	364	23	10	-	120	11
17 Inadequately described and not stated occupations	50	23	41	20	9	3	5	-
On a Government scheme	73	41	73	41			20	8

92. Economically active residents   (10% sample)

Socio-economic group	TOTAL PERSONS		Economic position				Persons with different address 1 year before census (migrants)	
			In employment		Unemployed			
	Males	Females	Males	Females	Males	Females	Males	Females
a	b	c	d	e	f	g	h	i

Rushmoor

TOTAL PERSONS	**2,650**	**1,972**	**2,483**	**1,885**	**167**	**87**	**492**	**344**
1.1 Employers in large establishments	-	-	-	-	-	-	-	-
1.2 Managers in large establishments	171	88	168	88	3	-	17	12
2.1 Employers in small establishments	49	16	48	16	1	-	4	-
2.2 Managers in small establishments	224	118	206	110	18	8	30	22
3 Professional workers - self-employed	9	3	9	3	-	-	-	-
4 Professional workers - employees	193	30	186	30	7	-	33	5
5.1 Ancillary workers and artists	211	263	204	259	7	4	32	46
5.2 Foremen and supervisors - non-manual	23	35	22	35	1	-	6	4
6 Junior non-manual workers	242	735	233	703	9	32	38	134
7 Personal service workers	38	177	35	173	3	4	11	25
8 Foremen and supervisors - manual	61	21	57	18	4	3	8	1
9 Skilled manual workers	405	44	374	40	31	4	50	12
10 Semi-skilled manual workers	241	178	215	168	26	10	39	27
11 Unskilled manual workers	90	127	72	125	18	2	21	16
12 Own account workers (other than professional)	236	40	223	39	13	1	27	5
13 Farmers - employers and managers	-	-	-	-	-	-	-	-
14 Farmers - own account	1	-	1	-	-	-	-	-
15 Agricultural workers	3	3	3	3	-	-	-	-
16 Members of armed forces	394	55	392	52	2	3	167	26
17 Inadequately described and not stated occupations	18	10	16	7	2	3	5	3
On a Government scheme	19	16	19	16			2	2

Southampton

TOTAL PERSONS	**5,523**	**3,983**	**4,692**	**3,712**	**831**	**271**	**785**	**580**
1.1 Employers in large establishments	1	-	1	-	-	-	-	-
1.2 Managers in large establishments	199	112	197	110	2	2	29	17
2.1 Employers in small establishments	129	43	128	43	1	-	9	4
2.2 Managers in small establishments	380	223	340	212	40	11	61	39
3 Professional workers - self-employed	39	9	39	9	-	-	5	1
4 Professional workers - employees	333	76	323	73	10	3	79	23
5.1 Ancillary workers and artists	463	603	438	596	25	7	80	108
5.2 Foremen and supervisors - non-manual	33	70	32	67	1	3	5	9
6 Junior non-manual workers	520	1,474	468	1,402	52	72	88	219
7 Personal service workers	110	376	86	345	24	31	24	47
8 Foremen and supervisors - manual	171	29	154	29	17	-	12	4
9 Skilled manual workers	1,168	75	989	71	179	4	121	10
10 Semi-skilled manual workers	798	325	663	292	135	33	106	42
11 Unskilled manual workers	308	316	201	298	107	18	42	25
12 Own account workers (other than professional)	575	97	515	95	60	2	67	6
13 Farmers - employers and managers	-	-	-	-	-	-	-	-
14 Farmers - own account	-	1	-	1	-	-	-	-
15 Agricultural workers	6	9	5	6	1	3	5	-
16 Members of armed forces	24	3	23	3	1	-	5	-
17 Inadequately described and not stated occupations	56	30	41	25	15	5	11	3
On a Government scheme	49	35	49	35			8	5

92. Economically active residents (10% sample)

Socio-economic group	TOTAL PERSONS		Economic position				Persons with different address 1 year before census (migrants)	
			In employment		Unemployed			
	Males	Females	Males	Females	Males	Females	Males	Females
a	b	c	d	e	f	g	h	i

Test Valley

TOTAL PERSONS	**3,124**	**2,219**	**2,940**	**2,129**	**184**	**90**	**458**	**312**
1.1 Employers in large establishments	-	-	-	-	-	-	-	-
1.2 Managers in large establishments	235	72	232	71	3	1	26	13
2.1 Employers in small establishments	124	40	124	40	-	-	14	5
2.2 Managers in small establishments	305	151	285	143	20	8	43	28
3 Professional workers - self-employed	60	8	60	8	-	-	8	-
4 Professional workers - employees	168	36	166	34	2	2	15	12
5.1 Ancillary workers and artists	264	335	258	330	6	5	28	43
5.2 Foremen and supervisors - non-manual	15	40	14	38	1	2	3	7
6 Junior non-manual workers	241	801	228	774	13	27	32	108
7 Personal service workers	40	210	38	202	2	8	9	29
8 Foremen and supervisors - manual	81	13	79	13	2	-	16	2
9 Skilled manual workers	509	50	473	46	36	4	69	8
10 Semi-skilled manual workers	281	163	265	155	16	8	29	22
11 Unskilled manual workers	104	154	79	150	25	4	11	20
12 Own account workers (other than professional)	294	62	284	62	10	-	36	4
13 Farmers - employers and managers	29	7	28	7	1	-	2	-
14 Farmers - own account	20	3	20	3	-	-	-	-
15 Agricultural workers	61	18	56	17	5	1	9	4
16 Members of armed forces	209	4	205	4	4	-	94	1
17 Inadequately described and not stated occupations	24	19	21	18	3	1	3	1
On a Government scheme	25	14	25	14			4	1

Winchester

TOTAL PERSONS	**2,792**	**2,017**	**2,625**	**1,933**	**167**	**84**	**358**	**278**
1.1 Employers in large establishments	-	1	-	1	-	-	-	-
1.2 Managers in large establishments	234	84	232	83	2	1	24	9
2.1 Employers in small establishments	119	43	119	43	-	-	7	1
2.2 Managers in small establishments	294	148	274	143	20	5	33	21
3 Professional workers - self-employed	83	12	83	12	-	-	6	1
4 Professional workers - employees	238	44	231	43	7	1	29	11
5.1 Ancillary workers and artists	303	395	288	383	15	12	45	58
5.2 Foremen and supervisors - non-manual	16	22	15	21	1	1	-	4
6 Junior non-manual workers	238	641	225	620	13	21	22	93
7 Personal service workers	42	187	33	171	9	16	7	31
8 Foremen and supervisors - manual	39	7	39	7	-	-	5	-
9 Skilled manual workers	321	26	292	23	29	3	31	3
10 Semi-skilled manual workers	209	113	193	110	16	3	26	13
11 Unskilled manual workers	78	132	65	126	13	6	8	9
12 Own account workers (other than professional)	237	78	224	77	13	1	21	7
13 Farmers - employers and managers	40	7	40	7	-	-	3	-
14 Farmers - own account	26	4	26	4	-	-	1	-
15 Agricultural workers	62	28	59	27	3	1	11	5
16 Members of armed forces	138	12	138	12	-	-	68	6
17 Inadequately described and not stated occupations	22	11	22	10	-	1	2	1
On a Government scheme	27	10	27	10			5	2

Table 93 SEG, social class and ethnic group (10% sample)

93. Residents aged 16 and over, employees and self-employed

(10% sample)

Socio-economic group and social class based on occupation	TOTAL PERSONS	Ethnic group										Persons born in Ireland
		White	Black Caribbean	Black African	Black other	Indian	Pakistani	Bangla-deshi	Chinese	Other groups Asian	Other groups Other	
a	b	c	d	e	f	g	h	i	j	k	l	m

HAMPSHIRE

Socio-economic group

TOTAL	**71,873**	**70,641**	**150**	**59**	**73**	**355**	**40**	**54**	**173**	**175**	**153**	**979**
1,2 Employers and managers	11,864	11,688	17	6	8	47	3	13	36	20	26	149
3,4 Professional workers	4,122	4,004	6	4	3	50	10	2	17	11	15	63
5 Intermediate non-manual workers	9,891	9,715	30	16	8	38	7	2	24	17	34	171
6 Junior non-manual workers	15,254	15,071	27	16	17	50	6	-	20	24	23	168
8,9,12 Manual workers (foremen, supervisors, skilled and own account)	13,744	13,564	21	7	14	78	7	4	19	9	21	176
7,10 Personal service and semi-skilled manual workers	9,802	9,570	32	5	10	63	5	32	47	17	21	138
11 Unskilled manual workers	3,334	3,281	8	2	8	20	1	1	5	3	5	63
13,14,15 Farmers and agricultural workers	838	836	-	-	-	1	-	-	-	1	-	3
16,17 Members of armed forces and inadequately described and not stated occupations	3,024	2,912	9	3	5	8	1	-	5	73	8	48

Social class based on occupation

TOTAL	**71,873**	**70,641**	**150**	**59**	**73**	**355**	**40**	**54**	**173**	**175**	**153**	**979**
I Professional etc occupations	4,132	4,014	6	4	3	50	10	2	17	11	15	63
II Managerial and technical	20,908	20,583	45	22	16	102	9	4	35	33	59	305
III(N) Skilled occupations - non-manual	16,815	16,576	31	17	18	57	7	10	46	27	26	180
III(M) Skilled occupations - manual	13,133	12,946	20	6	11	54	7	20	39	10	20	169
IV Partly skilled occupations	10,101	9,908	29	4	11	64	5	17	26	18	19	137
V Unskilled occupations	3,760	3,702	10	3	9	20	1	1	5	3	6	77
Armed forces	2,528	2,431	4	3	5	2	-	-	3	73	7	42
Occupation inadequately described or not stated	496	481	5	-	-	6	1	-	2	-	1	6

Table 93 SEG, social class and ethnic group (10% sample) – **continued**

93. Residents aged 16 and over, employees and self-employed

(10% sample)

Socio-economic group and social class based on occupation	TOTAL PERSONS	Ethnic group								Other groups		Persons born in Ireland
		White	Black Caribbean	Black African	Black other	Indian	Pakistani	Bangladeshi	Chinese	Asian	Other	
a	b	c	d	e	f	g	h	i	j	k	l	m
Basingstoke & Deane												
Socio-economic group												
TOTAL	**7,472**	**7,324**	**30**	**9**	**6**	**48**	**9**	**3**	**11**	**15**	**17**	**125**
1,2 Employers and managers	1,360	1,340	1	-	1	8	1	1	2	2	4	19
3,4 Professional workers	492	469	-	1	-	13	5	-	1	-	3	5
5 Intermediate non-manual workers	1,019	979	6	4	-	11	3	1	3	7	5	27
6 Junior non-manual workers	1,715	1,687	9	2	3	6	-	-	2	4	2	15
8,9,12 Manual workers (foremen, supervisors, skilled and own account)	1,411	1,397	5	1	1	5	-	-	-	-	2	29
7,10 Personal service and semi-skilled manual workers	968	949	7	1	-	4	-	1	3	2	1	24
11 Unskilled manual workers	327	326	-	-	-	1	-	-	-	-	-	6
13,14,15 Farmers and agricultural workers	97	97	-	-	-	-	-	-	-	-	-	-
16,17 Members of armed forces and inadequately described and not stated occupations	83	80	2	-	1	-	-	-	-	-	-	-
Social class based on occupation												
TOTAL	**7,472**	**7,324**	**30**	**9**	**6**	**48**	**9**	**3**	**11**	**15**	**17**	**125**
I Professional etc occupations	494	471	-	1	-	13	5	-	1	-	3	5
II Managerial and technical	2,254	2,196	6	4	1	22	4	-	3	9	9	42
III(N) Skilled occupations - non-manual	1,867	1,836	10	2	3	6	-	1	3	4	2	19
III(M) Skilled occupations - manual	1,380	1,362	7	1	1	2	-	2	3	-	2	28
IV Partly skilled occupations	1,023	1,009	5	1	-	4	-	-	1	2	1	22
V Unskilled occupations	371	370	-	-	-	1	-	-	-	-	-	9
Armed forces	34	33	-	1	1	-	-	-	-	-	-	-
Occupation inadequately described or not stated	49	47	2	-	-	-	-	-	-	-	-	-

Table 93 SEG, social class and ethnic group (10% sample) – continued

93. Residents aged 16 and over, employees and self-employed

(10% sample)

East Hampshire

Socio-economic group and social class based on occupation	TOTAL PERSONS	White	Black Caribbean	Black African	Black other	Indian	Pakistani	Bangladeshi	Chinese	Asian (Other groups)	Other (Other groups)	Persons born in Ireland
a	b	c	d	e	f	g	h	i	j	k	l	m
Socio-economic group												
TOTAL	**4,956**	**4,913**	**2**	**4**	**5**	**14**	**-**	**2**	**4**	**4**	**8**	**73**
1,2 Employers and managers	989	980	-	-	1	4	-	1	1	-	2	13
3,4 Professional workers	314	311	-	-	-	1	-	-	1	-	1	5
5 Intermediate non-manual workers	715	709	-	1	-	1	-	-	-	1	3	20
6 Junior non-manual workers	920	910	1	2	2	2	-	-	1	-	2	14
8,9,12 Manual workers (foremen, supervisors, skilled and own account)	908	904	-	-	1	3	-	-	-	-	-	6
7,10 Personal service and semi-skilled manual workers	566	560	1	-	-	2	-	1	1	1	-	7
11 Unskilled manual workers	195	194	-	-	-	1	-	-	-	-	-	5
13,14,15 Farmers and agricultural workers	140	140	-	-	-	-	-	-	-	-	-	-
16,17 Members of armed forces and inadequately described and not stated occupations	209	205	-	1	1	-	-	-	-	2	-	3
Social class based on occupation												
TOTAL	**4,956**	**4,913**	**2**	**4**	**5**	**14**	**-**	**2**	**4**	**4**	**8**	**73**
I Professional etc occupations	315	312	-	-	-	1	-	-	-	1	1	5
II Managerial and technical	1,707	1,693	-	1	1	6	-	-	1	-	5	34
III(N) Skilled occupations - non-manual	1,036	1,023	1	2	2	3	-	1	2	-	2	14
III(M) Skilled occupations - manual	827	824	1	-	1	1	-	-	-	1	-	7
IV Partly skilled occupations	632	627	-	-	1	2	-	1	1	-	-	5
V Unskilled occupations	230	229	-	-	-	1	-	-	-	-	-	5
Armed forces	182	178	-	1	1	-	-	-	-	2	-	3
Occupation inadequately described or not stated	27	27	-	-	-	-	-	-	-	-	-	-

Table 93 SEG, social class and ethnic group (10% sample) – **continued**

93. Residents aged 16 and over, employees and self-employed

(10% sample)

Eastleigh

Socio-economic group

Socio-economic group and social class based on occupation	TOTAL PERSONS	White	Black Caribbean	Black African	Black other	Indian	Pakistani	Bangla-deshi	Chinese	Asian	Other	Persons born in Ireland
a	b	c	d	e	f	g	h	i	j	k	l	m
TOTAL	**5,205**	**5,115**	**11**	**2**	**4**	**43**	**-**	**9**	**8**	**5**	**8**	**49**
1,2 Employers and managers	894	877	4	-	-	3	-	1	1	5	3	9
3,4 Professional workers	273	266	-	-	-	4	-	-	2	-	1	6
5 Intermediate non-manual workers	800	785	3	1	2	7	-	-	2	-	-	6
6 Junior non-manual workers	1,290	1,278	2	-	1	8	-	-	1	-	-	6
8,9,12 Manual workers (foremen, supervisors, skilled and own account)	1,045	1,029	-	1	1	9	-	2	1	-	2	6
7,10 Personal service and semi-skilled manual workers	627	604	2	-	-	12	-	6	1	-	2	11
11 Unskilled manual workers	194	194	-	-	-	-	-	-	-	-	-	-
13,14,15 Farmers and agricultural workers	27	27	-	-	-	-	-	-	-	-	-	-
16,17 Members of armed forces and inadequately described and not stated occupations	55	55	-	-	-	-	-	-	-	-	-	-

Social class based on occupation

Social class based on occupation	TOTAL PERSONS	White	Black Caribbean	Black African	Black other	Indian	Pakistani	Bangla-deshi	Chinese	Asian	Other	Persons born in Ireland
TOTAL	**5,205**	**5,115**	**11**	**2**	**4**	**43**	**-**	**9**	**8**	**5**	**8**	**49**
I Professional etc occupations	273	266	-	-	-	4	-	-	2	-	1	6
II Managerial and technical	1,587	1,560	7	1	2	9	-	-	2	4	2	15
III(N) Skilled occupations - non-manual	1,425	1,408	2	-	2	9	-	2	2	-	-	6
III(M) Skilled occupations - manual	995	977	-	1	-	10	-	4	1	-	2	6
IV Partly skilled occupations	646	626	2	-	-	11	-	3	1	1	2	10
V Unskilled occupations	224	223	-	-	-	-	-	-	-	-	1	6
Armed forces	32	32	-	-	-	-	-	-	-	-	-	-
Occupation inadequately described or not stated	23	23	-	-	-	-	-	-	-	-	-	-

Ethnic group — Other groups

Table 93 SEG, social class and ethnic group (10% sample) – **continued**

93. Residents aged 16 and over, employees and self-employed

(10% sample)

Fareham

Socio-economic group and social class based on occupation	TOTAL PERSONS	Ethnic group								Other groups		Persons born in Ireland
		White	Black Caribbean	Black African	Black other	Indian	Pakistani	Bangla-deshi	Chinese	Asian	Other	
a	b	c	d	e	f	g	h	i	j	k	l	m

Socio-economic group

	b	c	d	e	f	g	h	i	j	k	l	m
TOTAL	**4,790**	**4,755**	**6**	**-**	**3**	**4**	**2**	**2**	**10**	**7**	**1**	**49**
1,2 Employers and managers	858	850	2	-	1	1	-	-	2	2	-	6
3,4 Professional workers	297	289	-	-	-	2	1	-	3	2	-	6
5 Intermediate non-manual workers	751	747	1	-	1	1	1	-	1	1	-	8
6 Junior non-manual workers	1,020	1,015	-	-	1	-	-	-	3	1	-	14
8,9,12 Manual workers (foremen, supervisors, skilled and own account)	844	842	1	-	-	1	-	-	-	-	-	4
7,10 Personal service and semi-skilled manual workers	502	498	1	-	-	-	-	1	1	-	1	2
11 Unskilled manual workers	205	204	-	-	-	-	-	1	-	-	-	2
13,14,15 Farmers and agricultural workers	28	28	-	-	-	-	-	-	-	-	-	-
16,17 Members of armed forces and inadequately described and not stated occupations	285	282	1	-	-	-	-	-	-	2	-	7

Social class based on occupation

	b	c	d	e	f	g	h	i	j	k	l	m
TOTAL	**4,790**	**4,755**	**6**	**-**	**3**	**4**	**2**	**2**	**10**	**7**	**1**	**49**
I Professional etc occupations	297	289	3	-	2	2	1	-	3	2	-	6
II Managerial and technical	1,538	1,528	3	-	2	1	1	-	1	2	1	14
III(N) Skilled occupations - non-manual	1,126	1,120	1	-	1	1	1	-	4	1	-	13
III(M) Skilled occupations - manual	763	759	1	-	-	1	-	-	2	-	-	5
IV Partly skilled occupations	549	546	1	-	-	-	-	1	-	-	1	2
V Unskilled occupations	232	231	-	-	-	-	-	1	-	-	-	2
Armed forces	256	254	-	-	-	-	-	-	-	2	-	6
Occupation inadequately described or not stated	29	28	1	-	-	-	-	-	-	-	-	1

Table 93 SEG, social class and ethnic group (10% sample) – continued

93. Residents aged 16 and over, employees and self-employed

(10% sample)

Socio-economic group and social class based on occupation	TOTAL PERSONS	Ethnic group								Other groups		Persons born in Ireland
		White	Black Caribbean	Black African	Black other	Indian	Pakistani	Bangla-deshi	Chinese	Asian	Other	
a	b	c	d	e	f	g	h	i	j	k	l	m
Gosport												
Socio-economic group												
TOTAL	**3,390**	**3,365**	**1**	**1**	**5**	**1**	**-**	**-**	**8**	**1**	**8**	**48**
1,2 Employers and managers	362	358	-	-	1	1	-	-	1	-	1	8
3,4 Professional workers	98	98	-	-	1	1	-	-	1	-	-	1
5 Intermediate non-manual workers	380	377	-	-	1	-	-	-	1	-	1	8
6 Junior non-manual workers	678	670	-	1	1	-	-	-	2	1	4	7
8,9,12 Manual workers (foremen, supervisors, skilled and own account)	658	656	-	-	-	-	-	-	1	-	1	9
7,10 Personal service and semi-skilled manual workers	566	564	-	-	-	-	-	-	1	1	1	7
11 Unskilled manual workers	178	176	-	-	1	-	-	-	1	-	-	1
13,14,15 Farmers and agricultural workers	12	12	-	-	-	-	-	-	-	-	-	-
16,17 Members of armed forces and inadequately described and not stated occupations	458	454	1	-	2	-	-	-	1	-	-	7
Social class based on occupation												
TOTAL	**3,390**	**3,365**	**1**	**1**	**5**	**1**	**-**	**-**	**8**	**1**	**8**	**48**
I Professional etc occupations	98	98	-	-	-	-	-	-	-	-	-	1
II Managerial and technical	692	686	-	-	2	1	-	-	1	-	2	16
III(N) Skilled occupations - non-manual	741	731	-	1	-	-	-	-	3	1	5	8
III(M) Skilled occupations - manual	649	648	-	-	-	-	-	-	1	-	8	8
IV Partly skilled occupations	560	558	-	-	-	-	-	-	1	-	1	7
V Unskilled occupations	192	190	-	1	1	1	-	-	1	-	-	1
Armed forces	431	428	1	-	2	-	-	-	-	-	-	7
Occupation inadequately described or not stated	27	26	-	-	-	-	-	-	1	-	-	-

Table 93 SEG, social class and ethnic group (10% sample) – **continued**

County, districts

93. Residents aged 16 and over, employees and self-employed

(10% sample)

Hart

Socio-economic group and social class based on occupation	TOTAL PERSONS	Ethnic group								Other groups		Persons born in Ireland
		White	Black Caribbean	Black African	Black other	Indian	Pakistani	Bangla-deshi	Chinese	Asian	Other	
a	b	c	d	e	f	g	h	i	j	k	l	m

Socio-economic group

	b	c	d	e	f	g	h	i	j	k	l	m
TOTAL	**4,222**	**4,102**	**6**	**5**	**1**	**12**	**2**	**-**	**13**	**74**	**7**	**75**
1,2 Employers and managers	954	944	1	1	1	1	-	-	3	1	2	18
3,4 Professional workers	364	359	-	1	1	2	-	-	-	-	2	5
5 Intermediate non-manual workers	606	597	2	1	-	-	1	-	2	2	1	14
6 Junior non-manual workers	862	849	2	-	-	4	1	-	2	3	1	14
8,9,12 Manual workers (foremen, supervisors, skilled and own account)	633	630	-	-	-	3	-	-	-	-	-	12
7,10 Personal service and semi-skilled manua workers	386	378	-	1	-	-	-	-	6	-	1	6
11 Unskilled manual workers	122	122	-	-	-	-	-	-	-	-	-	3
13,14,15 Farmers and agricultural workers	41	41	-	-	-	-	-	-	-	-	-	-
16,17 Members of armed forces and inadequately described and not stated occupations	254	182	1	1	-	2	-	-	-	68	-	3

Social class based on occupation

	b	c	d	e	f	g	h	i	j	k	l	m
TOTAL	**4,222**	**4,102**	**6**	**5**	**1**	**12**	**2**	**-**	**13**	**74**	**7**	**75**
I Professional etc occupations	367	362	-	1	-	2	-	-	-	-	2	5
II Managerial and technical	1,517	1,498	3	2	1	4	1	-	2	3	3	30
III(N) Skilled occupations - non-manual	948	932	2	-	-	4	1	-	5	3	1	15
III(M) Skilled occupations - manual	612	606	-	-	-	-	-	-	5	-	1	13
IV Partly skilled occupations	389	387	-	1	-	-	-	-	1	-	-	6
V Unskilled occupations	135	135	-	-	-	-	-	-	-	-	-	3
Armed forces	231	159	1	1	-	2	-	-	-	68	-	3
Occupation inadequately described or not stated	23	23	-	-	-	-	-	-	-	-	-	-

Table 93 SEG, social class and ethnic group (10% sample) – **continued**

93. Residents aged 16 and over, employees and self-employed

(10% sample)

Havant

Socio-economic group and social class based on occupation	TOTAL PERSONS	Ethnic group								Other groups		Persons born in Ireland
		White	Black Caribbean	Black African	Black other	Indian	Pakistani	Bangla-deshi	Chinese	Asian	Other	
a	b	c	d	e	f	g	h	i	j	k	l	m

Socio-economic group

TOTAL	**5,177**	**5,127**	**6**	**4**	**7**	**5**	**1**	**3**	**10**	**4**	**10**	**49**
1,2 Employers and managers	794	786	1	-	-	2	-	1	3	-	1	6
3,4 Professional workers	287	281	1	-	-	2	1	-	1	1	-	2
5 Intermediate non-manual workers	683	677	2	1	1	-	1	1	-	1	1	6
6 Junior non-manual workers	1,052	1,046	1	-	1	-	-	1	1	1	2	7
8,9,12 Manual workers (foremen, supervisors, skilled and own account)	1,092	1,083	1	1	2	1	-	1	-	1	2	13
7,10 Personal service and semi-skilled manual workers	876	866	-	1	2	-	-	-	5	1	1	7
11 Unskilled manual workers	241	238	-	1	1	-	-	-	-	-	1	2
13,14,15 Farmers and agricultural workers	24	24	-	-	-	-	-	-	-	-	-	1
16,17 Members of armed forces and inadequately described and not stated occupations	128	126	-	-	-	-	-	-	-	-	2	5

Social class based on occupation

TOTAL	**5,177**	**5,127**	**6**	**4**	**7**	**5**	**1**	**3**	**10**	**4**	**10**	**49**
I Professional etc occupations	287	281	1	-	1	2	1	-	1	1	-	2
II Managerial and technical	1,381	1,371	3	-	1	2	-	1	1	1	2	10
III(N) Skilled occupations - non-manual	1,170	1,163	1	-	1	-	-	1	1	1	2	6
III(M) Skilled occupations - manual	1,032	1,017	-	2	1	1	-	-	7	1	2	15
IV Partly skilled occupations	908	902	-	-	2	-	-	1	1	1	1	8
V Unskilled occupations	271	267	-	1	2	-	-	-	-	-	1	3
Armed forces	83	81	-	-	-	-	-	-	-	-	-	3
Occupation inadequately described or not stated	45	45	-	-	-	-	-	-	-	-	-	2

Table 93 SEG, social class and ethnic group (10% sample) – **continued**

93. Residents aged 16 and over, employees and self-employed

(10% sample)

Socio-economic group and social class based on occupation	TOTAL PERSONS	Ethnic group										Persons born in Ireland
		White	Black Caribbean	Black African	Black other	Indian	Pakistani	Bangladeshi	Chinese	Asian (Other groups)	Other (Other groups)	
a	b	c	d	e	f	g	h	i	j	k	l	m
New Forest												
Socio-economic group												
TOTAL	6,894	6,853	6	4	-	6	-	3	9	6	7	69
1,2 Employers and managers	1,242	1,238	2	-	-	1	-	-	-	-	1	8
3,4 Professional workers	348	344	-	-	-	2	-	-	-	2	-	4
5 Intermediate non-manual workers	923	915	1	1	-	1	-	-	3	-	2	14
6 Junior non-manual workers	1,522	1,515	-	2	-	1	-	-	2	-	2	11
8,9,12 Manual workers (foremen, supervisors, skilled and own account)	1,365	1,360	-	1	-	1	-	-	1	1	1	15
7,10 Personal service and semi-skilled manual workers	926	918	1	-	-	-	-	3	3	1	-	8
11 Unskilled manual workers	306	302	2	-	-	-	-	-	-	1	1	7
13,14,15 Farmers and agricultural workers	147	146	-	-	-	-	-	-	-	1	-	2
16,17 Members of armed forces and inadequately described and not stated occupations	115	115	-	-	-	-	-	-	-	-	-	-
Social class based on occupation												
TOTAL	6,894	6,853	6	4	-	6	-	3	9	6	7	69
I Professional etc occupations	349	345	-	1	-	2	-	-	-	2	-	4
II Managerial and technical	2,118	2,108	3	1	-	2	-	-	3	-	1	23
III(N) Skilled occupations - non-manual	1,694	1,685	-	2	-	1	-	-	2	-	4	12
III(M) Skilled occupations - manual	1,291	1,283	1	1	-	1	-	2	1	2	1	14
IV Partly skilled occupations	969	963	1	-	-	-	-	1	3	1	-	9
V Unskilled occupations	358	354	2	-	-	-	-	-	-	1	1	7
Armed forces	63	63	-	-	-	-	-	-	-	-	-	-
Occupation inadequately described or not stated	52	52	-	-	-	-	-	-	-	-	-	-

Table 93 SEG, social class and ethnic group (10% sample) – continued

93. Residents aged 16 and over, employees and self-employed

(10% sample)

Socio-economic group and social class based on occupation	TOTAL PERSONS	White	Ethnic group							Other groups		Persons born in Ireland
			Black Caribbean	Black African	Black other	Indian	Pakistani	Bangla-deshi	Chinese	Asian	Other	
a	b	c	d	e	f	g	h	i	j	k	l	m

Portsmouth

Socio-economic group

TOTAL	**7,563**	**7,435**	**7**	**9**	**9**	**19**	**1**	**22**	**30**	**13**	**18**	**92**
1,2 Employers and managers	954	934	1	3	-	4	-	6	5	-	1	12
3,4 Professional workers	340	328	1	-	-	6	-	1	2	1	1	6
5 Intermediate non-manual workers	1,014	1,000	1	2	1	1	1	-	-	4	4	18
6 Junior non-manual workers	1,542	1,520	1	3	3	6	-	-	3	4	2	11
8,9,12 Manual workers (foremen, supervisors, skilled and own account)	1,565	1,547	2	-	2	2	-	-	7	2	3	12
7,10 Personal service and semi-skilled manual workers	1,241	1,210	1	-	1	-	-	15	9	2	3	19
11 Unskilled manual workers	450	445	-	1	2	-	-	-	1	-	1	8
13,14,15 Farmers and agricultural workers	9	9	-	-	-	-	-	-	-	-	-	-
16,17 Members of armed forces and inadequately described and not stated occupations	448	442	-	-	-	-	-	-	3	-	3	6

Social class based on occupation

TOTAL	**7,563**	**7,435**	**7**	**9**	**9**	**19**	**1**	**22**	**30**	**13**	**18**	**92**
I Professional etc occupations	340	328	1	-	-	6	-	1	2	1	1	6
II Managerial and technical	1,855	1,826	2	5	1	5	1	1	2	4	8	32
III(N) Skilled occupations - non-manual	1,693	1,662	1	3	3	6	-	4	8	4	2	12
III(M) Skilled occupations - manual	1,497	1,472	1	-	2	2	-	10	8	2	-	7
IV Partly skilled occupations	1,229	1,210	1	1	1	-	-	6	6	2	3	19
V Unskilled occupations	501	495	1	1	2	-	-	-	1	-	1	10
Armed forces	387	381	-	-	-	-	-	-	3	-	3	5
Occupation inadequately described or not stated	61	61	-	-	-	-	-	-	-	-	-	1

Table 93 SEG, social class and ethnic group (10% sample) – **continued**

93. Residents aged 16 and over, employees and self-employed

(10% sample)

Rushmoor

Socio-economic group and social class based on occupation	TOTAL PERSONS	Ethnic group								Other groups		Persons born in Ireland
		White	Black Caribbean	Black African	Black other	Indian	Pakistani	Bangla-deshi	Chinese	Asian	Other	
a	b	c	d	e	f	g	h	i	j	k	l	m

Socio-economic group

	TOTAL PERSONS	White	Black Caribbean	Black African	Black other	Indian	Pakistani	Bangla-deshi	Chinese	Asian	Other	Persons born in Ireland
TOTAL	**4,333**	**4,225**	**19**	**5**	**6**	**25**	**4**	**1**	**14**	**16**	**18**	**89**
1,2 Employers and managers	636	619	1	-	2	4	1	-	5	2	2	11
3,4 Professional workers	228	222	-	1	-	2	1	-	1	2	-	3
5 Intermediate non-manual workers	520	502	2	2	-	3	-	-	1	2	8	11
6 Junior non-manual workers	936	915	4	2	1	5	1	-	1	5	2	23
8,9,12 Manual workers (foremen, supervisors, skilled and own account)	751	734	4	-	2	2	1	-	2	2	4	15
7,10 Personal service and semi-skilled manual workers	591	576	4	-	4	4	1	1	4	1	1	9
11 Unskilled manual workers	197	191	2	-	-	2	1	-	-	1	-	7
13,14,15 Farmers and agricultural workers	7	7	-	-	-	-	-	-	-	-	-	-
16,17 Members of armed forces and inadequately described and not stated occupations	467	459	2	-	1	3	-	-	1	1	1	10

Social class based on occupation

	TOTAL PERSONS	White	Black Caribbean	Black African	Black other	Indian	Pakistani	Bangla-deshi	Chinese	Asian	Other	Persons born in Ireland
TOTAL	**4,333**	**4,225**	**19**	**5**	**6**	**25**	**4**	**1**	**14**	**16**	**18**	**89**
I Professional etc occupations	230	224	-	1	-	2	-	-	1	2	-	3
II Managerial and technical	1,085	1,052	3	2	2	8	-	-	4	4	10	21
III(N) Skilled occupations - non-manual	1,015	991	4	2	1	5	1	-	4	5	2	21
III(M) Skilled occupations - manual	739	722	4	-	1	2	2	-	2	2	4	15
IV Partly skilled occupations	571	557	4	-	1	3	-	1	3	1	1	11
V Unskilled occupations	226	220	2	-	-	2	1	-	-	1	-	8
Armed forces	444	440	1	-	1	-	-	-	-	1	1	9
Occupation inadequately described or not stated	23	19	1	-	-	3	-	-	-	-	-	1

Table 93   SEG, social class and ethnic group (10% sample) – continued

93. Residents aged 16 and over, employees and self-employed

(10% sample)

Southampton

Socio-economic group and social class based on occupation	TOTAL PERSONS	Ethnic group White	Black Caribbean	Black African	Black other	Indian	Pakistani	Bangla-deshi	Chinese	Other groups Asian	Other	Persons born in Ireland
a	b	c	d	e	f	g	h	i	j	k	l	m
Socio-economic group												
TOTAL	**8,320**	**7,974**	**48**	**10**	**21**	**154**	**17**	**5**	**33**	**25**	**33**	**148**
1,2 Employers and managers	1,031	996	3	2	-	11	-	2	5	7	5	15
3,4 Professional workers	444	411	2	1	3	13	1	-	6	1	6	10
5 Intermediate non-manual workers	1,133	1,092	11	1	1	12	1	-	6	2	7	24
6 Junior non-manual workers	1,870	1,833	7	2	3	17	3	-	-	4	1	24
8,9,12 Manual workers (foremen, supervisors, skilled and own account)	1,853	1,777	7	2	5	43	6	1	7	1	4	38
7,10 Personal service and semi-skilled manual workers	1,386	1,296	13	2	6	38	5	2	8	9	7	22
11 Unskilled manual workers	499	472	4	-	3	16	-	-	1	1	2	14
13,14,15 Farmers and agricultural workers	12	11	-	-	-	1	-	-	-	-	-	-
16,17 Members of armed forces and inadequately described and not stated occupations	92	86	1	-	-	3	1	-	-	-	1	1
Social class based on occupation												
TOTAL	**8,320**	**7,974**	**48**	**10**	**21**	**154**	**17**	**5**	**33**	**25**	**33**	**148**
I Professional etc occupations	444	411	2	1	3	13	1	-	6	1	6	10
II Managerial and technical	2,045	1,970	14	3	1	27	1	1	10	6	12	33
III(N) Skilled occupations - non-manual	2,041	1,988	9	2	3	20	4	1	6	7	1	28
III(M) Skilled occupations - manual	1,791	1,729	5	1	5	33	5	2	5	1	5	38
IV Partly skilled occupations	1,358	1,270	12	2	6	42	5	1	5	9	6	22
V Unskilled occupations	549	520	5	1	3	16	-	-	1	1	2	16
Armed forces	26	25	-	-	-	-	-	-	-	-	1	1
Occupation inadequately described or not stated	66	61	1	-	-	3	1	-	-	-	-	-

Table 93 SEG, social class and ethnic group (10% sample) – **continued**

County, districts

93. Residents aged 16 and over, employees and self-employed

(10% sample)

Test Valley

Socio-economic group and social class based on occupation	TOTAL PERSONS	Ethnic group								Other groups		Persons born in Ireland
		White	Black Caribbean	Black African	Black other	Indian	Pakistani	Bangla-deshi	Chinese	Asian	Other	
a	b	c	d	e	f	g	h	i	j	k	l	m

Socio-economic group

TOTAL	**5,030**	**4,973**	**6**	**4**	**3**	**14**	**4**	**-**	**16**	**3**	**7**	**59**
1,2 Employers and managers	895	881	1	-	1	1	1	-	7	1	2	12
3,4 Professional workers	268	261	1	-	-	3	2	-	1	-	-	3
5 Intermediate non-manual workers	640	634	1	-	1	1	-	-	2	-	1	8
6 Junior non-manual workers	1,002	993	-	2	1	1	1	-	1	1	2	13
8,9,12 Manual workers (foremen, supervisors, skilled and own account)	957	944	1	1	-	8	-	-	-	1	2	12
7,10 Personal service and semi-skilled manual workers	660	656	1	-	-	-	-	-	3	-	-	9
11 Unskilled manual workers	229	227	-	-	-	-	-	-	2	-	-	-
13,14,15 Farmers and agricultural workers	131	131	-	-	-	-	-	-	-	-	-	-
16,17 Members of armed forces and inadequately described and not stated occupations	248	246	1	1	-	-	-	-	-	-	-	2

Social class based on occupation

TOTAL	**5,030**	**4,973**	**6**	**4**	**3**	**14**	**4**	**-**	**16**	**3**	**7**	**59**
I Professional etc occupations	268	261	1	-	-	3	2	-	1	-	2	3
II Managerial and technical	1,507	1,487	1	-	2	10	1	-	3	1	3	17
III(N) Skilled occupations - non-manual	1,133	1,117	1	3	1	1	1	-	5	1	3	16
III(M) Skilled occupations - manual	917	911	1	-	-	-	-	-	3	-	2	10
IV Partly skilled occupations	703	699	1	-	-	-	-	-	2	1	-	9
V Unskilled occupations	254	252	-	-	-	-	-	-	2	-	-	2
Armed forces	209	207	1	1	-	-	-	-	-	-	-	2
Occupation inadequately described or not stated	39	39	-	-	-	-	-	-	-	-	-	-

93. Residents aged 16 and over, employees and self-employed

(10% sample)

Socio-economic group and social class based on occupation	TOTAL PERSONS	Ethnic group								Other groups		Persons born in Ireland
		White	Black Caribbean	Black African	Black other	Indian	Pakistani	Bangla-deshi	Chinese	Asian	Other	
a	b	c	d	e	f	g	h	i	j	k	l	m

Winchester

Socio-economic group

	b	c	d	e	f	g	h	i	j	k	l	m
TOTAL	**4,521**	**4,480**	**2**	**2**	**3**	**10**	**-**	**4**	**7**	**2**	**11**	**54**
1,2 Employers and managers	895	885	-	-	-	6	-	1	1	-	2	12
3,4 Professional workers	369	365	1	-	-	-	-	1	1	1	1	7
5 Intermediate non-manual workers	707	701	-	2	-	1	-	-	2	-	1	7
6 Junior non-manual workers	845	840	-	-	1	-	-	-	1	-	3	9
8,9,12 Manual workers (foremen, supervisors, skilled and own account)	662	661	-	-	-	-	-	-	-	1	-	5
7,10 Personal service and semi-skilled manual workers	507	495	1	-	1	3	-	2	2	-	3	7
11 Unskilled manual workers	191	190	-	-	1	-	-	-	-	-	-	3
13,14,15 Farmers and agricultural workers	163	163	-	-	-	-	-	-	-	-	-	-
16,17 Members of armed forces and inadequately described and not stated occupations	182	180	-	-	-	-	-	-	1	-	1	4

Social class based on occupation

	b	c	d	e	f	g	h	i	j	k	l	m
TOTAL	**4,521**	**4,480**	**2**	**2**	**3**	**10**	**-**	**4**	**7**	**2**	**11**	**54**
I Professional etc occupations	370	366	1	-	-	-	-	1	-	1	1	7
II Managerial and technical	1,622	1,608	-	2	-	5	-	1	3	-	3	18
III(N) Skilled occupations - non-manual	926	920	-	-	1	2	-	-	1	-	2	10
III(M) Skilled occupations - manual	640	636	-	-	-	1	-	-	1	1	1	3
IV Partly skilled occupations	564	554	1	-	1	2	-	2	1	-	3	7
V Unskilled occupations	217	216	-	-	1	-	-	-	-	-	-	5
Armed forces	150	150	-	-	-	-	-	-	-	-	-	3
Occupation inadequately described or not stated	32	30	-	-	-	-	-	-	1	-	1	1

Table 94 Former industry of unemployed (10% sample)

County, districts

(10% sample)

94. Residents on a Government scheme or unemployed

a	TOTAL PERSONS	Agriculture, forestry and fishing	Energy and water	Mining	Manufacturing metal etc	Other manufacturing	Construction	Distribution and catering	Transport	Banking and finance etc	Other services	Not stated, inadequately described or workplace outside UK
	b	c	d	e	f	g	h	i	j	k	l	m
HAMPSHIRE												
TOTAL PERSONS	**5,035**	**77**	**38**	**89**	**601**	**306**	**993**	**979**	**295**	**523**	**928**	**206**
Males	3,567	62	31	48	461	212	961	591	252	310	488	151
Females	1,468	15	7	41	140	94	32	388	43	213	440	55
Basingstoke & Deane												
TOTAL PERSONS	**447**	**6**	**3**	**9**	**57**	**29**	**74**	**89**	**24**	**56**	**87**	**13**
Males	305	4	3	5	43	21	72	54	20	27	45	11
Females	142	2	-	4	14	8	2	35	4	29	42	2
East Hampshire												
TOTAL PERSONS	**243**	**6**	**3**	**4**	**32**	**23**	**38**	**36**	**10**	**31**	**51**	**9**
Males	166	5	2	1	26	14	36	23	9	16	26	8
Females	77	1	1	3	6	9	2	13	1	15	25	1
Eastleigh												
TOTAL PERSONS	**264**	**4**	**1**	**4**	**31**	**13**	**60**	**53**	**18**	**27**	**48**	**5**
Males	193	3	-	2	28	12	54	35	15	23	17	4
Females	71	1	1	2	3	1	6	18	3	4	31	1
Fareham												
TOTAL PERSONS	**261**	**3**	**2**	**5**	**32**	**22**	**47**	**50**	**15**	**28**	**50**	**7**
Males	184	3	2	2	25	16	45	32	13	14	29	3
Females	77	-	-	3	7	6	2	18	2	14	21	4
Gosport												
TOTAL PERSONS	**259**	**4**	**1**	**7**	**42**	**10**	**44**	**47**	**14**	**15**	**65**	**10**
Males	162	3	1	5	24	6	43	23	11	8	34	4
Females	97	1	-	2	18	4	1	24	3	7	31	6

Industry of most recent job in last 10 years

Table 94 Former industry of unemployed (10% sample) – continued

94. Residents on a Government scheme or unemployed

a	TOTAL PERSONS	Agriculture, forestry and fishing	Energy and water	Mining	Manufacturing metal etc	Other manufacturing	Construction	Distribution and catering	Transport	Banking and finance etc	Other services	Not stated, inadequately described or workplace outside UK
	b	c	d	e	f	g	h	i	j	k	l	m
Hart												
TOTAL PERSONS	**186**	**-**	**2**	**3**	**18**	**12**	**29**	**26**	**14**	**35**	**34**	**13**
Males	123	-	2	1	10	8	25	13	12	20	21	11
Females	63	-	-	2	8	4	4	13	2	15	13	2
Havant												
TOTAL PERSONS	**460**	**5**	**-**	**4**	**84**	**42**	**94**	**77**	**15**	**49**	**68**	**22**
Males	347	5	-	1	64	31	91	49	14	30	42	20
Females	113	-	-	3	20	11	3	28	1	19	26	2
New Forest												
TOTAL PERSONS	**440**	**8**	**7**	**7**	**52**	**18**	**100**	**86**	**30**	**43**	**66**	**23**
Males	316	6	5	3	45	9	96	44	29	24	37	18
Females	124	2	2	4	7	9	4	42	1	19	29	5
Portsmouth												
TOTAL PERSONS	**798**	**10**	**4**	**17**	**81**	**42**	**168**	**161**	**45**	**69**	**160**	**41**
Males	562	9	3	7	56	25	166	94	36	41	93	32
Females	236	1	1	10	25	17	2	67	9	28	67	9
Rushmoor												
TOTAL PERSONS	**253**	**2**	**1**	**6**	**24**	**21**	**44**	**37**	**10**	**32**	**67**	**9**
Males	164	1	1	2	16	14	41	21	6	19	38	5
Females	89	1	-	4	8	7	3	16	4	13	29	4
Southampton												
TOTAL PERSONS	**929**	**11**	**13**	**18**	**106**	**48**	**210**	**205**	**80**	**74**	**132**	**32**
Males	711	8	12	15	95	37	207	135	68	48	63	23
Females	218	3	1	3	11	11	3	70	12	26	69	9

Industry of most recent job in last 10 years

Table 94 Former industry of unemployed (10% sample) – continued

94. Residents on a Government scheme or unemployed

	TOTAL PERSONS	Industry of most recent job in last 10 years										
		Agriculture, forestry and fishing	Energy and water	Mining	Manufacturing metal etc	Other manufacturing	Construction	Distribution and catering	Transport	Banking and finance etc	Other services	Not stated, inadequately described or workplace outside UK
a	b	c	d	e	f	g	h	i	j	k	l	m
Test Valley												
TOTAL PERSONS	**252**	**10**	**-**	**5**	**22**	**10**	**41**	**51**	**15**	**32**	**50**	**16**
Males	171	9	-	4	14	10	41	29	14	19	21	10
Females	81	1	-	1	8	-	-	22	1	13	29	6
Winchester												
TOTAL PERSONS	**243**	**8**	**1**	**-**	**20**	**16**	**44**	**61**	**5**	**32**	**50**	**6**
Males	163	6	-	-	15	9	44	39	5	21	22	2
Females	80	2	1	-	5	7	-	22	-	11	28	4

Table 95   Former occupation of unemployed (10% sample)   County, districts

95. Residents on a Government scheme or unemployed   (10% sample)

a	TOTAL PERSONS	Managers and administrators	Professional	Associate professional	Clerical and secretarial	Craft and related	Personal and protective service	Sales	Plant and machine operatives	Other occupations	Not stated or inadequately described
	b	c	d	e	f	g	h	i	j	k	l
HAMPSHIRE											
TOTAL PERSONS	5,035	516	172	288	611	1,143	513	371	633	686	102
Males	3,567	378	134	197	221	1,081	264	180	487	550	75
Females	1,468	138	38	91	390	62	249	191	146	136	27
Basingstoke & Deane											
TOTAL PERSONS	447	47	13	25	74	90	40	26	71	52	9
Males	305	32	11	15	30	85	19	14	52	40	7
Females	142	15	2	10	44	5	21	12	19	12	2
East Hampshire											
TOTAL PERSONS	243	39	14	15	31	42	27	17	27	28	3
Males	166	34	9	9	8	39	15	10	18	21	3
Females	77	5	5	6	23	3	12	7	9	7	-
Eastleigh											
TOTAL PERSONS	264	33	8	8	40	71	30	19	27	25	3
Males	193	23	7	7	13	71	11	10	25	23	3
Females	71	10	1	1	27	-	19	9	2	2	-
Fareham											
TOTAL PERSONS	261	38	22	24	33	62	15	20	25	19	3
Males	184	29	18	19	12	57	6	8	19	14	2
Females	77	9	4	5	21	5	9	12	6	5	1
Gosport											
TOTAL PERSONS	259	22	4	19	32	53	41	16	34	31	7
Males	162	14	3	8	11	51	24	6	22	19	4
Females	97	8	1	11	21	2	17	10	12	12	3
Hart											
TOTAL PERSONS	186	30	18	19	31	23	11	18	14	16	6
Males	123	21	15	11	11	21	4	9	13	12	6
Females	63	9	3	8	20	2	7	9	1	4	-
Havant											
TOTAL PERSONS	460	42	10	23	44	114	28	41	90	58	10
Males	347	30	8	19	17	110	20	22	66	46	9
Females	113	12	2	4	27	4	8	19	24	12	1

95. Residents on a Government scheme or unemployed   (10% sample)

a	TOTAL PERSONS	Occupation (SOC Major Groups) of most recent job in last 10 years									
		Managers and administrators	Professional	Associate professional	Clerical and secretarial	Craft and related	Personal and protective service	Sales	Plant and machine operatives	Other occupations	Not stated or inadequately described
a	b	c	d	e	f	g	h	i	j	k	l

New Forest

TOTAL PERSONS	440	54	17	31	44	92	31	41	52	65	13
Males	316	41	14	21	11	88	16	16	46	54	9
Females	124	13	3	10	33	4	15	25	6	11	4

Portsmouth

TOTAL PERSONS	798	53	13	42	84	221	102	55	102	110	16
Males	562	34	11	30	31	202	59	23	70	91	11
Females	236	19	2	12	53	19	43	32	32	19	5

Rushmoor

TOTAL PERSONS	253	33	10	14	40	45	33	15	27	31	5
Males	164	22	9	8	10	41	21	7	19	25	2
Females	89	11	1	6	30	4	12	8	8	6	3

Southampton

TOTAL PERSONS	929	61	21	33	99	240	93	69	114	179	20
Males	711	48	16	27	51	233	43	35	97	146	15
Females	218	13	5	6	48	7	50	34	17	33	5

Test Valley

TOTAL PERSONS	252	37	7	11	33	44	26	18	29	41	6
Males	171	30	4	5	9	43	12	8	21	35	4
Females	81	7	3	6	24	1	14	10	8	6	2

Winchester

TOTAL PERSONS	243	27	15	24	26	46	36	16	21	31	1
Males	163	20	9	18	7	40	14	12	19	24	-
Females	80	7	6	6	19	6	22	4	2	7	1

96. Residents in employment in armed forces   (10% sample)

Age	TOTAL PERSONS		In households		Not in households		With different address 1 year before census (migrants)					
							All migrants		From outside district		From outside county	
	Males	Females	Males	Females	Males	Females	In households	Not in households	In households	Not in households	In households	Not in households
a	b	c	d	e	f	g	h	i	j	k	l	m

HAMPSHIRE

Age	Males	Females	Males	Females	Males	Females	h	i	j	k	l	m
ALL AGES 16 AND OVER	2,331	175	1,621	89	710	86	502	427	330	377	262	351
16 - 19	230	42	22	6	208	36	9	181	5	173	4	163
20 - 24	479	58	177	25	302	33	111	158	62	137	45	130
25 - 29	494	37	379	22	115	15	158	56	111	44	89	39
30 - 34	423	23	363	21	60	2	106	21	67	16	53	13
35 - 39	280	7	269	7	11	-	64	7	46	6	40	5
40 - 44	210	5	201	5	9	-	33	3	25	1	20	1
45 - 49	122	2	121	2	1	-	11	-	8	-	7	-
50 - 54	54	1	52	1	2	-	10	1	6	-	4	-
55 and over	39	-	37	-	2	-	-	-	-	-	-	-

Basingstoke & Deane

Age	Males	Females	Males	Females	Males	Females	h	i	j	k	l	m
ALL AGES 16 AND OVER	32	2	32	2	-	-	6	-	5	-	3	-
16 - 19	1	-	1	-	-	-	1	-	1	-	1	-
20 - 24	4	-	4	-	-	-	1	-	1	-	-	-
25 - 29	8	-	8	-	-	-	2	-	2	-	1	-
30 - 34	8	1	8	1	-	-	1	-	-	-	-	-
35 - 39	3	-	3	-	-	-	-	-	-	-	-	-
40 - 44	1	-	1	-	-	-	-	-	-	-	-	-
45 - 49	4	1	4	1	-	-	-	-	-	-	-	-
50 - 54	2	-	2	-	-	-	1	-	1	-	1	-
55 and over	1	-	1	-	-	-	-	-	-	-	-	-

East Hampshire

Age	Males	Females	Males	Females	Males	Females	h	i	j	k	l	m
ALL AGES 16 AND OVER	163	12	98	5	65	7	45	59	35	58	29	58
16 - 19	29	4	2	-	27	4	2	27	-	27	-	27
20 - 24	33	2	7	-	26	2	3	19	2	19	1	19
25 - 29	29	2	22	1	7	1	18	8	17	7	15	7
30 - 34	25	4	21	4	4	-	12	4	8	4	7	4
35 - 39	18	-	17	-	1	-	3	1	3	1	3	1
40 - 44	12	-	12	-	-	-	5	-	4	-	2	-
45 - 49	10	-	10	-	-	-	1	-	-	-	-	-
50 - 54	6	-	6	-	-	-	1	-	1	-	1	-
55 and over	1	-	1	-	-	-	-	-	-	-	-	-

Eastleigh

Age	Males	Females	Males	Females	Males	Females	h	i	j	k	l	m
ALL AGES 16 AND OVER	30	2	30	2	-	-	3	-	3	-	1	-
16 - 19	3	1	3	1	-	-	-	-	-	-	-	-
20 - 24	2	-	2	-	-	-	-	-	-	-	-	-
25 - 29	4	1	4	1	-	-	-	-	-	-	-	-
30 - 34	5	-	5	-	-	-	-	-	-	-	-	-
35 - 39	7	-	7	-	-	-	3	-	3	-	1	-
40 - 44	2	-	2	-	-	-	-	-	-	-	-	-
45 - 49	6	-	6	-	-	-	-	-	-	-	-	-
50 - 54	1	-	1	-	-	-	-	-	-	-	-	-
55 and over	-	-	-	-	-	-	-	-	-	-	-	-

Table 96 Armed forces (10% sample) – **continued**

County, districts

96. Residents in employment in armed forces (10% sample)

Age	TOTAL PERSONS		In households		Not in households		With different address 1 year before census (migrants)					
							All migrants		From outside district		From outside county	
	Males	Females	Males	Females	Males	Females	In house-holds	Not in house-holds	In house-holds	Not in house-holds	In house-holds	Not in house-holds
a	b	c	d	e	f	g	h	i	j	k	l	m

Fareham

Age	Males	Females	Males	Females	Males	Females	h	i	j	k	l	m
ALL AGES 16 AND OVER	235	18	204	14	31	4	37	28	30	16	18	14
16 - 19	14	2	1	-	13	2	-	13	-	12	-	11
20 - 24	23	1	11	1	12	-	4	9	4	1	2	1
25 - 29	35	7	32	5	3	2	19	4	14	2	7	1
30 - 34	47	3	47	3	-	-	7	-	7	-	5	-
35 - 39	39	4	37	4	2	-	4	1	2	1	2	1
40 - 44	42	1	41	1	1	-	3	1	3	-	2	-
45 - 49	22	-	22	-	-	-	-	-	-	-	-	-
50 - 54	6	-	6	-	-	-	-	-	-	-	-	-
55 and over	7	-	7	-	-	-	-	-	-	-	-	-

Gosport

Age	Males	Females	Males	Females	Males	Females	h	i	j	k	l	m
ALL AGES 16 AND OVER	394	35	344	27	50	8	98	42	50	33	36	31
16 - 19	16	5	1	2	15	3	1	17	1	15	1	15
20 - 24	73	17	50	14	23	3	38	17	19	14	12	13
25 - 29	88	5	81	3	7	2	25	5	15	2	12	2
30 - 34	90	5	88	5	2	-	19	2	8	1	5	1
35 - 39	59	-	57	-	2	-	8	1	4	1	4	-
40 - 44	36	2	35	2	1	-	4	-	1	-	1	-
45 - 49	19	1	19	1	-	-	1	-	1	-	1	-
50 - 54	6	-	6	-	-	-	2	-	1	-	-	-
55 and over	7	-	7	-	-	-	-	-	-	-	-	-

Hart

Age	Males	Females	Males	Females	Males	Females	h	i	j	k	l	m
ALL AGES 16 AND OVER	221	6	97	2	124	4	37	36	29	35	27	34
16 - 19	15	2	-	1	15	1	1	13	-	12	-	12
20 - 24	51	3	10	-	41	3	9	17	7	17	6	16
25 - 29	59	-	17	-	42	-	9	5	8	5	7	5
30 - 34	50	-	27	-	23	-	6	-	5	-	5	-
35 - 39	18	1	17	1	1	-	6	-	5	-	5	-
40 - 44	15	-	13	-	2	-	3	1	2	1	2	1
45 - 49	10	-	10	-	-	-	3	-	2	-	2	-
50 - 54	2	-	2	-	-	-	-	-	-	-	-	-
55 and over	1	-	1	-	-	-	-	-	-	-	-	-

Havant

Age	Males	Females	Males	Females	Males	Females	h	i	j	k	l	m
ALL AGES 16 AND OVER	81	1	81	1	-	-	20	-	14	-	11	-
16 - 19	2	-	2	-	-	-	1	-	1	-	1	-
20 - 24	5	1	5	1	-	-	3	-	1	-	1	-
25 - 29	11	-	11	-	-	-	4	-	4	-	3	-
30 - 34	15	-	15	-	-	-	6	-	5	-	4	-
35 - 39	15	-	15	-	-	-	4	-	2	-	1	-
40 - 44	15	-	15	-	-	-	2	-	1	-	1	-
45 - 49	11	-	11	-	-	-	-	-	-	-	-	-
50 - 54	5	-	5	-	-	-	-	-	-	-	-	-
55 and over	2	-	2	-	-	-	-	-	-	-	-	-

Table 96 Armed forces (10% sample) – **continued**　　　　　　　　　　　　　　　　　　　　County, districts

96. Residents in employment in armed forces　　　　　　　　　　　　　　　　　　　　　　　　　　　　　(10% sample)

Age	TOTAL PERSONS		In households		Not in households		With different address 1 year before census (migrants)					
							All migrants		From outside district		From outside county	
	Males	Females	Males	Females	Males	Females	In house-holds	Not in house-holds	In house-holds	Not in house-holds	In house-holds	Not in house-holds
a	b	c	d	e	f	g	h	i	j	k	l	m

New Forest

ALL AGES 16 AND OVER	58	5	44	4	14	1	23	6	9	4	8	4
16 - 19	2	1	-	1	2	-	-	1	-	1	-	1
20 - 24	15	-	7	-	8	-	4	2	1	2	1	2
25 - 29	16	3	14	2	2	1	9	1	3	1	3	1
30 - 34	13	1	12	1	1	-	8	1	4	-	3	-
35 - 39	4	-	4	-	-	-	1	-	-	-	-	-
40 - 44	5	-	5	-	-	-	1	-	1	-	1	-
45 - 49	1	-	1	-	-	-	-	-	-	-	-	-
50 - 54	2	-	1	-	1	-	-	1	-	-	-	-
55 and over	-	-	-	-	-	-	-	-	-	-	-	-

Portsmouth

ALL AGES 16 AND OVER	363	23	259	17	104	6	76	51	37	40	27	28
16 - 19	38	5	3	1	35	4	1	23	1	21	1	17
20 - 24	90	6	43	5	47	1	24	16	12	11	7	7
25 - 29	81	7	76	6	5	1	23	4	11	3	10	1
30 - 34	59	4	51	4	8	-	13	5	4	3	3	1
35 - 39	43	-	40	-	3	-	7	2	4	2	3	2
40 - 44	29	1	26	1	3	-	4	1	3	-	2	-
45 - 49	11	-	10	-	1	-	2	-	2	-	1	-
50 - 54	4	-	4	-	-	-	2	-	-	-	-	-
55 and over	8	-	6	-	2	-	-	-	-	-	-	-

Rushmoor

ALL AGES 16 AND OVER	392	52	205	9	187	43	73	118	48	108	41	105
16 - 19	55	15	2	-	53	15	1	49	-	47	-	44
20 - 24	114	22	25	2	89	20	18	48	11	44	11	44
25 - 29	97	8	67	2	30	6	22	16	13	13	10	13
30 - 34	54	4	40	2	14	2	11	4	6	4	4	4
35 - 39	36	1	35	1	1	-	14	1	12	-	11	-
40 - 44	21	1	21	1	-	-	6	-	5	-	4	-
45 - 49	5	-	5	-	-	-	-	-	-	-	-	-
50 - 54	8	1	8	1	-	-	1	-	1	-	1	-
55 and over	2	-	2	-	-	-	-	-	-	-	-	-

Southampton

ALL AGES 16 AND OVER	23	3	23	3	-	-	4	-	4	-	2	-
16 - 19	3	-	3	-	-	-	-	-	-	-	-	-
20 - 24	3	1	3	1	-	-	-	-	-	-	-	-
25 - 29	9	1	9	1	-	-	4	-	4	-	2	-
30 - 34	5	1	5	1	-	-	-	-	-	-	-	-
35 - 39	2	-	2	-	-	-	-	-	-	-	-	-
40 - 44	1	-	1	-	-	-	-	-	-	-	-	-
45 - 49	-	-	-	-	-	-	-	-	-	-	-	-
50 - 54	-	-	-	-	-	-	-	-	-	-	-	-
55 and over	-	-	-	-	-	-	-	-	-	-	-	-

Table 96   Armed forces (10% sample) – **continued**   County, districts

96. Residents in employment in armed forces   (10% sample)

Age	TOTAL PERSONS		In households		Not in households		With different address 1 year before census (migrants)					
							All migrants		From outside district		From outside county	
	Males	Females	Males	Females	Males	Females	In house-holds	Not in house-holds	In house-holds	Not in house-holds	In house-holds	Not in house-holds
a	b	c	d	e	f	g	h	i	j	k	l	m

Test Valley

Age	Males	Females	Males	Females	Males	Females	h	i	j	k	l	m
ALL AGES 16 AND OVER	204	4	121	2	83	2	53	40	43	39	39	38
16 - 19	25	-	3	-	22	-	1	13	1	13	-	13
20 - 24	52	1	8	-	44	1	5	20	3	20	3	19
25 - 29	38	2	26	1	12	1	16	5	14	4	13	4
30 - 34	28	-	24	-	4	-	13	2	11	2	10	2
35 - 39	22	1	22	1	-	-	9	-	7	-	7	-
40 - 44	15	-	15	-	-	-	4	-	4	-	4	-
45 - 49	10	-	10	-	-	-	3	-	2	-	2	-
50 - 54	7	-	6	-	1	-	2	-	1	-	-	-
55 and over	7	-	7	-	-	-	-	-	-	-	-	-

Winchester

Age	Males	Females	Males	Females	Males	Females	h	i	j	k	l	m
ALL AGES 16 AND OVER	135	12	83	1	52	11	27	47	23	44	20	39
16 - 19	27	7	1	-	26	7	-	25	-	25	-	23
20 - 24	14	4	2	1	12	3	2	10	1	9	1	9
25 - 29	19	1	12	-	7	1	7	8	6	7	6	5
30 - 34	24	-	20	-	4	-	10	3	9	2	7	1
35 - 39	14	-	13	-	1	-	5	1	4	1	3	1
40 - 44	16	-	14	-	2	-	1	-	1	-	1	-
45 - 49	13	-	13	-	-	-	1	-	1	-	1	-
50 - 54	5	-	5	-	-	-	1	-	1	-	1	-
55 and over	3	-	3	-	-	-	-	-	-	-	-	-

Table 97 Armed forces: households (10% sample)

97. Residents in households with head in employment in armed forces

(10% sample)

Age	Marital status of household head								Marital status of all persons							
	Total		Single		Married		Widowed or divorced		Total		Single		Married		Widowed or divorced	
	Males	Females	Males	Females	Males	Females	Males	Females	Males	Females	Males	Females	Males	Females	Males	Females
a	b	c	d	e	f	g	h	i	j	k	l	m	n	o	p	q
HAMPSHIRE																
ALL AGES	1,391	31	83	16	1,270	10	38	5	2,374	2,224	1,046	928	1,280	1,267	48	29
0 - 15	-	-	-	-	-	-	-	-	774	712	774	712	-	-	-	-
16 - 44	1,197	30	79	15	1,086	10	32	5	1,399	1,353	267	214	1,095	1,121	37	18
45 up to pensionable age	194	1	4	1	184	-	6	-	196	141	5	2	184	136	7	3
Pensionable age and over	-	-	-	-	-	-	-	-	5	18	-	-	1	10	4	8
Persons with different address 1 year before census (migrants)	404	10	28	5	366	5	10	-	658	618	270	243	372	368	16	7
Basingstoke & Deane																
ALL AGES	25	-	2	-	21	-	2	-	44	42	21	18	21	22	2	2
0 - 15	-	-	-	-	-	-	-	-	17	13	17	13	-	-	-	-
16 - 44	18	-	2	-	15	-	1	-	20	21	4	5	15	15	1	1
45 up to pensionable age	7	-	-	-	6	-	1	-	7	6	-	-	6	6	1	-
Pensionable age and over	-	-	-	-	-	-	-	-	-	2	-	-	-	1	-	1
Persons with different address 1 year before census (migrants)	5	-	1	-	2	-	2	-	7	10	3	7	2	2	2	-
East Hampshire																
ALL AGES	88	1	6	-	82	-	-	1	138	141	53	59	82	81	3	1
0 - 15	-	-	-	-	-	-	-	-	38	46	38	46	-	-	-	-
16 - 44	72	1	6	-	66	-	-	1	83	83	15	13	66	69	2	1
45 up to pensionable age	16	-	-	-	16	-	-	-	17	10	-	-	16	10	1	-
Pensionable age and over	-	-	-	-	-	-	-	-	-	2	-	-	-	2	-	-
Persons with different address 1 year before census (migrants)	36	-	3	-	33	-	-	-	60	52	25	19	33	33	2	-

Table 97 Armed forces: households (10% sample) – **continued**

(10% sample)

97. Residents in households with head in employment in armed forces

Age	Marital status of household head								Marital status of all persons							
	Total		Single		Married		Widowed or divorced		Total		Single		Married		Widowed or divorced	
	Males	Females	Males	Females	Males	Females	Males	Females	Males	Females	Males	Females	Males	Females	Males	Females
a	b	c	d	e	f	g	h	i	j	k	l	m	n	o	p	q
Eastleigh																
ALL AGES	22	-	1	-	20	-	1	-	38	29	17	9	20	20	1	-
0 - 15									10	6	10	6	-	-	-	-
16 - 44	16	-	1	-	14	-	1	-	22	19	7	3	14	16	1	-
45 up to pensionable age	6	-	-	-	6	-	-	-	6	4	-	-	6	4	-	-
Pensionable age and over	-	-	-	-	-	-	-	-	-	-	-	-	-	-	-	-
Persons with different address																
1 year before census (migrants)	3	-	-	-	3	-	-	-	5	4	2	1	3	3	-	-
Fareham																
ALL AGES	185	3	8	1	176	1	1	1	327	296	149	119	177	174	1	3
0 - 15									113	90	113	90	-	-	-	-
16 - 44	151	3	8	1	142	1	1	1	180	176	36	28	143	146	1	2
45 up to pensionable age	34	-	-	-	34	-	-	-	34	28	-	-	34	27	-	-
Pensionable age and over	-	-	-	-	-	-	-	-	-	2	-	1	-	1	-	1
Persons with different address																
1 year before census (migrants)	29	2	2	1	27	1	-	-	51	54	23	24	28	30	-	-
Gosport																
ALL AGES	294	12	18	8	262	4	14	-	499	477	217	210	265	261	17	6
0 - 15									157	153	157	153	-	-	-	-
16 - 44	265	11	18	7	236	4	11	-	310	300	59	56	239	241	12	3
45 up to pensionable age	29	1	-	1	26	-	3	-	30	20	1	1	26	18	3	1
Pensionable age and over	-	-	-	-	-	-	-	-	2	4	-	-	-	2	2	2
Persons with different address																
1 year before census (migrants)	76	4	8	2	65	2	3	-	120	120	49	54	67	65	4	1

Table 97 Armed forces: households (10% sample) – **continued**

97. Residents in households with head in employment in armed forces

Age	Marital status of household head								Marital status of all persons							
	Total		Single		Married		Widowed or divorced		Total		Single		Married		Widowed or divorced	
	Males	Females	Males	Females	Males	Females	Males	Females	Males	Females	Males	Females	Males	Females	Males	Females
a	b	c	d	e	f	g	h	i	j	k	l	m	n	o	p	q
Hart																
ALL AGES	89	1	-	-	89	1	-	-	159	151	69	62	90	88	-	1
0 - 15	77	1	-	-	77	1	-	-	54	54	54	54	-	-	-	-
16 - 44	12	-	-	-	12	-	-	-	93	88	15	8	78	80	-	-
45 up to pensionable age	-	-	-	-	-	-	-	-	12	7	-	-	12	7	-	-
Pensionable age and over	-	-	-	-	-	-	-	-	-	2	-	-	-	1	-	1
Persons with different address 1 year before census (migrants)	33	1	-	-	33	1	-	-	55	55	21	21	34	34	-	-
Havant																
ALL AGES	62	1	3	-	58	1	1	-	113	112	53	50	59	60	1	2
0 - 15	44	1	3	-	41	1	-	-	40	33	40	33	-	-	-	-
16 - 44	18	-	-	-	17	-	1	-	55	63	13	17	42	46	-	-
45 up to pensionable age	-	-	-	-	-	-	-	-	18	15	-	-	17	14	1	1
Pensionable age and over	-	-	-	-	-	-	-	-	-	1	-	-	-	-	-	1
Persons with different address 1 year before census (migrants)	12	-	-	-	12	-	-	-	20	24	8	11	12	13	-	-
New Forest																
ALL AGES	32	2	3	2	28	-	1	-	56	48	26	20	28	28	2	-
0 - 15	30	2	2	2	27	-	1	-	18	14	18	14	-	-	-	-
16 - 44	2	-	1	-	1	-	-	-	36	33	7	6	27	27	2	-
45 up to pensionable age	-	-	-	-	-	-	-	-	2	1	1	-	1	1	-	-
Pensionable age and over	-	-	-	-	-	-	-	-	-	-	-	-	-	-	-	-
Persons with different address 1 year before census (migrants)	14	1	1	1	13	-	-	-	23	23	9	10	13	13	1	-

257

Table 97 Armed forces: households (10% sample) – continued

(10% sample)

97. Residents in households with head in employment in armed forces

Age	Marital status of household head								Marital status of all persons							
	Total		Single		Married		Widowed or divorced		Total		Single		Married		Widowed or divorced	
	Males	Females	Males	Females	Males	Females	Males	Females	Males	Females	Males	Females	Males	Females	Males	Females
a	b	c	d	e	f	g	h	i	j	k	l	m	n	o	p	q
Portsmouth																
ALL AGES	207	7	31	3	166	1	10	3	352	320	171	144	169	168	12	8
0 - 15									112	109	112	109	-	-	-	-
16 - 44	191	7	29	3	152	1	10	3	222	195	57	35	154	154	11	6
45 up to pensionable age	16	-	2	-	14	-	-	-	16	13	2	-	14	13	1	-
Pensionable age and over	-	-	-	-	-	-	-	-	2	3	-	-	1	1	-	2
Persons with different address																
1 year before census (migrants)	52	1	10	1	39	-	3	-	85	70	41	30	40	38	4	2
Rushmoor																
ALL AGES	191	2	3	-	185	2	3	-	311	306	122	120	186	184	3	2
0 - 15									99	104	99	104	-	-	-	-
16 - 44	177	2	3	-	171	2	3	-	198	191	23	16	172	174	3	1
45 up to pensionable age	14	-	-	-	14	-	-	-	14	11	-	-	14	10	-	1
Pensionable age and over	-	-	-	-	-	-	-	-	-	-	-	-	-	-	-	-
Persons with different address																
1 year before census (migrants)	70	1	1	1	69	1	-	-	105	97	35	29	70	67	-	1
Southampton																
ALL AGES	13	1	2	-	9	-	2	-	17	15	6	6	9	9	2	-
0 - 15									4	2	4	4	-	-	-	-
16 - 44	13	1	2	-	9	-	2	-	13	13	2	2	9	9	2	-
45 up to pensionable age	-	-	-	-	-	-	-	-	-	-	-	-	-	-	-	-
Pensionable age and over	-	-	-	-	-	-	-	-	-	-	-	-	-	-	-	-
Persons with different address																
1 year before census (migrants)	2	-	-	-	-	-	2	-	2	2	-	1	-	1	2	-

Table 97 Armed forces: households (10% sample) – continued

97. Residents in households with head in employment in armed forces

(10% sample)

Age	Marital status of household head								Marital status of all persons							
	Total		Single		Married		Widowed or divorced		Total		Single		Married		Widowed or divorced	
	Males	Females	Males	Females	Males	Females	Males	Females	Males	Females	Males	Females	Males	Females	Males	Females
a	b	c	d	e	f	g	h	i	j	k	l	m	n	o	p	q
Test Valley																
ALL AGES	107	1	5	1	101	-	1	-	183	167	81	65	101	99	1	3
0 - 15									61	50	61	50				
16 - 44	86	1	4	1	81	-	1	-	101	101	19	15	81	83	1	3
45 up to pensionable age	21	-	1	-	20	-	-	-	21	15	1	-	20	15	-	-
Pensionable age and over	-	-	-	-	-	-	-	-	-	1	-	-	-	1	-	-
Persons with different address 1 year before census (migrants)	45	-	2	-	43	-	-	-	78	63	35	19	43	42	-	2
Winchester																
ALL AGES	76	-	1	-	73	-	2	-	137	120	61	46	73	73	3	1
0 - 15									51	38	51	38			1	1
16 - 44	57	-	1	-	55	-	1	-	66	70	10	8	55	61	1	-
45 up to pensionable age	19	-	-	-	18	-	1	-	19	11	-	-	18	11	1	-
Pensionable age and over	-	-	-	-	-	-	-	-	1	1	-	-	-	1	-	-
Persons with different address 1 year before census (migrants)	27	-	-	-	27	-	-	-	47	44	19	17	27	27	1	-

98. Residents aged 16 and over, employees and self-employed   (10% sample)

1980 occupation orders	TOTAL PERSONS	Males	Females
a	b	c	d

HAMPSHIRE

		TOTAL PERSONS	Males	Females
	ALL OCCUPATIONS	71,873	40,790	31,083
1	Professional and related supporting management; senior national and local government managers	5,540	3,739	1,801
2	Professional and related in education, welfare and health	5,931	1,756	4,175
3	Literary, artistic and sports	848	491	357
4	Professional and related in science, engineering, technology and similar fields	4,792	4,151	641
5	Managerial	8,939	6,195	2,744
6	Clerical and related	11,812	2,262	9,550
7	Selling	4,583	1,682	2,901
8	Security and protective services	3,003	2,729	274
9	Catering, cleaning, hairdressing and other personal services	7,640	1,738	5,902
10	Farming, fishing and related	946	766	180
11	Materials processing: making and repairing (excluding metal and electrical)	2,849	2,207	642
12	Processing, making, repairing and related (metal and electrical)	5,978	5,624	354
13	Painting, repetitive assembling, product inspecting, packaging and related	2,250	1,367	883
14	Construction, mining and related, not identified elsewhere	2,166	2,139	27
15	Transport operating, materials moving and storing and related	3,549	3,233	316
16	Miscellaneous	483	399	84
17	Inadequately described and not stated	564	312	252

Basingstoke & Deane

		TOTAL PERSONS	Males	Females
	ALL OCCUPATIONS	7,472	4,237	3,235
1	Professional and related supporting management; senior national and local government managers	734	500	234
2	Professional and related in education, welfare and health	477	137	340
3	Literary, artistic and sports	86	44	42
4	Professional and related in science, engineering, technology and similar fields	610	518	92
5	Managerial	883	589	294
6	Clerical and related	1,426	253	1,173
7	Selling	429	173	256
8	Security and protective services	125	113	12
9	Catering, cleaning, hairdressing and other personal services	731	191	540
10	Farming, fishing and related	126	112	14
11	Materials processing: making and repairing (excluding metal and electrical)	300	241	59
12	Processing, making, repairing and related (metal and electrical)	567	546	21
13	Painting, repetitive assembling, product inspecting, packaging and related	218	128	90
14	Construction, mining and related, not identified elsewhere	220	215	5
15	Transport operating, materials moving and storing and related	444	405	39
16	Miscellaneous	43	39	4
17	Inadequately described and not stated	53	33	20

East Hampshire

		TOTAL PERSONS	Males	Females
	ALL OCCUPATIONS	4,956	2,821	2,135
1	Professional and related supporting management; senior national and local government managers	463	316	147
2	Professional and related in education, welfare and health	509	156	353
3	Literary, artistic and sports	82	44	38
4	Professional and related in science, engineering, technology and similar fields	292	263	29
5	Managerial	734	533	201
6	Clerical and related	729	116	613
7	Selling	276	121	155
8	Security and protective services	199	183	16
9	Catering, cleaning, hairdressing and other personal services	491	96	395
10	Farming, fishing and related	130	103	27
11	Materials processing: making and repairing (excluding metal and electrical)	195	148	47
12	Processing, making, repairing and related (metal and electrical)	312	286	26
13	Painting, repetitive assembling, product inspecting, packaging and related	121	76	45
14	Construction, mining and related, not identified elsewhere	183	180	3
15	Transport operating, materials moving and storing and related	182	162	20
16	Miscellaneous	29	24	5
17	Inadequately described and not stated	29	14	15

98. Residents aged 16 and over, employees and self-employed   (10% sample)

1980 occupation orders	TOTAL PERSONS	Males	Females
a	b	c	d

Eastleigh

		TOTAL PERSONS	Males	Females
	ALL OCCUPATIONS	**5,205**	**2,945**	**2,260**
1	Professional and related supporting management; senior national and local government managers	453	297	156
2	Professional and related in education, welfare and health	419	126	293
3	Literary, artistic and sports	60	35	25
4	Professional and related in science, engineering, technology and similar fields	363	319	44
5	Managerial	631	437	194
6	Clerical and related	970	167	803
7	Selling	397	160	237
8	Security and protective services	90	84	6
9	Catering, cleaning, hairdressing and other personal services	458	100	358
10	Farming, fishing and related	46	40	6
11	Materials processing: making and repairing (excluding metal and electrical)	223	194	29
12	Processing, making, repairing and related (metal and electrical)	489	476	13
13	Painting, repetitive assembling, product inspecting, packaging and related	157	93	64
14	Construction, mining and related, not identified elsewhere	127	126	1
15	Transport operating, materials moving and storing and related	265	249	16
16	Miscellaneous	30	29	1
17	Inadequately described and not stated	27	13	14

Fareham

		TOTAL PERSONS	Males	Females
	ALL OCCUPATIONS	**4,790**	**2,698**	**2,092**
1	Professional and related supporting management; senior national and local government managers	408	276	132
2	Professional and related in education, welfare and health	450	131	319
3	Literary, artistic and sports	58	36	22
4	Professional and related in science, engineering, technology and similar fields	372	320	52
5	Managerial	633	462	171
6	Clerical and related	794	123	671
7	Selling	289	98	191
8	Security and protective services	275	249	26
9	Catering, cleaning, hairdressing and other personal services	432	76	356
10	Farming, fishing and related	39	28	11
11	Materials processing: making and repairing (excluding metal and electrical)	168	130	38
12	Processing, making, repairing and related (metal and electrical)	386	364	22
13	Painting, repetitive assembling, product inspecting, packaging and related	116	77	39
14	Construction, mining and related, not identified elsewhere	127	125	2
15	Transport operating, materials moving and storing and related	176	160	16
16	Miscellaneous	29	24	5
17	Inadequately described and not stated	38	19	19

Gosport

		TOTAL PERSONS	Males	Females
	ALL OCCUPATIONS	**3,390**	**1,931**	**1,459**
1	Professional and related supporting management; senior national and local government managers	130	89	41
2	Professional and related in education, welfare and health	233	68	165
3	Literary, artistic and sports	30	19	11
4	Professional and related in science, engineering, technology and similar fields	156	134	22
5	Managerial	316	205	111
6	Clerical and related	493	81	412
7	Selling	213	59	154
8	Security and protective services	455	409	46
9	Catering, cleaning, hairdressing and other personal services	407	79	328
10	Farming, fishing and related	30	26	4
11	Materials processing: making and repairing (excluding metal and electrical)	138	102	36
12	Processing, making, repairing and related (metal and electrical)	380	347	33
13	Painting, repetitive assembling, product inspecting, packaging and related	114	59	55
14	Construction, mining and related, not identified elsewhere	80	80	-
15	Transport operating, materials moving and storing and related	157	131	26
16	Miscellaneous	29	27	2
17	Inadequately described and not stated	29	16	13

98. Residents aged 16 and over, employees and self-employed   (10% sample)

1980 occupation orders	TOTAL PERSONS	Males	Females
a	b	c	d

Hart

ALL OCCUPATIONS	**4,222**	**2,485**	**1,737**
1 Professional and related supporting management; senior national and local government managers	514	352	162
2 Professional and related in education, welfare and health	326	92	234
3 Literary, artistic and sports	56	26	30
4 Professional and related in science, engineering, technology and similar fields	377	322	55
5 Managerial	665	489	176
6 Clerical and related	676	108	568
7 Selling	263	113	150
8 Security and protective services	221	210	11
9 Catering, cleaning, hairdressing and other personal services	344	88	256
10 Farming, fishing and related	53	41	12
11 Materials processing: making and repairing (excluding metal and electrical)	108	91	17
12 Processing, making, repairing and related (metal and electrical)	276	262	14
13 Painting, repetitive assembling, product inspecting, packaging and related	65	44	21
14 Construction, mining and related, not identified elsewhere	92	90	2
15 Transport operating, materials moving and storing and related	141	133	8
16 Miscellaneous	12	9	3
17 Inadequately described and not stated	33	15	18

Havant

ALL OCCUPATIONS	**5,177**	**2,918**	**2,259**
1 Professional and related supporting management; senior national and local government managers	334	226	108
2 Professional and related in education, welfare and health	384	110	274
3 Literary, artistic and sports	59	35	24
4 Professional and related in science, engineering, technology and similar fields	371	330	41
5 Managerial	603	417	186
6 Clerical and related	765	173	592
7 Selling	361	106	255
8 Security and protective services	115	107	8
9 Catering, cleaning, hairdressing and other personal services	527	111	416
10 Farming, fishing and related	42	32	10
11 Materials processing: making and repairing (excluding metal and electrical)	258	194	64
12 Processing, making, repairing and related (metal and electrical)	531	463	68
13 Painting, repetitive assembling, product inspecting, packaging and related	292	129	163
14 Construction, mining and related, not identified elsewhere	212	209	3
15 Transport operating, materials moving and storing and related	238	218	20
16 Miscellaneous	37	31	6
17 Inadequately described and not stated	48	27	21

New Forest

ALL OCCUPATIONS	**6,894**	**3,847**	**3,047**
1 Professional and related supporting management; senior national and local government managers	471	314	157
2 Professional and related in education, welfare and health	596	173	423
3 Literary, artistic and sports	103	61	42
4 Professional and related in science, engineering, technology and similar fields	443	402	41
5 Managerial	952	650	302
6 Clerical and related	1,129	187	942
7 Selling	475	174	301
8 Security and protective services	121	107	14
9 Catering, cleaning, hairdressing and other personal services	760	158	602
10 Farming, fishing and related	143	110	33
11 Materials processing: making and repairing (excluding metal and electrical)	333	269	64
12 Processing, making, repairing and related (metal and electrical)	572	549	23
13 Painting, repetitive assembling, product inspecting, packaging and related	169	116	53
14 Construction, mining and related, not identified elsewhere	223	220	3
15 Transport operating, materials moving and storing and related	307	287	20
16 Miscellaneous	43	36	7
17 Inadequately described and not stated	54	34	20

98. Residents aged 16 and over, employees and self-employed   (10% sample)

1980 occupation orders	TOTAL PERSONS	Males	Females
a	b	c	d

Portsmouth

		TOTAL PERSONS	Males	Females
	ALL OCCUPATIONS	**7,563**	**4,288**	**3,275**
1	Professional and related supporting management; senior national and local government managers	407	271	136
2	Professional and related in education, welfare and health	619	181	438
3	Literary, artistic and sports	68	46	22
4	Professional and related in science, engineering, technology and similar fields	408	361	47
5	Managerial	778	509	269
6	Clerical and related	1,181	249	932
7	Selling	515	179	336
8	Security and protective services	445	413	32
9	Catering, cleaning, hairdressing and other personal services	978	257	721
10	Farming, fishing and related	37	34	3
11	Materials processing: making and repairing (excluding metal and electrical)	333	222	111
12	Processing, making, repairing and related (metal and electrical)	676	638	38
13	Painting, repetitive assembling, product inspecting, packaging and related	293	182	111
14	Construction, mining and related, not identified elsewhere	243	240	3
15	Transport operating, materials moving and storing and related	434	396	38
16	Miscellaneous	74	69	5
17	Inadequately described and not stated	74	41	33

Rushmoor

		TOTAL PERSONS	Males	Females
	ALL OCCUPATIONS	**4,333**	**2,464**	**1,869**
1	Professional and related supporting management; senior national and local government managers	318	201	117
2	Professional and related in education, welfare and health	247	60	187
3	Literary, artistic and sports	48	30	18
4	Professional and related in science, engineering, technology and similar fields	308	258	50
5	Managerial	473	325	148
6	Clerical and related	749	145	604
7	Selling	248	97	151
8	Security and protective services	467	412	55
9	Catering, cleaning, hairdressing and other personal services	458	106	352
10	Farming, fishing and related	21	17	4
11	Materials processing: making and repairing (excluding metal and electrical)	110	81	29
12	Processing, making, repairing and related (metal and electrical)	369	340	29
13	Painting, repetitive assembling, product inspecting, packaging and related	137	76	61
14	Construction, mining and related, not identified elsewhere	112	112	-
15	Transport operating, materials moving and storing and related	220	173	47
16	Miscellaneous	23	15	8
17	Inadequately described and not stated	25	16	9

Southampton

		TOTAL PERSONS	Males	Females
	ALL OCCUPATIONS	**8,320**	**4,643**	**3,677**
1	Professional and related supporting management; senior national and local government managers	458	287	171
2	Professional and related in education, welfare and health	773	262	511
3	Literary, artistic and sports	94	57	37
4	Professional and related in science, engineering, technology and similar fields	474	391	83
5	Managerial	782	496	286
6	Clerical and related	1,432	376	1,056
7	Selling	625	198	427
8	Security and protective services	120	95	25
9	Catering, cleaning, hairdressing and other personal services	1,052	265	787
10	Farming, fishing and related	51	45	6
11	Materials processing: making and repairing (excluding metal and electrical)	357	280	77
12	Processing, making, repairing and related (metal and electrical)	822	778	44
13	Painting, repetitive assembling, product inspecting, packaging and related	292	222	70
14	Construction, mining and related, not identified elsewhere	260	259	1
15	Transport operating, materials moving and storing and related	574	533	41
16	Miscellaneous	81	58	23
17	Inadequately described and not stated	73	41	32

98. Residents aged 16 and over, employees and self-employed   (10% sample)

1980 occupation orders	TOTAL PERSONS	Males	Females
a	b	c	d

Test Valley

ALL OCCUPATIONS	**5,030**	**2,915**	**2,115**
1 Professional and related supporting management; senior national and local government managers	384	274	110
2 Professional and related in education, welfare and health	406	113	293
3 Literary, artistic and sports	50	28	22
4 Professional and related in science, engineering, technology and similar fields	301	258	43
5 Managerial	743	549	194
6 Clerical and related	811	143	668
7 Selling	264	112	152
8 Security and protective services	206	198	8
9 Catering, cleaning, hairdressing and other personal services	502	95	407
10 Farming, fishing and related	105	84	21
11 Materials processing: making and repairing (excluding metal and electrical)	211	167	44
12 Processing, making, repairing and related (metal and electrical)	378	364	14
13 Painting, repetitive assembling, product inspecting, packaging and related	183	98	85
14 Construction, mining and related, not identified elsewhere	152	150	2
15 Transport operating, materials moving and storing and related	250	234	16
16 Miscellaneous	38	27	11
17 Inadequately described and not stated	46	21	25

Winchester

ALL OCCUPATIONS	**4,521**	**2,598**	**1,923**
1 Professional and related supporting management; senior national and local government managers	466	336	130
2 Professional and related in education, welfare and health	492	147	345
3 Literary, artistic and sports	54	30	24
4 Professional and related in science, engineering, technology and similar fields	317	275	42
5 Managerial	746	534	212
6 Clerical and related	657	141	516
7 Selling	228	92	136
8 Security and protective services	164	149	15
9 Catering, cleaning, hairdressing and other personal services	500	116	384
10 Farming, fishing and related	123	94	29
11 Materials processing: making and repairing (excluding metal and electrical)	115	88	27
12 Processing, making, repairing and related (metal and electrical)	220	211	9
13 Painting, repetitive assembling, product inspecting, packaging and related	93	67	26
14 Construction, mining and related, not identified elsewhere	135	133	2
15 Transport operating, materials moving and storing and related	161	152	9
16 Miscellaneous	15	11	4
17 Inadequately described and not stated	35	22	13

99. Residents aged 16 and over, employees and self-employed			(10% sample)
Standard Occupational Classification Minor Groups	TOTAL PERSONS	Males	Females
a	b	c	d

HAMPSHIRE

ALL OCCUPATIONS	**71,873**	**40,790**	**31,083**
1. Managers and administrators			
a) Corporate managers and administrators	**8,237**	**5,872**	**2,365**
10 General managers and administrators in national and local government, large companies and organisations	374	238	136
11 Production managers in manufacturing, construction, mining and energy industries	2,134	1,896	238
12 Specialist managers	2,464	1,662	802
13 Financial institution and office managers, civil service executive officers	1,573	780	793
14 Managers in transport and storing	527	436	91
15 Protective service officers	490	467	23
19 Managers and administrators nec	675	393	282
b) Managers/proprietors in agriculture and services	**3,933**	**2,387**	**1,546**
16 Managers in farming, horticulture, forestry and fishing	376	297	79
17 Managers and proprietors in service industries	3,557	2,090	1,467
2. Professional occupations			
a) Science and engineering professionals	**2,462**	**2,251**	**211**
20 Natural scientists	419	316	103
21 Engineers and technologists	2,043	1,935	108
b) Health professionals	**389**	**243**	**146**
22 Health professionals	389	243	146
c) Teaching professionals	**2,237**	**784**	**1,453**
23 Teaching professionals	2,237	784	1,453
d) Other professional occupations	**1,401**	**955**	**446**
24 Legal professionals	164	118	46
25 Business and financial professionals	565	428	137
26 Architects, town planners and surveyors	285	257	28
27 Librarians and related professionals	49	10	39
29 Professional occupations nec	338	142	196
3. Associate professional and technical occupations			
a) Science and engineering associate professionals	**2,504**	**1,973**	**531**
30 Scientific technicians	1,246	928	318
31 Draughtspersons, quantity and other surveyors	446	402	44
32 Computer analysts/programmers	812	643	169
b) Health associate professions	**1,566**	**141**	**1,425**
34 Health associate professionals	1,566	141	1,425
c) Other associate professional occupations	**2,737**	**1,670**	**1,067**
33 Ship and aircraft officers, air traffic planners and controllers	150	147	3
35 Legal associate professionals	97	40	57
36 Business and financial associate professionals	809	547	262
37 Social welfare associate professionals	373	82	291
38 Literary, artistic and sports professionals	780	505	275
39 Associate professional and technical occupations nec	528	349	179
4. Clerical and secretarial occupations			
a) Clerical occupations	**8,079**	**2,428**	**5,651**
40 Administrative/clerical officers and assistants in civil service and local government	1,225	301	924
41 Numerical clerks and cashiers	2,900	668	2,232
42 Filing and records clerks	800	213	587
43 Clerks (not otherwise specified)	1,647	285	1,362
44 Stores and despatch clerks, storekeepers	1,032	832	200
49 Clerical and secretarial occupations nec	475	129	346
b) Secretarial occupations	**3,496**	**105**	**3,391**
45 Secretaries, personal assistants, typists, word processor operators	2,645	33	2,612
46 Receptionists, telephonists and related occupations	851	72	779

99. Residents aged 16 and over, employees and self-employed   (10% sample)

Standard Occupational Classification Minor Groups	TOTAL PERSONS	Males	Females
a	b	c	d

HAMPSHIRE – *continued*

5. Craft and related occupations

a) Skilled construction trades	**1,888**	**1,860**	**28**
50 Construction trades	1,888	1,860	28
b) Skilled engineering trades	**3,135**	**3,040**	**95**
51 Metal machining, fitting and instrument making trades	1,790	1,744	46
52 Electrical/electronic trades	1,345	1,296	49
c) Other skilled trades	**4,466**	**3,891**	**575**
53 Metal forming, welding and related trades	1,131	1,091	40
54 Vehicle trades	755	729	26
55 Textiles, garments and related trades	338	112	226
56 Printing and related trades	370	253	117
57 Woodworking trades	880	869	11
58 Food preparation trades	201	164	37
59 Other craft and related occupations nec	791	673	118

6. Personal and protective service occupations

a) Protective service occupations	**3,035**	**2,752**	**283**
60 NCOs and other ranks, armed forces	2,077	1,920	157
61 Security and protective service occupations	958	832	126
b) Personal service occupations	**4,924**	**1,014**	**3,910**
62 Catering occupations	1,367	450	917
63 Travel attendants and related occupations	182	89	93
64 Health and related occupations	1,444	125	1,319
65 Childcare and related occupations	994	12	982
66 Hairdressers, beauticians and related occupations	269	19	250
67 Domestic staff and related occupations	452	176	276
69 Personal and protective service occupations nec	216	143	73

7. Sales occupations

a) Buyers, brokers and sales representatives	**1,362**	**1,015**	**347**
70 Buyers, brokers and related agents	210	152	58
71 Sales representatives	1,152	863	289
b) Other sales occupations	**3,935**	**832**	**3,103**
72 Sales assistants and check-out operators	3,555	656	2,899
73 Mobile, market and door-to-door salespersons and agents	162	141	21
79 Sales occupations nec	218	35	183

8. Plant and machine operatives

a) Industrial plant and machine operators, assemblers	**3,671**	**2,409**	**1,262**
80 Food, drink and tobacco process operatives	167	102	65
81 Textiles and tannery process operatives	25	11	14
82 Chemicals, paper, plastics and related process operatives	441	335	106
83 Metal making and treating process operatives	41	37	4
84 Metal working process operatives	438	370	68
85 Assemblers/lineworkers	672	314	358
86 Other routine process operatives	991	462	529
89 Plant and machine operatives nec	896	778	118
b) Drivers and mobile machine operators	**2,321**	**2,159**	**162**
87 Road transport operatives	1,721	1,585	136
88 Other transport and machinery operatives	600	574	26

9. Other occupations

a) Other occupations in agriculture, forestry and fishing	**433**	**326**	**107**
90 Other occupations in agriculture, forestry and fishing	433	326	107
b) Other elementary occupations	**5,166**	**2,371**	**2,795**
91 Other occupations in mining and manufacturing	281	215	66
92 Other occupations in construction	564	555	9
93 Other occupations in transport	255	249	6
94 Other occupations in communication	480	389	91
95 Other occupations in sales and services	3,334	739	2,595
99 Other occupations nec	252	224	28
Occupation not stated or inadequately described	**496**	**312**	**184**

99. Residents aged 16 and over, employees and self-employed

(10% sample)

Standard Occupational Classification Minor Groups	TOTAL PERSONS	Males	Females
a	b	c	d

Basingstoke & Deane

	TOTAL PERSONS	Males	Females
ALL OCCUPATIONS	7,472	4,237	3,235
1. Managers and administrators			
a) Corporate managers and administrators	**1,028**	**703**	**325**
10 General managers and administrators in national and local government, large companies and organisations	48	37	11
11 Production managers in manufacturing, construction, mining and energy industries	243	207	36
12 Specialist managers	385	268	117
13 Financial institution and office managers, civil service executive officers	213	103	110
14 Managers in transport and storing	51	38	13
15 Protective service officers	12	12	-
19 Managers and administrators nec	76	38	38
b) Managers/proprietors in agriculture and services	**313**	**198**	**115**
16 Managers in farming, horticulture, forestry and fishing	34	31	3
17 Managers and proprietors in service industries	279	167	112
2. Professional occupations			
a) Science and engineering professionals	**337**	**296**	**41**
20 Natural scientists	81	61	20
21 Engineers and technologists	256	235	21
b) Health professionals	**30**	**17**	**13**
22 Health professionals	30	17	13
c) Teaching professionals	**164**	**48**	**116**
23 Teaching professionals	164	48	116
d) Other professional occupations	**146**	**100**	**46**
24 Legal professionals	14	11	3
25 Business and financial professionals	74	51	23
26 Architects, town planners and surveyors	29	27	2
27 Librarians and related professionals	4	-	4
29 Professional occupations nec	25	11	14
3. Associate professional and technical occupations			
a) Science and engineering associate professionals	**303**	**237**	**66**
30 Scientific technicians	161	124	37
31 Draughtspersons, quantity and other surveyors	35	33	2
32 Computer analysts/programmers	107	80	27
b) Health associate professions	**146**	**19**	**127**
34 Health associate professionals	146	19	127
c) Other associate professional occupations	**278**	**165**	**113**
33 Ship and aircraft officers, air traffic planners and controllers	5	5	-
35 Legal associate professionals	10	1	9
36 Business and financial associate professionals	101	68	33
37 Social welfare associate professionals	19	4	15
38 Literary, artistic and sports professionals	86	48	38
39 Associate professional and technical occupations nec	57	39	18
4. Clerical and secretarial occupations			
a) Clerical occupations	**1,011**	**323**	**688**
40 Administrative/clerical officers and assistants in civil service and local government	147	40	107
41 Numerical clerks and cashiers	312	63	249
42 Filing and records clerks	100	22	78
43 Clerks (not otherwise specified)	202	40	162
44 Stores and despatch clerks, storekeepers	166	134	32
49 Clerical and secretarial occupations nec	84	24	60
b) Secretarial occupations	**458**	**12**	**446**
45 Secretaries, personal assistants, typists, word processor operators	350	3	347
46 Receptionists, telephonists and related occupations	108	9	99

99. Residents aged 16 and over, employees and self-employed (10% sample)

Standard Occupational Classification Minor Groups	TOTAL PERSONS	Males	Females
a	b	c	d

Basingstoke & Deane – *continued*

5. Craft and related occupations

a) Skilled construction trades | **187** | **185** | **2**
50   Construction trades | 187 | 185 | 2

b) Skilled engineering trades | **307** | **302** | **5**
51   Metal machining, fitting and instrument making trades | 159 | 157 | 2
52   Electrical/electronic trades | 148 | 145 | 3

c) Other skilled trades | **425** | **387** | **38**
53   Metal forming, welding and related trades | 81 | 77 | 4
54   Vehicle trades | 85 | 83 | 2
55   Textiles, garments and related trades | 24 | 14 | 10
56   Printing and related trades | 41 | 30 | 11
57   Woodworking trades | 97 | 95 | 2
58   Food preparation trades | 13 | 12 | 1
59   Other craft and related occupations nec | 84 | 76 | 8

6. Personal and protective service occupations

a) Protective service occupations | **126** | **114** | **12**
60   NCOs and other ranks, armed forces | 23 | 21 | 2
61   Security and protective service occupations | 103 | 93 | 10

b) Personal service occupations | **429** | **118** | **311**
62   Catering occupations | 119 | 49 | 70
63   Travel attendants and related occupations | 23 | 16 | 7
64   Health and related occupations | 95 | 13 | 82
65   Childcare and related occupations | 102 | 1 | 101
66   Hairdressers, beauticians and related occupations | 12 | 2 | 10
67   Domestic staff and related occupations | 60 | 26 | 34
69   Personal and protective service occupations nec | 18 | 11 | 7

7. Sales occupations

a) Buyers, brokers and sales representatives | **135** | **101** | **34**
70   Buyers, brokers and related agents | 17 | 12 | 5
71   Sales representatives | 118 | 89 | 29

b) Other sales occupations | **357** | **86** | **271**
72   Sales assistants and check-out operators | 324 | 74 | 250
73   Mobile, market and door-to-door salespersons and agents | 10 | 8 | 2
79   Sales occupations nec | 23 | 4 | 19

8. Plant and machine operatives

a) Industrial plant and machine operators, assemblers | **403** | **269** | **134**
80   Food, drink and tobacco process operatives | 9 | 4 | 5
81   Textiles and tannery process operatives | 4 | 2 | 2
82   Chemicals, paper, plastics and related process operatives | 78 | 56 | 22
83   Metal making and treating process operatives | 3 | 3 | -
84   Metal working process operatives | 38 | 34 | 4
85   Assemblers/lineworkers | 66 | 36 | 30
86   Other routine process operatives | 124 | 61 | 63
89   Plant and machine operatives nec | 81 | 73 | 8

b) Drivers and mobile machine operators | **264** | **249** | **15**
87   Road transport operatives | 209 | 198 | 11
88   Other transport and machinery operatives | 55 | 51 | 4

9. Other occupations

a) Other occupations in agriculture, forestry and fishing | **64** | **55** | **9**
90   Other occupations in agriculture, forestry and fishing | 64 | 55 | 9

b) Other elementary occupations | **512** | **220** | **292**
91   Other occupations in mining and manufacturing | 15 | 13 | 2
92   Other occupations in construction | 47 | 46 | 1
93   Other occupations in transport | 22 | 21 | 1
94   Other occupations in communication | 54 | 42 | 12
95   Other occupations in sales and services | 345 | 71 | 274
99   Other occupations nec | 29 | 27 | 2

Occupation not stated or inadequately described | **49** | **33** | **16**

99. Residents aged 16 and over, employees and self-employed (10% sample)

Standard Occupational Classification Minor Groups	TOTAL PERSONS	Males	Females
a	b	c	d

East Hampshire

ALL OCCUPATIONS	**4,956**	**2,821**	**2,135**
1. Managers and administrators			
a) Corporate managers and administrators	**673**	**511**	**162**
10 General managers and administrators in national and local government, large companies and organisations	33	23	10
11 Production managers in manufacturing, construction, mining and energy industries	182	165	17
12 Specialist managers	241	177	64
13 Financial institution and office managers, civil service executive officers	106	61	45
14 Managers in transport and storing	30	24	6
15 Protective service officers	32	30	2
19 Managers and administrators nec	49	31	18
b) Managers/proprietors in agriculture and services	**357**	**233**	**124**
16 Managers in farming, horticulture, forestry and fishing	65	45	20
17 Managers and proprietors in service industries	292	188	104
2. Professional occupations			
a) Science and engineering professionals	**167**	**156**	**11**
20 Natural scientists	25	23	2
21 Engineers and technologists	142	133	9
b) Health professionals	**35**	**21**	**14**
22 Health professionals	35	21	14
c) Teaching professionals	**230**	**67**	**163**
23 Teaching professionals	230	67	163
d) Other professional occupations	**116**	**85**	**31**
24 Legal professionals	18	13	5
25 Business and financial professionals	46	36	10
26 Architects, town planners and surveyors	24	23	1
27 Librarians and related professionals	1	1	-
29 Professional occupations nec	27	12	15
3. Associate professional and technical occupations			
a) Science and engineering associate professionals	**129**	**97**	**32**
30 Scientific technicians	56	42	14
31 Draughtspersons, quantity and other surveyors	22	21	1
32 Computer analysts/programmers	51	34	17
b) Health associate professions	**98**	**6**	**92**
34 Health associate professionals	98	6	92
c) Other associate professional occupations	**230**	**141**	**89**
33 Ship and aircraft officers, air traffic planners and controllers	12	12	-
35 Legal associate professionals	9	3	6
36 Business and financial associate professionals	58	39	19
37 Social welfare associate professionals	30	3	27
38 Literary, artistic and sports professionals	81	48	33
39 Associate professional and technical occupations nec	40	36	4
4. Clerical and secretarial occupations			
a) Clerical occupations	**441**	**122**	**319**
40 Administrative/clerical officers and assistants in civil service and local government	50	10	40
41 Numerical clerks and cashiers	200	43	157
42 Filing and records clerks	46	10	36
43 Clerks (not otherwise specified)	71	10	61
44 Stores and despatch clerks, storekeepers	60	45	15
49 Clerical and secretarial occupations nec	14	4	10
b) Secretarial occupations	**280**	**5**	**275**
45 Secretaries, personal assistants, typists, word processor operators	211	4	207
46 Receptionists, telephonists and related occupations	69	1	68

99. Residents aged 16 and over, employees and self-employed   (10% sample)

Standard Occupational Classification Minor Groups	TOTAL PERSONS	Males	Females
a	b	c	d

East Hampshire – *continued*

5. Craft and related occupations

a) Skilled construction trades	**153**	**151**	**2**
50 Construction trades	153	151	2
b) Skilled engineering trades	**167**	**156**	**11**
51 Metal machining, fitting and instrument making trades	85	81	4
52 Electrical/electronic trades	82	75	7
c) Other skilled trades	**310**	**265**	**45**
53 Metal forming, welding and related trades	53	51	2
54 Vehicle trades	47	46	1
55 Textiles, garments and related trades	31	11	20
56 Printing and related trades	17	11	6
57 Woodworking trades	56	56	-
58 Food preparation trades	15	13	2
59 Other craft and related occupations nec	91	77	14

6. Personal and protective service occupations

a) Protective service occupations	**200**	**183**	**17**
60 NCOs and other ranks, armed forces	152	142	10
61 Security and protective service occupations	48	41	7
b) Personal service occupations	**339**	**52**	**287**
62 Catering occupations	84	21	63
63 Travel attendants and related occupations	19	6	13
64 Health and related occupations	112	7	105
65 Childcare and related occupations	72	1	71
66 Hairdressers, beauticians and related occupations	10	1	9
67 Domestic staff and related occupations	34	11	23
69 Personal and protective service occupations nec	8	5	3

7. Sales occupations

a) Buyers, brokers and sales representatives	**102**	**77**	**25**
70 Buyers, brokers and related agents	12	7	5
71 Sales representatives	90	70	20
b) Other sales occupations	**208**	**49**	**159**
72 Sales assistants and check-out operators	182	37	145
73 Mobile, market and door-to-door salespersons and agents	11	11	-
79 Sales occupations nec	15	1	14

8. Plant and machine operatives

a) Industrial plant and machine operators, assemblers	**202**	**131**	**71**
80 Food, drink and tobacco process operatives	13	10	3
81 Textiles and tannery process operatives	1	1	-
82 Chemicals, paper, plastics and related process operatives	28	18	10
83 Metal making and treating process operatives	1	1	-
84 Metal working process operatives	27	22	5
85 Assemblers/lineworkers	32	15	17
86 Other routine process operatives	54	25	29
89 Plant and machine operatives nec	46	39	7
b) Drivers and mobile machine operators	**125**	**113**	**12**
87 Road transport operatives	85	76	9
88 Other transport and machinery operatives	40	37	3

9. Other occupations

a) Other occupations in agriculture, forestry and fishing	**69**	**51**	**18**
90 Other occupations in agriculture, forestry and fishing	69	51	18
b) Other elementary occupations	**298**	**135**	**163**
91 Other occupations in mining and manufacturing	8	7	1
92 Other occupations in construction	41	40	1
93 Other occupations in transport	5	5	-
94 Other occupations in communication	27	22	5
95 Other occupations in sales and services	196	44	152
99 Other occupations nec	21	17	4
Occupation not stated or inadequately described	**27**	**14**	**13**

99. Residents aged 16 and over, employees and self-employed
(10% sample)

Standard Occupational Classification Minor Groups	TOTAL PERSONS	Males	Females
a	b	c	d

Eastleigh

	TOTAL PERSONS	Males	Females
ALL OCCUPATIONS	5,205	2,945	2,260
1. Managers and administrators			
a) Corporate managers and administrators	619	436	183
10 General managers and administrators in national and local government, large companies and organisations	30	14	16
11 Production managers in manufacturing, construction, mining and energy industries	173	153	20
12 Specialist managers	186	126	60
13 Financial institution and office managers, civil service executive officers	103	48	55
14 Managers in transport and storing	42	37	5
15 Protective service officers	19	19	-
19 Managers and administrators nec	66	39	27
b) Managers/proprietors in agriculture and services	254	146	108
16 Managers in farming, horticulture, forestry and fishing	11	9	2
17 Managers and proprietors in service industries	243	137	106
2. Professional occupations			
a) Science and engineering professionals	164	158	6
20 Natural scientists	14	13	1
21 Engineers and technologists	150	145	5
b) Health professionals	18	9	9
22 Health professionals	18	9	9
c) Teaching professionals	179	77	102
23 Teaching professionals	179	77	102
d) Other professional occupations	106	70	36
24 Legal professionals	10	7	3
25 Business and financial professionals	46	36	10
26 Architects, town planners and surveyors	22	20	2
27 Librarians and related professionals	3	-	3
29 Professional occupations nec	25	7	18
3. Associate professional and technical occupations			
a) Science and engineering associate professionals	222	176	46
30 Scientific technicians	105	78	27
31 Draughtspersons, quantity and other surveyors	44	39	5
32 Computer analysts/programmers	73	59	14
b) Health associate professions	112	11	101
34 Health associate professionals	112	11	101
c) Other associate professional occupations	194	119	75
33 Ship and aircraft officers, air traffic planners and controllers	12	12	-
35 Legal associate professionals	9	5	4
36 Business and financial associate professionals	64	43	21
37 Social welfare associate professionals	23	3	20
38 Literary, artistic and sports professionals	51	34	17
39 Associate professional and technical occupations nec	35	22	13
4. Clerical and secretarial occupations			
a) Clerical occupations	641	179	462
40 Administrative/clerical officers and assistants in civil service and local government	62	11	51
41 Numerical clerks and cashiers	261	61	200
42 Filing and records clerks	68	22	46
43 Clerks (not otherwise specified)	142	24	118
44 Stores and despatch clerks, storekeepers	64	53	11
49 Clerical and secretarial occupations nec	44	8	36
b) Secretarial occupations	300	9	291
45 Secretaries, personal assistants, typists, word processor operators	234	1	233
46 Receptionists, telephonists and related occupations	66	8	58

99. Residents aged 16 and over, employees and self-employed

(10% sample)

Standard Occupational Classification Minor Groups	TOTAL PERSONS	Males	Females
a	b	c	d

Eastleigh – continued

5. Craft and related occupations

a) Skilled construction trades	**108**	**105**	**3**
50 Construction trades	108	105	3
b) Skilled engineering trades	**257**	**255**	**2**
51 Metal machining, fitting and instrument making trades	149	149	-
52 Electrical/electronic trades	108	106	2
c) Other skilled trades	**364**	**335**	**29**
53 Metal forming, welding and related trades	105	104	1
54 Vehicle trades	60	55	5
55 Textiles, garments and related trades	20	13	7
56 Printing and related trades	24	18	6
57 Woodworking trades	87	87	-
58 Food preparation trades	13	9	4
59 Other craft and related occupations nec	55	49	6

6. Personal and protective service occupations

a) Protective service occupations	**96**	**88**	**8**
60 NCOs and other ranks, armed forces	20	18	2
61 Security and protective service occupations	76	70	6
b) Personal service occupations	**312**	**53**	**259**
62 Catering occupations	92	27	65
63 Travel attendants and related occupations	14	6	8
64 Health and related occupations	87	7	80
65 Childcare and related occupations	76	1	75
66 Hairdressers, beauticians and related occupations	14	-	14
67 Domestic staff and related occupations	22	7	15
69 Personal and protective service occupations nec	7	5	2

7. Sales occupations

a) Buyers, brokers and sales representatives	**137**	**103**	**34**
70 Buyers, brokers and related agents	20	12	8
71 Sales representatives	117	91	26
b) Other sales occupations	**324**	**69**	**255**
72 Sales assistants and check-out operators	294	57	237
73 Mobile, market and door-to-door salespersons and agents	11	8	3
79 Sales occupations nec	19	4	15

8. Plant and machine operatives

a) Industrial plant and machine operators, assemblers	**259**	**183**	**76**
80 Food, drink and tobacco process operatives	15	9	6
81 Textiles and tannery process operatives	1	1	-
82 Chemicals, paper, plastics and related process operatives	18	16	2
83 Metal making and treating process operatives	2	2	-
84 Metal working process operatives	38	35	3
85 Assemblers/lineworkers	33	25	8
86 Other routine process operatives	84	30	54
89 Plant and machine operatives nec	68	65	3
b) Drivers and mobile machine operators	**191**	**181**	**10**
87 Road transport operatives	139	131	8
88 Other transport and machinery operatives	52	50	2

9. Other occupations

a) Other occupations in agriculture, forestry and fishing	**12**	**10**	**2**
90 Other occupations in agriculture, forestry and fishing	12	10	2
b) Other elementary occupations	**313**	**160**	**153**
91 Other occupations in mining and manufacturing	18	17	1
92 Other occupations in construction	38	37	1
93 Other occupations in transport	17	17	-
94 Other occupations in communication	29	21	8
95 Other occupations in sales and services	194	51	143
99 Other occupations nec	17	17	-
Occupation not stated or inadequately described	**23**	**13**	**10**

99. Residents aged 16 and over, employees and self-employed			(10% sample)
Standard Occupational Classification Minor Groups	TOTAL PERSONS	Males	Females
a	b	c	d

Fareham

	TOTAL PERSONS	Males	Females
ALL OCCUPATIONS	4,790	2,698	2,092
1. Managers and administrators			
a) Corporate managers and administrators	659	497	162
10 General managers and administrators in national and local government, large companies and organisations	42	31	11
11 Production managers in manufacturing, construction, mining and energy industries	178	166	12
12 Specialist managers	170	114	56
13 Financial institution and office managers, civil service executive officers	131	67	64
14 Managers in transport and storing	30	27	3
15 Protective service officers	68	65	3
19 Managers and administrators nec	40	27	13
b) Managers/proprietors in agriculture and services	229	131	98
16 Managers in farming, horticulture, forestry and fishing	12	9	3
17 Managers and proprietors in service industries	217	122	95
2. Professional occupations			
a) Science and engineering professionals	199	177	22
20 Natural scientists	30	16	14
21 Engineers and technologists	169	161	8
b) Health professionals	25	18	7
22 Health professionals	25	18	7
c) Teaching professionals	181	61	120
23 Teaching professionals	181	61	120
d) Other professional occupations	88	54	34
24 Legal professionals	11	6	5
25 Business and financial professionals	34	28	6
26 Architects, town planners and surveyors	19	15	4
27 Librarians and related professionals	4	-	4
29 Professional occupations nec	20	5	15
3. Associate professional and technical occupations			
a) Science and engineering associate professionals	176	136	40
30 Scientific technicians	94	71	23
31 Draughtspersons, quantity and other surveyors	27	25	2
32 Computer analysts/programmers	55	40	15
b) Health associate professions	138	14	124
34 Health associate professionals	138	14	124
c) Other associate professional occupations	213	143	70
33 Ship and aircraft officers, air traffic planners and controllers	18	18	-
35 Legal associate professionals	10	3	7
36 Business and financial associate professionals	74	55	19
37 Social welfare associate professionals	24	7	17
38 Literary, artistic and sports professionals	49	36	13
39 Associate professional and technical occupations nec	38	24	14
4. Clerical and secretarial occupations			
a) Clerical occupations	524	129	395
40 Administrative/clerical officers and assistants in civil service and local government	117	24	93
41 Numerical clerks and cashiers	198	39	159
42 Filing and records clerks	51	13	38
43 Clerks (not otherwise specified)	90	9	81
44 Stores and despatch clerks, storekeepers	50	41	9
49 Clerical and secretarial occupations nec	18	3	15
b) Secretarial occupations	239	2	237
45 Secretaries, personal assistants, typists, word processor operators	174	-	174
46 Receptionists, telephonists and related occupations	65	2	63

99. Residents aged 16 and over, employees and self-employed

(10% sample)

Standard Occupational Classification Minor Groups	TOTAL PERSONS	Males	Females
a	b	c	d

Fareham – continued

5. Craft and related occupations

a) Skilled construction trades | **93** | **93** | **-**

50 Construction trades | 93 | 93 | -

b) Skilled engineering trades | **222** | **218** | **4**

51 Metal machining, fitting and instrument making trades | 136 | 135 | 1
52 Electrical/electronic trades | 86 | 83 | 3

c) Other skilled trades | **285** | **249** | **36**

53 Metal forming, welding and related trades | 79 | 78 | 1
54 Vehicle trades | 33 | 33 | -
55 Textiles, garments and related trades | 29 | 8 | 21
56 Printing and related trades | 18 | 14 | 4

57 Woodworking trades | 72 | 72 | -
58 Food preparation trades | 7 | 7 | -
59 Other craft and related occupations nec | 47 | 37 | 10

6. Personal and protective service occupations

a) Protective service occupations | **279** | **251** | **28**

60 NCOs and other ranks, armed forces | 194 | 178 | 16
61 Security and protective service occupations | 85 | 73 | 12

b) Personal service occupations | **270** | **38** | **232**

62 Catering occupations | 66 | 18 | 48
63 Travel attendants and related occupations | 8 | 3 | 5
64 Health and related occupations | 82 | 7 | 75
65 Childcare and related occupations | 71 | - | 71

66 Hairdressers, beauticians and related occupations | 14 | - | 14
67 Domestic staff and related occupations | 17 | 3 | 14
69 Personal and protective service occupations nec | 12 | 7 | 5

7. Sales occupations

a) Buyers, brokers and sales representatives | **90** | **58** | **32**

70 Buyers, brokers and related agents | 14 | 9 | 5
71 Sales representatives | 76 | 49 | 27

b) Other sales occupations | **239** | **46** | **193**

72 Sales assistants and check-out operators | 211 | 35 | 176
73 Mobile, market and door-to-door salespersons and agents | 11 | 11 | -
79 Sales occupations nec | 17 | - | 17

8. Plant and machine operatives

a) Industrial plant and machine operators, assemblers | **187** | **121** | **66**

80 Food, drink and tobacco process operatives | 6 | 4 | 2
81 Textiles and tannery process operatives | 2 | 1 | 1
82 Chemicals, paper, plastics and related process operatives | 15 | 9 | 6
83 Metal making and treating process operatives | 2 | 1 | 1

84 Metal working process operatives | 27 | 24 | 3
85 Assemblers/lineworkers | 33 | 12 | 21
86 Other routine process operatives | 46 | 27 | 19
89 Plant and machine operatives nec | 56 | 43 | 13

b) Drivers and mobile machine operators | **116** | **109** | **7**

87 Road transport operatives | 81 | 75 | 6
88 Other transport and machinery operatives | 35 | 34 | 1

9. Other occupations

a) Other occupations in agriculture, forestry and fishing | **9** | **5** | **4**

90 Other occupations in agriculture, forestry and fishing | 9 | 5 | 4

b) Other elementary occupations | **300** | **129** | **171**

91 Other occupations in mining and manufacturing | 15 | 11 | 4
92 Other occupations in construction | 39 | 38 | 1
93 Other occupations in transport | 10 | 9 | 1
94 Other occupations in communication | 25 | 19 | 6
95 Other occupations in sales and services | 195 | 38 | 157
99 Other occupations nec | 16 | 14 | 2

Occupation not stated or inadequately described | **29** | **19** | **10**

99. Residents aged 16 and over, employees and self-employed   (10% sample)

Standard Occupational Classification Minor Groups	TOTAL PERSONS	Males	Females
a	b	c	d

Gosport

	TOTAL PERSONS	Males	Females
ALL OCCUPATIONS	3,390	1,931	1,459
1. Managers and administrators			
a) Corporate managers and administrators	273	187	86
10 General managers and administrators in national and local government, large companies and organisations	19	15	4
11 Production managers in manufacturing, construction, mining and energy industries	62	52	10
12 Specialist managers	52	35	17
13 Financial institution and office managers, civil service executive officers	59	16	43
14 Managers in transport and storing	15	11	4
15 Protective service officers	52	49	3
19 Managers and administrators nec	14	9	5
b) Managers/proprietors in agriculture and services	138	73	65
16 Managers in farming, horticulture, forestry and fishing	3	3	-
17 Managers and proprietors in service industries	135	70	65
2. Professional occupations			
a) Science and engineering professionals	65	60	5
20 Natural scientists	12	8	4
21 Engineers and technologists	53	52	1
b) Health professionals	11	9	2
22 Health professionals	11	9	2
c) Teaching professionals	59	22	37
23 Teaching professionals	59	22	37
d) Other professional occupations	28	20	8
24 Legal professionals	5	3	2
25 Business and financial professionals	3	3	-
26 Architects, town planners and surveyors	8	8	-
27 Librarians and related professionals	1	-	1
29 Professional occupations nec	11	6	5
3. Associate professional and technical occupations			
a) Science and engineering associate professionals	89	70	19
30 Scientific technicians	57	43	14
31 Draughtspersons, quantity and other surveyors	13	13	-
32 Computer analysts/programmers	19	14	5
b) Health associate professions	74	5	69
34 Health associate professionals	74	5	69
c) Other associate professional occupations	101	68	33
33 Ship and aircraft officers, air traffic planners and controllers	8	8	-
35 Legal associate professionals	3	1	2
36 Business and financial associate professionals	23	19	4
37 Social welfare associate professionals	16	3	13
38 Literary, artistic and sports professionals	22	18	4
39 Associate professional and technical occupations nec	29	19	10
4. Clerical and secretarial occupations			
a) Clerical occupations	370	94	276
40 Administrative/clerical officers and assistants in civil service and local government	110	18	92
41 Numerical clerks and cashiers	106	20	86
42 Filing and records clerks	26	4	22
43 Clerks (not otherwise specified)	52	6	46
44 Stores and despatch clerks, storekeepers	59	41	18
49 Clerical and secretarial occupations nec	17	5	12
b) Secretarial occupations	115	6	109
45 Secretaries, personal assistants, typists, word processor operators	79	2	77
46 Receptionists, telephonists and related occupations	36	4	32

99. Residents aged 16 and over, employees and self-employed   (10% sample)

Standard Occupational Classification Minor Groups	TOTAL PERSONS	Males	Females
a	b	c	d

Gosport – continued

5. Craft and related occupations

a) Skilled construction trades | **69** | **68** | **1** |
50 Construction trades	69	68	1
b) Skilled engineering trades	**216**	**212**	**4**
51 Metal machining, fitting and instrument making trades	147	144	3
52 Electrical/electronic trades	69	68	1
c) Other skilled trades	**206**	**180**	**26**
53 Metal forming, welding and related trades	63	60	3
54 Vehicle trades	34	31	3
55 Textiles, garments and related trades	15	1	14
56 Printing and related trades	11	9	2
57 Woodworking trades	37	37	-
58 Food preparation trades	12	9	3
59 Other craft and related occupations nec	34	33	1

6. Personal and protective service occupations

a) Protective service occupations	**455**	**409**	**46**
60 NCOs and other ranks, armed forces	380	347	33
61 Security and protective service occupations	75	62	13
b) Personal service occupations	**260**	**44**	**216**
62 Catering occupations	56	21	35
63 Travel attendants and related occupations	8	1	7
64 Health and related occupations	86	6	80
65 Childcare and related occupations	66	2	64
66 Hairdressers, beauticians and related occupations	15	-	15
67 Domestic staff and related occupations	22	9	13
69 Personal and protective service occupations nec	7	5	2

7. Sales occupations

a) Buyers, brokers and sales representatives	**36**	**27**	**9**
70 Buyers, brokers and related agents	5	4	1
71 Sales representatives	31	23	8
b) Other sales occupations	**214**	**37**	**177**
72 Sales assistants and check-out operators	193	26	167
73 Mobile, market and door-to-door salespersons and agents	11	10	1
79 Sales occupations nec	10	1	9

8. Plant and machine operatives

a) Industrial plant and machine operators, assemblers	**228**	**135**	**93**
80 Food, drink and tobacco process operatives	6	5	1
81 Textiles and tannery process operatives	9	2	7
82 Chemicals, paper, plastics and related process operatives	30	21	9
83 Metal making and treating process operatives	5	5	-
84 Metal working process operatives	20	18	2
85 Assemblers/lineworkers	37	13	24
86 Other routine process operatives	56	26	30
89 Plant and machine operatives nec	65	45	20
b) Drivers and mobile machine operators	**92**	**82**	**10**
87 Road transport operatives	71	61	10
88 Other transport and machinery operatives	21	21	-

9. Other occupations

a) Other occupations in agriculture, forestry and fishing	**7**	**4**	**3**
90 Other occupations in agriculture, forestry and fishing	7	4	3
b) Other elementary occupations	**257**	**103**	**154**
91 Other occupations in mining and manufacturing	19	16	3
92 Other occupations in construction	12	12	-
93 Other occupations in transport	10	9	1
94 Other occupations in communication	21	16	5
95 Other occupations in sales and services	181	36	145
99 Other occupations nec	14	14	-
Occupation not stated or inadequately described	**27**	**16**	**11**

99. Residents aged 16 and over, employees and self-employed (10% sample)

Standard Occupational Classification Minor Groups	TOTAL PERSONS	Males	Females
a	b	c	d

Hart

	TOTAL PERSONS	Males	Females
ALL OCCUPATIONS	4,222	2,485	1,737
1. Managers and administrators			
a) Corporate managers and administrators	733	548	185
10 General managers and administrators in national and local government, large companies and organisations	24	16	8
11 Production managers in manufacturing, construction, mining and energy industries	161	144	17
12 Specialist managers	279	200	79
13 Financial institution and office managers, civil service executive officers	132	83	49
14 Managers in transport and storing	26	23	3
15 Protective service officers	48	47	1
19 Managers and administrators nec	63	35	28
b) Managers/proprietors in agriculture and services	234	149	85
16 Managers in farming, horticulture, forestry and fishing	19	13	6
17 Managers and proprietors in service industries	215	136	79
2. Professional occupations			
a) Science and engineering professionals	233	211	22
20 Natural scientists	42	34	8
21 Engineers and technologists	191	177	14
b) Health professionals	30	18	12
22 Health professionals	30	18	12
c) Teaching professionals	139	35	104
23 Teaching professionals	139	35	104
d) Other professional occupations	120	79	41
24 Legal professionals	14	10	4
25 Business and financial professionals	64	45	19
26 Architects, town planners and surveyors	21	16	5
27 Librarians and related professionals	6	1	5
29 Professional occupations nec	15	7	8
3. Associate professional and technical occupations			
a) Science and engineering associate professionals	150	111	39
30 Scientific technicians	67	42	25
31 Draughtspersons, quantity and other surveyors	25	23	2
32 Computer analysts/programmers	58	46	12
b) Health associate professions	81	3	78
34 Health associate professionals	81	3	78
c) Other associate professional occupations	192	117	75
33 Ship and aircraft officers, air traffic planners and controllers	13	13	-
35 Legal associate professionals	5	1	4
36 Business and financial associate professionals	67	47	20
37 Social welfare associate professionals	9	1	8
38 Literary, artistic and sports professionals	57	29	28
39 Associate professional and technical occupations nec	41	26	15
4. Clerical and secretarial occupations			
a) Clerical occupations	402	100	302
40 Administrative/clerical officers and assistants in civil service and local government	52	18	34
41 Numerical clerks and cashiers	152	29	123
42 Filing and records clerks	49	10	39
43 Clerks (not otherwise specified)	105	17	88
44 Stores and despatch clerks, storekeepers	26	23	3
49 Clerical and secretarial occupations nec	18	3	15
b) Secretarial occupations	238	6	232
45 Secretaries, personal assistants, typists, word processor operators	199	5	194
46 Receptionists, telephonists and related occupations	39	1	38

99. Residents aged 16 and over, employees and self-employed			(10% sample)
Standard Occupational Classification Minor Groups	TOTAL PERSONS	Males	Females
a	b	c	d

Hart – *continued*

5. Craft and related occupations			
a) Skilled construction trades	**79**	**77**	**2**
50 Construction trades	79	77	2
b) Skilled engineering trades	**156**	**152**	**4**
51 Metal machining, fitting and instrument making trades	96	95	1
52 Electrical/electronic trades	60	57	3
c) Other skilled trades	**205**	**184**	**21**
53 Metal forming, welding and related trades	44	43	1
54 Vehicle trades	41	40	1
55 Textiles, garments and related trades	4	3	1
56 Printing and related trades	24	18	6
57 Woodworking trades	40	38	2
58 Food preparation trades	6	6	-
59 Other craft and related occupations nec	46	36	10
6. Personal and protective service occupations			
a) Protective service occupations	**224**	**212**	**12**
60 NCOs and other ranks, armed forces	184	176	8
61 Security and protective service occupations	40	36	4
b) Personal service occupations	**229**	**55**	**174**
62 Catering occupations	65	24	41
63 Travel attendants and related occupations	17	10	7
64 Health and related occupations	45	7	38
65 Childcare and related occupations	56	-	56
66 Hairdressers, beauticians and related occupations	18	3	15
67 Domestic staff and related occupations	18	2	16
69 Personal and protective service occupations nec	10	9	1
7. Sales occupations			
a) Buyers, brokers and sales representatives	**109**	**85**	**24**
70 Buyers, brokers and related agents	21	15	6
71 Sales representatives	88	70	18
b) Other sales occupations	**204**	**43**	**161**
72 Sales assistants and check-out operators	189	35	154
73 Mobile, market and door-to-door salespersons and agents	4	4	-
79 Sales occupations nec	11	4	7
8. Plant and machine operatives			
a) Industrial plant and machine operators, assemblers	**115**	**84**	**31**
80 Food, drink and tobacco process operatives	2	1	1
81 Textiles and tannery process operatives	2	2	-
82 Chemicals, paper, plastics and related process operatives	7	4	3
83 Metal making and treating process operatives	3	2	1
84 Metal working process operatives	20	19	1
85 Assemblers/lineworkers	14	4	10
86 Other routine process operatives	30	19	11
89 Plant and machine operatives nec	37	33	4
b) Drivers and mobile machine operators	**102**	**95**	**7**
87 Road transport operatives	76	69	7
88 Other transport and machinery operatives	26	26	-
9. Other occupations			
a) Other occupations in agriculture, forestry and fishing	**23**	**16**	**7**
90 Other occupations in agriculture, forestry and fishing	23	16	7
b) Other elementary occupations	**201**	**90**	**111**
91 Other occupations in mining and manufacturing	3	2	1
92 Other occupations in construction	17	17	-
93 Other occupations in transport	12	12	-
94 Other occupations in communication	21	18	3
95 Other occupations in sales and services	137	33	104
99 Other occupations nec	11	8	3
Occupation not stated or inadequately described	**23**	**15**	**8**

99. Residents aged 16 and over, employees and self-employed

(10% sample)

Standard Occupational Classification Minor Groups	TOTAL PERSONS	Males	Females
a	b	c	d

Havant

	TOTAL PERSONS	Males	Females
ALL OCCUPATIONS	**5,177**	**2,918**	**2,259**
1. Managers and administrators			
a) Corporate managers and administrators	**541**	**374**	**167**
10 General managers and administrators in national and local government, large companies and organisations	17	8	9
11 Production managers in manufacturing, construction, mining and energy industries	174	149	25
12 Specialist managers	128	86	42
13 Financial institution and office managers, civil service executive officers	99	41	58
14 Managers in transport and storing	44	32	12
15 Protective service officers	36	36	-
19 Managers and administrators nec	43	22	21
b) Managers/proprietors in agriculture and services	**235**	**146**	**89**
16 Managers in farming, horticulture, forestry and fishing	11	9	2
17 Managers and proprietors in service industries	224	137	87
2. Professional occupations			
a) Science and engineering professionals	**190**	**182**	**8**
20 Natural scientists	22	19	3
21 Engineers and technologists	168	163	5
b) Health professionals	**24**	**14**	**10**
22 Health professionals	24	14	10
c) Teaching professionals	**150**	**53**	**97**
23 Teaching professionals	150	53	97
d) Other professional occupations	**78**	**55**	**23**
24 Legal professionals	6	5	1
25 Business and financial professionals	35	27	8
26 Architects, town planners and surveyors	18	16	2
27 Librarians and related professionals	2	-	2
29 Professional occupations nec	17	7	10
3. Associate professional and technical occupations			
a) Science and engineering associate professionals	**210**	**168**	**42**
30 Scientific technicians	113	87	26
31 Draughtspersons, quantity and other surveyors	29	24	5
32 Computer analysts/programmers	68	57	11
b) Health associate professions	**93**	**8**	**85**
34 Health associate professionals	93	8	85
c) Other associate professional occupations	**168**	**108**	**60**
33 Ship and aircraft officers, air traffic planners and controllers	11	11	-
35 Legal associate professionals	4	-	4
36 Business and financial associate professionals	40	26	14
37 Social welfare associate professionals	28	9	19
38 Literary, artistic and sports professionals	50	36	14
39 Associate professional and technical occupations nec	35	26	9
4. Clerical and secretarial occupations			
a) Clerical occupations	**532**	**177**	**355**
40 Administrative/clerical officers and assistants in civil service and local government	70	28	42
41 Numerical clerks and cashiers	199	57	142
42 Filing and records clerks	51	18	33
43 Clerks (not otherwise specified)	125	19	106
44 Stores and despatch clerks, storekeepers	62	48	14
49 Clerical and secretarial occupations nec	25	7	18
b) Secretarial occupations	**199**	**8**	**191**
45 Secretaries, personal assistants, typists, word processor operators	146	3	143
46 Receptionists, telephonists and related occupations	53	5	48

99. Residents aged 16 and over, employees and self-employed (10% sample)

Standard Occupational Classification Minor Groups	TOTAL PERSONS	Males	Females
a	b	c	d

Havant – continued

5. Craft and related occupations

a) Skilled construction trades | **165** | **159** | **6**

| 50 | Construction trades | 165 | 159 | 6 |

b) Skilled engineering trades | **278** | **262** | **16**

| 51 | Metal machining, fitting and instrument making trades | 170 | 162 | 8 |
| 52 | Electrical/electronic trades | 108 | 100 | 8 |

c) Other skilled trades | **374** | **309** | **65**

53	Metal forming, welding and related trades	96	86	10
54	Vehicle trades	47	45	2
55	Textiles, garments and related trades	44	11	33
56	Printing and related trades	31	21	10
57	Woodworking trades	83	83	-
58	Food preparation trades	21	20	1
59	Other craft and related occupations nec	52	43	9

6. Personal and protective service occupations

a) Protective service occupations | **117** | **109** | **8**

| 60 | NCOs and other ranks, armed forces | 50 | 49 | 1 |
| 61 | Security and protective service occupations | 67 | 60 | 7 |

b) Personal service occupations | **360** | **71** | **289**

62	Catering occupations	95	30	65
63	Travel attendants and related occupations	10	4	6
64	Health and related occupations	120	9	111
65	Childcare and related occupations	63	-	63
66	Hairdressers, beauticians and related occupations	27	1	26
67	Domestic staff and related occupations	24	11	13
69	Personal and protective service occupations nec	21	16	5

7. Sales occupations

a) Buyers, brokers and sales representatives | **101** | **69** | **32**

| 70 | Buyers, brokers and related agents | 20 | 14 | 6 |
| 71 | Sales representatives | 81 | 55 | 26 |

b) Other sales occupations | **327** | **52** | **275**

72	Sales assistants and check-out operators	300	44	256
73	Mobile, market and door-to-door salespersons and agents	8	6	2
79	Sales occupations nec	19	2	17

8. Plant and machine operatives

a) Industrial plant and machine operators, assemblers | **448** | **234** | **214**

80	Food, drink and tobacco process operatives	12	8	4
81	Textiles and tannery process operatives	1	-	1
82	Chemicals, paper, plastics and related process operatives	42	32	10
83	Metal making and treating process operatives	2	2	-
84	Metal working process operatives	62	38	24
85	Assemblers/lineworkers	116	31	85
86	Other routine process operatives	131	53	78
89	Plant and machine operatives nec	82	70	12

b) Drivers and mobile machine operators | **159** | **146** | **13**

| 87 | Road transport operatives | 102 | 94 | 8 |
| 88 | Other transport and machinery operatives | 57 | 52 | 5 |

9. Other occupations

a) Other occupations in agriculture, forestry and fishing | **12** | **8** | **4**

| 90 | Other occupations in agriculture, forestry and fishing | 12 | 8 | 4 |

b) Other elementary occupations | **371** | **179** | **192**

91	Other occupations in mining and manufacturing	31	22	9
92	Other occupations in construction	53	53	-
93	Other occupations in transport	26	26	-
94	Other occupations in communication	32	26	6
95	Other occupations in sales and services	217	40	177
99	Other occupations nec	12	12	-

Occupation not stated or inadequately described | **45** | **27** | **18**

99. Residents aged 16 and over, employees and self-employed   (10% sample)

Standard Occupational Classification Minor Groups	TOTAL PERSONS	Males	Females
a	b	c	d

New Forest

	TOTAL PERSONS	Males	Females
ALL OCCUPATIONS	**6,894**	**3,847**	**3,047**
1. Managers and administrators			
a) Corporate managers and administrators	**735**	**538**	**197**
10 General managers and administrators in national and local government, large companies and organisations	26	15	11
11 Production managers in manufacturing, construction, mining and energy industries	244	223	21
12 Specialist managers	215	133	82
13 Financial institution and office managers, civil service executive officers	122	68	54
14 Managers in transport and storing	58	53	5
15 Protective service officers	14	13	1
19 Managers and administrators nec	56	33	23
b) Managers/proprietors in agriculture and services	**502**	**289**	**213**
16 Managers in farming, horticulture, forestry and fishing	62	51	11
17 Managers and proprietors in service industries	440	238	202
2. Professional occupations			
a) Science and engineering professionals	**192**	**178**	**14**
20 Natural scientists	21	15	6
21 Engineers and technologists	171	163	8
b) Health professionals	**53**	**37**	**16**
22 Health professionals	53	37	16
c) Teaching professionals	**199**	**67**	**132**
23 Teaching professionals	199	67	132
d) Other professional occupations	**121**	**90**	**31**
24 Legal professionals	22	18	4
25 Business and financial professionals	39	37	2
26 Architects, town planners and surveyors	24	21	3
27 Librarians and related professionals	4	-	4
29 Professional occupations nec	32	14	18
3. Associate professional and technical occupations			
a) Science and engineering associate professionals	**222**	**193**	**29**
30 Scientific technicians	141	123	18
31 Draughtspersons, quantity and other surveyors	47	44	3
32 Computer analysts/programmers	34	26	8
b) Health associate professions	**152**	**12**	**140**
34 Health associate professionals	152	12	140
c) Other associate professional occupations	**292**	**186**	**106**
33 Ship and aircraft officers, air traffic planners and controllers	28	26	2
35 Legal associate professionals	15	6	9
36 Business and financial associate professionals	82	58	24
37 Social welfare associate professionals	38	13	25
38 Literary, artistic and sports professionals	83	55	28
39 Associate professional and technical occupations nec	46	28	18
4. Clerical and secretarial occupations			
a) Clerical occupations	**715**	**199**	**516**
40 Administrative/clerical officers and assistants in civil service and local government	69	15	54
41 Numerical clerks and cashiers	315	76	239
42 Filing and records clerks	77	20	57
43 Clerks (not otherwise specified)	144	22	122
44 Stores and despatch clerks, storekeepers	66	54	12
49 Clerical and secretarial occupations nec	44	12	32
b) Secretarial occupations	**382**	**12**	**370**
45 Secretaries, personal assistants, typists, word processor operators	284	1	283
46 Receptionists, telephonists and related occupations	98	11	87

99. Residents aged 16 and over, employees and self-employed
(10% sample)

Standard Occupational Classification Minor Groups	TOTAL PERSONS	Males	Females
a	b	c	d

New Forest – continued

5. Craft and related occupations

a) Skilled construction trades | **199** | **196** | **3**

50 | Construction trades | 199 | 196 | 3

b) Skilled engineering trades | **282** | **274** | **8**

51 | Metal machining, fitting and instrument making trades | 167 | 164 | 3
52 | Electrical/electronic trades | 115 | 110 | 5

c) Other skilled trades | **452** | **387** | **65**

53 | Metal forming, welding and related trades | 106 | 104 | 2
54 | Vehicle trades | 83 | 80 | 3
55 | Textiles, garments and related trades | 21 | 9 | 12
56 | Printing and related trades | 36 | 18 | 18

57 | Woodworking trades | 81 | 80 | 1
58 | Food preparation trades | 34 | 22 | 12
59 | Other craft and related occupations nec | 91 | 74 | 17

6. Personal and protective service occupations

a) Protective service occupations | **124** | **109** | **15**

60 | NCOs and other ranks, armed forces | 51 | 47 | 4
61 | Security and protective service occupations | 73 | 62 | 11

b) Personal service occupations | **556** | **98** | **458**

62 | Catering occupations | 166 | 58 | 108
63 | Travel attendants and related occupations | 10 | 2 | 8
64 | Health and related occupations | 198 | 11 | 187
65 | Childcare and related occupations | 87 | 1 | 86

66 | Hairdressers, beauticians and related occupations | 33 | 2 | 31
67 | Domestic staff and related occupations | 40 | 10 | 30
69 | Personal and protective service occupations nec | 22 | 14 | 8

7. Sales occupations

a) Buyers, brokers and sales representatives | **139** | **110** | **29**

70 | Buyers, brokers and related agents | 17 | 13 | 4
71 | Sales representatives | 122 | 97 | 25

b) Other sales occupations | **415** | **81** | **334**

72 | Sales assistants and check-out operators | 378 | 67 | 311
73 | Mobile, market and door-to-door salespersons and agents | 14 | 9 | 5
79 | Sales occupations nec | 23 | 5 | 18

8. Plant and machine operatives

a) Industrial plant and machine operators, assemblers | **361** | **282** | **79**

80 | Food, drink and tobacco process operatives | 30 | 18 | 12
81 | Textiles and tannery process operatives | 1 | - | 1
82 | Chemicals, paper, plastics and related process operatives | 89 | 84 | 5
83 | Metal making and treating process operatives | 6 | 5 | 1

84 | Metal working process operatives | 46 | 42 | 4
85 | Assemblers/lineworkers | 46 | 20 | 26
86 | Other routine process operatives | 52 | 26 | 26
89 | Plant and machine operatives nec | 91 | 87 | 4

b) Drivers and mobile machine operators | **219** | **207** | **12**

87 | Road transport operatives | 159 | 148 | 11
88 | Other transport and machinery operatives | 60 | 59 | 1

9. Other occupations

a) Other occupations in agriculture, forestry and fishing | **73** | **54** | **19**

90 | Other occupations in agriculture, forestry and fishing | 73 | 54 | 19

b) Other elementary occupations | **457** | **214** | **243**

91 | Other occupations in mining and manufacturing | 30 | 24 | 6
92 | Other occupations in construction | 70 | 68 | 2
93 | Other occupations in transport | 27 | 26 | 1
94 | Other occupations in communication | 28 | 17 | 11
95 | Other occupations in sales and services | 285 | 63 | 222
99 | Other occupations nec | 17 | 16 | 1

Occupation not stated or inadequately described | **52** | **34** | **18**

99. Residents aged 16 and over, employees and self-employed   (10% sample)

Standard Occupational Classification Minor Groups	TOTAL PERSONS	Males	Females
a	b	c	d

Portsmouth

	TOTAL PERSONS	Males	Females
ALL OCCUPATIONS	**7,563**	**4,288**	**3,275**
1. Managers and administrators			
a) Corporate managers and administrators	**603**	**388**	**215**
10 General managers and administrators in national and local government, large companies and organisations	31	15	16
11 Production managers in manufacturing, construction, mining and energy industries	135	118	17
12 Specialist managers	126	70	56
13 Financial institution and office managers, civil service executive officers	151	62	89
14 Managers in transport and storing	58	47	11
15 Protective service officers	43	41	2
19 Managers and administrators nec	59	35	24
b) Managers/proprietors in agriculture and services	**398**	**239**	**159**
16 Managers in farming, horticulture, forestry and fishing	-	-	-
17 Managers and proprietors in service industries	398	239	159
2. Professional occupations			
a) Science and engineering professionals	**228**	**209**	**19**
20 Natural scientists	35	28	7
21 Engineers and technologists	193	181	12
b) Health professionals	**27**	**16**	**11**
22 Health professionals	27	16	11
c) Teaching professionals	**192**	**80**	**112**
23 Teaching professionals	192	80	112
d) Other professional occupations	**99**	**60**	**39**
24 Legal professionals	15	11	4
25 Business and financial professionals	30	19	11
26 Architects, town planners and surveyors	14	12	2
27 Librarians and related professionals	5	3	2
29 Professional occupations nec	35	15	20
3. Associate professional and technical occupations			
a) Science and engineering associate professionals	**240**	**198**	**42**
30 Scientific technicians	108	86	22
31 Draughtspersons, quantity and other surveyors	31	29	2
32 Computer analysts/programmers	101	83	18
b) Health associate professions	**191**	**19**	**172**
34 Health associate professionals	191	19	172
c) Other associate professional occupations	**258**	**157**	**101**
33 Ship and aircraft officers, air traffic planners and controllers	13	13	-
35 Legal associate professionals	12	7	5
36 Business and financial associate professionals	61	43	18
37 Social welfare associate professionals	55	11	44
38 Literary, artistic and sports professionals	64	52	12
39 Associate professional and technical occupations nec	53	31	22
4. Clerical and secretarial occupations			
a) Clerical occupations	**858**	**272**	**586**
40 Administrative/clerical officers and assistants in civil service and local government	152	35	117
41 Numerical clerks and cashiers	279	62	217
42 Filing and records clerks	73	18	55
43 Clerks (not otherwise specified)	172	32	140
44 Stores and despatch clerks, storekeepers	128	108	20
49 Clerical and secretarial occupations nec	54	17	37
b) Secretarial occupations	**276**	**9**	**267**
45 Secretaries, personal assistants, typists, word processor operators	196	2	194
46 Receptionists, telephonists and related occupations	80	7	73

99. Residents aged 16 and over, employees and self-employed   (10% sample)

Standard Occupational Classification Minor Groups	TOTAL PERSONS	Males	Females
a	b	c	d

Portsmouth – continued

5. Craft and related occupations

a) Skilled construction trades | **228** | **227** | **1**

| 50 | Construction trades | 228 | 227 | 1 |

b) Skilled engineering trades | **362** | **352** | **10**

| 51 | Metal machining, fitting and instrument making trades | 205 | 202 | 3 |
| 52 | Electrical/electronic trades | 157 | 150 | 7 |

c) Other skilled trades | **495** | **397** | **98**

53	Metal forming, welding and related trades	135	127	8
54	Vehicle trades	70	69	1
55	Textiles, garments and related trades	70	11	59
56	Printing and related trades	57	40	17
57	Woodworking trades	85	85	-
58	Food preparation trades	19	18	1
59	Other craft and related occupations nec	59	47	12

6. Personal and protective service occupations

a) Protective service occupations | **450** | **418** | **32**

| 60 | NCOs and other ranks, armed forces | 344 | 323 | 21 |
| 61 | Security and protective service occupations | 106 | 95 | 11 |

b) Personal service occupations | **608** | **156** | **452**

62	Catering occupations	171	67	104
63	Travel attendants and related occupations	23	17	6
64	Health and related occupations	188	14	174
65	Childcare and related occupations	103	3	100
66	Hairdressers, beauticians and related occupations	32	3	29
67	Domestic staff and related occupations	50	24	26
69	Personal and protective service occupations nec	41	28	13

7. Sales occupations

a) Buyers, brokers and sales representatives | **109** | **86** | **23**

| 70 | Buyers, brokers and related agents | 26 | 18 | 8 |
| 71 | Sales representatives | 83 | 68 | 15 |

b) Other sales occupations | **490** | **108** | **382**

72	Sales assistants and check-out operators	439	80	359
73	Mobile, market and door-to-door salespersons and agents	30	27	3
79	Sales occupations nec	21	1	20

8. Plant and machine operatives

a) Industrial plant and machine operators, assemblers | **413** | **261** | **152**

80	Food, drink and tobacco process operatives	13	8	5
81	Textiles and tannery process operatives	3	2	1
82	Chemicals, paper, plastics and related process operatives	39	23	16
83	Metal making and treating process operatives	4	4	-
84	Metal working process operatives	45	37	8
85	Assemblers/lineworkers	86	37	49
86	Other routine process operatives	125	62	63
89	Plant and machine operatives nec	98	88	10

b) Drivers and mobile machine operators | **279** | **256** | **23**

| 87 | Road transport operatives | 211 | 190 | 21 |
| 88 | Other transport and machinery operatives | 68 | 66 | 2 |

9. Other occupations

a) Other occupations in agriculture, forestry and fishing | **9** | **8** | **1**

| 90 | Other occupations in agriculture, forestry and fishing | 9 | 8 | 1 |

b) Other elementary occupations | **689** | **331** | **358**

91	Other occupations in mining and manufacturing	40	35	5
92	Other occupations in construction	73	71	2
93	Other occupations in transport	35	35	-
94	Other occupations in communication	55	46	9
95	Other occupations in sales and services	449	109	340
99	Other occupations nec	37	35	2

Occupation not stated or inadequately described | **61** | **41** | **20**

99. Residents aged 16 and over, employees and self-employed   (10% sample)

Standard Occupational Classification Minor Groups	TOTAL PERSONS	Males	Females
a	b	c	d

Rushmoor

ALL OCCUPATIONS	**4,333**	**2,464**	**1,869**
1. Managers and administrators			
a) Corporate managers and administrators	**494**	**336**	**158**
10 General managers and administrators in national and local government, large companies and organisations	24	15	9
11 Production managers in manufacturing, construction, mining and energy industries	102	90	12
12 Specialist managers	147	95	52
13 Financial institution and office managers, civil service executive officers	101	48	53
14 Managers in transport and storing	35	28	7
15 Protective service officers	47	41	6
19 Managers and administrators nec	38	19	19
b) Managers/proprietors in agriculture and services	**165**	**100**	**65**
16 Managers in farming, horticulture, forestry and fishing	1	1	-
17 Managers and proprietors in service industries	164	99	65
2. Professional occupations			
a) Science and engineering professionals	**180**	**164**	**16**
20 Natural scientists	46	37	9
21 Engineers and technologists	134	127	7
b) Health professionals	**9**	**4**	**5**
22 Health professionals	9	4	5
c) Teaching professionals	**80**	**20**	**60**
23 Teaching professionals	80	20	60
d) Other professional occupations	**51**	**31**	**20**
24 Legal professionals	2	1	1
25 Business and financial professionals	28	19	9
26 Architects, town planners and surveyors	6	6	-
27 Librarians and related professionals	2	-	2
29 Professional occupations nec	13	5	8
3. Associate professional and technical occupations			
a) Science and engineering associate professionals	**149**	**113**	**36**
30 Scientific technicians	69	46	23
31 Draughtspersons, quantity and other surveyors	30	27	3
32 Computer analysts/programmers	50	40	10
b) Health associate professions	**74**	**12**	**62**
34 Health associate professionals	74	12	62
c) Other associate professional occupations	**163**	**92**	**71**
33 Ship and aircraft officers, air traffic planners and controllers	5	4	1
35 Legal associate professionals	4	2	2
36 Business and financial associate professionals	47	28	19
37 Social welfare associate professionals	14	1	13
38 Literary, artistic and sports professionals	54	35	19
39 Associate professional and technical occupations nec	39	22	17
4. Clerical and secretarial occupations			
a) Clerical occupations	**549**	**152**	**397**
40 Administrative/clerical officers and assistants in civil service and local government	92	21	71
41 Numerical clerks and cashiers	175	32	143
42 Filing and records clerks	44	16	28
43 Clerks (not otherwise specified)	112	23	89
44 Stores and despatch clerks, storekeepers	89	49	40
49 Clerical and secretarial occupations nec	37	11	26
b) Secretarial occupations	**205**	**6**	**199**
45 Secretaries, personal assistants, typists, word processor operators	154	2	152
46 Receptionists, telephonists and related occupations	51	4	47

99. Residents aged 16 and over, employees and self-employed (10% sample)

Standard Occupational Classification Minor Groups	TOTAL PERSONS	Males	Females
a	b	c	d

Rushmoor – continued

5. Craft and related occupations

a) Skilled construction trades | **105** | **104** | **1**

| 50 | Construction trades | 105 | 104 | 1 |

b) Skilled engineering trades | **197** | **190** | **7**

| 51 | Metal machining, fitting and instrument making trades | 114 | 108 | 6 |
| 52 | Electrical/electronic trades | 83 | 82 | 1 |

c) Other skilled trades | **219** | **190** | **29**

53	Metal forming, welding and related trades	60	57	3
54	Vehicle trades	49	47	2
55	Textiles, garments and related trades	12	5	7
56	Printing and related trades	29	21	8
57	Woodworking trades	29	28	1
58	Food preparation trades	8	6	2
59	Other craft and related occupations nec	32	26	6

6. Personal and protective service occupations

a) Protective service occupations | **468** | **412** | **56**

| 60 | NCOs and other ranks, armed forces | 400 | 354 | 46 |
| 61 | Security and protective service occupations | 68 | 58 | 10 |

b) Personal service occupations | **282** | **59** | **223**

62	Catering occupations	96	24	72
63	Travel attendants and related occupations	11	6	5
64	Health and related occupations	69	6	63
65	Childcare and related occupations	51	1	50
66	Hairdressers, beauticians and related occupations	16	1	15
67	Domestic staff and related occupations	27	13	14
69	Personal and protective service occupations nec	12	8	4

7. Sales occupations

a) Buyers, brokers and sales representatives | **87** | **58** | **29**

| 70 | Buyers, brokers and related agents | 9 | 6 | 3 |
| 71 | Sales representatives | 78 | 52 | 26 |

b) Other sales occupations | **195** | **47** | **148**

72	Sales assistants and check-out operators	182	41	141
73	Mobile, market and door-to-door salespersons and agents	4	4	-
79	Sales occupations nec	9	2	7

8. Plant and machine operatives

a) Industrial plant and machine operators, assemblers | **191** | **107** | **84**

80	Food, drink and tobacco process operatives	3	2	1
81	Textiles and tannery process operatives	-	-	-
82	Chemicals, paper, plastics and related process operatives	14	8	6
83	Metal making and treating process operatives	3	3	-
84	Metal working process operatives	29	22	7
85	Assemblers/lineworkers	42	13	29
86	Other routine process operatives	60	25	35
89	Plant and machine operatives nec	40	34	6

b) Drivers and mobile machine operators | **117** | **107** | **10**

| 87 | Road transport operatives | 88 | 79 | 9 |
| 88 | Other transport and machinery operatives | 29 | 28 | 1 |

9. Other occupations

a) Other occupations in agriculture, forestry and fishing | **4** | **2** | **2**

| 90 | Other occupations in agriculture, forestry and fishing | 4 | 2 | 2 |

b) Other elementary occupations | **326** | **142** | **184**

91	Other occupations in mining and manufacturing	8	4	4
92	Other occupations in construction	33	33	-
93	Other occupations in transport	17	17	-
94	Other occupations in communication	42	33	9
95	Other occupations in sales and services	210	43	167
99	Other occupations nec	16	12	4

Occupation not stated or inadequately described | **23** | **16** | **7**

99. Residents aged 16 and over, employees and self-employed   (10% sample)

Standard Occupational Classification Minor Groups	TOTAL PERSONS	Males	Females
a	b	c	d

Southampton

ALL OCCUPATIONS	**8,320**	**4,643**	**3,677**
1. Managers and administrators			
a) Corporate managers and administrators	**611**	**400**	**211**
10 General managers and administrators in national and local government, large companies and organisations	25	15	10
11 Production managers in manufacturing, construction, mining and energy industries	151	133	18
12 Specialist managers	170	96	74
13 Financial institution and office managers, civil service executive officers	125	58	67
14 Managers in transport and storing	66	59	7
15 Protective service officers	7	6	1
19 Managers and administrators nec	67	33	34
b) Managers/proprietors in agriculture and services	**413**	**233**	**180**
16 Managers in farming, horticulture, forestry and fishing	6	3	3
17 Managers and proprietors in service industries	407	230	177
2. Professional occupations			
a) Science and engineering professionals	**196**	**178**	**18**
20 Natural scientists	44	31	13
21 Engineers and technologists	152	147	5
b) Health professionals	**49**	**32**	**17**
22 Health professionals	49	32	17
c) Teaching professionals	**269**	**133**	**136**
23 Teaching professionals	269	133	136
d) Other professional occupations	**161**	**104**	**57**
24 Legal professionals	13	6	7
25 Business and financial professionals	60	45	15
26 Architects, town planners and surveyors	23	20	3
27 Librarians and related professionals	8	3	5
29 Professional occupations nec	57	30	27
3. Associate professional and technical occupations			
a) Science and engineering associate professionals	**301**	**230**	**71**
30 Scientific technicians	157	105	52
31 Draughtspersons, quantity and other surveyors	74	65	9
32 Computer analysts/programmers	70	60	10
b) Health associate professions	**220**	**19**	**201**
34 Health associate professionals	220	19	201
c) Other associate professional occupations	**283**	**154**	**129**
33 Ship and aircraft officers, air traffic planners and controllers	12	12	-
35 Legal associate professionals	4	3	1
36 Business and financial associate professionals	73	37	36
37 Social welfare associate professionals	59	15	44
38 Literary, artistic and sports professionals	83	54	29
39 Associate professional and technical occupations nec	52	33	19
4. Clerical and secretarial occupations			
a) Clerical occupations	**1,001**	**362**	**639**
40 Administrative/clerical officers and assistants in civil service and local government	116	33	83
41 Numerical clerks and cashiers	348	94	254
42 Filing and records clerks	110	33	77
43 Clerks (not otherwise specified)	227	48	179
44 Stores and despatch clerks, storekeepers	144	134	10
49 Clerical and secretarial occupations nec	56	20	36
b) Secretarial occupations	**374**	**27**	**347**
45 Secretaries, personal assistants, typists, word processor operators	270	7	263
46 Receptionists, telephonists and related occupations	104	20	84

99. Residents aged 16 and over, employees and self-employed

(10% sample)

Standard Occupational Classification Minor Groups	TOTAL PERSONS	Males	Females
a	b	c	d

Southampton – *continued*

5. *Craft and related occupations*

a) Skilled construction trades | **271** | **268** | **3**

| 50 | Construction trades | 271 | 268 | 3 |

b) Skilled engineering trades | **402** | **387** | **15**

| 51 | Metal machining, fitting and instrument making trades | 202 | 190 | 12 |
| 52 | Electrical/electronic trades | 200 | 197 | 3 |

c) Other skilled trades | **571** | **518** | **53**

53	Metal forming, welding and related trades	169	166	3
54	Vehicle trades	111	110	1
55	Textiles, garments and related trades	40	18	22
56	Printing and related trades	41	28	13
57	Woodworking trades	98	96	2
58	Food preparation trades	29	21	8
59	Other craft and related occupations nec	83	79	4

6. *Personal and protective service occupations*

a) Protective service occupations | **126** | **100** | **26**

| 60 | NCOs and other ranks, armed forces | 22 | 20 | 2 |
| 61 | Security and protective service occupations | 104 | 80 | 24 |

b) Personal service occupations | **645** | **153** | **492**

62	Catering occupations	172	62	110
63	Travel attendants and related occupations	20	11	9
64	Health and related occupations	205	24	181
65	Childcare and related occupations	116	1	115
66	Hairdressers, beauticians and related occupations	42	4	38
67	Domestic staff and related occupations	56	31	25
69	Personal and protective service occupations nec	34	20	14

7. *Sales occupations*

a) Buyers, brokers and sales representatives | **149** | **113** | **36**

| 70 | Buyers, brokers and related agents | 20 | 17 | 3 |
| 71 | Sales representatives | 129 | 96 | 33 |

b) Other sales occupations | **563** | **113** | **450**

72	Sales assistants and check-out operators	510	78	432
73	Mobile, market and door-to-door salespersons and agents	28	26	2
79	Sales occupations nec	25	9	16

8. *Plant and machine operatives*

a) Industrial plant and machine operators, assemblers | **447** | **324** | **123**

80	Food, drink and tobacco process operatives	39	21	18
81	Textiles and tannery process operatives	-	-	-
82	Chemicals, paper, plastics and related process operatives	42	35	7
83	Metal making and treating process operatives	6	6	-
84	Metal working process operatives	41	35	6
85	Assemblers/lineworkers	96	72	24
86	Other routine process operatives	92	46	46
89	Plant and machine operatives nec	131	109	22

b) Drivers and mobile machine operators | **385** | **353** | **32**

| 87 | Road transport operatives | 297 | 272 | 25 |
| 88 | Other transport and machinery operatives | 88 | 81 | 7 |

9. *Other occupations*

a) Other occupations in agriculture, forestry and fishing | **10** | **6** | **4**

| 90 | Other occupations in agriculture, forestry and fishing | 10 | 6 | 4 |

b) Other elementary occupations | **807** | **395** | **412**

91	Other occupations in mining and manufacturing	63	44	19
92	Other occupations in construction	67	67	-
93	Other occupations in transport	50	50	-
94	Other occupations in communication	98	88	10
95	Other occupations in sales and services	496	117	379
99	Other occupations nec	33	29	4

Occupation not stated or inadequately described | **66** | **41** | **25**

99. Residents aged 16 and over, employees and self-employed   (10% sample)

Standard Occupational Classification Minor Groups	TOTAL PERSONS	Males	Females
a	b	c	d

Test Valley

	TOTAL PERSONS	Males	Females
ALL OCCUPATIONS	**5,030**	**2,915**	**2,115**
1. Managers and administrators			
a) Corporate managers and administrators	**631**	**482**	**149**
10 General managers and administrators in national and local government, large companies and organisations	31	21	10
11 Production managers in manufacturing, construction, mining and energy industries	156	145	11
12 Specialist managers	173	128	45
13 Financial institution and office managers, civil service executive officers	129	72	57
14 Managers in transport and storing	46	35	11
15 Protective service officers	58	55	3
19 Managers and administrators nec	38	26	12
b) Managers/proprietors in agriculture and services	**337**	**222**	**115**
16 Managers in farming, horticulture, forestry and fishing	65	52	13
17 Managers and proprietors in service industries	272	170	102
2. Professional occupations			
a) Science and engineering professionals	**128**	**115**	**13**
20 Natural scientists	17	9	8
21 Engineers and technologists	111	106	5
b) Health professionals	**38**	**25**	**13**
22 Health professionals	38	25	13
c) Teaching professionals	**171**	**54**	**117**
23 Teaching professionals	171	54	117
d) Other professional occupations	**119**	**85**	**34**
24 Legal professionals	20	18	2
25 Business and financial professionals	35	25	10
26 Architects, town planners and surveyors	34	32	2
27 Librarians and related professionals	4	2	2
29 Professional occupations nec	26	8	18
3. Associate professional and technical occupations			
a) Science and engineering associate professionals	**171**	**136**	**35**
30 Scientific technicians	72	51	21
31 Draughtspersons, quantity and other surveyors	47	42	5
32 Computer analysts/programmers	52	43	9
b) Health associate professions	**88**	**1**	**87**
34 Health associate professionals	88	1	87
c) Other associate professional occupations	**170**	**97**	**73**
33 Ship and aircraft officers, air traffic planners and controllers	8	8	-
35 Legal associate professionals	4	2	2
36 Business and financial associate professionals	53	37	16
37 Social welfare associate professionals	28	6	22
38 Literary, artistic and sports professionals	45	27	18
39 Associate professional and technical occupations nec	32	17	15
4. Clerical and secretarial occupations			
a) Clerical occupations	**594**	**176**	**418**
40 Administrative/clerical officers and assistants in civil service and local government	94	22	72
41 Numerical clerks and cashiers	202	47	155
42 Filing and records clerks	62	15	47
43 Clerks (not otherwise specified)	118	15	103
44 Stores and despatch clerks, storekeepers	81	69	12
49 Clerical and secretarial occupations nec	37	8	29
b) Secretarial occupations	**227**	**1**	**226**
45 Secretaries, personal assistants, typists, word processor operators	178	1	177
46 Receptionists, telephonists and related occupations	49	-	49

99. Residents aged 16 and over, employees and self-employed   (10% sample)

Standard Occupational Classification Minor Groups	TOTAL PERSONS	Males	Females
a	b	c	d

Test Valley – *continued*

5. Craft and related occupations

a) Skilled construction trades | **122** | **120** | **2**

| 50 | Construction trades | 122 | 120 | 2 |

b) Skilled engineering trades | **192** | **186** | **6**

| 51 | Metal machining, fitting and instrument making trades | 109 | 107 | 2 |
| 52 | Electrical/electronic trades | 83 | 79 | 4 |

c) Other skilled trades | **314** | **277** | **37**

53	Metal forming, welding and related trades	78	77	1
54	Vehicle trades	61	56	5
55	Textiles, garments and related trades	19	7	12
56	Printing and related trades	22	16	6
57	Woodworking trades	66	66	-
58	Food preparation trades	12	11	1
59	Other craft and related occupations nec	56	44	12

6. Personal and protective service occupations

a) Protective service occupations | **206** | **198** | **8**

| 60 | NCOs and other ranks, armed forces | 155 | 154 | 1 |
| 61 | Security and protective service occupations | 51 | 44 | 7 |

b) Personal service occupations | **309** | **50** | **259**

62	Catering occupations	101	25	76
63	Travel attendants and related occupations	8	1	7
64	Health and related occupations	66	6	60
65	Childcare and related occupations	77	1	76
66	Hairdressers, beauticians and related occupations	15	-	15
67	Domestic staff and related occupations	29	9	20
69	Personal and protective service occupations nec	13	8	5

7. Sales occupations

a) Buyers, brokers and sales representatives | **108** | **80** | **28**

| 70 | Buyers, brokers and related agents | 21 | 19 | 2 |
| 71 | Sales representatives | 87 | 61 | 26 |

b) Other sales occupations | **205** | **49** | **156**

72	Sales assistants and check-out operators	177	37	140
73	Mobile, market and door-to-door salespersons and agents	13	11	2
79	Sales occupations nec	15	1	14

8. Plant and machine operatives

a) Industrial plant and machine operators, assemblers | **296** | **190** | **106**

80	Food, drink and tobacco process operatives	11	8	3
81	Textiles and tannery process operatives	1	-	1
82	Chemicals, paper, plastics and related process operatives	32	22	10
83	Metal making and treating process operatives	2	2	-
84	Metal working process operatives	29	29	-
85	Assemblers/lineworkers	60	29	31
86	Other routine process operatives	94	41	53
89	Plant and machine operatives nec	67	59	8

b) Drivers and mobile machine operators | **156** | **150** | **6**

| 87 | Road transport operatives | 114 | 108 | 6 |
| 88 | Other transport and machinery operatives | 42 | 42 | - |

9. Other occupations

a) Other occupations in agriculture, forestry and fishing | **65** | **51** | **14**

| 90 | Other occupations in agriculture, forestry and fishing | 65 | 51 | 14 |

b) Other elementary occupations | **344** | **149** | **195**

91	Other occupations in mining and manufacturing	19	13	6
92	Other occupations in construction	39	38	1
93	Other occupations in transport	18	16	2
94	Other occupations in communication	26	21	5
95	Other occupations in sales and services	221	45	176
99	Other occupations nec	21	16	5

Occupation not stated or inadequately described | **39** | **21** | **18**

99. Residents aged 16 and over, employees and self-employed

(10% sample)

Standard Occupational Classification Minor Groups	TOTAL PERSONS	Males	Females
a	b	c	d

Winchester

	TOTAL PERSONS	Males	Females
ALL OCCUPATIONS	4,521	2,598	1,923
1. Managers and administrators			
a) Corporate managers and administrators	637	472	165
10 General managers and administrators in national and local government, large companies and organisations	24	13	11
11 Production managers in manufacturing, construction, mining and energy industries	173	151	22
12 Specialist managers	192	134	58
13 Financial institution and office managers, civil service executive officers	102	53	49
14 Managers in transport and storing	26	22	4
15 Protective service officers	54	53	1
19 Managers and administrators nec	66	46	20
b) Managers/proprietors in agriculture and services	358	228	130
16 Managers in farming, horticulture, forestry and fishing	87	71	16
17 Managers and proprietors in service industries	271	157	114
2. Professional occupations			
a) Science and engineering professionals	183	167	16
20 Natural scientists	30	22	8
21 Engineers and technologists	153	145	8
b) Health professionals	40	23	17
22 Health professionals	40	23	17
c) Teaching professionals	224	67	157
23 Teaching professionals	224	67	157
d) Other professional occupations	168	122	46
24 Legal professionals	14	9	5
25 Business and financial professionals	71	57	14
26 Architects, town planners and surveyors	43	41	2
27 Librarians and related professionals	5	-	5
29 Professional occupations nec	35	15	20
3. Associate professional and technical occupations			
a) Science and engineering associate professionals	142	108	34
30 Scientific technicians	46	30	16
31 Draughtspersons, quantity and other surveyors	22	17	5
32 Computer analysts/programmers	74	61	13
b) Health associate professions	99	12	87
34 Health associate professionals	99	12	87
c) Other associate professional occupations	195	123	72
33 Ship and aircraft officers, air traffic planners and controllers	5	5	-
35 Legal associate professionals	8	6	2
36 Business and financial associate professionals	66	47	19
37 Social welfare associate professionals	30	6	24
38 Literary, artistic and sports professionals	55	33	22
39 Associate professional and technical occupations nec	31	26	5
4. Clerical and secretarial occupations			
a) Clerical occupations	441	143	298
40 Administrative/clerical officers and assistants in civil service and local government	94	26	68
41 Numerical clerks and cashiers	153	45	108
42 Filing and records clerks	43	12	31
43 Clerks (not otherwise specified)	87	20	67
44 Stores and despatch clerks, storekeepers	37	33	4
49 Clerical and secretarial occupations nec	27	7	20
b) Secretarial occupations	203	2	201
45 Secretaries, personal assistants, typists, word processor operators	170	2	168
46 Receptionists, telephonists and related occupations	33	-	33

99. Residents aged 16 and over, employees and self-employed   (10% sample)

Standard Occupational Classification Minor Groups	TOTAL PERSONS	Males	Females
a	b	c	d

Winchester – continued

	TOTAL PERSONS	Males	Females
5. Craft and related occupations			
a) Skilled construction trades	**109**	**107**	**2**
50 Construction trades	109	107	2
b) Skilled engineering trades	**97**	**94**	**3**
51 Metal machining, fitting and instrument making trades	51	50	1
52 Electrical/electronic trades	46	44	2
c) Other skilled trades	**246**	**213**	**33**
53 Metal forming, welding and related trades	62	61	1
54 Vehicle trades	34	34	-
55 Textiles, garments and related trades	9	1	8
56 Printing and related trades	19	9	10
57 Woodworking trades	49	46	3
58 Food preparation trades	12	10	2
59 Other craft and related occupations nec	61	52	9
6. Personal and protective service occupations			
a) Protective service occupations	**164**	**149**	**15**
60 NCOs and other ranks, armed forces	102	91	11
61 Security and protective service occupations	62	58	4
b) Personal service occupations	**325**	**67**	**258**
62 Catering occupations	84	24	60
63 Travel attendants and related occupations	11	6	5
64 Health and related occupations	91	8	83
65 Childcare and related occupations	54	-	54
66 Hairdressers, beauticians and related occupations	21	2	19
67 Domestic staff and related occupations	53	20	33
69 Personal and protective service occupations nec	11	7	4
7. Sales occupations			
a) Buyers, brokers and sales representatives	**60**	**48**	**12**
70 Buyers, brokers and related agents	8	6	2
71 Sales representatives	52	42	10
b) Other sales occupations	**194**	**52**	**142**
72 Sales assistants and check-out operators	176	45	131
73 Mobile, market and door-to-door salespersons and agents	7	6	1
79 Sales occupations nec	11	1	10
8. Plant and machine operatives			
a) Industrial plant and machine operators, assemblers	**121**	**88**	**33**
80 Food, drink and tobacco process operatives	8	4	4
81 Textiles and tannery process operatives	-	-	-
82 Chemicals, paper, plastics and related process operatives	7	7	-
83 Metal making and treating process operatives	2	1	1
84 Metal working process operatives	16	15	1
85 Assemblers/lineworkers	11	7	4
86 Other routine process operatives	43	21	22
89 Plant and machine operatives nec	34	33	1
b) Drivers and mobile machine operators	**116**	**111**	**5**
87 Road transport operatives	89	84	5
88 Other transport and machinery operatives	27	27	-
9. Other occupations			
a) Other occupations in agriculture, forestry and fishing	**76**	**56**	**20**
90 Other occupations in agriculture, forestry and fishing	76	56	20
b) Other elementary occupations	**291**	**124**	**167**
91 Other occupations in mining and manufacturing	12	7	5
92 Other occupations in construction	35	35	-
93 Other occupations in transport	6	6	-
94 Other occupations in communication	22	20	2
95 Other occupations in sales and services	208	49	159
99 Other occupations nec	8	7	1
Occupation not stated or inadequately described	**32**	**22**	**10**

Date of change	Authority for change	Existing area i.e. as constituted at 21st April 1991 (names or descriptions not existing on 5th April 1981 are marked *)	Composition of existing area in terms of areas as constituted at 5th April 1981 (names or descriptions of counties/districts which have now ceased to exist are marked #)	Present population 1981	Existing areas in which the balance (if any) of the area named in col d is now situated
a	b	c	d	e	f
1st April 1991	The Berkshire, Buckinghamshire, Hampshire, Oxfordshire and Surrey (County Boundaries) Order 1991	HAMPSHIRE	Hampshire	1,467,142 1,466,385	
			except:		
			Basingstoke and Deane (pt)		
			Silchester Ward (pt)	− 264	†Berkshire
			Hart (pt)		†Berkshire
			Eversley Ward (pt)	-	
			Berkshire (pt)		
			viz:		
			Newbury (pt)		†Berkshire
			No 7 Ward (pt)	-	
			No 11 Ward (pt)	+1,021	
			Wokingham (pt)		†Berkshire
			Finchampstead Ward (pt)	-	
1st April 1985	The Hampshire (Areas) Order 1985	Basingstoke and Deane	Basingstoke and Deane	131,264 130,526	Winchester
			except:		
			North Waltham Ward (pt)	− 19	
1st April 1991	The Berkshire, Buckinghamshire, Hampshire, Oxfordshire and Surrey (County Boundaries) Order 1991		Basingstoke and Deane		Newbury †(Berkshire)
			except:		
			Silchester Ward (pt)	− 264	
			Newbury (pt)		Newbury †(Berkshire)
			viz:		
			No 7 Ward (pt)	-	
			No 11 Ward (pt)	+1,021	
1st April 1984	The East Hampshire and Havant (Areas) Order 1983	East Hampshire	East Hampshire	90,585 90,613	Havant
			except:		
			Horndean-Hazleton Ward (pt)	− 8	
			Horndean-Kings Ward (pt)	− 45	
			Havant (pt)		Havant
			viz:		
			Cowplain Ward (pt)	+21	
			Hart Plain Ward (pt)	+11	
1st April 1985	The Hampshire (Areas) Order 1985		East Hampshire		Winchester
			except:		
			Clanfield and Buriton Ward (pt)	− 11	
			Froxfield and Steep Ward (pt)	-	
			Medstead Ward (pt)	-	
			Winchester (pt)		Winchester
			viz:		
			Bishops Sutton Ward (pt)	+2	
			Upper Meon Valley Ward (pt)	+2	

†See relevant County Report

Notes:- Hectare measurements for those areas affected by boundary changes have not been included because the figures are not routinely available.

Changes of boundaries may involve areas of land with no population present in 1981, this is shown by a dash in Column e.

Where changes have affected ward or parish boundaries and/or names, details can be obtained from the Office of Population Censuses and Surveys, Census Customer Services, Titchfield, Fareham, Hants. PO15 5RR.

Date of change	Authority for change	Existing area i.e. as constituted at 21st April 1991 (names or descriptions not existing on 5th April 1981 are marked *)	Composition of existing area in terms of areas as constituted at 5th April 1981 (names or descriptions of counties/districts which have now ceased to exist are marked #)	Present population 1981	Existing areas in which the balance (if any) of the area named in col d is now situated
a	b	c	d	e	f
1st April 1985	The Hampshire (Areas) Order 1985	Eastleigh		92,952	
			Eastleigh	92,954	Winchester
			except:		
			Eastleigh North Ward (pt)	− 6	
			Winchester (pt)		Winchester
			viz:		
			Otterbourne and Hursley Ward (pt)	+4	
1st April 1990	The Hampshire (District Boundaries) Order 1990	Hart		72,717	
			Hart	76,158	Rushmoor
			except:		
			Hawley Ward (pt)	− 3,441	
			Rushmoor (pt)		Rushmoor
			viz:		
			Cove Ward (pt)	-	
1st April 1991	The Berkshire, Buckinghamshire, Hampshire, Oxfordshire and Surrey (County Boundaries) Order 1991		Hart		Wokingham †(Berkshire)
			except:		
			Eversley Ward (pt)	-	
			Wokingham (pt)		Wokingham †(Berkshire)
			viz:		
			Finchampstead Ward (pt)	-	
1st April 1984	The East Hampshire and Havant (Areas) Order 1983	Havant		117,449	
			Havant	117,428	East Hampshire
			except:		
			Cowplain Ward (pt)	− 21	
			Hart Plain Ward (pt)	− 11	
			East Hampshire (pt)		East Hampshire
			viz:		
			Horndean-Hazleton Ward (pt)	+8	
			Horndean-Kings Ward (pt)	+45	
1st April 1990	The Hampshire (District Boundaries) Order 1990	Rushmoor		81,684	
			Rushmoor	78,243	Hart
			except:		
			Cove Ward (pt)	-	
			Hart (pt)		Hart
			viz:		
			Hawley Ward (pt)	+3,441	
1st April 1985	The Hampshire (Areas) Order 1985	Test Valley		91,436	
			Test Valley	91,407	
			Winchester (pt)		Winchester
			viz:		
			Sparsholt Ward (pt)	+29	

†See relevant County Report

Notes:- Hectare measurements for those areas affected by boundary changes have not been included because the figures are not routinely available.

Changes of boundaries may involve areas of land with no population present in 1981, this is shown by a dash in Column e.

Where changes have affected ward or parish boundaries and/or names, details can be obtained from the Office of Population Censuses and Surveys, Census Customer Services, Titchfield, Fareham, Hants. PO15 5RR.

Date of change	Authority for change	Existing area i.e. as constituted at 21st April 1991 (names or descriptions not existing on 5th April 1981 are marked *)	Composition of existing area in terms of areas as constituted at 5th April 1981 (names or descriptions of counties/districts which have now ceased to exist are marked #)	Present population 1981	Existing areas in which the balance (if any) of the area named in col d is now situated
a	b	c	d	e	f
1st April 1985	The Hampshire (Areas) Order 1985	Winchester		90,826	
			Winchester except:	90,827	East Hampshire, Eastleigh, Test Valley
			Bishops Sutton Ward (pt)	− 2	
			Otterbourne and Hursley Ward (pt)	− 4	
			Sparsholt Ward (pt)	− 29	
			Upper Meon Valley Ward (pt)	− 2	
			Basingstoke and Deane (pt) viz:		Basingstoke and Deane
			North Waltham Ward (pt)	+19	
			East Hampshire (pt) viz:		East Hampshire
			Clanfield and Buriton Ward (pt)	+11	
			Froxfield and Steep Ward (pt)	-	
			Medstead Ward (pt)	-	
			Eastleigh (pt) viz:		Eastleigh
			Eastleigh North Ward (pt)	+6	

Notes:- Hectare measurements for those areas affected by boundary changes have not been included because the figures are not routinely available.

Changes of boundaries may involve areas of land with no population present in 1981, this is shown by a dash in Column e.

Where changes have affected ward or parish boundaries and/or names, details can be obtained from the Office of Population Censuses and Surveys, Census Customer Services, Titchfield, Fareham, Hants. PO15 5RR.

Annex B   How to obtain 1991 Census results

The products described in this Annex become available in the period May 1992 until mid-1994. Dates of availability are not given, to avoid any confusion as this Report continues to be used during and after the period 1992-94. All products are described as if available, but, in any case of doubt, a check should be made with OPCS Census Customer Services at the address given at the end of this Annex.

The form of results

The statistical results of the Census are made available in two ways:

(a)   in printed *reports* sold by HMSO bookshops (or, in a few cases, directly from the Census Offices); or

(b)   in *statistical abstracts* available, on request and for a charge, from the Census offices.

The *reports* take three general forms:

*   volumes - such as this Report - containing substantial and detailed tables;

*   *key statistics*, which give around 200 summary statistics for particular types of areas throughout the country, with national and regional figures, laid out for easy comparison between areas; and

*   *Monitors*, pamphlets which either give between 20 and 60 summary statistics for particular types of area in parts of the country, sometimes issued before main reports to give early results, or provide summaries for the country as a whole.

Statistical abstracts are supplied mainly in machine-readable form, although small quantities can be supplied as hard copies, and are generally either:

*   in a standard form, commissioned by a number of customers sharing costs, particularly to provide results for areas and populations smaller than those covered in reports; or

*   specially designed output commissioned by individual customers.

The Census Offices also supply supplementary products, for example to provide information on the geographical base of the Census, and documentation in a series of OPCS/GRO(S) *1991 Census User Guides*.

There are two broad types of results:

(a)   *local statistics*, which cover the full range of census topics - such as this Report; and

(b)   *topic statistics*, which focus on particular census topics in more detail, mainly at national and regional level.

All the main statistical results and products are described in *Prospectuses* in the *User Guides* series, available from the addresses given in section 13 and at the end of this Annex. Prospectuses for reports and abstracts contain complete outlines of the tables which will become available.

All areas for which results are provided in reports and abstracts are as at the time of the 1991 Census (unless otherwise indicated).

Local statistics

Local authorities

Results for smaller areas within the local authorities covered in this Report, or within local authorities elsewhere, are available as:

Ward and Civil Parish Monitors (England) or *Ward and Community Monitors* (Wales): pamphlets for each county in England and Wales which give some 30 statistics for each ward and civil parish/community, with figures for counties and districts/boroughs for comparison (see *Prospectus/User Guide* 32).

Local and Small Area Statistics are standard abstracts available from a variety of areas throughout Britain from the smallest - the Census Enumeration District - upwards. They are introduced in section 3 of this Report, and further information is available in *Prospectus/User Guide* 3. Further *User Guides* give: the file specification (number 21); the cell numbering system (24 and 25); and explanatory notes (38).

Results for local authorities in other parts of the country are available, with full comparability, as:

County Reports (England and Wales) and *Region Reports* (Scotland): issued separately in two parts for each County in England and Wales and for each Region in Scotland.

Key Statistics (Great Britain): a single report giving around 200 summary statistics, with some 1981/91 comparisons, for each local authority (see *Prospectus/User Guide* 29).

County Monitors (England and Wales) and *Region Monitors* (Scotland): pamphlets issued separately for each County or Region in advance of the main *Reports*, with contents as section 15 of this Report. Welsh County Monitors will be produced in bi-lingual format (Welsh and English).

Local and Small Area Statistics are also available at local authority level.

Results for other types of area, in forms comparable with those for local authorities listed above, are available for:

Health authority areas

Health Regions Report: a single report, in the form of a County Report, for Regional Health Authorities in England (elsewhere in Britain health authority boundaries coincided with those of local authorities at the time of the 1991 Census).

Key Statistics: a single report giving some 200 summary statistics for each Regional and District Health Authority in England (see *Prospectus/User Guide* 30).

Health Authority Monitors: pamphlets, in the form of County Monitors, for Regional and District Health Authorities.

Local and Small Area Statistics are also available at health authority level.

Urban and Rural Areas

Key Statistics: a single report for the larger urban areas and the rural areas in Great Britain, giving some 200 summary statistics for each area, with six 'regional' reports covering urban areas of all sizes and the rural areas in various parts of England and, separately, for Wales and Scotland (see *Prospectus/User Guide* 31).

Urban and rural areas have been specially defined for both the 1981 and 1991 Censuses, and a further report will give figures on change over the decade. 'Urban areas' cover conurbations, cities and towns of all sizes defined on a land use ('bricks and mortar') basis, so, for example, Census results are available for smaller towns *within* the larger local authority areas.

Small Area Statistics are also available for each urban and rural area.

Parliamentary and European Constituencies

Parliamentary Constituency Monitors: pamphlets, in the form of County Monitors, but with some additional '10 per cent' statistics, with results for each Parliamentary Constituency (and with figures for Britain for comparison). There are separate Monitors for each standard statistical region in England, and for Wales and Scotland (see *Prospectus/User Guide* 34). A single pamphlet in the same form is available for the European Parliamentary Constituencies in Great Britain.

Postcode areas

Postcode Sector Monitors: pamphlets for counties or groups of counties in England and Wales, giving some 30 '100 per cent' and '10 per cent' summary statistics at postcode sector level (see *Prospectus/User Guide* 33).

Small Area Statistics are also available for postcode sectors.

The 1991 Census records for England and Wales are re-sorted to give exact counts for postcode sectors. Results for a wide range of postcode based areas are available in Scotland.

National versions of local results

Results for Great Britain, regions in England, and Wales and Scotland, for these areas as a whole in forms comparable with those for local authorities and other types of area listed above, are available as:

National Reports: issued in two parts, on the lines of this Report, for Great Britain as a whole, including results for standard statistical regions in England and for Wales and Scotland; there is also a *Report for Wales*, and a *Report for Scotland*.

National and Regional Summary Monitor: pamphlet for Great Britain, including results for standard statistical regions in England and for Wales and Scotland, with contents as section 15 of this Report. Similar summary Monitors will be issued for Wales (bi-lingual) and Scotland, including summary results at County/Region level.

Topic statistics

Results for particular census topics are available in a series of reports summarised in the table on the following page. The reports present results mainly at the national level, but the following table shows those which have results at regional level, or at a county or district (or equivalent) level. Prospectuses should be checked for detailed information. The Regional Migration Reports comprise separate volumes for each standard statistical region of England, and for Wales and for Scotland.

Workplace and migration statistics

The analysis of the Census questions on 'address of workplace' and 'usual address one year before the Census' gives results on journeys from residences to workplaces and on migration moves, together with figures on people with workplaces in an area and out-migrants from an area, not only for the larger areas covered by the Reports listed above but also for smaller local areas. The latter are:

Special Migration Statistics: which provide information (in machine-readable form only) on migrants within and between local areas (see *Prospectus/User Guide* 35).

Special Workplace Statistics: which provide information (in machine-readable form only) on workforces in areas of workplace and residence for customer defined zones, and on journeys from residence to workplace between the zones (see *Prospectus/User Guide* 36).

Other products

Commissioned tables

In addition to the standard tables prepared for the local and topic statistics, the Census Offices also supply tables, on request, to a customer's own specification, at a charge which meets the marginal cost of production. *Prospectus/User Guide* 14 explains how customers may specify and order commissioned tables, and provides guidance on estimation of costs.

Topic	Processing level (per cent)	Prospectus (number)	With some results for:		
			Standard Statistical Regions*	Counties/ Scottish regions	Districts
Sex, Age and Marital Status (GB)	100	2	yes	yes	no
Historical Tables (GB)	100	4	yes	yes	no
Usual Residence (GB)	100	7	yes	yes	yes
Persons Aged 60 and Over (GB)	100	6	yes	no	no
Housing and Availability of Cars (GB and S)	100	12	yes	yes	yes
Communal Establishments (GB)	100	15	yes	no	no
Household Composition (GB)	100	11	yes	no	no
Limiting Long-term Illness (GB)	100	5	yes	no	no
Ethnic Group and Country of Birth (GB)	100/10	9	yes	yes	yes
Welsh Language in Wales	100/10	10	n/a	yes	yes
Gaelic Language in Scotland	100/10	18	n/a	yes	yes
National Migration (Part 1) (GB)	100	17	yes**	no	no
National Migration (Part 2) (GB)	10	17	yes**	no	no
Regional Migration (Part 1)	100	22	yes**	yes	yes
Regional Migration (Part 2)	10	22	yes**	yes	no
Report for Health Areas (GB)	100	39	n/a	n/a	n/a
Economic Activity (GB and S)	10	16	yes	no	no
Workplace and Transport to Work (GB and S)	10	20	yes	yes	yes***
Household and Family Composition (GB)	10	23	no	no	no
Qualified Manpower (GB)	10	8	yes	no	no
Children and Young Adults (GB)	100/10	13	yes	no	no

GB   Volumes for Great Britain
GB and S   Volumes for Great Britain together with additional volumes for Scotland

*   includes Metropolitan Counties in England
**   includes main urban areas
***   includes city centres

Enumeration District/Postcode Directory

This Directory provides a means of associating enumeration districts to postcodes to enable users to undertake their own linkage between census and other datasets. It is available, on magnetic media only, separately for each county. Alternatively, customers may purchase a National Directory. Further details of the file specification, information on availability, cost and ordering are provided in *Prospectus/User Guide* 26.

User Guide Catalogue

This catalogue is available from the Census Customer Services at the address given below. The catalogue is regularly revised to provide up-to-date information on all Prospectuses/User Guides.

Census Newsletter

The Newsletter is published several times a year to provide a link with users. It gives information on many aspects of the 1991 Census, including details of relevant publications and census-related activities. The Newsletter is a major source of information about the availability of census results and also reports on the main findings from evaluations of coverage and quality. Customers wishing to be included on the mailing list for future copies of the Newsletter should contact Census Customer Services.

Information on all products described in this Annex may be obtained from

Census Customer Services
OPCS
Segensworth Road
Titchfield
Fareham
Hampshire
PO15 5RR

telephone 0329 813800

Please mention this Report when making an enquiry.

VI 10 per cent topics

Reference should be made to section 8 of the introductory text of this part of the Report for notes on the '10 per cent' sample.

Government employment and training schemes

During processing of the County Reports, a situation was found in which some people who gave their occupation as armed forces also mistakenly stated that they were 'on a government employment or training scheme' in response to the question asking what they were doing in the week up to Census night. Such people have been classified as 'on a government employment or training scheme' and not as members of the armed forces. The effect is an understatement of the number of people in the armed forces and those in full-time employment, and a consequent overstatement of those on a government employment or training scheme. At the time of printing, the number of people so mis-classified in the 10 per cent sample was thought to be fewer than one thousand nationwide. This affects figures in Tables 72-83 and 90-99. In Tables 72 and 90-92, in any area where people have been mis-classified, the numbers of people in the 'on a government scheme' category will be overstated, and the numbers in the 'employees' category will be consequently understated. In Tables 73-83, 93, 96, 98, and 99 the total numbers of persons will be understated, and the total numbers of persons in Table 97 is also likely to be understated, whereas in Tables 94 and 95 the total numbers of persons will be overstated.

A table presenting the effect for each local authority district will be given in Part 2 of the National Report for Great Britain. This table will be available on request from Census Customer Services (for address see section 13) in advance of Part 2 of the National Report.

Table 71

(i)   This table compares the 100 per cent counts of residents and households (as used in part 1 of the Report) with the corresponding '10 per cent' sample counts. Thus, the '100 per cent' line repeats the resident and household counts from part 1 tables.

(ii) Imputed households, and residents in imputed households are omitted from the '10 per cent' sample - see sections 6 and 8 of the introductory text for notes on the effect of the omission.

Table 72*

This table combines information from the Census question on 'Whether working, retired, looking after the home, etc, last week' (number 13 on the Census form) with the questions on 'Hours worked per week' (number 14) and 'Occupation' (number 15). The information on hours worked is from question 14, which was processed in the 10 per cent sample,

rather than from question 13, so that it covers a sample of all those in employment in the week before the Census, rather than employees alone.

Table 73*

The information on industry in this table is based on the written-in answers to the question on 'Name and business of employer (if self-employed give the name and nature of the person's business)' (number 16 on the Census form), and brief notes on coding and categories are given in paragraphs 7.41 to 7.50 of *1991 Census Definitions* - see section 7 of the introductory text.

Table 74*

The information on occupations in this table is based on the written-in answers to the Census question on 'Occupation' (number 15 on the Census form), and brief notes on coding and categories, together with notes on continuity with the Classification of occupations used in the 1981 Census, are given in paragraphs 7.28 to 7.40 of *1991 Census Definitions* - see section 7 of the introductory text.

Table 76*

(i)   For 'industry' see note on Table 73, and for 'occupations' see note on Table 74.

(ii) 'Working outside district of usual residence' refers to residents of an area with a stated workplace outside the local authority district in which they were resident.

Table 77*

For 'industry' see note on Table 73.

Table 78*

(i)   For 'occupations' see note on Table 74.

(ii) 'Working outside district of usual residence' refers to residents of an area with a stated workplace outside a local authority district in which they are resident.

Table 79*

(i)   For 'industry' see note on Table 73.

(ii) The information on hours worked by employees is from the Census question on 'Hours worked per week' (number 14 on the Census form), which was processed in the 10 per cent sample.

---

*See also note on government employment and training schemes, at the head of this section.

Table 80[*]

(i) Information on 'couple families' and 'lone parents', and on 'dependent child in the family' is from the Census question on 'Relationship in household' (number 5 on the Census form), which was processed in the 10 per cent sample. Further notes on household and family composition are given in paragraphs 7.3 to 7.21 of *1991 Census Definitions* - see section 7 of the introductory text.

(ii) A 'family', in so far as can be determined from the relationship of the person in the first column of the Census form to each other person on the form, is

- *either* a married couple with or without their never married child(ren) - including a childless married couple,

- *or* a cohabiting couple - two persons of the opposite sex stating that they were 'living together as a couple' in answer to question 5 - with or without their never married child(ren) - including a childless cohabiting couple,

- *or* a lone parent - a father or mother - together with his or her never married child(ren).

A 'family' therefore contains only one or two generations. Grandparent(s) with grandchild(ren), if there are no apparent parents of the grandchild(ren) resident in the household, are classified as a family. 'Childless' in this context means that no child(ren) of the couple is/are apparent and resident in the household.

(iii) 'Couple families' comprise married couples and cohabiting couples.

(iv) 'Dependent child(ren)' are in the second generation of a family and are aged 0-15, or aged 16-18 and never married, and in full-time education and economically inactive.

Table 81[*]

(i) For 'occupations' see note on Table 74.

(ii) The information on hours worked by employees is from the Census question on 'Hours worked per week' (number 14 on the Census form), which was processed in the 10 per cent sample.

Table 82[*]

(i) A person's usual residence may differ from the address from which he or she went to work in the week before the Census; hence seemingly unlikely means of 'transport' may be shown in an area.

(ii) Some people may be shown as 'working outside district of usual residence', yet also as 'working at home' under 'means of transport to work'. These are people who gave a work address (HQ, office, factory, depot, etc) outside the district of usual residence in answer to the Census question on 'Address of place of work' (number 17 on the Census form) and who ticked 'Work mainly at home' in response to the question on 'Daily journey to work' (number 18 on the Census form). It should be noted that this is not a complete count of persons who work mainly at home but whose workplace address is based outside the district of usual residence - many such people would have ticked 'mainly at home' in response to the question on address of workplace.

(iii) 'Bus' includes minibuses or coaches (public or private).

(iv) 'Car' as a 'Means of transport to work' includes vans, three-wheeled cars and motor caravans.

(v) 'Working outside district of usual residence' refers to residents of an area with a stated workplace outside the local authority district in which they are resident.

(vi) The 'socio-economic group' of a person is determined by considering their employment status and occupation. Brief notes on the classification are given in paragraphs 7.61 to 7.64 of *1991 Census Definitions* - see Section 7 of the introductory text.

(vii) 'Car(s)' available to households include vans.

Table 83[*]

(i) This table gives the *combinations* of the main means of journey to work among members of households.

(ii) 'Car' as a means of transport comprises drivers and car passengers.

(iii) 'Public transport' comprises British Rail train, other rail, and bus.

(iv) 'Other' (means of journeys to work) comprises motor cycle, pedal cycle, on foot, other means, working at home, and not stated.

(v) 'Car(s)' available to households include vans.

Table 84

The information on qualified persons in this table is based on the written-in answers to the Census question on 'Degrees, professional and vocational qualifications' (number 19 on the Census form), and brief notes on the coding of responses and on categorisation to educational levels 'a', 'b' and 'c' are given in paragraphs 7.88 to 7.97 to *1991 Census Definitions* - see section 7 of the introductory text.

---

[*]See also note on government employment and training schemes, at the head of this section.

Table 85

(i)   Paragraphs 6.33 to 6.39 in *1991 Census Definitions* - see section 7 of the introductory text - give notes on the coding of information from the Census question on 'Ethnic Group' (number 11 on the Census form) to the categories used in this table.

(ii)   For 'persons qualified' see note on Table 84.

Table 86

(i)   The categories of tenure given in this table do not include households in permanent buildings renting, or occupying rent free, with a job, farm, shop or other business. A count of such households together with households not in permanent buildings may be derived by subtracting the sum of the given tenure categories from the relevant 'TOTAL HOUSEHOLDS' figure.

(ii)   A 'migrant head of household' is a resident head of household with a different usual address one year before that at the time of the Census, whether or not any other members of the household are migrants.

(iii)   'Dependent children' in *households* are persons aged 0-15 in a household or persons aged 16-18 and never married and in full-time education and economically inactive.

(iv)   For 'families' see note (ii) for Table 80.

(v)   Information on 'lone parents with dependent child(ren)' is from the Census question on 'Relationship in household' (number 5 on the Census form), which was processed in the 10 per cent sample. 'Dependent child(ren)' in a *family* are in the second generation of a family and are aged 0-15, or aged 16-18 and never married and in full-time education and economically inactive.

(vi)   'Head of family' is the head of the household if the family contains the head of the household, otherwise; in a couple family, the head is the first member of the couple on the form; or, in a lone parent family, the head is the parent.

(vii)   Further notes on household and family composition are given in paragraphs 7.3 to 7.21 of *1991 Census Definitions* - see section 7 of the introductory text.

(viii)   For 'socio-economic group' (SEG) see note (v) on Table 82. Households where the head in unemployed or on a Government scheme are assigned to SEGs on the basis of the head's most recent job in the previous ten years; otherwise they are included in the 'TOTAL' row only. This also applies to the cross-tabulations of SEG for 'persons' and 'families'.

Table 87

(i)   For tenure categories see note (i) on Table 86.

(ii)   For 'migrant head of household' see note (ii) on Table 86.

(iii)   For 'families' see note (ii) to Table 80.

(iv)   Further notes on household and family composition are given in paragraphs 7.3 to 7.21 *1991 Census Definitions* - see section 7 of the introductory text.

Table 88

(i)   For 'families' see note (ii) for Table 80.

(ii)   For 'head of family' see note (viii) on Table 86.

(iii)   The figures in the 'all 16 and over' columns may contain a small number of households and/or family heads aged under 16. They are not included in any other column.

(iv)   A 'concealed family' is any family which does not contain the head of a household.

(v)   An 'unconcealed family' contains the head of the household.

(vi)   For 'dependent child(ren)' see note (iv) for Table 80.

(vii)   'Couple families' comprise married couples and cohabiting couples.

(viii)   Further notes on household and family composition are given in paragraphs 7.3 to 7.21 to *1991 Census Definitions* - see section 7 of the introductory text.

Table 89

(i)   For 'families' see note (ii) for Table 80.

(ii)   For 'dependent child(ren)' see note (iv) for Table 80.

(iii)   Further notes on household and family composition are given in paragraphs 7.3 to 7.21 of *1991 Census Definitions* - see section 7 of the introductory text.

Table 90[*]

(i)   The 'social class' of a person is assigned on the basis of occupation in the week before the Census, or where there was no paid job, on the basis of the most recent paid job held within the previous ten years. A further short description of the procedure is given in paragraphs 7.51 to 7.57 of *1991 Census Definitions* - see section 7 of the introductory text.

---

[*]See also note on government employment and training schemes, at the head of this section.

(ii) Unemployed heads of households are assigned to a social class on the basis of their most recent paid job in the previous ten years. Otherwise they are included in the 'inadequately described' category.

(iii) 'Females in couples' include those in both married and cohabiting couples.

Table 91[*]

See notes on Table 90.

Table 92[*]

For 'socio-economic group' see note (viii) on Table 86, except that economically active persons on a Government scheme are shown separately in Table 92.

Table 93[*]

(i) Paragraphs 6.33 to 6.39 in *1991 Census Definitions* - see section 7 of the introductory text - give notes on the coding of information from the Census question in 'Ethnic Group' (number 11 on the Census form) to the categories used in this table.

(ii) For 'socio-economic group' see note (v) on Table 82; for 'social class' see note (i) on Table 90.

(iii) Persons on a Government scheme are excluded from this table/are included in TOTAL rows only.

Table 94[*]

(i) For 'industry' see note on Table 73.

(ii) A person who is on a Government scheme, or who is unemployed, and who has had no paid job in the previous ten years, is included in the 'not stated' category.

Table 95[*]

(i) For 'occupation' see note on Table 74.

(ii) A person who is on a Government scheme, or who is unemployed and who has had no paid job in the previous ten years, is included in the 'not stated' category.

Table 96[*]

(i) The persons counted in this table had the occupation of 'armed forces' and were in full-time employment in the week before the Census, that is they were serving members of the armed forces. The numbers of persons shown to be in the armed forces may therefore differ from the counts made in other tables on a different basis.

(ii) 'In households' means resident in households at the time of the 1991 Census. 'Not in households' means resident in communal establishments.

(iii) A 'migrant' 'from outside district' had a usual address one year before the Census in a different local government district *within* the area which is the subject of this Report.

Table 97[*]

The persons counted in this table are residents in households where the heads had the occupation of 'armed forces' and were in full-time employment in the week before the Census, that is the heads were serving members of the armed forces.

Table 98[*]

This table provides 1991 Census figures of persons in the categories of occupation used in the 1981 Census County Reports to enable comparisons between the Censuses. Annex A should be checked to see whether boundary changes may affect 1981-91 comparisons.

Table 99[*]

For 'occupation' see note on Table 74.

---

[*]See also note on government employment and training schemes, at the head of this section.

Printed in the United Kingdom for HMSO
Dd296126 3/93 C6 G3397 10170